THE JEWISH HOLIDAYS

COMMENTARIES BY:
ARNOLD EISEN · EVERETT GENDLER · ARTHUR GREEN
EDWARD L. GREENSTEIN · ZALMAN SCHACHTER-SHALOMI

THE JEWISH HOLIDAYS

A GUIDE AND COMMENTARY

BY MICHAEL STRASSFELD
ILLUSTRATED BY BETSY PLATKIN TEUTSCH

Quill
A HarperResource Book
An Imprint of HarperCollins*Publishers*

HarperCollins books may be purchased for educational, business, or sales promotional use. For information please write: Special Markets Department, HarperCollins Publishers Inc., 10 East 53rd Street, New York, NY 10022.

First HarperResource Quill paperback edition published 2001

Designer: Charlotte Staub

Library of Congress Cataloging in Publication Data

Srassfield, Michael.
    The Jewish holidays..

    1. Feasts and feasts—Judaism. I. Teutsch, Betsy Platkin.
II. Eisen, Arnold M., 1951-   . III. Title.
BM690.576   1985   296.4'3   84-48196
ISBN 0-06-015406-3
ISBN 0-06-272008-2

88 89 10 9 8 7 6 5
02 CW 16

CONTENTS

When asked how we are to act in this world, the rabbis responded:

> Just as the Holy One is merciful, so shall you be merciful;
> just as the Holy One seeks justice, so shall you seek justice. . . .

This book is dedicated to Saul Pavlin,
who lives that tradition as one

> who arouses the sleeping
> who causes the speechless to speak
> who frees those that are bound up
> who aids the fallen
> who raises those that are bowed down.

INTRODUCTION

In our lives, we are all ceaseless time-travelers as we move from moment to moment, event to event. But the maps of time are hard to attain and even harder to read. Many of us find ourselves seeming to stand still in our lives and yet time whizzes by until suddenly we approach our end of days.

The Jewish people, perhaps because we have done so much traveling in space, have developed a map for traveling in time. Called the "festival cycle," this map has its origin in the Torah and has continued to develop and change even in our era. The special days of the festival cycle are not random moments scattered over the year, but purposeful occurrences that draw their power from multiple sources—the natural world and its seasons, myth, religious traditions, folk customs, and decisive historical events in the life of our people. As such, the festivals operate on several levels at one and the same time, and hence can serve as a guide for travelers moving through the several dimensions of existence. One can also say that the festivals act as lodgings for travelers making their way through the year. These festival inns are special accommodations not solely for rest or retreat from the world, but also places to halt and take our bearings to make sure we are traveling and not just going around in circles. These are inns not for sleeping but rather for awakening from obliviousness. The cycle comes to remind us of both eternal

1

nature and its order, and the ever-recurring history of an eternal people. Even more fundamentally, the festival cycle causes us to focus on how our human life cycle parallels that of the natural and historical cycles of this world. The festivals bring us into contact with the great human themes of food, shelter, and security; birth, growth, and death; freedom and responsibility; the earthly and the transcendent.

It is part of the richness of the festival cycle that any one holiday can mean different things to different people. Each of us will find that some holidays will speak more clearly than others at different times in our lives; however, each also provides a sustaining continuity to our lives as we celebrate it once again. Similarly, each of us will approach this book and the festivals with his or her mix of viewpoint, sensibility, and experience. This book attempts to provide the reader with the raw material with which to create her or his own celebration, while remaining attached to the tradition that gives the cycle its power to guide us. That is why the commentators who appear in the margins are so important: They make clear that there is no one authority—no one interpretation of a holiday's meaning. This book invites you to join in the discussion that takes place between the margin and the text and thereby develop your own guide to the festival cycle.

How to Read This Book

Each chapter is devoted to one holiday or specific time period. The chapters have been set up in a uniform fashion to help you find your way more easily. Each one begins with an introduction to the history, themes, and practices of the holiday. A section entitled "Traditions" follows, which provides a detailed description of the traditional rituals and customs, thus serving as a "how-to" for observance. This is followed by a section entitled "Kavvanot." *Kavvanot,* meaning intentions, are suggestions for those seeking either a contemporary approach to the holiday or places to focus their observance amid the large number of traditional rituals associated with the holidays. Whether celebrating a holiday for the first or fiftieth time, kavvanot can help to initiate or renew our thinking about a holiday. The final section on each holiday is entitled "Derash"—interpretation—and discusses in greater depth the key themes and questions raised by the holiday.

Derash is a time-honored Jewish method of dealing with a text. The important texts in Jewish tradition such as the Bible and the Talmud are kept alive by being endlessly studied and interpreted rather than by being slavishly followed. It is this commitment, if not commandment, to interpret that makes the one Torah given to all Jews at Sinai a personal Torah for each and every one. *Derash,* as the process of interpretation, allows for the weeding out of those parts of the tradition that are no longer vital components of this generation's Torah while simultaneously calling for the creation of new pieces to be added to the Torah as an *etz hayyim*—a living and growing tree.

Placed around the text of this book you will find two kinds of material.

The first is the art, the work of Betsy Platkin Teutsch. The art borrows from the style of medieval illuminated manuscripts but transforms that style into a contemporary mode. Thus while illustrating and illuminating the book and adding an aesthetic dimension, the artwork also reflects the goal of the book itself—restating the tradition to make it ours.

The second type of material is the commentaries, which serve as examples of the living process of *derash.* For the most part, the written material in the margins is the comments of five individuals who were asked to respond to the "text" of this book by expressing their own thoughts about the holidays. They are Arnold Eisen, Everett Gendler, Arthur Green, Edward L. Greenstein, and Zalman Schachter-Shalomi. It should be made clear that they bear no responsibility for my interpretations even when they do not demur in their commentary. One of my chief regrets in regard to this book is that the three women who were asked to comment were unable to do so because of time pressure. Each of the commentators is credited by the initials appearing at the end of the commentary (E.Ge. is Everett Gendler; E.Gr. is Edward Greenstein). Comments initialed M.S. are those of the author and are usually detailed discussions of an issue found in the text of the book.

At the end of this book, there are appendixes on the Jewish calendar and on the halakhah of the holidays. The latter sets forth the details of Jewish law for each holiday. It is meant to provide more of that kind of information for those particularly interested in Jewish law as well as to serve as a handy reference for specific questions—e.g., If the baby blows out the Hanukkah candles, are you supposed to relight them? There is also a Torah reading chart for all the festivals, a list of the commonly said blessings in Hebrew, and a glossary of Hebrew words frequently used in the text.

I wish to thank all those who were involved in this project, ranging from the library staff of the Jewish Theological Seminary of America to my typists Helen Nakdiman and Joyce Gottlieb. Special thanks go to each of the commentators, whose work is an intrinsic part of the book and who also provided important critiques and advice at various stages of it; to Betsy Platkin Teutsch, who transformed the idea of a modern medieval illuminated book into brilliant reality; and to my editor, Ted Solotaroff, who with great patience and skill helped develop the final form of this book and who elevated the honing of a phrase to a form of art. Last and most important is my wife, Sharon, who with equal measures of assistance and forbearance immeasurably aided me in this book, which I would like to believe is a reflection of the Jewish life we have created together.

PESAH

FEASTING FOR FREEDOM

assover (Pesah), which celebrates the Exodus of the Israelites from Egypt, begins on the fifteenth of the month of Nisan and continues for seven days, through Nisan 21, though many Diaspora communities celebrate it for eight days (see discussion of the second day of festivals in Appendixes 1 and 2). The name Passover is taken from the Exodus story: During the tenth and ultimate plague inflicted on Pharaoh to break his will, God passed over the Israelites and struck down only the Egyptian firstborn. That night Pharaoh finally agreed to let the Israelites go; and ever since then, we gather together on that night to commemorate that time, and to contemplate the meaning of being freed by the "mighty hand and outstretched arm" of the Holy One.

The central meaning of Passover is liberation, and hence it is also called *zeman heiruteinu*—the season of our liberation. Another name for Passover is *hag ha-aviv*—the holiday of spring. The Jewish calendar is set so that certain holidays always occur in a particular season of the year (unlike, for instance, the Moslem calendar). Thus, the holiday of liberation is also the holiday of spring, not simply by coincidence but by design. Following the bleakness of winter when everything is covered with the shrouds of snow, spring marks the rebirth of the earth with the bursting forth of green life. Similarly, a people enshackled in oppressive slavery, doomed to a slow process of degra-

True and incontestable for the Northern Hemisphere. However, for the international edition of this work you had better solicit comments from someone who resides south of the equator. As I personally discovered while living in Rio de Janeiro, our traditional midrashim require not only translation into a different language but adaptation to a cycle of seasons quite the opposite of our northern.

In regions south of the equator, Pesah comes at harvest time and Sukkot is the springtime celebration! Pretty disorienting at first hearing, isn't it? But take heart! Has midrashic ingenuity ever failed us? Through millennia it has come to our rescue, and will surely guide us past this challenge as well—though how *I* cannot say.

E.Ge.

And thus we establish, in this the firstborn of Jewish festivals, the special character of Jewish memory. We are commanded to recall the past, in order to remember the *present*—to see it clearly, to know it fully, in all its possibilities—in the light of our future redemption. We Jews stand between redemptions, as it were, looking back in order to look forward: We thus come to see that we also stand *among* redemptions—acts of freedom, births of possibility—that we might not have seen, or assisted in, without the paradigm of Pesah. Messianic hope would not be credible in the world as we know it were it not for the fact—rehearsed at Pesah—that redemption has occurred. Because it has, because the events of liberation that we recall are as real as acts of cruelty or arbitrariness of which we need no reminder, we are made bold enough to hope for the Messiah. And that reservoir of faith, the gift of memory, makes all the difference as we go about the business of living in the world, and trying to redeem it.

A.E.

dation or even extinction, bursts forth out of Egypt into a new life's journey leading to a land flowing with milk and honey. The watchwords of both spring and Pesah are *rebirth* and *hope.* Thus, the spirit of renewed optimism aroused by the sights and smells of spring are reinforced in a Jewish context by Passover with its trumpeting of the possibilities of liberation. Passover reminds us annually that no matter how terrible our situation, we must not lose hope. Passover holds out the possibility of renewal, proclaiming that such change is as intrinsic to human nature as are blossoming trees to the natural world.

Another name for Pesah is *hag ha-matzot*—the holiday of the unleavened bread. The matzah evokes images of that night when the Israelites ate the sacrificial lamb in fearful and eager anticipation of the future. Around them arose the wails of Egyptians mourning the deaths of their firstborn. Suddenly, the word came from Moses to hurry forth. The Israelites had no time to let the dough rise for bread, and so they carried with them this "matzah" as their only provisions.

Matzah as a symbol of liberation is meant to trigger in our minds the whole story, which began in slavery and ended in freedom. It also reminds us of God's role in the Exodus, for it recalls the simple faith of the Israelites, who were willing to leave the home they knew and go off into the desert. Having seen God's redemptive power, they trusted in His promise. As *His* people, they were willing to follow after Him into "an unsown land" (Jer. 2:2).

It is this act of redemption by God that establishes the Covenant between Israel and God. Prior to the Exodus, the covenantal relationship existed only between God and individuals—for example, between God and Abraham. Passover marks the beginning of the relationship between God and the Jews as a people. God's claim to the Covenant lies in His having fulfilled His promise to bring us out of Egypt. Having redeemed us, God promises: "And I will take you to be My people, and I will be your God. And you shall know that I, the Lord, am your God who freed you from the burdens of the Egyptians" (Exod. 6:7).

From generation to generation

This covenantal relationship lies at the heart of the celebration of Passover. We rejoice for the past liberation from Egypt and for other redemptions by God since then. And because of the fulfillment of past promises, we anticipate at Passover the future final redemption. We create a special role for the prophet Elijah at the seder (see below) as the symbol of our faith in the redemption soon to come.

Because it is the crucial event that marks the beginning of our sacred history, the Exodus is referred to repeatedly in Jewish liturgy and thought. For example, the shema (the central prayer in Jewish liturgy) concludes "I, the Lord, am your God who brought you out of the land of Egypt to be your God: I the Lord your God" (Num. 15:41). At Passover we are commanded to tell the story of the Exodus. This commandment, unique to this holiday, leads us not simply to remember the Exodus but to expand upon the tale, to explore its complexities and develop its meaning. Thus the Haggadah, the liturgy we use at the seder, states:

> In every generation, each person should feel as though she or he were redeemed from Egypt, as it is said: "You shall tell your children on that day saying, 'It is because of what the Lord did for me when I went free out of Egypt.' For the Holy One redeemed not only our ancestors; He redeemed us with them."

The uniqueness of Passover is encapsulated in the above passage. It teaches us that Jewish history is also a timeless present, that Passover is not simply a commemoration of an important event in our past—analogous to the Fourth of July or Bastille Day—but an event in which *we* participated and in which we *continue* to participate. We are meant to reexperience the slavery and the redemption that occurs in each day of our lives. It is our own story, not just some ancient history that we retell at Passover.

To relive the experience, we are commanded to observe three rituals:

1. To tell the story of the Exodus. As the Torah states: "Remember this day, on which you went free from Egypt, the house of bondage, how the Lord freed you from it with a mighty hand . . ." (Exod. 13:3).

The biblical story models the Exodus of Israel from Egypt (birth of the nation) on the pattern of an ancient Creation myth (birth of the world) that is preserved in fragmentary allusions in the books of Isaiah, Psalms, Job, and others. In that myth, God created the land by vanquishing the dragon of the sea, forcing it back, restraining it from inundating the land. In defeating the dragon, God would cleave it and/or dry it up, leaving room for the dry land below to surface. When the Lord liberated the Israelites, he brought them to safety by defeating his, and their, human enemy, Pharaoh; by splitting the sea, allowing the Israelites to pass through on dry land; and by bringing the sea back together and drowning the king of Egypt and his cohort. The redeeming of Israel from Egypt was perceived in the Bible as another Creation. This theme is developed by the so-called Second Isaiah, a prophet of the Babylonian Exile (circa 540 B.C.E.), who adds yet a third event to the pattern, the impending return of the exiled Judeans from Babylonia to Judea: "Arise, arise, clothe yourself in force, O arm of the Lord! Arise, as in days of yore, times primeval! For you are the one that cut Rahab, that ran through Tanin! For you are the one that dried up the sea, the waters of the great deep! The one that turned the bottom of the sea into a way for the redeemed to pass through! Yes, the redeemed of the Lord will return, they will enter Zion in jubilation, with joy forever on their heads. Merriment and joy will overcome them. Fled are anxiety and sighing" (Isa. 51:9–11). Pesah places all the redemptions, past and future, into the same mold: Creation, Exodus, Return from exiles past, the Return of the Messianic Age.

E.Gr.

The seder is really not about the reexperiencing of the slavery and redemption of the Hebrews. As we see below, we all have our own Egypt to leave, and we do leave "Egypt." It is not a reexperience, which cannot really be, but an experience. It is not theater but life.

E.GR.

Words are powerful beyond words, and the Haggadah both testifies to that power and makes use of it as it helps us to conjure up events that otherwise would be unreal. The Telling re-presents the Exodus to us, makes it present; to get us into the spirit of that act of magic, it begins by telling the words of a previous generation of rabbis as they told the story of Passover, at a time when the words seemed especially meaningful because the messianic era seemed very near. The heart of the narrative is built upon the declaration "My father was a wandering Aramean . . ." (Deut. 26), and thus recalls the powerful set of words uttered by the Israelite who, as he brought the fruit of God's bounty in the land to the temple, acknowledged that he had tasted of the redemption. We recite his words, as the Torah did, that we might conjure up the future as well as the past. They help us to speak of a redemption that, like the Exodus from Egypt itself, would otherwise be unreal. All this through words.

A.E.

Marvelous: We place the matzah on the table in order to remember—why we have placed the matzah on the table! But that is how symbols work, after all: raising questions we might never have asked, and so pointing us to answers we can never exhaust. Abraham Joshua Heschel was fond of saying that the important thing in life is to ask the right questions. For this we need an occasion, a structure, a set of symbols to prod us, all of which are provided by the sensory delights of the seder table—first of all by the matzah so utterly lacking in those delights.

A.E.

2. To eat matzah—unleavened bread. As the Torah states: "At evening, you shall eat unleavened bread" (Exodus 12:18).

3. To refrain from eating or owning hametz—leavened bread. As the Torah states: "On the very first day, you shall remove leaven from your houses, for whoever eats leavened bread from the first day to the seventh day, that person shall be cut off from Israel" (Exod. 12:15).

The focus for this reliving is the seder. On the first night of Passover, we gather together in families or groups to celebrate this ritual meal. The Hebrew word *seder* means "order," and the meal has a very carefully constructed order to it. The seder includes many rituals, such as eating matzah and maror (the bitter herbs), drinking four cups of wine, and eating a sumptuous feast. Its many symbols are meant to remind us, on the one hand, of the bitterness of slavery and, on the other, of the great joy of our liberation.

In the midst of these rituals, we recite a special pedagogic and liturgical text, the Haggadah. *Haggadah* comes from the root meaning "to tell" and reflects the purpose of the evening—the retelling of the story of the Exodus. Celebrating the seder by reading the Haggadah is one of the most widely observed practices in American Judaism. Eagerly anticipated, the Haggadah includes such parts as the Four Questions (Mah Nishtanah), the Four Children, the songs (e.g., "Dayyeinu"), and the custom of stealing the afikomen matzah. But underlying the fun and the warmth of families and friends gathered together is an important religious drama in which the props are the symbols, the script is the Haggadah, and the actors are our families, our friends, whosoever would understand the drama.

Passover is also a family holiday because of the importance it places on conveying the story and meaning of Passover to the next generation. It is the children's role to ask the Four Questions; it is our role to impress upon them the significance of the answers, for we understand fully what our children do not: that the future of the Jewish people lies with them. For that people to continue its 3000-year history, in every generation each of us and each of our children must feel as though they themselves were slaves in Egypt and were redeemed. In this way, each new generation can take its place in the chain of the Jewish people leading down from the Exodus to the present.

Matzah, a flat bread (similar to a cracker) whose only ingredients are flour and water, can be either rectangular or round, and is made from a dough whose leavening process is interrupted. Basically, this is accomplished by making and baking matzah very quickly, so quickly that we stop the dough from rising.

The reason we eat matzah during Pesah is given by Rabban Gamliel in the Haggadah as follows:

Matzah: Why do we eat it? To remind ourselves that even before the dough of our ancestors could become leavened bread, the Holy One revealed Himself and redeemed them, as it is written: "And they baked the dough which they had brought from Egypt into matzah, because it did not rise since they were driven out of Egypt and they could not delay, nor had they prepared provisions for themselves."

Matzah, then, is a reminder of the moment of Exodus from Egypt. Although we may eat matzah all during Passover, we are *commanded* to eat it only during the seder.

Hametz is a mixture of flour and water that is allowed to rise, thus becoming what we normally call "bread." The laws of hametz are very strict, and prohibit not only eating it but even owning it during Passover. Thus, during the weeks before Pesah, we dispose of our hametz. The night before Passover, there is a final search for hametz, followed the next morning by a ritual burning of what remains. We also make a formal declaration renouncing ownership of any hametz and declaring any that remains in our homes null and void.

Since no food is permitted to have hametz in it, the tradition states that most of the processed foods we eat during the year are not "kosher for Passover" without rabbinic supervision. Similarly, we are supposed to store away all kitchen utensils used throughout the year and use, instead, pots and dishes reserved for Passover.

All these prohibitions on hametz are meant to mark off matzah as something special. Since we eat matzah in remembrance of the Exodus, we further refrain from eating hametz to emphasize the importance of matzah and its symbolism.

Further, we refrain from hametz as part of the process of personal liberation. In rabbinic interpretation, hametz is seen as symbolic of the *yetzer ha-ra* —the evil inclination. The removal of all hametz is a metaphor for an inner process of purging and freeing ourselves of impurity—the hametz that lies within us. This is why we go to such lengths to remove even the tiniest amount of material hametz; it is meant to signify the difficulty of the struggle to remove those negative parts of our selves.

Philo, a Greek-Jewish philosopher, described hametz as pride because leavened bread is puffed up. To remove hametz, then, is to struggle with our sense of self-importance. Philo's sense of hametz also fits well with an interpretation of the Exodus story as a struggle between Pharaoh, a man who thinks he is divine, and God, the being who is divine. Thus, it was necessary to bring about the plagues to humble Pharaoh and to teach him the answer to the question he so flippantly posed to Moses at their first encounter: "Who is the Lord that I should listen to His voice to let Israel go? I do not know the Lord and I will not let Israel go" (Exod. 5:2). The Exodus story teaches us that it is God and not humans, not even a king, who controls destiny. In searching for hametz, we search for the pieces of Pharaoh's arrogance that lie within each of us.

TRADITIONS

The following is a ten-step approach to removing hametz. Each of us is free to decide whether to do less or more than is presented here.

1. Do a thorough cleaning of the house, with special attention to those

The gathering of Jews at the seder is an archetypal event. Much goes on this night beneath the surface of the text. Like the mysterious force returning the swallows to Capistrano, even those Jews alienated from the tradition gather together on the full moon of the vernal equinox for the seder. It is, to use the phrase of Mordecai Kaplan, a moment when "the reconstitution of the Jewish people" takes place.

Z.S.

The point, I think, is that true liberation binds us, false service giving way to true. Unredeemed daily existence filled with its own pretenses gives way to more modest fare; the prohibition on bread, of course, also reminds us that human beings "cannot live on bread alone, but upon all that goes forth from the mouth of the Lord." If hametz represents our *yetzer ha-ra*, so does that evil impulse fuel our desire to cast off all bonds, all obligations, all authority; the atrocities committed in our day in the name of "liberation" are staggering. So: *davka* when we celebrate redemption, we are limited in the satisfaction of the most primal human desire (food), and are focused on the modest fare of matzah. Freedom, in this tradition, means subjection to the "yoke of mitzvah" rather than the human yokes of either Pharaohs *or* false messiahs.

A.E.

From generation to generation

areas where hametz might have been eaten or stored. To facilitate this process, you may want to clean a room at a time and then allow no further eating in a room once it is "Pesahdik." Hametz may be lurking in such places as your car, coat pockets, handbags, baby carriages, or under the sofa cushions. If you have small children, the possibilities are endless.

Many people have assimilated the removal of hametz into a general spring cleaning. On the one hand, the greater the sense of preparation for Passover, the more we become cognizant of the holiday's approach and are confronted with the holiday's themes. Spring cleaning fits in with the sense of removing the old (hametz) and welcoming the new (spring and Passover). In Eastern Europe, Jews living in villages used to whitewash the walls of their homes before Pesah, not because they thought there was hametz in the walls but as preparation for the holiday. On the other hand, there is no real reason to wash your curtains because of the laws of hametz. This should be remembered if Pesah cleaning begins to become overwhelming. The removal of hametz and the celebration of Passover are the essential; the housecleaning is peripheral and should not work to the detriment of the essential.

2. If you are certain that no one has brought hametz into an area—for example, the cellar, attic, or studio/office—you don't have to clean it.

3. The dining room and kitchen require special attention. The table(s) should be cleaned, particularly the crack between the halves of a table that opens. While some "kasher" their tables by scouring them and pouring hot water over them, others simply wash them and then cover them. Many people cover the kitchen counters, and some line the shelves of their kitchen cabinets.

4. All hametz should be eaten, disposed of, or, if it is to be sold, put into separate cabinets/storage space. To prevent the accidental eating of hametz during the holiday, many people tie or tape the hametz cabinets closed. (Even if according to your observance you are not going to remove or sell your hametz, it would still seem important to set it aside to prevent eating it by mistake.)

5. All dishes, silverware, pots, dish drainers, food processors, etc., that are used during the year are considered "hametzdik" and should be put away. (For rules on kashering, see below.)

6. The refrigerator should be emptied of all hametz and washed out. The freezer should be defrosted. Some people line the refrigerator shelves with foil or newspaper. (Care should be taken to punch holes in the liner to allow the circulation of air necessary for the refrigerator's operation.)

7. Certain things may be kashered for Passover rather than replaced. (In our situation, this means making hametz utensils permissible for use on Pesah.) Unless you have an extra stove used only for Passover (believe it or not, a growing practice among the ultra-Orthodox), the most difficult task is kashering your stove/oven/broiler. To do so requires an understanding of the general rules of kashering—which, by the way, are the same for transforming a nonkosher utensil to kosher. The principles are as follows:

a. Utensils are kashered the way they are used—that is, utensils used with heat are kashered by heat.

From generation to generation

b. Heat during normal use of utensils causes the absorption of food material into their walls. Further heat will cause the walls to exude it.

Cold does not cause any absorption. Thus, a refrigerator can simply be washed since it is used only, or mostly, with cold things. On the other hand, since the oven uses heat, its walls will absorb particles of the food being cooked in it. Also, hot food will often spill or bubble over onto the oven's surfaces. Therefore, an oven must be kashered with heat to draw out the hametz food particles.

8. To kasher an oven:

a. Do not use the oven for twenty-four hours before you plan to kasher it. (Food particles absorbed into the walls are believed to decay after twenty-four hours so that the rabbis no longer considered them real food, though the particles still must be removed for the kashering process.)

b. Clean the oven thoroughly so that no grease or large lumps of burnt food remain.

c. Clean the oven racks and put them back into the oven. (We have found that soaking the racks overnight in the bathtub makes the grease brittle so that it cracks and comes off easily with steel wool.)

d. Turn the oven to its highest temperature and leave it on for one hour.

For microwave ovens, follow steps 1–3, then turn on the oven, place a pot of water inside, and allow a thick steam to fill the oven. Self-cleaning ovens can simply be turned on to their self-cleaning cycle—and *voilà!* Continuous-cleaning ovens, however, are considered regular ovens and should be kashered accordingly. (For rules on kashering silverware, pots and pans, see p. 211)

9. The stovetop and burners should be kashered in a similar fashion. They should be unused for twenty-four hours, thoroughly cleaned, and burners turned to the highest temperature for about fifteen minutes for a gas stove, five minutes for an electric stove. (In addition, some cover the burners and/or the burner pans with foil liners.)

10. The sink: If it is metal, scour it well and pour boiling water over it. If it is porcelain or enamel, pour boiling water on it and then put a sink liner at the bottom.

Or (11) go to a relative or a hotel and forget the whole thing. (But even if you do go away, you are required to sell all the hametz in your home to a non-Jew. You are also required to recite the nullification [*bittul*] formula.)

MEKHIRAT HAMETZ

While the ideal is to destroy all your hametz, many people feel they have too much to do so. Tradition provides us with a process called *mekhirat hametz*

To kasher utensils that cannot be kashered in other ways, such as plastics that would melt under high heat, I use chemistry rather than the physics of the traditional kashering process. Chemical kashering uses strong acids such as lye and sulfuric acid to leach out and dissolve the food substances contained in the walls of a utensil. To use this process, fill a bathtub with Drano and then submerge the utensil. In the case of metal utensils, be careful not to leave them in too long, because eventually the acid will eat the metal itself.

Z.S.

It is also a good example, à la the "Shabbas goy," of how Jews depend upon non-Jews for help in observing laws binding only upon the Jew! Nothing could better highlight our anomalous position among the nations or the partial character of our redemption. Maybe it will change once the Messiah comes? Then again, there might not be Pesah then, for why look forward to a redemption that has already come? It is hard to say. In the meantime, we sell our hametz.

A.E.

From generation to generation

—the selling of hametz. Originally, this process was devised for those Jews in the food or liquor business with substantial quantities of hametz. To avoid serious financial loss, *mekhirat hametz* was devised to allow the sale of hametz to a non-Jew. It is an example of how Jewish law can respond in a humane way to a problem created by its own legal system. Today, *mekhirat hametz* can be performed by anyone.

While the form of the sale has changed over time, today it involves the real sale of hametz to a non-Jew before Passover. The seller writes down the type of hametz, though not necessarily the exact amounts; where it is located; and how access can be gained to it. A price is set and a down payment is made by the non-Jew. The balance of the purchase price is considered a loan to the non-Jew. After Passover, if the non-Jew does not want to pay the balance, he resells the hametz to the Jew for a small amount of money. It is a real sale in the sense that the non-Jew could pay the purchase price and keep the hametz. Also, during Passover, the non-Jew has the right to come and eat as much of the hametz as she/he wants.

Because it is complicated, the sale is usually done through a rabbi, who acts as your agent in the transaction. The rabbi needs an authorization from you, which should be in writing but if necessary can be by phone, just as the written list of hametz is not an absolute necessity. (While some people will not sell hard-core hametz such as bread, most authorities state that any hametz can be sold.) Only food is sold, not pots or dishes.

A PASSOVER SHOPPING LIST

A word to the consumer: Some "kosher" food packagers exploit Passover by selling items that either require no supervision or are available from national brands at normal prices. For example, some national brands of apple juice are available with a "Kosher for Passover" label, and therefore it is unnecessary to buy a more expensive "Jewish" brand.

A decision should also be made about which foods you really need for Passover. Each year more new foods are available for Pesah, but is it really necessary to buy Passover potato chips or ice cream? Part of the experience of Pesah is that the food for the week should be different from that of the rest of the year. To have kosher-for-Passover substitutes for our whole regular diet negates the distinctive *ta'am* or taste of this holiday and obfuscates the significance of the removal of hametz.

Foods that require no special supervision for Passover are coffee, tea, sugar, eggs, meat, fish, fresh fruits and vegetables (except *kitniyot*—see below), salt (some will not used iodized salt, which may contain dextrose), and dates. Also requiring no supervision are Valley Lea and Alba white powdered milk and Pillsbury Sweet 10 (a dietetic sweetener). Some authorities also include honey; dried fruits; frozen fruits and vegetables without any additional ingredients (e.g., corn syrup); garlic; pepper; onion and garlic powders; nuts;

and milk. Such things as aluminum foil, plastic wrap, garbage bags, scouring powder and pads, detergents (all-purpose, laundry, and dishwashing powders and liquids), and metal (silver, etc.) polishes also require no supervision.

By custom, Ashkenazic Jews do not eat *kitniyot* during Passover. *Kitniyot* are legumes and include beans, peas, lentils, rice, millet, sesame and sunflower seeds, corn, and, according to some authorities, peanuts. (String beans are not *kitniyot* according to the Rabbinical Assembly Law Committee—Conservative). Since corn syrup, derivatives of soybeans, etc., are used in many foods, this complicates the kashrut picture for Pesah.

Among the common foods that may be problematic are ketchup and mayonnaise because of the vinegar in them; confectioner's sugar because it may contain corn syrup; and brown sugar because it may contain yeast. Foods like vinegar, baking soda, baking powder, Postum and most liquors are made from grain and are not kosher for Passover.

Foods that are kosher if under rabbinic supervision for Passover: matzot, matzah products, candies, cakes, beverages, canned and processed foods, jams, cheeses, jellies, relishes, salad oils, vinegar, wine and liquors.

Each year the Union of Orthodox Jewish Congregations of America publishes a Kosher for Passover Products Directory that lists all the products under their supervision. It is available from Orthodox Union, Dept. K, 45 West 36th Street, New York, N.Y. 10018. Unfortunately, no complete list exists of the products supervised by all the various groups and individuals that provide such supervision; the above pamphlet covers only *their* supervised products and those that require no supervision.

"Baking soda" forbidden during Passover? There are at least two arguments to the contrary, one chemical, one theological.

1. The chemical: Since baking soda is a salt derivative formed by carbonic acid, what would make it forbidden? Its components are found in salt water and seltzer water, neither forbidden for Pesah. Perhaps baking *powder* has been confused with baking *soda*, the former suspect due to possible starch-from-grain ingredients, the latter beyond reproach?

2. The theological: How is it imaginable that a humanly concerned, liberating Deity would prescribe eight, or even seven, heavily fried, cholesterol- and fat-filled-food days, without permitting bicarbonate of soda as chaser for the unavoidable indigestion?

E.Ge.

THE WEEK BEFORE PESAH

The Shabbat before Passover is called Shabbat ha-Gadol—the great Sabbath—because the special haftarah for this Shabbat refers to the great and awesome day at the final redemption (see Mal. 3:23). Even before we recount the redemption from Egypt at Passover, we look forward to the final redemption, which will be heralded by Elijah. In many traditional synagogues in Eastern Europe, the rabbi gave a sermon twice a year—once on the Shabbat between Rosh ha-Shanah and Yom Kippur and the other on Shabbat ha-Gadol. The sermon on Shabbat ha-Gadol was *very long* because it spelled out all the laws of hametz and Passover, hence Shabbat ha-Gadol.

On Shabbat ha-Gadol, it is the custom of some Ashkenazic Jews to read through the Haggadah in the afternoon until the end of the section when Rabban Gamliel enumerates the three symbols Pesah, matzah, maror. The custom arose because people wanted to familiarize themselves with the text of the Haggadah before the actual seder. If Erev Pesah (see below) falls on Shabbat, that Shabbat is still called Shabbat ha-Gadol but the sermon is moved up a week so that the laws can be explained in time to be useful for preparing for Passover.

Rabbi Levi Yizhak of Berdichev (eighteenth-century Hasidic master) comments that the true miracle of the Exodus, the "great" miracle, in fact took place on the tenth of Nisan, not later. When Israel decided that they would slaughter sheep (which according to tradition were gods in Egypt) without regard for what their Egyptian taskmasters would say or do to them, their liberation had begun. That God can wreak plagues, split the sea, and all the rest—these are no source of surprise to the person of faith. But Israel's courage to defy the Egyptians—that is truly worthy of being called miraculous.

A.G.

From generation to generation

EREV PESAH— THE DAY BEFORE PASSOVER

The day before Passover, called "Erev Pesah"—literally, the eve of Passover—presents us with the final stages of removing the hametz, involving three rituals:

1. *Bedikat hametz*—the search for hametz
2. *Bittul hametz*—the nullification of hametz
3. *Bi-ur hametz*—the destruction of hametz

BEDIKAT HAMETZ

By nightfall of the day before Passover, it is customary to have finished cleaning the house. Soon after sundown we conduct a final, mostly symbolic search of our homes for hametz. Many people hide a few pieces of bread so that the children, who participate in the search, will have something to find. There is a kabbalistic tradition of hiding ten pieces of bread to reflect the ten *sefirot*—the spheres that make up the universe. Make sure to collect all the crumbs from the pieces you discover.

The search is conducted at night, since that is when everyone is at home. There are bedikat hametz kits including a candle, a feather for brushing the hametz, and a spoon into which the hametz is brushed. All of the kit can be burned the next day with the hametz. While a candle is customary, a flashlight can also be used. You must search everywhere in the house where hametz might have been eaten or used during the year. Before the search, we recite the following blessing:

> Praised are You, Lord our God, Ruler of the universe, who has sanctified us through His commandments, commanding us to remove all hametz.

It is customary not to speak during bedikat hametz except for matters related to the search. All the hametz that is found should be collected and set aside for the morning. After the search is completed, the formula of *bittul* (see below) is recited.

BITTUL HAMETZ

While bedikat hametz—the search—is the better-known ritual, *bittul hametz*—the formula of nullification—is the one grounded in a biblical law. The *bittul* formula is recited after the search at night:

> All leaven in my possession which I have not seen or removed or of which I am unaware is hereby nullified and ownerless as the dust of the earth.

Bittul is written in Aramaic but should be recited in a language you understand. It declares that the hametz in our possession is of no value and ownerless. This embodies two concepts of *bittul:* first, that we nullify hametz by making it worthless; and, second, that by making hametz *hefker*—free for the taking—we renounce all claims to ownership. According to the Torah, the removal of hametz requires not so much action as intention: By making a firm declaration of *bittul,* we successfully eliminate hametz from our possession. This reflects a rabbinic belief in the power of the word even without action to change reality.

The *bittul* formula is recited again next morning after *bi-ur hametz* (see below). The wording is slightly changed in the morning since the version recited at night is not intended to include the hametz that we know about and intend to eat for breakfast.

During the actual day before Pesah—that is, from sunrise to sunset— tradition provides for a progressive restriction on hametz as we make the transitions from hametz to matzah and from a regular day to a holiday.

During the first four hours of the day, hametz is permitted. Beginning with the fifth hour, the eating of hametz is prohibited, but we are still allowed to benefit from it. Beyond the fact that we can still close deals in grain on the commodity market, we perform *bi-ur hametz*—the destruction of the hametz —at this time, since fulfilling a mitzvah (commandment) is considered to be gaining a benefit and in this case it is the hametz that is the cause of our gain. Beginning with the sixth hour, it is forbidden to eat or gain benefit from hametz.

Bi-ur Hametz

The ritual destruction of hametz should take place no later than the fifth hour on that day. The hametz collected the night before during bedikat hametz, plus whatever hametz is left over from breakfast, is gathered together, brought outside, and burned. While other methods of destruction are permitted (e.g., breaking bread into crumbs and scattering it in the wind or flushing it down the toilet), the common method is to burn it. Those unfamiliar with the ritual will discover that it is not easy to burn bread, but at least the hametz should be rendered inedible (lighter fluid can be helpful).

After the burning, the *bittul* formula is recited again:

All leaven in my possession, whether I have seen it or not, whether I have removed it or not, is hereby nullified and ownerless as the dust of the earth.

Some have the custom of adding the following kavvanah (meditation):

Lord, our God and God of our ancestors, just as I have removed all hametz from my home and from my ownership, so may it be Your will that I merit the removal of the evil inclination from my heart.

One custom associated with *bi-ur hametz* is to use part of the lulav (palm branch) saved from Sukkot (or alternatively the willows of Hoshana Rabbah) to light the fire. Alternatively, some use a piece of a lulav to sweep up the

As the Israelites purified their camp in the wilderness, so we, at Pesah, symbolically cleanse our homes. As they eliminated ritual impurity from their ordered space by returning it to one of the four elements, so we burn our hametz—and employ the magic of words to declare whatever remains "as the dust of the earth." Unlike the ancient Israelites, however, we moderns tend to be uncomfortable with the whole notion of symbolic purification, and tend to chafe at procedures such as this one. So we do well to remember two things. One: The great advantage of ritual over ethical purity is that it is attainable. No matter how complex the procedure, it is far simpler than acting ethically. The difficulty of knowing the right thing is surpassed only by the difficulty of doing it. Symbolic purity, like atonement, is a necessary compensation for our imperfection. Two: The symbol reminds us of things we do not want to remember, such as that we do not really own anything, including ourselves, and that we resemble hametz insofar as we return to "the dust of the earth." The ritual has us see all that, and then go on. At this point our words, our symbolic purity, are all that is demanded.

A.E.

As stated, it sounds a bit magical, which might put some people off. In fact, it is by words that we define situations, declare ownership, convey intentions. The meaning of a raised hand might be aggressive or affectionate; words will define the meaning. The item displayed might be offered for sale, as a gift, or merely to be seen and admired; words will define the situation. The primordial power of words to define and determine situations is strikingly, if surprisingly, illustrated in this ritual act.

Cf. And out of the ground the Lord God formed every beast of the field, and every fowl of the air; and brought them unto the man to see what he would call them; and whatsoever the man would call every living creature, that was to be the name thereof. [Gen. 2:19]

E.Ge.

hametz during bedikat hametz. Others use a part of the lulav to light the oven to bake matzot. Thus the end of the pilgrimage festival cycle (Sukkot) is linked with the beginning of next year's festival cycle and so we bridge the gap between the end and the beginning and come to understand that these cycles continue.

OTHER CUSTOMS OF EREV PESAH

FAST OF THE FIRSTBORN (TA'ANIT BEKHORIM)

Custom has it that all firstborn fast on the day before Passover to commemorate having been spared during the plague of the firstborn at the time of the Exodus. (According to some traditional authorities, firstborn females should fast as well, even though, in general, a female never acquires the status of firstborn in Jewish law.) The fast begins at sunrise rather than the previous night.

Ta'anit Bekhorim is one of the minor fast days, no longer as widely observed as it once was. Many people who still observe Ta'anit Bekhorim use the halakhic principle regarding the importance of Torah study to override and cut short the fast. There is a custom that whenever the study of a body of Jewish text is completed (for example, a tractate of Talmud), a siyyum takes place. A siyyum (literally, completion) is a celebration with food and drink of a special occasion. On Ta'anit Bekhorim the last lines of a text that have been completed are studied at the siyyum, and this study is followed by a seudat mitzvah—a meal in honor of a mitzvah. This meal and its siyyum bring the fast to an end.

Some people who are nonfirstborn choose to fast in order to heighten the taste of matzah at the seder meal or in commemoration of the three-day fast in the time of Queen Esther (see Esther 3:7, 4:16). Some people end work at noon or even earlier. One custom is to read the biblical description of the Pesah sacrifice during the afternoon as a reminder of the sacrifice and the temple. Some traditional Jews go to the mikveh—ritual bath—to purify themselves before the holiday.

The rest of the day is devoted to preparing physically, mentally, and spiritually for Passover and the seder. The foods eaten for lunch should be kosher for Passover. However, in order to make the eating of matzah special at the seder, no matzah is eaten on Erev Pesah. Some people elaborate on this custom and do not eat matzah for two weeks or a month before Passover. In this way, the matzah we are commanded to eat on Pesah is made distinct from any other.

Tradition recommends eating lightly to make us hungry for the seder. The seder should start as soon as possible after sundown, since we want the children to be awake for as much of it as possible.

PREPARING THE SEDER TABLE

The preparation should involve the whole group or family if possible. Children can help set the table, color place cards, make matzah covers from napkins, and take charge of the salt water. The more that people participate, the greater their sense of involvement—and the lighter the burden on those doing the planning and cooking. In honor of the festival, and in celebration of freedom, many people set the table with their finest dishes. In honor of spring and the festival, some buy or pick flowers for the table.

Besides the Haggadot and whatever food will be served at the meal, the main items needed for the seder are the seder plate, matzot, and wine.

THE SEDER PLATE

The seder plate—*k'arah*—contains all the symbols of the seder. While any dish can be used, many people own special ceremonial plates with places marked for each item. One seder plate will suffice, but people often lay out individual ones.

The foods on the seder plate are *not* eaten during the seder:

1. *Karpas*—a vegetable, usually green such as parsley, symbolizing spring and rebirth. It is dipped in salt water near the beginning of the seder.
2. *Haroset*—a mixture of chopped apples, nuts, wine, and spices. We dip the maror into haroset to lessen the bitter herbs' taste. It also symbolizes the mortar that the slaves made for bricks in Egypt. Recipes for haroset vary widely among Jews, though the above list of ingredients is the most common among Ashkenazic Jews. One Sephardic recipe includes bananas, dates, raisins, apples, nuts, wine, and cinnamon.
3. *Maror*—the bitter herbs. Either romaine lettuce or freshly ground horseradish is used as a symbol of the bitterness of slavery. If using romaine lettuce, carefully wash it to remove any small insects that often infest it. Horseradish should be unadulterated—that is, without beets or vinegar found in most commercially prepared horseradish. If grating your own, do so in a well-ventilated area long before the seder and leave the horseradish uncovered so it will lose some of its strength. The rabbis listed an order of preference for maror as follows: romaine lettuce, horseradish, endive, or escarole. They prefered romaine lettuce because, like the Egyptian experience, it first tastes sweet and only later becomes bitter. (If none of these is available, use any bitter vegetable but do not recite the blessing "to eat maror.")
4. *Beitzah*—a roasted egg, symbol of the festival sacrifice *(korban hagigah)*

I am a firstborn, and for many years now—at least since the late Sixties, which has something to do with it—I never attend a *siyyum* to avoid the fast. I am conscious of three reasons. First, I object to the legal loophole of the *siyyum*. It smacks of insincerity and corruption. Torah should be studied for its own sake. Second, I applaud observances that help make us sensitive to the suffering of others, even our enemies, for whom we need special sensitizing. As a firstborn spared, I want to feel for the firstborn of Egypt, who were singled out as victims so that God could make a point. And third, the seder food, that first matzah, tastes extra good following a day of fasting.

E.GR.

Begin the seder by asking everyone to make their own seder plate. Have bowls ready with all the needed ingredients—maror, eggs, etc. Provide everyone with an extra napkin to cover the three matzot. The seder leader should tell the participants where to place the item on the plate (two o'clock position, etc.). This encourages people to ask about the rituals of the seder.

Z.S.

Instead of a beet, we use a pascal yam just for the sound of it.

Z.S.

The symbols of the seder plate can be related to a schematic description of the *sefirot* as a human shape. The shank bone and the egg are the right and left arms. Maror is in the center with the three matzot *(hokhmah, binah, da'at)* underneath. Haroset and karpas are the right and left legs. *Hazeret* is at the base *(yesod).* The plate itself is the *sefirah* of *malkhut.*

Z.S.

On Shabbat and festivals, it is traditional to use whole loaves of bread for the *motzi* (the blessing over bread). Since during the early part of the seder we divide the middle matzah, we need three matzot to begin with if we are to have two whole ones left for *motzi.*

M.S.

Traditionally, each matzah represents one of the tribal statuses of Jews, but these divisions offend me today. In the ritual practices of my religious community, they play no role. I certainly can appreciate the universal classes of the Four Children: wise, wicked, simple, inexperienced. We should develop a different perception of the three matzot. What about the unfree, the free who don't care, and the free who care? Put the apathetic free on the bottom, the unfree in the middle. When we break the middle matzah, we can hope, as in sympathetic magic, for the breaking out of the as yet unfree. The retrieval of half of this matzah as the afikomen toward the end of the seder can symbolize—as it does for those who have customarily identified the hidden half as the Messiah—the future redemption of the unfree by us, the committed free, resting on the top of the matzah stack, unfettered and ready to act.

E.GR.

offered by each Jew going up to the temple in Jerusalem. The egg should be hard-boiled and then, still in its shell, placed on a stove burner until a part of it is scorched.

5. *Zeroa*—a roasted bone, commonly a shank bone, symbol of the Passover sacrifice *(korban pesah).* The bone is roasted and then scorched in a similar manner as the egg to simulate the Passover sacrifice, which was roasted. For vegetarians and others who prefer not to use a bone, the rabbis have suggested an alternative: a broiled beet (see Pesahim 114b).

Some seder plates have a sixth symbol, *hazeret,* which is additional maror to be used for the *koreikh* sandwich (see "Outline of the Seder" below).

There are a number of traditional arrangements of these symbols on the seder plate. One common one is as follows:

egg		shank bone
	maror	
karpas		haroset
	(hazeret)	

MATZOT

Three matzot, placed one atop the other, are used during the seder. Many people use special cloth "matzah covers" that have three compartments. If not using a matzah cover, it is customary to cover the matzot with a napkin during the seder. The matzot are placed next to the seder plate (as with the seder plate, anyone can have his or her own set of matzot). The three matzot are seen as symbolic of the three categories of Jews: priests *(kohanim),* Levites, and Israelites.

At the seder we use the plain flour-and-water type of matzah since the seder requires *lehem oni*—the plain bread of affliction (see below). Even if you eat egg matzah during Passover, all authorities agree you will not be fulfilling the commandment concerning matzah if you use it at the seder. Egg matzah is seen as "rich" matzah that is better tasting and easier to eat and should only be used at the seder by those who really cannot digest regular matzah. Some people prefer to use *matzah shemurah* (watched matzah) for the seder. These are made from flour/grain that has been watched from the time of harvest to prevent any possible contact with water, which could lead to leavening. Regular matzah is watched only from the time the grain is ground.

While most matzot are the square, machine-made variety, there are hand-baked matzot that are round and have a special quality all their own. For directions to bake your own matzah, see the *First Jewish Catalog,* p. 145. If your edition says the temperature required is 2000°, you have one of the more interesting mistakes of the catalog since this is the temperature used to heat steel. The correct temperature is 600° to 800°, so you still may find it difficult to bake matzot in a regular oven.

WINE

"Kosher for Passover" wine is needed for the Four Cups. Since each person is required to drink four cups, everyone should have his or her own glass. The drinking of the four cups is a mitzvah (of rabbinic origin), not an endurance test. Since it is important to be fully conscious at the seder, rather than sleepy or tipsy, you may use "Kosher for Passover" grape juice instead of wine. If, for reasons of health, you cannot drink grape wine or juice, raisin wine or any drink you would serve guests can be used.

There is no one clear reason why we have specifically four cups of wine at the seder. The most common explanation connects the Four Cups with the four expressions of redemption found in Exodus 6:6–7: "I am the Lord. I will *free* you from the burdens of the Egyptians and *deliver* you from their bondage. I will *redeem* you with an outstretched arm . . . and I will *take* you to be My people. . . ."

OTHER ITEMS AND PRACTICES FOR THE SEDER

Salt water We dip vegetables (karpas) into salt water, symbol of the tears of slavery. Prepare enough bowls of salted water before the seder.

Reclining It is a rabbinic mitzvah to recline during the seder, since reclining while eating was a sign of freedom in the ancient world. We recline to our left side (an armchair or pillows can facilitate the reclining) when we partake of the four cups, matzah, *koreikh,* and the afikomen. We do not recline when eating symbols of slavery such as maror.

Elijah's cup A large, ornate goblet is set aside for Elijah since, according to legend, Elijah visits every home on Passover and drinks from his cup.

Kittel In some households, the leader of the seder wears a kittel—a white robe that reminds us of the priestly garments worn during the temple service and thus of the Passover sacrifice as well.

AN OUTLINE OF THE SEDER

There is a traditional list of key words to remind us of the order of the seder.

I. *Kadesh.* Over the first cup of wine, kiddush (the sanctification of the day) is recited. This wine is drunk while reclining. Additional paragraphs for Shabbat are recited if Passover begins on Friday night. Havdalah is recited if Passover begins on Saturday night. The kiddush concludes with the recitation of the *she-he-heyanu* blessing.

I have learned from a friend that the kittel is worn to symbolize a new beginning, as on the High Holy Days, when we repent and acquire a new chance in life. The father of a newborn boy wears a kittel at the *brit millah,* acting as proxy for the boy who is entering the Covenant. A bridegroom wears a kittel, opening a new life for himself and his prospective family. When we die, we pass into Life Eternal buried in a kittel. At Pesah, we each free ourselves from Egypt, and, as befits this renewal, we wear a kittel.

E.GR.

Another association: This garment, associated with death also, suggests that any profound transition requires the dying of the old as the new is being born. The older generation from Egypt perishes in the desert as the new generation approaches the land; old attachments must die before new ones can develop; old ideas perish so that new ones can establish themselves.

Liberation, itself a transition, involves a death and rebirth, the dying of the old as the new comes into being; hence it is frightening. No wonder the Israelites had mixed reactions toward their liberation; it is rarely easy to adjust to the new, and the perishing of the familiar is often painful.

As for them, so for us: The dying of the old entrapments still causes fright, still provokes resistance. Death, the age-old price of liberation, is still the price today. Wearing the kittel reminds me of that ancient truth, and perhaps helps me fear it somewhat less.

E.GE.

Why is haroset on the seder plate, but salt water, which is used in our first dipping, absent? Salt water can be counted the tenth sefirotic element (instead of counting the seder plate itself) needed for completion. This element, which has been lacking for too many years, is the feminine. The salt water, symbolizing the amniotic fluid, heralds the bursting forth both of the spring of karpas and of the Jewish people from Egypt. In our time, we need to make a place for the salt water on the seder plate.

Z.S.

II. *Ur-hatz.* Traditionally, before a meal we wash our hands and recite the blessing *al netilat ya-dayim.* For *ur-hatz* we wash our hands but do not recite a blessing since this washing is related to the laws of ritual impurity, most of which have fallen into disuse. A vegetable dipped into liquid was a possible conveyer of impurity, hence a purification by washing is included to precede the dipping of vegetables that follows. Incidentally, this washing was probably retained at the seder to make the children curious.

III. *Karpas.* We dip a vegetable, symbol of the renewal of the earth at springtime, into salt water, symbol of the bitter tears shed by the slaves in Egypt. This ritual evokes the imagery of the birth of the Jewish people at the time of the Exodus.

During the seder we dip twice (the second time, we dip maror into the haroset) to provoke the children to ask about this unusual practice. In ancient times it was customary to begin a meal with a course of dips. A number of the seder customs are derived from Greco-Roman banquet customs that were seen as the way free people would eat. At first what was unusual about the seder was that we dipped twice, not just once. Later, when the general custom of dipping fell into disuse, the practice of dipping at all was unusual, hence one of the Four Questions asks, "Why do we dip twice?"

If one of the three matzot signifies our liberation from Egypt, and the second the messianic redemption yet to come, the middle matzah stands for our present situation in between. We break off a piece and hide it, as redemption is still hidden from us—though, because of the Exodus, we know that it is there—and then at the end of the meal our children find the piece we have hidden, so that we can all eat of it and so taste the redemption yet to come. We are forbidden to eat anything after that afikomen, so that we leave the seder with the taste of redemption on our lips.

A.E.

IV. *Yahatz.* We take the middle one of the three matzot and break it in two. The larger piece is wrapped in a napkin and set aside as the afikomen—the matzah eaten at the end of the meal; the smaller piece is replaced between the other two matzot. This practice is commonly explained as linked to the term *lehem oni*—the bread of affliction—which appears in the next paragraph of the Haggadah. Matzah, symbol of the slave food in Egypt, is broken in half to stress the extreme poverty of our lives in Egypt.

A common practice is for the children to steal the afikomen and hold it for ransom since the seder cannot end until the afikomen is eaten. This game was encouraged in order to keep the children awake for the seder. (It should

When we break the middle matzah of *binah* (a *sefirah* of wisdom), the smaller part we retain symbolizes how we understood before eating the afikomen, the larger part that we set aside symbolizes how we understand after the afikomen.

Or put another way, the top matzah symbolizes the right hemisphere of the brain. The middle is the left hemisphere, which is broken, reflecting the characteristic of analysis *(binah),* which involves the breakdown of things. Thus matzah has to do with consciousness. Rabbi Shneur Zalman of Liadi (eighteenth-century founder of Lubavitch Hasidism) said that a child cannot call Him Father until he has had a taste of grain. For us there can be no connection with God as parent until we eat the matzah, food of faith and healing.

Z.S.

be noted that, in extremis, any matzah can be used for the afikomen, not just the one set aside at *yahatz.*)

The prescribed ritual at the beginning of the seder seems similar to that of any Shabbat or festival eve, and yet there are differences. We begin with kiddush, but then we wash without a blessing. And instead of following the washing by the eating of bread, which would be customary, we dip vegetables and break bread without eating it. Next, we invite the hungry to join us, but instead of eating, we remove the seder plate that is the symbol of the seder meal. All these curious doings are a prelude to the Mah Nishtanah—the Four Questions. Rabbi Akiva at this point used to hand out treats to the children both to retain their interest and to make them wonder why they were getting dessert before the meal.

V. *Maggid.* This is the heart of the Haggadah—the story of the Exodus. The main structure is as follows:

A. *Ha lahma anya*—"This is the bread of affliction that our ancestors ate in Egypt." This paragraph—which is in Aramaic, the spoken language of the Jews in the early centuries of the Common Era—invites all who are hungry to join with us and ends with a hope that next year we will be free and in the land of Israel. It should be noted that the seder begins and ends with a hope for the return to Israel and Jerusalem. Confidence in that redemption helps us to celebrate the seder despite the reality we acknowledge when we say, "This year we are slaves, next year we will be free." Despite our present condition, we still celebrate the redemption of the Exodus as a foreshadowing of the redemption to come.

B. *Mah Nishtanah*—The Four Questions. This famous section is usually recited by the youngest child, though in fact anyone can ask "Why is this night different?" As mentioned, much of the previous ritual is to provoke children to ask questions, and the Talmud states that any question fulfills the purpose and makes Mah Nishtanah unnecessary.

The most challenging and exciting method I know for concealing the afikomen was employed by the leader of a seder I attended as a boy. Every year he would insert the half-matzah into the lining of the pillow on which he reclined. Everyone knew where it was; the problem was how to get it. The various children around the table would compete, often in collusion with another child or two, to sneak up and steal the afikomen when the leader was distracted. Often one would be caught in the act and forced to back down. But one would try, try again!

E.Gr.

Ha lahma anya—"Let all who are hungry come and eat; let all who are in need come share our Passover." Its recital in the common language of the day was to ensure that even those less well educated be able to understand its intent: that none be excluded from the celebrative feast.

And today? In our trim and economically segregated suburban neighborhoods, *Ha lahma anya,* even if recited in English with the door wide open, is unlikely to be heard by the poor, for they live elsewhere. In cities, who opens doors so unguardedly? Besides, even if we could contact the poor in our immediate areas, what about the desperately poor in many parts of the world, at least some portion of whose poverty is the result of policies pursued by our own government, our own corporations, and other agencies that we support and from which we benefit?

Yet if we fail, in truth, to open our doors at *Ha lahma anya,* if we permit the poor to remain unfed, how can we expect Elijah to enter when we open our doors for his messianic coming?

Along with the traditional pre-Pesah custom of *ma'ot hittim,* I have added the sending of contributions to Oxfam and Food First, two organizations whose integrity, programs, and perspicacity I trust. Perhaps in this way our symbolic opening of the door for *Ha lahma anya* has somewhat more reality to it, and Elijah may feel slightly more inclined to enter when later we open our door to him.

Addresses: Oxfam America, 115 Broadway, Boston, Mass. 02116

Food First Institute for Food and Development Policy, 1885 Mission Street, San Francisco, Calif. 94103

E.Ge.

Without in any way detracting from the concrete image of Jewish redemption in the land of Israel, we may still view Zion and Jerusalem as more abstract symbols of our personal and national fulfillment—just as Egypt symbolizes not only the place of our physical oppression but also the state of our enslavement by many different things. "Next year in Jerusalem" looks forward to a future of greater freedom just as leaving Egypt does.

E.GR.

Ask yourself: What are your four questions? Your four questions about Judaism? If I want to *know* something this night, what is it I really want to know? Why is it *different?* Life, I mean; why is it different from what I expected?

Z.S.

And even the wisest were not so wise as to stand aloof from the hope for imminent redemption and therefore were cruelly disappointed when the Bar Kochba rebellion was crushed. The question of whether Passover would be observed after the Messiah's coming ("all the days of your life . . . *all* the days includes the messianic era") was a real one for them; the pain that fueled such expectation was all too real as well. And the problem is to share their perfect faith in redemption, keeping the hope alive, without succumbing to false messiahs. Better to tell of the exodus from Egypt, all the way till the morning shema.

A.E.

Incidentally, the meal originally preceded the maggid section, which is why there are questions about matzah and maror although in our seders the child has not yet tasted them. It is customary to fill the second cup of wine and to remove the seder plate before Mah Nishtanah is recited—again to encourage questions.

C. *Avadim hayinu*—"We were slaves to Pharaoh. . . ." The Four Questions are never answered directly in the Haggadah. This paragraph begins the indirect answer by telling the story of the Exodus. It sets forth two essential themes of the Haggadah:

1. We, not just our ancestors, were slaves to Pharaoh in Egypt, and if God had not redeemed us, we and our descendants would still be enslaved to Pharaoh.

2. No matter how learned we are, it is still incumbent upon us to tell the story of the Exodus. Whoever expands upon the telling is considered praiseworthy. *Avadim hayinu* points to the fact that the Egyptian experience is our own as well and therefore the story must be retold and expanded upon, since we are still struggling to be free. Each year we try to expand the frontiers of our freedom a little farther, since we understand that if we simply recite the story as a tale told about others, we can easily slip into being enslaved to the "pharaohs" of our own creation.

   Avadim hayinu is followed by a paragraph telling of five talmudic scholars who stayed up all night discussing the Exodus, thus giving us an example of how even the wisest expanded upon the tale.

D. *Arba banim*—the Four Children. The rabbis use four biblical references to children asking or being told about the Exodus to construct this exposition of four types of children. Much commentary has been written on this section discussing such issues as the difference between the wise and wicked child, whether the simple child is stupid or innocent, etc. An underlying motif of this section is that each child is different and should be told the story on the level of his or her own understanding.

E. *Mi-tehilah ovdei*—"In the beginning our ancestors worshiped idols." In the Talmud it states that the Haggadah should "begin with degradation and end with praise." There is disagreement over what is "degradation." One opinion is that we were slaves, hence *Avadim hayinu.* The other is that we were idol-worshipers, hence this paragraph.

F. *Barukh shomeir*—two paragraphs stating that God has kept His promise and redeemed us in Egypt and will redeem us from the foes that arise against us in every age.

G. *Arami oveid avi*—"My father was a wandering Aramean." These verses from Deuteronomy (26:5–8), the core of the telling of the story, were recited by Jews bringing their first fruits to the temple in Jerusalem and therefore were familiar to everyone. In the Haggadah each verse is recited and then interpretations of individual phrases are offered.

   This part of the Haggadah requires the most preparation by the seder leader(s). The midrashic style of commentary can be foreign to people unfamiliar with it, and the interpretations may add little to their understanding of the verses. This section can be handled in a number of ways as outlined below in "Kavvanot." You may also want to playact or begin a discussion on an important Passover theme instead of focusing on the text. Some modern Haggadot have changed the text in this section, and you may find a revised text that appeals to you.

This section ends with a recitation of the ten plagues. It is customary to remove a drop of wine from your cup at the mention of each plague. This is to show that we are cognizant of the humanity of our enemies and rejoice over their downfall with less than a full heart.

H. "Dayyeinu"—a song that recounts all the great deeds God performed for the Israelites. Each line ends with the refrain *dayyeinu*—"It would have been enough."

I. *Rabban Gamliel hayah omeir*—"Rabban Gamliel would say . . ." Gamliel requires an explanation of the central symbols of the seder—the Passover sacrifice, matzah, and maror. There is a custom of pointing to the matzah and maror as we refer to them. We do not point to the shank bone to show it is only a symbol of the Passover sacrifice.

J. *Be-khol dor ve-dor*—"In each generation, every individual should feel personally redeemed. . . ." This paragraph is the clearest statement that *we* were redeemed from Egypt, not just our ancestors. Thus the Haggadah stresses the mythical notion that we, living today, are slaves and *are* redeemed. This Passover myth continues to live in our lives since all of us in different ways are still enslaved and still striving to be free.

K. *Le-fikhakh*—"Therefore, since God redeemed us, we must glorify the Holy One and sing praise before Him." Following this paragraph are two sections of the hallel service. The second section speaks of the Exodus, which is why it was placed here, while the rest of hallel is recited after the meal.

L. The concluding blessing of the maggid section praises God for being our redeemer and speaks of our hope for future redemption. The maggid section concludes with the second cup of wine, over which we recite the blessing and which we drink while reclining.

VI. *Rohtzah.* We ritually wash our hands and recite the blessing *al netilat ya-dayim.*

VII & VIII. *Motzi, Matzah.* We take the three matzot and recite two blessings—the regular blessing for bread and a special one for matzah. We eat from the top and middle matzot while reclining.

IX. *Maror.* We take the bitter herbs, dip them in haroset, and recite the blessing for maror. We do not recline while eating.

X. *Koreikh.* We use the bottom matzah to make a sandwich with maror. By way of explanation, we recite a paragraph describing temple practice; then we eat the sandwich while reclining. The sage Hillel believed that matzah and maror (and the Passover sacrifice) were eaten together in temple times. Our

The wicked child, like the others, quotes the exact words of Torah—and that is precisely the point. For in order to twist the words to his purpose, he utters them in a tone of voice and gives them a meaning far different from those intended, thereby standing above the text, detached from it. He has distanced himself by his irony. Therefore, says the Haggadah, the child denies a cardinal principle of Jewish faith, and the very essence of Pesah: that God acts in history to redeem us.

Had such a person been present in Egypt, he would never have stopped to smear blood on the lintel; at Sinai he would probably have overslept on the morning of Revelation; today he puts redemption far off by his failure to say the word *we.*

How different is the simple person who, though he cannot follow most of what goes on, still gets the essential point. Like the Hasid of Rabbi Levi Yitzhak of Berdichev, who knew only that "our fathers and mothers were in captivity in the land of the Gypsies, and we have a God, and He led them out, and into freedom. And see: Now we are again in captivity and I know, and I tell you, that God will lead us to freedom, too."

A.E.

practice is to eat matzah and maror separately, but then, to fulfill Hillel's opinion as well, we eat a sandwich *(koreikh)*.

XI. *Shulhan Oreikh.* At last! We eat the festive meal. Some people begin the meal with eggs dipped in salt water. Different but not very convincing reasons have been given for this custom, including that eggs are

    A. a sign of mourning for the temple and its sacrificial system;

    B. a symbol of joy and fertility;

    C. a metaphor for the Jewish people: The more they are heated, oppressed, the harder they get.

The meal can be a social time or used for further discussions of the seder themes. There are no requirements concerning what to eat, though some people refrain from eating any roasted meat (or even any roasted food). This is to avoid any suggestion that we are actually eating the Pesah sacrifice.

XII. *Tzafun.* We ransom the afikomen and eat it while reclining. In temple times, the Passover sacrifice was eaten at the end of the meal, when everyone was almost satiated. In remembrance of this, we partake of the afikomen as the very last food to be eaten at the seder. There is a folk belief that the afikomen acts as a powerful "amulet" for good luck, and some people save a piece throughout the year.

XIII. *Bareikh.* The grace after meals is recited. At the conclusion, the blessing for wine is recited over the third cup of wine, which is drunk while reclining.

The last part of the Haggadah ends with praise and song. We praise the past redemption and look forward to the future redemption as symbolized by the figure of Elijah.

XIV. *Hallel.* The rest of hallel is recited. Preceding hallel, the door is opened for Elijah—usually by a child—and *shefokh hamatka* (Pour out your wrath) is recited. A goblet is placed on the table to be used as Elijah's cup. The genesis of this custom is complex. According to tradition, Elijah will come to herald the Messiah and the final redemption. One tradition has it that the final redemption will take place at the same time of the year that the first redemption took place—i.e., Nisan. Therefore we open the door hoping that this year will be the one when Elijah appears.

There is also a debate in the Talmud as to whether there should be four or five cups at the seder based on the word *ve-heiveiti*—"I will bring you"—in Exodus 6:8 (see "Wine," p. 19). The resolution of the debate is one of those issues in the Talmud left for Elijah to resolve in messianic times, and thus Elijah's cup is really the fifth cup, which is not drunk, because its status remains in doubt.

Shefokh hamatkha, a harsh and bitter cry for revenge against the nations seems to have little connection with Elijah. The custom of reciting these verses began in the Middle Ages in response to the violent persecution of the

The halakhah states that nothing else may be eaten after the afikomen in order that the taste linger in our mouths. Some authorities, however, allow the drinking of tea, apple juice, and seltzer after the afikomen.

M.S.

Jews that began with the Crusades. Some scholars speculate that the Jews in the Middle Ages opened their doors to give the lie to the blood accusation that Jews killed Christians to use their blood to bake matzot. The connection of these verses with Elijah, then, is that the nations will be punished at the final redemption for their persecution of Israel. Psalm 136 as well as the prayers nishmat and yishtabah (taken from the traditional liturgy) are recited after hallel. Then the blessing over wine is recited and the fourth cup is drunk while reclining. The blessing said *after* drinking wine is also recited.

XV. *Nirtzah*—the conclusion. We finish the seder with part of a poem called "Hasal Siddur Pesah." We then say or sing *le-shanah ha-ba-ah*—"Next year in Jerusalem."

After this, there are a number of songs such as "Ki lo Na'eh," "Adir Hu," "Ehad mi Yodea" ("Who Knows One"), and "Had Gadya" ("One Kid"). These are medieval additions to the Haggadah but have become very popular. Recently some people have reversed the order and first sing the songs, then drink the fourth cup, and finally conclude the seder with *nirtzah,* feeling that the songs appear after *nirtzah* only because they are late additions.

The perfect ending, the summation of Pesah themes and hopes: a children's song, chanted with laughter and gusto, the words of which are utterly terrifying. Death after death, destruction after destruction, cheerfully sung because we know the ending: The Holy One, Blessed be He, comes and slaughters the angel of death, thereby bringing complete redemption. Without that ending, the lot of little kids (and their parents) would be less joyful. But, the Haggadah reassures us, that *is* how the story ends.

A.E.

THE REST OF PASSOVER

The synagogue services the morning after the seder are similar to all holiday services and include hallel, a special Torah reading, and musaf—the additional service. The first day of Passover is also distinguished by the addition of Tal during the repetition of the musaf amidah. Tal is a special prayer for dew recited as the rainy season ends in the land of Israel. (Both the prayer for dew and the prayer for rain on Shemini Atzeret are recited only on the first day, ignoring the question of the second days of festivals.) For the crops to survive the dry summer, a substantial dew is necessary. The words *mashiv ha-ruah u-morid ha-gashem*—He who causes the blowing of winds and the falling of rain—which are added to every amidah beginning on Shemini Atzeret, are no longer recited beginning with the first day of Pesah. (Sephardim replace those words in the amidah with the phrase *morid ha-tal*— He who causes the falling of the dew.)

Since the success of the crops affects the sustenance of our lives, these prayers are recited with special seriousness. It is customary for the service leader to wear a white robe during the musaf service, and for the ark to be opened during the repetition of the amidah. The melodies used are similar to those of the High Holidays, reflecting how much our lives depend on the amount of rainfall. The prayer itself was composed by Rabbi Elazar ha-Kallir (c. eighth century) and is added to the second blessing of the musaf amidah during its repetition. The text can be found in most prayer books.

SECOND DAY OF PASSOVER

If you observe "the second day of the festivals in the Diaspora," then the observance of this day is the same as the first day of yom tov, with the following exceptions:

- The Haggadah text is the same as for the first seder except for two piyyutim (liturgical poems) recited near the end of the seder. *U-be-khen va-yehi ba-hatzi ha-lailah* is recited the first night, and *u-be-khen ve-amarteim zevah Pesah* is recited the second night.
- We begin to count the omer at the second seder (this ritual will be found near the end of the Haggadah). The omer was a specific measure of the new wheat harvest that was harvested the second night of Passover and brought to the temple as a special offering. Connected with this was the counting of the omer—that is, counting the days between Passover and Shavuot. Today, without a temple, there is no omer offering, but we are still rabbinically commanded to count the days between Passover and Shavuot. (For more details and explanations of the Omer, see the next chapter.)

Therefore on the second night we recite:

Praised are You, Lord our God, King of the universe who sanctified us through His commandments, commanding us to count the omer.
Today is the first day of the omer.

The omer should be counted whether one observes the second day as a yom tov (festival day) or as the first of the intermediate days.

- The morning services are the same as the first day except for a different Torah reading and for the fact that the Tal prayer is not recited again.

HOL HA-MOED—

THE INTERMEDIATE DAYS OF PASSOVER

The days that lie between the first and last days of Pesah are semiholidays. Traditionally, work was discouraged on these days, but for most people today these days are marked only by the noteworthy features of the holiday—that is, the eating of matzah and abstinence from hametz. (For more on *hol ha-moed*, see p. 133.)

Most other differences between normal weekdays and yom tov are found in the synagogue liturgy—e.g., a Torah reading and the recital of musaf every day. On Passover, unlike the intermediate days of Sukkot, only a partial hallel *(hatzi hallel)* is recited. The reason for this is obscure. The most common explanation is that because we recite a partial hallel on the seventh day, which is a yom tov, we recite only a partial hallel on the intermediate ones in order not to elevate the intermediate days above a full festival day. The reason only a partial hallel is recited on the seventh day is that it commemorates the day that the Israelites crossed the Red Sea. We temper our happiness because of the drowning of the Egyptians, who were human even though our enemies.

On the Shabbat that falls during the intermediate days, many congregations recite the Song of Songs (Shir ha-Shirim) before the Torah reading. (Another custom is to read it after the seder.)

THE SEVENTH DAY

The seventh day of Passover is a yom tov—a full festival day. For those who observe the second day of festivals, the eighth day of Passover is also a full festival day. These days have the same sanctity and regulations as the first days except that since they are not seen to have a special character of their own, the she-he-heyanu blessing is omitted.

The seventh day, according to tradition, marks the crossing of the Red Sea by the Israelites. Some people, particularly Hasidim, follow the custom of pouring water on the floor and singing and dancing to commemorate the crossing of the sea.

Yizkor, the memorial prayer for the dead, is recited on the last day (seventh or eighth, depending on your observance) of the festival.

There is a kabbalistic custom of staying up all night of the seventh day of Passover to recite and study a tikkun—a prescribed course of study. Unlike the tikkun leil shavuot (see Shavuot), this is observed by very few people.

ON REJOICING AT THE DOWNFALL OF AN ENEMY

Passover is replete with examples of the tension between rejoicing at the suffering and death of those who persecute us and yet feeling sorrow that human life is being tormented and destroyed. Thus in one section of the Haggadah, the rabbis elaborate on the number of plagues that befell the Egyptians, raising it from 10 to 250—but there is also the custom of taking out one drop for each of the ten plagues so that our cup is not full because of their suffering. Similarly, as noted above, we recite only a partial hallel, except for the first days of Passover. The tradition seems to be teaching us that while it is only human to rejoice at the downfall of an enemy, such rejoicing must be qualified by awareness of the suffering—necessary perhaps, but suffering nonetheless—of our foes.

This tension is best captured in comparing the exultant Song at the Sea (Exod. 15) recited by the Israelites after the drowning of the Egyptians with the following midrash:

> At that moment [of the crossing], the ministering angels wanted to sing praises to God. But God silenced them, saying: "My children are drowning in the sea and you want to sing before me!"

If you find hametz during Pesah, you must remove it immediately. Since you are not allowed to burn it on a yom tov, if you find it on the first day(s) of Passover, you are to cover it with a bowl to prevent anyone from accidentally eating it. Once yom tov is over, you should burn it.
M.S.

The midrash states: "A humble maidservant saw more [of a vision of God] at the crossing of the sea than Ezekiel saw in his vision [of the chariot]." During the tikkun of the seventh day of Passover, each person should get a chance to sit in the "rebbe's seat" and hold forth for five minutes. Everyone has something to say that is a reflection of what the Shekhinah is sending down into the world at this time. After each person gets a chance, sing and dance around the table, then sit down with everyone moving over one chair. There should be no response to what people say, to prevent any feelings of intimidation.
Z.S.

Yes, we are only human. But we are obliged to be holy, like God: "Holy shall you be, for holy am I," says the Lord in Leviticus 19:2. The angels should not be seen on a level above what we should be, but as models of what we should be. The lessons in holiness that God teaches the angels are lessons we must graduate to learn. God knows we are only human, but we are bidden to adopt more and more of God's behavior. Angels are agents of God, "messengers" in the idiom of the Bible. That is our mission, too.
E.GR.

POST-PESAH

Restoring your house to hametz is a simple matter consisting mainly of putting away Pesah utensils and returning hametz ones to their regular places.

The one law that lingers after Passover pertains to *hametz she-avar alav ha-pesah.* As mentioned earlier, any hametz owned by a Jew during Passover is permanently forbidden by rabbinic decree. Therefore, some people will not eat bread from Jewish-owned bakeries or food stores the first day or so after Pesah until they are reasonably sure whatever bread was baked on Passover has already been sold.

Pesah is concluded by havdalah said over wine. (The blessings over the candle and spices are said only upon the conclusion of Shabbat.) Some people have the custom of eating a heavily hametz meal such as pizza, or at least eating some food that they sorely missed during Passover. For others the transition back to hametz is a slow one, taking place during the omer period. As we shall see, there is a transition from the Pesah meals of matzah and meat to the Shavuot meals of dairy food and leavened bread. This transition, reflecting the spiritual growth that takes place between Pesah and the giving of the Torah on Shavuot, will be more fully discussed in the following chapter. (For a discussion of Isru Hag—the day after Pesah—see p. 77.)

MAIMUNA

Jews of North Africa celebrate Maimuna the evening and day after Pesah. According to tradition, it is the anniversary of the death of Maimon ben Joseph, the father of Maimonides (twelfth century). Pitchers of milk, garlands of leaves and flowers, branches of fig trees, ears of wheat, and a fishbowl complete with fish are placed on the table. The menu is made up of dairy foods, particularly pancakes known as *muflita.* During the day, Jews gather together for picnics. In Israel there is a central gathering of Moroccan Jews in Jerusalem. How this festival originated and its connection with Maimon are obscure—though, interestingly, it reflects an immediate transition to the agricultural themes and dairy foods of the omer period and Shavuot respectively.

KAVVANOT

PREPARING FOR THE HOLIDAY

The basic preparations for Pesah involve the total removal of hametz from our possession. Because of the strictness of the hametz prohibitions, much thought and effort are required for this enterprise. Each one of us, together with the people with whom we celebrate Passover, must decide what we want to do, or feel commanded to do, in removing hametz. Similar questions arise in regard to how to observe the prohibition of hametz *during* the holiday. For some, the full range of traditional laws about hametz will seem the correct approach; for others, they will seem excessive, irrelevant, or counterproductive to the celebration of Passover.

Those of us who find ourselves somewhere between total acceptance and total rejection of the hametz laws will have to struggle with the tradition and with ourselves to create a mode of observance that feels right for each of us. There have been many extra restrictions added over time to the laws of hametz. These restrictions can be seen as arising from a deep concern about not violating the laws of hametz and thus as reflecting a love of the tradition and a desire to embellish it. On the other hand, these restrictions can also be seen as arising from an obsessive compulsiveness that borders on making the tradition into an idolatry.

The process of removing hametz involves us in the change that Passover brings to our lives. It is important to eat or throw away or give away at least some of our old hametz to make room for the newness and sense of freedom that Passover brings. Even after Passover is over, our cabinets should be somewhat different from before as a sign that Passover is not altogether gone from our minds and souls. Even if the can way at the back of the top shelf that has been there so long the label is hard to read is *not* hametz, by removing it we remind ourselves of how necessary periodic reviews of our own souls' "canned goods" are for growth. For this reason, participating in the removal of hametz, no matter to what degree, is vitally important in really experiencing Pesah. The most frequent slavery in our lives is slavery to old routines, old feelings, old habits. Pesah brings a taste of freedom, declaring that we must give away or put away the normal, the routine, and try something different for a week. Then when we go back to the old and familiar, it may be transformed for us.

In the Beginning In our family, the first sign of the approaching holiday (besides looks of dread at the inside of our oven) is the conscious effort to consume as much of our hametz as possible before Passover. Besides being a nonwasteful way of getting rid of hametz, this concern announces to each of us that Passover is upon us. Some individuals and groups have hametz parties ("pasta parties" for the alliterative) to remove their hametz in an enjoyable and creative way.

We have found that careful planning combined with doing the cleaning/-preparations over a period of time helps prevent overdosing on the work leading up to the holiday. In particular, the final days before Passover are a fine balancing act between still needing space for hametz and yet beginning to buy and cook foods for Passover.

We have found it helpful to make notes about how the preparations worked out, how much Pesah food (e.g., matzah) we used, etc., to facilitate the planning and the buying for the following year. Certain Pesah products we save from year to year. We make a list of such things to prevent us from buying the fifth container of black pepper. Such lists also include whatever utensils could be added to our Pesah kitchen supplies.

The Exodus occurred so that there might be Sinai, and our answer to the words *(devarim)* that God spoke at Sinai comes in the facts *(devarim)* that we create in accordance with His words. Facts, too, speak: Widows and orphans who are not cared for make a mockery of our words about God's merciful providence; injustice and poverty threaten the meaning that we seek to find in the world. It would therefore be inconceivable that the Haggadah *not* begin by inviting "all who are hungry" to come and eat with us; redemption cannot even be imagined, let alone achieved, if the "we" that we speak does not include those outside the door as well as those within. The fear of letting them in must be overcome.

A.E.

A story is told of Rabbi Hayyim Brisker (nineteenth-century talmudist). He was approached by a person who asked him whether he could fulfill the mitzvah of the Four Cups at the seder with milk instead of wine. Rabbi Hayyim answered no and gave the man twenty rubles and sent him on his way. Rabbi Hayyim's wife queried him: "What kind of *psak* [religious decision] is that? Everyone knows that if you have no choice, you can fulfill the mitzvah with milk!" Rabbi Hayyim responded: "I knew this person asked about milk because he could not afford wine or meat for the seder, therefore the question was not one of halakhah but of money."

Z.S.

In the End At the conclusion of all our preparations comes the ritual search for hametz on the night before Passover. Coming at the end of all the hametz preparations, this ritual is a good moment to take a deep breath before plunging into Pesah itself and is also an important symbol of completing a difficult task. It is customary for someone to hide a few pieces of bread before the search. Make sure to remember how many and where you hid them, or you will find the tenth, as we did one year, during Passover itself. The search is particularly enjoyable for children, who go from room to room with flashlight in hand looking for any trace of hametz. The search also serves as an introduction to the key role the children will play at the seder itself. In general, the children should be involved as much as possible in the holiday preparations, such as cleaning their rooms and helping to unpack the Passover dishes. It is memories of this kind of involvement that partly explain why Passover remains meaningful to many Jews who have discarded much of the rest of the holiday cycle.

Besides removing hametz, another important activity before the holiday is *ma'ot hittim* (literally money for bread). A special tzedakah (charity) collection is made during the month of Nisan for money to be given to the poor before Passover. Since Passover involves extra food costs, tzedakah is particularly important for this holiday. Even scholars, who were usually exempt from taxes in the medieval communities *(kehillot)*, were obligated to give to *ma'ot hittim;* indeed, we are told that we must give even if we have already given money to tzedakah.

The theme of hospitality and caring for the poor and the stranger is found throughout this period surrounding Passover. At the beginning of the seder, we invite all who are hungry to join us, and later we open our doors to Elijah, the eternal wanderer. We collect *ma'ot hittim* not only because Pesah food is expensive but because every Jew should be "free" to celebrate the festival of liberation. Therefore, Jewish law insists that even those poor who subsist on charity must have enough wine for the Four Cups. This is not an unrealistic legalism, but rather a recognition that we must work toward social justice, especially on this day. If one Jew were to go hungry at Passover, it would be a mockery of the whole story of Pesah, showing that we had truly come to forget that we were once slaves in the land of Egypt.

Recently, some people have combined these two aspects of the holiday preparation—removing hametz and showing concern for the needy—by giving away unopened containers of hametz to non-Jews. Local churches and social-service agencies are good sources for distribution to those in need.

PREPARING FOR THE SEDER

Just as important as the preparations involving hametz are those for the seder. It is not just the menu of the seder meal that requires forethought. If the seder is to be a meaningful reexperiencing of the Exodus rather than a rote reading of the Haggadah, then it requires real planning. Some questions to consider:

- Do you want the seder to be conducted by a leader or by the group? If the former, do you want to divide the role of leader so that different people are in charge of different sections of the Haggadah?
- How will the others be involved? Will the reading of the Haggadah be rotated or done in unison? Will people be asked to raise questions and make comments?
- How will accommodation be made for people with a variety of backgrounds?
- How will children be involved and yet the experience remain meaningful for adults?
- How will the experience be made "new" to those familiar with it from many past years' observance?
- What do you want to add to or delete from the Haggadah text?

Following are some general guidelines that our family has found useful over the years:

- Try to make everyone feel included by encouraging participation, even if only by getting people to ask questions about the reasons for various rituals.
- Whether one person is leading or that role is shared, try to keep in mind a general time frame. It is easy to spend so much time on the first few pages that you have to skip or race through the rest of the text.
- Whatever emphasis you want to give the seder, try to include all the essential elements—especially the telling of the Exodus story. This could mean skipping ahead while the children are still awake so they can be present for their favorite parts, and then returning later to the bypassed material.

One of the problems at many seders is that some people become hungry and desire to rush through the Haggadah text in order to arrive at the meal. To assuage hunger, we treat karpas—vegetables dipped in salt water near the beginning of the seder—as hors d'oeuvres. We serve platters of vegetables with different kinds of dips, thus allowing the seder to continue at a leisurely pace. (Care should be taken not to fill up completely before you have gotten to the meal.)

According to halakhah, the key elements of the seder are telling the story, eating matzah, drinking four cups of wine, eating maror, and reciting hallel. But as the Haggadah states, "Whoever expands upon the story of the Exodus deserves praise," hence the Haggadah itself consists of more than the bare-bones rituals sketched above. Some of its most popular parts are not, strictly speaking, part of the required observance—for example, the Four Questions or the parable of the Four Children or the songs, such as "Dayyeinu" or "Had Gadya"—but most people would feel something essential was missing from the seder if these were lacking.

- Each person should have a Haggadah. Depending on the participants' familiarity with the seder, you may want one edition for everyone (enabling the leader to announce pages) or several editions (providing

Before you actually start the seder, ask everyone to share their expectations. Some may want a seder with a lot of singing; others a lot of discussion. Some may want to stick close to the text; others may want to be very contemporary. Having everyone state aloud their expectations allows the group to work together to satisfy the variety of needs during the course of the evening.

Z.S.

Among some Jews of North African origin, the seder begins with each member of the family taking a staff in his hand, holding a matzah on his shoulders and a pack on his back, and walking in a circle about the seder table—a dramatic reliving of the walk out of Egypt.

A.G.

It should be emphasized that the real mitzvah of telling the tale is one of real communication. The language and content of the tale as told must be understood both by the one who tells it and by its hearers. Those who simply mumble through the Haggadah text in a Hebrew they do not understand are literally not fulfilling the commandment of the seder.

A.G.

Central to an understanding of Pesah is the commandment of *ve-higadeta le-vinkha*—you should tell your child [about the Exodus]. Matzah itself symbolizes the need for a dialogue between one generation and the next, for *lehem oni* can be interpreted as the bread *(lehem)* over which much is answered *(onim)*.

Every generation must reinterpret the Torah for itself. This occurs at the seder as each parent realizes that they are obligated to tell the story in a meaningful way to their children. In order to be understood, they must find the right language—that is, they must communicate in the words of the next generation. The children are obligated as well, obligated to ask questions according to their understanding.

This conversation must take place on the level of *emet*—truth. For the parents to tell the children pious untruths would result in a weakening of the transmission that is to take place this night. For one night a year, at least, the generations must meet and hear each other clearly. Since we usually avoid this, the tradition has created the setting of the seder to facilitate this happening. Whosoever has not really spoken to his children on this night has not fulfilled the mitzvah of *maggid*— telling.

Z.S.

a variety of perspectives to be drawn upon). Even if you use a number of editions, you may want enough copies of one edition for those who need direction.

There are over 3,000 editions of the Haggadah, and more appearing each year. Those in print run the gamut from reproductions of medieval texts to secular modern retellings. Spend some time in a library or bookstore looking through the available editions. Keep in mind your requirements: Do you want a Haggadah that is traditional or one that is contemporary? With English readings or with traditional commentary? With artwork?

Below are a number of recent Haggadot that may be of interest.

A Passover Haggadah. Edited by Herbert Bronstein. New York: Central Conference of American Rabbis (Reform), 1974. An interesting mixture of text and readings, beautifully illustrated.

The Haggadah. Edited by Joseph Elias. New York: Mesorah Publications, 1977. A collection of comments of traditional interpreters from an Orthodox viewpoint.

The Passover Haggadah. Edited by Nahum Glatzer. New York: Schocken Books, revised 1979. Traditional text with brief scholarly notes and a good introduction.

Passover Haggadah. Edited by Rachel Rabinowicz. New York: Rabbinical Assembly (Conservative), 1982. A clear set of instructions for the seder, with commentary.

Why Is This Night Different? Edited by Zev Schostak. New York: Judaica Press, 1981. A guide to Passover and the Haggadah from an Orthodox viewpoint.

Gates of Freedom. Edited by Chaim Stern. Bedford, N.Y.: New Star Press, 1981. Another interesting mixture of readings and text from a liberal viewpoint.

- While the seder is important for both adults and children, there is, as we have said, a special role for children this night. We want to encourage them to firmly associate themselves with the Jewish people and their heritage; thus, we tell them of Egypt and the Exodus to impress upon them their history. But beyond teaching them, children give *us* insights into the meaning of freedom, because they take nothing for granted. They are constantly questioning the hows and whys, and thereby make us reexamine our complacent explanations, which are often forms of subtle enslavement.

  The beginning of the seder is replete with rituals meant to provoke children into asking. One of the challenges we face is to provoke that questioning year after year. One family I know of began to serve the meal and then removed it. Try to create practices that will provoke *your* children to ask, "Why . . . ?"

- The telling of the story (the central part of the maggid section in the Haggadah) can be handled in many ways. You may wish to use the traditional text, or the revised versions of some recent Haggadot. You can use selections from the Book of Exodus or try having the participants take turns telling the story as they might have experienced it, each in his or her own fashion. Among Sephardic Jews, there are traditions of acting out the Exodus. One tradition has someone go out of the room and begin a question-and-answer ritual: Who's there? Where are you from? etc. Games and plays tell the story in ways both children and adults can relate to and help us all become involved in the experience of the seder.

· The after-the-meal section can also be a place to make additions to enhance the traditional Haggadah text. The simplest way to do this is to add appropriate songs (even English songs such as "Go Down, Moses") to those found in the Haggadah.

The figure of Elijah lends a motif of redemption to this section. Therefore, the after-the-meal section can be seen as a continuation of the Passover story. This can be implemented by adding material about Jews in later times, ranging from the Middle Ages to Israel and the Soviet Union today. You may also want to include material that looks toward the final redemption and the coming of the Messiah. Two recent customs are related to this motif. One is the matzah of hope—a prayer on behalf of the persecuted Jews in the Soviet Union. Some people even leave an empty chair and place setting for a Soviet Jew who cannot join them at the seder. (The matzah-of-hope prayer is available from the National Conference for Soviet Jewry, 10 East 40th Street, New York, N.Y. 10016.) The second custom is based on Hasidic practice: Rabbi Harold Schulweis has suggested filling Elijah's cup by passing it around the table for everyone to pour some of his or her wine into it, thus symbolically stating that all of us must join together to bring about the final redemption.

· Since the seder is preeminently a family celebration, you may want to join some appropriate segment of family history to the Passover story. The seder story is a never-ending one, for as the Haggadah states, "in every generation enemies rise up against us." Then, too, if Passover marks the beginning of the Jewish people, there is no more appropriate time to tell some of the history of your own little segment of the people. Uncle Jake could be asked to relate how he escaped from Europe before the war, or more-random reminiscences can be told (with each relative remembering a different version of the same event, of course). These, too, are parts of our priceless heritage and help children feel part of a people by describing a small and readily understood component of their history.

· For those holding a seder on the second night, preparation is even more important to maintain interest. Variety can be introduced in many ways. One night can hew to the traditional text; the other night can take it as a jumping-off point for wide-ranging discussion. A different theme or part of the story can be emphasized each night—for example, exploring slavery one night and liberation the next. Some material, songs, etc., can be set aside for the second night.

· There is a custom of reciting the Song of Songs after the seder. This

In clear weather, a fine way to begin the seder is to step outside, look eastward, and try to catch sight of the moon rising in the east just at sunset. Since on the fifteenth night of the lunar month the moon is always full, this provides the opportunity to entertain questions about the Jewish calendar, lunar rhythms, etc. [Cf. *The First Jewish Catalog,* pp. 96–100.]

Actually, a view of the full moon rising is sufficiently wondrous that even without questions or discussion, it's a fine way to begin any seder.

E.Ge.

book is seen as a metaphor for the love between God and Israel and is particularly appropriate to Passover as the time of spring and the birth of that love. Another custom is to recite only part of the shema recited at bedtime. Traditionally, every night before bed the shema and other prayers are recited. Part of the purpose of these prayers is to ask God for protection from harm while we sleep. Since the seder night is referred to as Leil Shimurim—a night of watching—there is a belief that God watches over us this night just as He protected the Israelites from harm on this night long ago in Egypt. Therefore, we need recite only the blessing *ha-mapil* and the first paragraph of the shema.

- There are a number of crafts associated with the seder, including the making and decorating of matzah covers, seder plates, and goblets for Elijah. The matzah covers, as explained earlier, are used to hold the three matzot used in the seder and can range from napkins decorated by the children to cloth embroidered by fine artists. Seder plates also come in many different media and styles. One can also fashion dishes for salt water and embroider pillowcases to be used for reclining at the seder. (The particular foods needed for the seder-plate ritual are described on pp. 17–18.)

DERASH

Like many adventure stories, the tale of the Exodus begins in crisis and ends happily. Yet it is not just the progression from slavery to freedom that is important; each component of the tale is significant.

SLAVERY

At some point in the seder, we should talk about how bad slavery is. What is the difference between slavery and righteous work—for there is work that makes us feel, if we do it and then eat, that we are not freeloaders on the universe. At which point does work break your body, at which point does it give you zest? When do you feel this is not the work I want to do, this is not the work I am meant to accomplish, these conditions are not *working* conditions?

Z.S.

We begin the retelling by proclaiming *"Avadim hayinu"*—"We were slaves to Pharaoh in Egypt." The sacred history of our people does not start with the tales of great heroes, or of the righteous founding fathers, or the stories of innocent babes (for example Romulus and Remus, the legendary founders of Rome), but with the tale of slaves. We begin not with a heroic chapter but with a bleak one. We know that slaves were the lowest social group in the ancient world, but instead of trying to rewrite history and hide or erase this tainted beginning, each generation of Jews proclaims the fact that not only our ancestors but *we ourselves* were slaves to Pharaoh.

We are meant to remember the pain of the lash and the degradation of slavery to make us sensitive to the pain of others. We who were slaves and strangers should understand hopelessness, fear, and insecurity. Thus, the Torah persistently admonishes us to take care of the poor, the orphan, the widow, and the stranger. We are told to leave behind the fallen gleanings of the field for them, to ensure that they receive equal justice. Why? "Because you were slaves in the land of Egypt" (Deut. 24:22).

The lesson of slavery could have been one of self-pity: to flaunt our suffering before other peoples so as to convince them that we are "owed" because of our experience. We could have wallowed in our role of victim. Or we could have learned to be more "realistic" about this harsh world, maintaining that the only way to survive is to be constantly on guard. We could say, "Having been enslaved by a people who at first welcomed us, we must never again let our guard down. Now we know we can trust only each other; everyone else is out to get us. . . ."

But we understand that to believe these things, to act in this fashion, would mean that the Egyptians had taught us to be wary of the stranger and thus to be like Pharaoh. Instead we are commanded:

> You shall not oppress a stranger, for you know the feelings of the stranger, having yourself been strangers in the land of Egypt. [Exod. 23:9]

and

> When a stranger resides with you in your land, you shall not wrong him. The stranger who resides with you shall be to you as one of your citizens; you shall love him as yourself, for you were strangers in the land of Egypt. I, the Lord, am your God. [Lev. 19:33,34]

The lesson is to act not like the Egyptians but differently from them, not to fear the alien but to welcome him.

The most striking commandment of all is "You shall not abhor an Egyptian because you were a stranger in his land" (Deut. 23:8). It is not just the alien but even your oppressor whom you should not hate. Why? Rashi, the medieval Jewish commentator, states that despite everything the Egyptians later did to us, at first they took us in when there was a famine in the land of Canaan. We are not meant to turn the other cheek, nor to expect the best from everyone we meet in this world. Nor are we prohibited from rejoicing over the downfall of our enemies (as we can see from the song recited by the Israelites after the Egyptians drowned in the Red Sea).

Nonetheless, we must care for even the stranger who oppressed us, not only out of gratitude but because to hate the Egyptians is to remain enslaved to them by the consuming passion of our hatred. We would be locked together in a death struggle from which neither party could exit whole. To free ourselves from them, to leave behind the bitterness that would consume us and carry away only the matzah of memory, is to be really free. Our ideal is to be able to deal humanely with the stranger, neither out of fear nor out of a need to dominate or patronize, but out of deep caring, having ourselves once been strangers in a strange land.

FREEDOM

We are told to begin the retelling of the Exodus story with our degradation and to end it with praise to God, without whom we would still be slaves to Pharaoh in Egypt. Being slaves has branded us forever, reminding us of the

humanity we share with all people. This miraculous redemption has also affected the ongoing character of the Jewish people: Once having been set free, we can never be spiritually enslaved again.

The tradition stresses that it was God alone who redeemed us from Egypt. This is why Moses is omitted from the Haggadah, and why Passover plays an important role in creating the covenant between God and Israel. God's "right" to establish that covenant rests on the fulfillment of His promise to Israel to save His people.

While stressing God's redemptive role, the Passover story serves as a model for any struggle for freedom. The message of God's role is not that only He can redeem us, thereby laying on us a fatalistic view of the world. Rather, the Exodus teaches us about the possibilities and potentialities for change in our lives. It serves as a striking example of how a person's life can change radically. Before the Exodus, it was natural to believe that once born a slave, you would remain one all your life, and your children and all your descendants would be slaves as well. While an occasional gracious act by a master could free a slave, in all likelihood an inexorable fate had permanently fixed you as a slave. To believe that your life could change or, even more, to contemplate that *you* could change your life was as laughable as believing the mighty Nile could turn into blood.

The story of the Exodus challenges the idea of a permanent identity and denies that there is an inexorable fate. Things do not always have to remain as they are. It is in our hands to change our lives, now that God has shown us that radical change is possible. Life is a flowing river whose course can be altered, not an image cast in stone.

The Exodus transformed the Jewish people by making us free forever. Once lit, the flame of freedom can never be fully extinguished. We must strive to become more and more liberated. Having shown us His redemptive powers, God leaves it to us to bring about redemption for ourselves and for this imperfect world. The Hatam Sofer (an early-nineteenth-century Hungarian rabbinic scholar) commented that while God alone took us out of Egypt, in exile we ourselves must bring redemption. As it says, "Zion shall be redeemed with righteousness" (Isa. 1:27)—that is, by our own good deeds. Yet we needed God to free us that first time, to set an example and give us our first taste of freedom.

That is why at the seder we eat matzah before we eat maror. We would expect to eat them in the opposite order, for the bitterness of slavery (represented by the maror) preceded the redemption (represented by the unleavened bread eaten during the hurried exodus). However, chronology is not followed at the seder, for we first need that taste of freedom to truly know and feel how bitter is slavery. Without that taste of freedom, it would be easy to accept slavery as part of the human fate. The midrash states: "By far the worst part of the slavery in Egypt was the fact that the Israelites had come to accept it."

The concept that things can change, that there is always hope, is reflected in a ritual aspect unique to Passover. On Pesah Sheni, the fourteenth day of Iyyar, the Hebrew month following Passover, the Second Passover occurs (see

Yes: It is not that history would have stopped had there been no divine redemption, but that it would have gone on as before, its changes signifying only the move from one form of servitude to another. By taking the Jews out of Egypt, giving them the Torah, leading them through the wilderness, and bringing them into the land of Israel—all the blessings we recall in the Haggadah—God opened up the possibility of a life unlike any the human race had ever known.

A.E.

Num. 9:1–13). It is a one-day miniversion of Passover for people who were ritually impure at the Passover sacrifice. Bringing that sacrifice was so important that people were given a second chance to offer it a month later. The idea of a "makeup" festival for those who missed it is unique to Passover, and it reinforces this message of Passover—that in life we can receive more than one chance.

THE TALE WITHOUT END

A striking passage in the Haggadah states: "And if the Holy One, praised be He, had not taken our ancestors out of Egypt, then we, and our children, and our children's children would still be enslaved to Pharaoh in Egypt. Now even if all of us were scholars, all of us sages, all of us elders, all of us learned in Torah, it still would be our duty to tell the story of the Exodus from Egypt. And whoever expands upon the story of the Exodus deserves praise."

On one level, this passage serves to remind us of the praise due to God for delivering His people. On another, it states that without that example of redemption we and our descendants would still be enslaved to the Pharaohs of the world—whether external or internal. Therefore, even if we think we know all the details of the story, we *must* retell it to remind ourselves not only that freedom is possible but that in an unredeemed world we must continue to strive for liberation in both personal and national ways. And whoever elaborates on the story—that is, whoever understands that the story is not just about a Pharaoh way back then or even the modern Pharaohs of our day, but about all the different ways we can be enslaved—he or she is deserving of praise.

For the Haggadah also explores how we have become enslaved to objects, routines, and patterns of behavior. There is a talmudic debate over what constitutes the "degradation" that should begin the recital of the Haggadah. One opinion is the obvious one—that we were slaves in Egypt, and that this is the degradation we tell about. The other opinion is that we should begin by telling how our ancestors were idol-worshipers. (In typical rabbinic fashion, both passages are found in the Haggadah: *Avadim hayinu*—"We were slaves"—and *Mi-tehilah ovdei avodah zarah hayu avoteinu*—"In the beginning our ancestors worshiped idols.")

Why is that latter piece of shameful family history relevant to Passover? Idol worship symbolizes the other kind of enslavement. Unlike the slavery in Egypt, it is voluntary, not forced. It is also basically internal rather than external. Idols are those things that humans perceive as powerful in this world. They represent those forces over which we seem to have no control, and which therefore must be placated. *Avodah zarah*—idol worship—literally means worship of the other, the alien. Instead of being able to accept the alien (or even to care for the human alien as mentioned earlier), we come to fear the unknown other. The Hebrew word *avodah*—worship or service—is also the word for slavery. Idol worship is a form of self-enslavement to those things that we fear and thus come to serve. This is why both meanings of

There are four levels of *mitzrayim*—Egypts—related to the four worlds of kabbalah. In the world of *assiyah,* the focus is on my addiction to things. I begin by examining how I nourish my body. By shifting my diet, I can discover what are my dependencies and addictions when it comes to food. Food as *the* element that keeps me alive is symbolic of any tangible item upon which I am dependent. On the second level, you examine your addictions and dependencies in the realm of the interpersonal *(yetzirah).* Have you locked yourself into a submissive role? Do you need the approval of other people? On the third level, *beriah,* Jews must look at the world around them and see clearly all the terrible things that make up reality, from oppression to pollution to nuclear weapons. To do so is to discover a world of inadequate ideas without the means to escape from an Egypt that is always arming, etc. Our task is not to respond in despair but to find a way to function in a hopeful fashion. On the fourth level, *azilut,* there remains the final Egypt, the barrier between God and ourselves. In this world of doubt, we must search for a path leading out of the eclipse of God. During the seder, all four Egypts must be acknowledged if not struggled with.

Z.S.

An idol is an icon, not the thing itself but an image of the thing, or the being. We worship idols when we fetishize the symbol rather than serve that which the symbol represents. Even God, as T. H. Gaster has often taught, is worshiped as an idol when we worship not what God is or stands for but the images in which we conceive of God (superperson, father, judge, king, soldier, power of nature, or whatever). We live in a culture of images, images that distance us from that which the image seeks to convey. Pesah, the personal experience of God's liberating power, calls our attention to the real thing. I, and not an angel, God says, bring you out of Egypt.

E.GR.

The words of Erich Fromm seem appropriate:

. . . the history of mankind up to the present time is primarily the history of idol worship, from the primitive idols of clay and wood to the modern idols of the state, the leader, production and consumption—sanctified by the blessing of an idolized God.

Man transfers his own passions and qualities to the idol. The more he impoverishes himself, the greater and stronger becomes the idol. The idol is the alienated form of man's experience of himself. In worshiping the idol, man worships himself. But this self is a partial, limited aspect of man: his intelligence, his physical strength, power, fame, and so on. By identifying himself with a partial aspect of himself, man limits himself to this aspect; he loses his totality as a human being and ceases to grow. He is dependent on the idol, since only in submission to the idol does he find the shadow, although not the substance, of himself. [*You Shall Be as Gods,* pp. 43–44]

E.GE.

There is indeed a strange contrast between the simplicity of the *essential* Passover foods and the luxury with which we often surround them. Passover, when stripped to its essentials, has about it a character of true primitive socialism that should not be overlooked: Every Jew, rich or poor, is eating the same simple matzah and maror. And no Jew may fulfill his or her own Passover obligation without seeing to it that the poorest of Jews—in spirit as well as in material needs—has the provisions required for Pesah.

A.G.

Rabbi Nahman of Bratslav [eighteenth-century Hasidic master] comments on "and they made no provisions for the way": "When you are about to leave Egypt—*any* Egypt—do not stop to think 'But how will I earn a living out there? . . .' One who stops to 'make provisions for the way' will never get out of Egypt." A comment to be repeated annually for college seniors, midlife-crisis confronters, and all the rest of us "wage-slaves," as Marx would have it.

A.G.

degradation—that is, slavery *and* idol worship—must be mentioned in the Haggadah. Both physical oppression and the more subtle internal oppressions must be explored through the retelling of the Passover story.

MATZAH

Matzah, as mentioned earlier, is most commonly seen as a symbol of freedom, being the food the Israelites took with them as they hurriedly left Egypt. At the seder we remember the first food we ate as a free people, which, while plain, must have tasted glorious. Perhaps that is why matzah is so striking a symbol: Amid the luxuriousness of the seder meal, with its many courses served on our finest china, matzah tells us that freedom can be plain as well. The rabbis borrowed certain practices (such as the many cups of wine and the reclining) from Roman banquet customs as signs of our freedom. Yet it is not sumptuous food or the dining customs of the rich that provide the central symbol of the seder. The choice of matzah as this symbol cautions us not to equate freedom with wealth. Tradition recognizes that money increases our freedom of choice, and that poverty can limit choices and in effect enslave us to our economic circumstances. Yet tradition still maintains that the deepest sense of freedom is internal and can lie in a flat, unsophisticated, and relatively tasteless food called "matzah." Matzah proclaims that freedom is a kingdom whose gates are open to all.

Matzah is also a symbol of peoples' trust in God. The people were ordered to hasten from Egypt. There was no time for a meeting to debate the question; there was no time even for second thoughts. The people faithfully awaited the signal with girded loins and staffs in their hands. They did not ask "Where are we going?" or "How will we get there?" They did not ask the most obvious question, "What should we take along for the journey?" They had only matzot and their faith in God, who would provide for them on their journey. Matzah is thus a symbol of the complete trust the Israelites had that night.

It would seem simple then. Matzah is the symbol both of a freedom available to all who would taste of it and of the perfect faith of Israel in their God. Perhaps this is why the halakhah requires that the matzot used in the seder ritual be whole and unbroken—as a symbol of that perfect faith.

The Broken Matzah And yet, near the beginning of the seder (at *yahatz*), we take the middle matzah and break it in half. Why? Because there is an underlying reality to our lives that cannot be denied, even during the seder. That reality changes with each generation of Jews and is different for Jews in various countries. Essentially, however, we as Jews and as humans are not totally free. The oppression of Soviet Jews is obvious, but even here in America, the *goldeneh medinah,* we are subtly enslaved. The enslavement is real, whether it is to other people (parents, spouses, children, bosses), or to old habits, or to our jobs, or to self-fulfillment, or to any of our fears and insecurities. To tell of the Exodus ensures that it is impossible ever again to be totally enslaved—but then again, neither are we, even now, totally free.

Though we hold on to the matzah as a symbol of hope, we break it as a sign that the perfect faith of our ancestors on that night in Egypt is not ours. We live in a world where God's outstretched arm is difficult to perceive. We take the broken matzah and put away one-half for the afikomen. The afikomen is eaten at *tzafun,* at the end of the meal. It is the very last thing we are allowed to eat on the seder night, and its taste is meant to linger in our mouths. *Tzafun* literally means "hidden" and probably refers to the afikomen, which is hidden away until we are ready to eat it. The hiddenness of *tzafun* has also been interpreted to refer to the Messiah, the Hidden One, who will bring about the final redemption.

Thus, the broken matzah is a reflection of the tragic reality of our world and our shattered faith in God, and at the same time a sign of hope. A hope that just as once there was a moment of complete redemption and perfect faith, so shall there be such a time again—a time when that which is hidden, the Messiah, and the potential concealed within us, will both be revealed. Therefore, near the beginning of the seder (right after *yahatz*), in the para-

The narrative portion of the Haggadah ends with the blessing, just before the second cup of wine, "Blessed are You, O Lord, who has redeemed Israel." Asked Rabbi Levi Yitzhak of Berdichev: "How dare we recite this blessing in the past tense? The true redemption is yet to come!" And he replies with a parable: A child asks his father for a cookie, but the father refuses to let him have one. If the child is smart and nervy, he will call out the blessing 'Blessed are You . . . who creates the species of grain.' Since his father will not want him to have recited the Lord's blessing in vain, he will have to let him eat the cookie. So we challenge God and call out: 'Blessed are You, Lord, who has redeemed Israel!' The rest is up to Him."

A.G.

How strange that we should begin our tale of liberation with the statement "This year we are slaves"! The point is, according to one Hasidic reading, that while we recognize our current enslavements, we also recognize the great distance we have traversed from Egyptian bondage to the sort of slavery we feel in our current lives. Had someone come to us while we were in Egypt and said, "You know, someday you and your children will be telling this tale as though it were all in the past," we would hardly have believed him. See how far we have come! And for those of us who have gone this far in the path of liberation—remembering that we once were carriers of bricks and mortar—nothing in the liberation that lies ahead should seem impossible to us.

A.G.

graph *Ha lahma anya,* we proclaim, "This year we are slaves, next year we will be free. This year we are here, next year in Jerusalem." Proclaiming our slavery at the beginning of the seder is not meant to undercut what follows. While recognizing the reality of our lives, it is a hopeful assertion that next year we will be totally free.

Matzah, then, is both a symbol of freedom and an expression of our future hopes. But that is not all. For right after we break the middle matzah, we recite, as mentioned above, the paragraph of *Ha lahma anya,* which not only proclaims that we are all slaves and in exile, but also says, "This [the matzah] is the bread of affliction which our ancestors ate as slaves in the land of Egypt." This seems to contradict the opinion of Rabban Gamliel, cited in the Haggadah, that we eat matzah because the dough of our ancestors did not have time to rise before leaving Egypt. Matzah, according to Rabban Gamliel, is a sign of freedom, and yet here it is described as the bread our ancestors ate as slaves in Egypt! Is matzah the cheap but filling food given to the Israelite slaves or the food those Israelites ate upon being liberated? Is matzah a symbol of slavery or of freedom?

We learn that matzah is both a slave's and a free person's bread. It is the dual nature of matzah that is the secret of its importance, for matzah was there from the beginning. Matzah, which was the bread of slaves, became the sole sustenance of a free people. Matzah changes from *lehem oni* (the bread of affliction) to the afikomen, from slave past to messianic future. All the blows of the taskmasters can be seen on its pockmarked surface; yet fragile as it is, matzah survives unbroken (until *we* are ready to break it). Matzah, in its very plainness, is the symbol of change for all. Freedom is not just for the wealthy but for the lowly as well. Yet despite this radical change from slavery to freedom, matzah always looks exactly the same. It is not in appearance that freedom is to be found. Matzah is watched to prevent its contamination with the yeast of pride, the lust for wealth, or the thirst for praise. No water is allowed to puff matzah up artificially, to make it appear to be more than what it naturally is. Simple, plain, and flat, matzah is the eternal symbol of freedom, for freedom lies in intoxication with the idea, not with the self.

HAMETZ

The most difficult Passover ritual to explain is hametz. Why should a food we happily consume fifty-one weeks a year become something that we diligently search out and destroy before the one week of Passover? Even if matzah is the symbol of the Exodus, could we not abstain from hametz at the seder but eat it during the rest of the week? Why go to such great lengths outlawing even the possession of hametz mixed with permitted food? What, after all, does removing hametz have to do with God redeeming us from Egypt?

According to the rabbinic view mentioned earlier, there is something wrong with hametz. Hametz is seen as symbolic of the *yetzer ha-ra*—evil inclination—in particular, the prompting of pride. Therefore the search for hametz must be extensive and intensive, for even the smallest particle of hametz in no matter how large a food mixture will corrupt. Similarly, no matter how small or deeply hidden the evil inclination is within us, it will fester and grow and eventually poison everything else. The process of removing hametz from the home is meant to arouse us to remove those negative inclinations within us as well.

We take a candle to search for the hametz the night before Pesah because "The soul of a human is the lamp of the Lord, searching all the innermost parts" (Prov. 20:27). Into the darkest recesses we carry a light searching for that which is hidden deep within each of us. We remove it and burn it and nullify it in an attempt to destroy its significance in our lives. We might think one method of removal would suffice, but the *yetzer ha-ra* will not disappear so easily. Just as hametz requires many attempts to eradicate it, so too will the *yetzer ha-ra.*

Why, then, can we eat hametz during the rest of the year if it is to some degree "evil"? The tradition demands a great deal from us, but not the impossible. It knows that we, being human, will always have pieces of the *yetzer ha-ra,* of the negative, within us. We would be deceiving ourselves if we thought we could be perfect. To abstain from hametz all year round would be to deny this truth. Having to refrain from hametz for a week reminds us that removing the *yetzer ha-ra* can never be fully accomplished. Yet we are not free to desist from the struggle, no matter how difficult and fruitless it sometimes seems. Having gained the perspective of a week free of hametz—a week "free" of the negative—we are then ready to reenter our everyday world where both are so prevalent.

Recognizing the impossibility of a complete ban on hametz, the tradition settles for prohibiting it at special times. Besides the ban at Passover, there was also a prohibition against offering any hametz on the altar in the temple. Meal offerings were made of matzah, as the verse states: "No meal offering that you offer to the Lord shall be made with leaven, for you must not turn into smoke any leaven or any honey as an offering by fire to the Lord" (Lev. 2:11). Thus, for most of the year hametz was permitted; inside the temple, however, the place of sacred eating and of purification, hametz was not allowed.

The connection between Passover and hametz, then, is that we must purify ourselves and clear away the old to be ready for the creation of the covenant between God and His people. Just as spring renews the earth, so must we renew ourselves to become free again at Passover. By removing the shackles of hametz, we are no longer the slaves of Pharaoh but become the servants of God.

Is Hametz Evil? If we reexamine the laws of hametz, there emerges another way of looking at hametz and its connection to Passover. There are many unique stringencies associated with hametz, perhaps the most remarkable being the prohibition against even owning hametz during Passover. At its most extreme, this means that even if you had hametz locked away in a safe with a time lock set to open only after Passover, you would still violate the

The fact is that the ritual use of matzah rather than hametz, for sacrifices as well as for Passover, probably points back to the most ancient collective memories of those tribes that were to form the nation of Israel. Leavened bread requires an oven, which means a home that is permanently fixed in one place. This happened only as our earliest ancestors made the transition from the life of the hunting and wandering nomad to that of the settled farmer. In his ritual memory, the farmer preserved a memory of that earlier and idealized state, the time when he was a free wanderer, eating no bread that could not be baked by the sun as he carried it on his back.

A.G.

law. It is important to note, however, that you are not prohibited from owning someone else's hametz.

Why all these regulations? Passover, as explained earlier, is a central festival of the year. Being slaves transformed the way we look at the world, and we are told to relive the experience of both slavery and freedom. The seder is an attempt, through tasting and telling, to do so. So, too, is the effort to remove hametz.

For some of us, cleaning the stove, refrigerator, cabinets, and the rest of the house is the hardest physical work we do all year. For everyone, it is a great deal of work in a concentrated period of time. At moments during this preparation, some of us feel a small taste of slavery, a sense of being obligated to do work that seems of little purpose. In the midst of cleaning the oven, with your nostrils filled with the fragrant odor of oven cleaner, such thoughts come to mind as "Do I really care about that spot on the back wall?" or "What kind of freedom is this? Am I not at this very moment enslaved to Jewish law?"

While giving us a small taste of slavery, the preparation shows us that freedom comes only through effort. It is not enough to wish for freedom.

The arduous preparation also reminds us of our changed status after the Exodus. We who were once slaves of Pharaoh are now the servants of God. We are a people who serve only one master, the Master of the world. Service to Him is to make us genuinely free human beings and not to constrict us.

How do Passover and the laws of hametz accomplish this loosening of the ties that normally bind us?

Pesah makes us reexamine our sense of the world. It takes what is permissible and makes it forbidden. It takes something so basic as to be taken for granted—our food—and completely changes how we regard it and use it. It is not simply that the permitted becomes the forbidden; we are not even allowed to *own* the forbidden—i.e., hametz. This prohibition strikes at the very notion of slavery by attacking our notion of possession: To own people is in subtle ways to be owned by that owning. That we must remove slavery from our lives is exemplified by the removal of hametz. We must not be possessed by our possessions—even that most basic possession, our food. Hametz cannot be hidden away during Pesah; it must be removed, taken out of our lives. We must be freed from all those things we think we possess, which in fact possess us. Therefore, *our* hametz must be removed, not someone else's. Passover begins at home, with me and with my things.

This parallels the experience of Sukkot, which questions our understanding of shelter, another basic necessity of our lives. It raises questions about our sense of security based on buildings made to keep others out. Sukkot asks us to leave our dwellings of fifty-one weeks a year and live in temporary booths that are fragile and open to the heavens. It forces us to ask the question "In what does my security lie? In strong walls or the structure of my inner self?"

Pesah asks us to remove what we eat fifty-one weeks a year in order to make us look at food and its significance and, more broadly, the morality of our lives. It asks us how we want to live—as free beings or as slaves? Further, it forces us to ask "How have I enslaved others or been enslaved by them?

Pesah focuses our attention on food. In ancient times, Pesah called upon the Israelites to slaughter sheep, grind grain for flour, bake matzot, gather herbs, etc. At least once in our lifetime (perhaps the year of bar or bat mitzvah), we should involve ourselves with food on its most basic level. We should go off into the woods with only some grain. The experience of collecting wild onions for karpas, finding the right stones to grind the grain, and then heating stones to bake matzah would enable us to understand why food is the central theme of this holiday.

Z.S.

How have I enslaved myself to my fears, to my hatreds, even to my rituals or those of Judaism itself?"

We must also not lose sight of the political dimensions of Passover. Hametz is not solely our personal sins and slaveries; it is found in injustice and oppression in our homes and in society. The hametz outside of us also needs to be cleansed away. We are meant to emulate Moses, who struck down a taskmaster beating a slave and thereby lost his princely sinecure and discovered his real identity. Rather than inveighing against human weakness, Passover proclaims that positive change is possible, since one who was once a slave can become free, and what was once permitted can be prohibited.

On Pesah, we question all of our daily assumptions, for Pesah stands not for blacks and whites but for life's complexities, for all the colors of the rainbow. Each of Pesah's symbols have double meanings. Hametz is both permitted and prohibited. Maror tastes good at first and becomes bitter at the end. Haroset—the mixture of apple, nuts, and wine—reminds us of the mortar the slaves used in Egypt and yet is also meant to sweeten the bitter taste of maror. Most of all, as we have seen, matzah is both the bread of affliction eaten by the slaves in Egypt and the bread of redemption eaten by the Israelites hurrying to freedom in the desert.

Pesah tries to show us that there is little difference between the permitted and the prohibited, the bitter and the sweet, and most of all between hametz and matzah. The Hebrew words for hametz and matzah are made up of the same letters except for one. A small piece of line would transform the letter *heh* of hametz into the letter *het* of matzah. This is symbolic of the minute difference between them.

Pesah attacks that security rooted in our sense of possession and calls upon us to declare our hametz null and void and as worthless as the dust of the earth. We are to carry into freedom *only* matzah—slave bread/free bread. Matzah is a symbol that is both transformed and remains the same. What was slave bread becomes food for the Exodus; yet matzah's very nature is unchanged. Unlike hametz, which is made from dough that constantly rises and expands, matzah is flat and constant, always remaining unleavened. It hides nothing. Its simpleness reflects the same question repeated over and over: Are you free?

MAH NISHTANAH

Why is this night different from all other nights? Most of all because it provokes us to question. We are to question our cherished notions and beliefs to discover if somehow slavery and oppression have crept in. How do we treat the other people in our lives? How many have we helped trap in stereotypes of their personalities ("Oh, she's a barrel of laughs," or "He's really a facile guy"), thus forcing them to play roles as "the jester," "the intellectual," "the unemotional," etc.? How do we treat those over whom we have authority—our employees, our children, etc.? Do we use it as a power trip? How do we feel about those outside our community—the Orthodox and the Reconstruc-

Referring to the male and female gentile, respectively, as "shegetz" and "shiksa" reminds me of another area in which we must wrestle free. These Yiddish epithets derive from Hebrew and mean "abomination," contact with which pollutes. The liberation from the shackles of our prejudices that Pesah betokens could well begin by removing the connotations of fear, dislike, and insult that our vocabulary concerning gentiles possesses. We need to break out of words and their poisonous associations just as we need to break out of ideas that prevent the free flow of the divine spirit in the world.

E.GR.

The going out from *mitzrayim* (Egypt) is an experience that every child must successfully pass through. Just as Abraham was commanded to leave his country, his birthplace, and the home of his parents (see Gen. 12:1), so must every child who is to become an adult. Every parent must be ready for this Exodus and balance the ability to let the child go with a continuing concern and love.

                                   Z.S.

tionist, the shegetz and the shiksa, the racial minorities and the foreigner? Do we remember that we, too, were once strangers and slaves in the land of Egypt? How do we serve God? Is it a service of the heart, or has it become idolatry?

The importance of questioning explains the central role of children at the seder. Young and naïve, they ask the basic questions, the ones we thought long settled or the ones so challenging to fundamentals that we could never risk asking them. The contrast, then, is clear between the wise child of the Haggadah and the wicked.

The wise child asks, "What are these laws, statutes, ordinances which God commanded?" That is, what is the purpose of these laws? We are told to answer by explaining all the Passover laws from beginning to end, in order that *we* understand why we are obeying them. Explaining to the children is as much for our benefit as for theirs.

The wicked child asks, "What is this service to you?" For this child, Pesah has become *avodah*—slavery; even *avodat hashem*—the service of God—has become a burdensome task. There are those who think all of Judaism is meaningless ritual. There is also the wicked child who is so complacent in having perfectly cleaned the stove or having bought "Kosher for Passover" potato chips that he or she does not know that his/her *avodah* has changed from service to the slavery of rote ritual. Therefore, we are told to answer either type of wicked child by slapping the complacent fool and proclaiming that this child would not have survived the purging process of Egypt and would have remained a slave to a pharaoh of his/her own creation.

We should finally locate each of these questioning children in ourselves. As Maimonides states, "If he has no child, then let his wife ask him [the Four Questions]; if he has no wife, then let one person ask the other even if they are all sages. If he is alone, then *he asks himself* 'Why is this night different?' "

SUMMARY

Unless we strenuously interrogate ourselves throughout the eight days of Pesah, we will have let the seder lapse into another pleasant but meaningless ritual. At the seder, we must be telling our own story, our own experience. Telling the story of others is not enough. We must relive slavery and freedom, and we must question our values. We must understand the narrow distinction that separates hametz from matzah by a small line, and an arbitrariness that turns hametz from permitted into forbidden. We must strive to be seared by the knowledge that we were slaves in Egypt, to know that we rejoiced at the sea when our enemies drowned, and yet to know that the Torah commands, "Do not abhor the Egyptian for you were a stranger. . . ." Until we can accept the *ger*—alien—outside of us, we will not be ready to accept the alien within. Only by having experienced all this can we then go back to "normal" and eat hametz. Only by having experienced the arbitrariness of what is permitted and what is prohibited can we begin on our way to accepting the Torah at Mount Sinai on Shavuot. Without the freedom of Pesah, the Torah could easily become a device for enslavement, not a path to freedom. By refraining from hametz for one week, we become freed to eat it the rest of the year.

This explains the concept of *hametz she-avar alav ha-pesah*—leavened bread owned by a Jew during Pesah and therefore forbidden even after Pesah is over. This is hametz that at the moment of freedom, at the moment of the seder, is still locked into slavery. It becomes frozen forever in that state. Having missed the chance for freedom, it becomes eternally enslaved. It is hametz that Pesah has passed over. On Pesah, God passed over the Israelites and gave us eternal freedom. Pesah passes over this hametz in our possession and condemns it to eternal slavery. Therefore the obligation to search for hametz continues for someone who did not perform bedikat hametz—the ritual search for hametz the night before Passover. As Maimonides states, "Whoever forgot or did not search [for hametz] on the night of the fourteenth [of Nisan] should do so in the morning of the fourteenth. If he did not search for it as the first thing in the morning he should search at the time of the burning of the hametz. If not, then let him search during the holiday. If the holiday passed then let him still search for any hametz."

The search continues.

כוס ישועות אשא

THE OMER
COUNTDOWN TO SINAI

The period called "the omer" begins the second night of Passover and continues until Shavuot. The omer (literally "a measure") was an offering of the first of the new grain harvest, which was brought to the temple on the sixteenth of Nisan (the second day of Passover). The Torah commanded that seven weeks be counted from the time of the offering of the omer, as it says:

> From the day after the sabbath, the day that you bring the sheaf of wave-offering, you shall keep count until seven full [*temimot*] weeks have elapsed: you shall count fifty days until the day after the seventh week, then you shall bring an offering of new grain to the Lord. You shall bring from your settlements two full loaves of bread as a wave-offering. . . . On that same day you shall hold a celebration, it shall be a sacred occasion for you. . . . [Lev. 23:15–21]

Because of this ritual of counting, the period between Passover and Shavuot came to be known as the omer. In fact, Shavuot does not have a fixed calendar date in the Bible, but rather falls on the day after the completion of the omer count—that is, the fiftieth day after the omer offering is brought. The period also became known as *sefirah*—literally, "the counting"—because of the nightly ritual of *sefirat ha-omer*—counting (the days of) the omer.

The omer ends after a count of seven weeks, seven times seven days from Pesah to Shavuot. The symmetry of the period (7×7) symbolizes a special degree of holiness for Shavuot, the day of the great revelation on Mount Sinai. Similarly, the especially sacred parts of the tabernacle—the portable sanctuary in the wilderness—were square in shape, symmetrical: the altar and the holy of holies. What has symmetry to do with the holy? It is stable, even, balanced, harmonious, sharing the same measure.

E.Gr.

47

THE SIGNIFICANCE OF COUNTING

The farmer stands in awe of the miraculous gift he has been given, the produce that his soil and labors have brought forth. "Is it mine?" he asks in wonder, hesitating to partake of it despite all the effort he has put into its growth. Only the gift to God at the beginning, parallel to that of the firstborn among flocks and children and the first fruits of the trees, gives him the ability to partake of earth's blessing.

The symbol of manna, "bread from heaven," underlies the pious person's attitude toward food and sustenance. Work at it as we may, we still see it as the gift of God, our daily survival as miracle. As we begin and end our meals with blessings to God, so did the farmer start and conclude his harvest with a sacred gift.

A.G.

Why was it important to count the days from the bringing of the omer until Shavuot? The Torah does not state a reason. Perhaps the simplest explanation has to do with the harvest. The bringing of the omer was the first harvesting of the new grain crop. This harvesting continued throughout the omer period and was brought to a climax at Shavuot with the offering of *shtei ha-lehem*—two loaves of bread.

Shavuot in the Bible is not connected with the giving of the Torah at Sinai; as we shall see in the next chapter, the association of Shavuot with the revelation of Sinai appears to belong to a later tradition. In the Torah, Shavuot is an agricultural festival marking the end of the harvest begun on Passover. Its name, meaning "weeks," refers to the seven weeks of omer counting. According to the biblical verse quoted above, it was forbidden to eat of the new grain crop until the omer was offered on Passover. Similarly, the tradition states that the meal offerings in the temple could not be made from the new grain crop until after the offering of the two loaves on Shavuot. Thus the omer offering on Pesah allowed people to eat from the new grain crop, and the two-loaves offering on Shavuot allowed for sacrificial offerings from the new grain crop in the temple. The omer period, then, was a marking of the time of harvest with its concern for a successful crop. The offerings that began and concluded it expressed that hope for the harvest and also expressed a thanksgiving to God for the land and its bounty.

As Shavuot became more and more associated with the revelation of the Torah at Mount Sinai, other reasons emerged for linking Passover and Shavuot. According to one tradition, the Israelites in the desert were so eager to receive the Torah that they counted the days from the Exodus until Sinai. Others see in Shavuot the culmination of the experience of the Exodus. For the consequence of the deliverance from Egypt was not simply to free a people but to transform them into a holy nation. The covenant between God and Israel, which began in Egypt, is then clearly spelled out in all its details at Sinai and is accepted by the Israelites. Sinai is the answer to the question "For what purpose were the Israelites freed from Egypt?" Sinai gave them goals to strive for and obligations to fulfill. They were transformed from *avdei pharaoh*—slaves of Pharaoh—to *avdei hashem*—servants of the Lord. Thus Pesah without Shavuot would have been incomplete, and the omer is the chain that links the two together.

Specifically, the kabbalists saw the omer period as one of preparation for the great event of Sinai. In this period those who had lived for so long as slaves surrounded by the *tum'ah* (immorality) of the Egyptians had to transform themselves into people worthy of receiving the gift of the Torah. For the kabbalists, each day of this period was an ascension from one of the forty-nine levels of the impurity of Egypt. This was expressed by seeing each day as a combination of the aspects of two of the mystical *sefirot* (attributes), such as the attribute of *hesed* (mercy) with that of *hod* (glory).

מֹשֶׁה קִבֵּל תּוֹרָה
מִסִּינַי וּמְסָרָהּ
פרקי אבות ו׳׳ו

Moses received the Torah at Sinai and transmitted it to . . .
Ethics of the Fathers 1:1

TRADITIONS

THE COUNTING

While there is no longer the temple or omer offering, the rabbis decreed that we should still count the days between Passover and Shavuot. (A few authorities maintain that it is still a biblical commandment.) The procedure for counting is as follows:

While standing, we recite the blessing:

> Praised are You, Lord our God, Ruler of the universe who has sanctified us with His commandments, commanding us to count the omer.

This is followed by the count for the day: "Today is the first day of the omer."

Weeks are counted as well—for example: "Today is the seventeenth day of the omer, which equals two weeks and three days of the omer."

This counting is done at night as the new day begins. Some people recite Psalm 67 after the counting, since it consists of seven verses and a total of forty-nine words.

The Omer Controversy A sharp controversy existed between the rabbis and a variety of Jewish sects over the interpretation of the words *the day after the sabbath* in the verse commanding the counting of the omer. According to the rabbis, "the sabbath" refers not to the seventh day of the week but rather to the first festival day of Passover; hence the omer count begins on the second night of Passover.

Various groups, beginning with the first-century Sadducees and continuing with the Karaites of the early Middle Ages, interpreted the word *sabbath* in different ways. Most commonly, it was interpreted as the first Shabbat after the beginning of Passover. The implication of this interpretation is that Shavuot, which falls on the day after the omer count of forty-nine days, would always occur on a Sunday. It would also occur on different days of the month since the first Shabbat during Passover could be, for instance, the third day of Passover (Nisan 17) or the fifth day (Nisan 19).

This argument over the omer was one of the basic ones between the Sadducees and the early rabbis (Pharisees). But other interpretations of the omer verse exist as well. The Falashas of Ethiopia interpret the words to mean the day after Passover is over; thus they celebrate Shavuot on Sivan 12 each year rather than Sivan 6, as we observe it.

This polemic prompted the early rabbis to emphasize their interpretation in the ritual surrounding the cutting of the barley to be brought as the omer offering. The ritual is described in detail in the Talmud (*Menahot* 65a), which tells us that the barley was harvested near Jerusalem and then brought to the temple, where it was ground and made into a meal offering. It was then ritually "waved" before the altar. A ritualized formula of question and answer was recited by the harvesters, emphasizing the rabbis' opinion that the

Kabbalists see the period of the omer as a time of intense preparation for the renewed receiving of the Torah that will take place on Shavuot. Some see it as a penitential period, others as a time for the uplifting of consciousness to make the mind ready to receive revelation.

The forty-nine days form a multiplication of seven times the seven *sefirot*, which represent aspects of both the divine and human personalities: *hesed* (love), *gevurah* (power, judgment, including anger), *tiferet* (glory, pride, also inner balance), *netzah* (triumph, aggrandizement), *hod* (beauty), *yesod*, (the "foundation," including sexual energy), and *malkhut* (kingship, authority, but also the feminine component in the male personality). Each of these seven in turn contains all seven within itself, making a total of forty-nine inner aspects of the divine/human self. On each day of the counting, the kabbalist seeks to restore or elevate within himself the combination of *sefirot* that belong to that day. This is readily comprehensible on a moralistic or psychological level, which is the way many Hasidim read the kabbalistic system. Thus on the first day of the omer (the count begins from above), one works on the *hesed* within *hesed*, on the purest love the soul can find within itself. On the second day, attention is focused on *gevurah* within *hesed*, the anger or judgment within one's love; the third day on *tiferet* in *hesed*, the glory or perhaps the self-glorification that lies within love; and so forth. In the second week the focus is on *gevurah*, beginning with *hesed* in *gevurah*, the love inside the judgment, and proceeding through the system. Thus the counting becomes a series of meditative and morally restorative exercises, purging the self and preparing it to stand again at Sinai.

A.G.

During the omer, we are dealing with a movement from the forty-nine Gates of Defilement through the Gates of Understanding on the way to Sinai. Each day we examine the virtues and vices embodied in that day's combination of the *sefirot*. One way of looking at this is, as follows:

DIVINE SEFIROT	ARCHETYPAL PERSON	VIRTUE	VICE
Hesed (Grace)	Abraham	Love	Lust
Gevurah (Severity)	Isaac	Respect	Fear
Tiferet (Beauty)	Israel	Compassion	Indulgence
Netzah (Victory)	Moses	Efficiency	Pedantry
Hod (Glory)	Aaron	Aesthetics	Vanity
Yesod (Foundation)	Joseph	Loyalty	Promiscuity
Malkhut (Majesty)	David	Surrender	Stubbornness

"When a person pays attention to what happens to him during the days of the *sefirah* period, he soon becomes aware that all he sees and hears on that day is but the activity of that *sefirah* and that it can serve to align him to God's blessed will" (Rabbi Nahman of Bratslav).

Z.S.

There seems to be a consensus that approximately thirty-three days of mourning are required. According to Karo, the mourning should end fifteen days before Shavuot, hence beginning with the thirty-fourth day of the omer. For others, Lag B'Omer is a special day and marks the end of the mourning begun at Passover. For others, the thirty-three days lie from Rosh Hodesh Iyyar until Shavuot. According to the last opinion, either Lag B'Omer marks a one-day suspension of the plague or it is chosen because the number 33 signifies the actual days of mourning. If you subtract from the forty-nine days of omer the seven days of Passover, the Shabbatot, and Rosh Hodesh (on these days mourning is forbidden), then you are left with thirty-two days when mourning customs can be observed. Therefore we celebrate Lag B'Omer, the thirty-third day, as a symbolic rather than literal end to the plague.

M.S.

second night of Passover was "the day after the sabbath." This was felt so strongly by the rabbis that even if the second day fell on Shabbat when harvesting is prohibited by Sabbath law, the harvesting of the omer still took place.

MOURNING DURING THE OMER PERIOD

Tradition mandates the observance of mourning customs during part or all of the omer period. It is forbidden to marry, have your hair cut, or attend concerts during this period. Some people do not shave. While these practices may date from talmudic times, authorities as late as Maimonides seem unaware of them. The reasons for this mourning are very obscure. The most common explanation derives from a talmudic passage stating that thousands of disciples of Rabbi Akiva (second century of the Christian Era) died in a plague because they did not treat each other with the appropriate respect. This passage, however, does not mandate any mourning practices, which are not mentioned in traditional sources before the eighth century. In the Middle Ages this observance of mourning was reinforced by the persecutions and massacres of Jews in Europe during the Crusades. Another later influence was the massacre of Ukrainian Jewry in 1648, which also took place during the omer period.

Lag B'Omer The obscurity of the reason for mourning is borne out by the discussion concerning the minor festival Lag B'Omer. Lag B'Omer occurs on the thirty-third day of the omer count (Iyyar 18). The name comes from the numerical values assigned to the Hebrew letters *lamed* (30) and *gimel* (3), hence "Lag," the thirty-third day in the omer. Lag B'Omer today is a minor festival celebrated usually by picnics and other outings during which mourning practices are lifted. There is also an old custom whereby children play with bows and arrows on this day. The most frequent explanation of Lag B'Omer is that the plague that killed Akiva's students either ended on this day or was suspended during it. Yet a closer examination of the different traditions about Lag B'Omer and their connection to varying practices in regard to mourning during the omer period raises questions specifically about Lag B'Omer and more generally about the omer.

If we look at the *Shulhan Arukh* (the classic code of Jewish law), we find a divergence of opinion about Lag B'Omer between its authors, Joseph Karo and R. Moses Isserles. Based on the interpretation of a phrase *(pros atzeret)*, Karo believes the mourning period of omer should end fifteen days *(pros)* before Shavuot *(atzeret)*. Therefore, beginning with the thirty-fourth day of the omer, we are allowed to hold wedding celebrations, etc. According to Karo, then, Lag B'Omer is the last day of mourning and not a semiholiday. Isserles, on the other hand, states the more familiar tradition that the thirty-third day of the omer marks a suspension or cessation of mourning.

Even for those who follow Isserles's opinion, there are varying practices:

• Some observe the mourning practices only from the beginning of the omer until Lag B'Omer. Between Lag B'Omer and Shavuot, they observe no mourning practices.

- Others observe the mourning from Rosh Hodesh Iyyar through Shavuot with a suspension at Lag B'Omer.
- Some observe mourning from Pesah to Shavuot, with a suspension at Lag B'Omer.

All of these variations raise doubts about the nature of Lag B'Omer and the mourning practices of the omer. When was the plague and when did it stop? What is Lag B'Omer—a celebration of the end of the plague, a temporary suspension, or even the literal last day of the plague (Karo's opinion)?

Many authorities have wrestled with these questions and have offered a variety of suggestions. Some believe that the story about Rabbi Akiva's students is a cryptic reference to the unsuccessful revolt of Bar Kochba against the Romans. This revolt (A.D. 132–35) was supported by Akiva and according to these scholars the mourning practices were for those killed during the revolt, including perhaps some of Akiva's students. The custom of playing with bows and arrows fits with this theory.

Other scholars suggest that the story refers to the persecutions of Emperor Hadrian during which Akiva and other sages were martyred. Still others find the origin of the mourning period in folk customs that have parallels in other cultures. One scholar cites Ovid to show that the Romans did not solemnize weddings during the month of May because the souls of the dead returned to earth at that time and rites were held to appease them. Theodor Gaster suggests that Lag B'Omer is the equivalent of May Day. There is an old German and English custom of shooting bows and arrows at demons on May Day, which followed Walpurgis night, the Witches' Sabbath. More generally, Gaster suggests that the mourning of the omer period derives from uncertainty about the harvest, and this, in turn, was extended to human fertility by prohibiting weddings.

The lack of clarity about the omer practices is reflected even in later authorities. The Taz (an eighteenth-century commentator on the *Shulhan Arukh*) attributes the mourning to the tragedies that befell the Jews during the Crusades. The Hatam Sofer attributes the celebration of Lag B'Omer not to a cessation of the plague but rather to a commemoration of the first time the manna fell in the desert. This requires a little juggling of the biblical text, which seems to place it on the sixteenth not the eighteenth of Iyyar (see Exod. 16:1).

I have always found the connection of omer period abstinence to Christian Lent and its pagan precursors (see T. H. Gaster, *Festivals of the Jewish Year*) to be persuasive. Anxiety over whether things will grow on schedule takes on outward symbolic actions. Lag B'Omer, parallel to May Day, breaks the tension as people work up the courage to defy the anxiety-producing forces of frustration. The Book of Ruth, which we read at the conclusion of the omer period, on Shavuot, reflects the same transition, from famine one year to a full and successful harvest the next.

E.GR.

Lag B'Omer the equivalent of May Day? If not the equivalent, they are surely related, and they syncretize most harmoniously.

For more than a decade, we (my wife, our daughters, and I) have held an annual May Day–Lag B'Omer celebration up in our small hayfield. Selecting a Sunday more or less near both dates—with, of course, allowance for New England's inclement spring weather—we've invited friends and neighbors to join us for a variety of outdoor activities. Most distinctive is a ritual procession around the periphery of the field, each person carrying some freshly cut winter rye, while at the head of the procession is carried a recently cut, eighteen-foot-high tree with eighteen ribbons stapled to it near the top (the *chai* motif). Also at the head of the procession is carried a *keter*—a crown for the May/Omer Pole—constructed earlier in the week from freshly cut branches. Attached to it are brightly colored pieces of fabric inscribed with appropriate verses from the Bible, from Chaucer, or from e. e. cummings, or whatever choices our fantasy may dictate that particular year.

After marching around the edges of the field, we head for the center, place the crown atop the pole, then erect and plant the May/Omer Pole securely. At this point everyone joins in dance to do the traditional weaving of the ribbons 'round the pole.

If subjective reactions of repeated delight may be given some weight, Gaster is surely right on this one: May Day and Lag B'Omer make a wonderful *shiddakh* (match)!

E.GE.

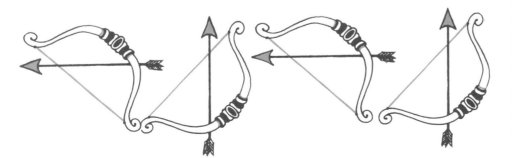

The mourning of this period is necessary to rid yourself of old habits. You
can not arrive at Sinai until you dispose
of *mitzrayim.* Yet, each *mitzrayim* was
a necessary stage for a certain period of
time, and therefore, we must mourn
each *mitzrayim*/habit in order to be
able to finally let go of it.
                                              Z.S.

The more Torah, the more life.
        Ethics of the Fathers 2:8

Hillula of Rabbi Shimon bar Yohai Mention should be made of another associ-
ation with Lag B'Omer—the *hillula* (celebration) of Rabbi Shimon bar Yohai.
This celebration takes place at the reputed site of his grave in Meron in the
Galilee. Rabbi Shimon bar Yohai was one of the leading disciples of Rabbi
Akiva. The classic mystical work the *Zohar* is attributed to him and thus he
is a central figure in Jewish mysticism. (Most modern scholars believe that the
Zohar was in fact written in the Middle Ages.)

The celebration involves much feasting and dancing and the lighting of
bonfires. Parents bring their three-year-old sons to Meron to cut their hair
for the first time. This ceremony is called *halaka* (Arabic for "cutting hair")
and is based on an old custom of not cutting the hair of male children until
they are three years old. Some rabbinic authorities in the past have attacked
this celebration as inappropriate to honor the memory of Rabbi Shimon bar
Yohai. Others have attacked it because some of the participants have the
custom of throwing expensive clothes into the bonfires. This, in their opinion,
violates the prohibition against wasteful or wanton destruction *(bal tashhit).*
Yet the celebration has continued and today attracts thousand of people,
particularly Oriental Jews.

As with all the omer observances, there is uncertainty here as well, for the
connection with Shimon bar Yohai is not clear. There are varying beliefs as
to whether Lag B'Omer is the anniversary of the death of bar Yohai or
commemorates another event in his life. While the *Zohar* mentions the *hillula*
of bar Yohai, it is not connected to Lag B'Omer until Rabbi Chaim Vital of
the seventeenth century. Incidentally, the kabbalists interpret the bow given
to children on Lag B'Omer as symbolic of the rainbow (in Hebrew the same
word is used for both), since there is a tradition that a rainbow will appear
in the sky as a harbinger of the final redemption.

Today, more and more people have come to disregard the mourning
practices because of their unclear origin. There has also been a general de-
emphasis of fasting, asceticism, etc., in our times. The mourning practices are
still observed in traditional circles, but the Rabbinical Assembly Law Committee (Conservative) recently ruled that the marriage prohibition and other
mourning practices need no longer apply, partly because the original reasons
are so obscure. They still maintain the mourning practices during the week-
end before Yom ha-Shoah.

Unrelated to the confusion about the mourning practices, the counting of
the omer remains a commandment. And although it may not seem so, remembering to count is in fact very difficult. One item of traditional folk art that
grew out of this difficulty is the *sefirah* counter—a device or chart used to help
with the counting of the omer. Even with this aid, in those years that I have
attempted to count, I have usually forgotten sometime during the first week!

CUSTOMS

One custom that is still widely observed during the omer period is the study of *Pirkei Avot—Ethics of the Fathers.* The study begins after Pesah, and one chapter is studied each week after the minhah service on Shabbat afternoons. There are six chapters and six Shabbatot between Passover and Shavuot. The sixth chapter is about Torah and is therefore an appropriate prelude to Shavuot, which commemorates the giving of the Torah at Sinai. It has become customary in some places to continue studying Pirkei Avot through Sukkot.

According to an old custom that has fallen into disuse, women did not work after sunset during the omer period. Some followed the custom that men as well did not work. According to one explanation, women were rewarded because women buried all of Akiva's students who had died in the plague. Another explanation bases the custom on the phrase *sheva shabbatot* used in reference to the omer period, literally meaning seven sabbaths rather than seven weeks as usually interpreted.

On the Shabbat following Passover, the dates of the new month of Iyyar are announced. For that Shabbat, one custom is to prepare a hallah in the shape of a key and sprinkle sesame seeds on it as a reminder that manna began to fall during the month of Iyyar in the desert. Another custom is to study the talmudic tractate *Shavuot* during the omer period; the reason for this custom is that its name is identical to the word for the holiday Shavuot (even though it means vows instead of weeks). The tractate also has forty-nine pages, which correspond conveniently to the forty-nine days of the omer.

Pesah Sheni: The Second Passover (Iyyar 14) Any person who, because of ritual impurity, was unable to offer the Passover sacrifice on the fourteenth of Nisan is supposed to offer it one month later on Iyyar 14 (see Num. 9:6–13). Since the destruction of the temple, Pesah Sheni is marked only by the omission of Tahanun (a petitionary prayer) from the daily liturgy. Some people eat matzah on Second Passover as a symbolic remembrance. There is also a custom of having a *hillula* (celebration) at the grave of Rabbi Meir Ba'al ha-Nes (Meir master of miracles) near Tiberias. While it is not clear which Rabbi Meir was supposed to have been buried in the tomb (miracles are associated with more than one Rabbi Meir in traditional sources), it is the yahrzeit (anniversary) of whoever-it-is's death. The custom is similar to the *hillula* of Rabbi Shimon bar Yohai at Meron on Lag B'Omer (described above), but not as widely observed.

Another old custom that has fallen into disuse is fasting on the days of *beit, heh, beit* (Monday, Thursday, and the following Monday). These fast days follow Pesah and Sukkot and are intended to atone for any excesses of eating and drinking during these holidays. Since the month of Nisan is traditionally a time of celebration, these fasts are not held until the following month of Iyyar. The parallel fasts for Sukkot are held in the following month of Heshvan. Since Shavuot is so brief compared to the other pilgrimage festivals, there apparently is little time for mischief-making and therefore no compensatory fasts are required.

A fact that gives pause to those who argue that Jewish tradition is thoroughly antiascetic. Still, it is comforting to know that our ancestors suffered from the same guilt that we have when we worry that we are enjoying ourselves too much, thereby bringing down the inevitable recompense.

A.E.

The fasts on Monday-Thursday-Monday can be used to check on what you promised yourself during the preceding festival. Fast half a day while contemplating unfulfilled promises.

Z.S.

Flowers, plants, and bean sprouts are nice; grains are also nice, and especially appropriate when dealing with a grain-cycle ceremonial. Perhaps include some wheat grains in the sprouting for the period after Pesah?

Further possibilities exist for giving substance to the otherwise abstract ceremony of numbering. For some years now, both at home in the garden and at temple with the students, I've planted winter rye during Sukkot. The rye generally germinates within ten days, grows a bit, then braces itself for the winter. In early spring, well before the ground can be worked, the rye resumes its growth. Depending on seasonal conditions and how early or late Pesah occurs, by the time omer counting begins, one can cut each night (or prior to each Shabbat) a good handful of rye for the numbering. As the counting continues, the rye grows steadily taller, and usually begins to head out before Shavuot, forming spikelets and revealing the grain-in-formation.

Not only is the steady development of the grain exciting to watch, one can make use of the lengthening stalks, bound into sheaves, to perform the beautiful acts of "waving" prescribed in Leviticus (23:15–16, 20).

In these ways one can achieve a renewed sense of the wondrous and life-sustaining power of the grain cycle, a central seasonal theme of the Pesah-Shavuot seven weeks.

E.Ge.

KAVVANOT

As a reminder of the harvest, some people buy flowers or plants each week or sprout beans in water to be eaten during the omer or on Shavuot. To reflect the importance of numbers in the omer count, others give to tzedakah (charity) the exact number of that night's count—that is, one cent, two cents . . . forty-nine cents, or one dollar, two dollars, etc.

Some people have remarked on an interesting change from the beginning of the omer to its end. We begin with the most elaborate and sumptuous meal of the year—the Pesah seder—and move gradually to the simple meals of Shavuot, which are traditionally dairy. We thus move from Passover, with its emphasis on the Pesah sacrifice, to the milk of Shavuot. Some people believe that our meals during the omer should reflect this shift from the very physical joy of Passover to the oncoming spiritual joy of the revelation at Sinai. Meals could emphasize grains as a reflection of the wheat harvest and, in general, be simpler during the omer. Mondays and Thursdays, in particular, could be meatless days. Even the ancient custom of women not working during the omer evenings could be revived in a limited way—that is, everyone might spend less time with food preparation and more time in self-preparation for God's revelation at Sinai.

Even more broadly, some people have begun to use this period as a time to reflect on how we use food and on the world food situation. This is appropriate not only because of the shift from meat to dairy described above but also because of the symbolism of the manna that began to fall during this period in the desert. This concern for world hunger has involved the avoidance of wasteful food products (processed foods) during the omer, the study of both Jewish and general materials on food and related issues, and the supporting of groups involved with world hunger relief. The goal is to bring about a time when, just as God sustained all Israel with manna, we will be able to sustain all the people of this planet with enough food so that, as in the desert, on that messianic Shabbat, no one will have to go out and search for manna/food. (Credit is due Robert Agus for many of the contemporary omer ideas described above.)

DERASH

If we do not observe the mourning practices and if we feel remote from the agricultural underpinnings of the omer, then how are we to relate to this period? Why does counting the omer remain important?

The omer, as mentioned earlier, serves as a link between Passover and Shavuot. Each day of the omer brings us that much closer to the event of Sinai. It is a form of countdown—except that in Judaism, everything is a "countup" (for example the number of Hanukkah candles). It is also a reminder of the Pesah liberation that has just passed, and a reminder that it is very easy to slide back into slavery. It is not only the generation of the desert

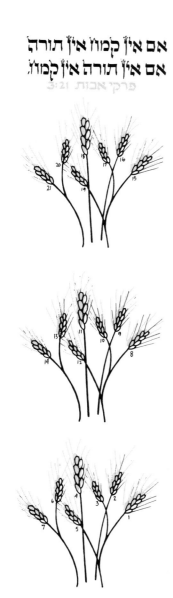

אם אין קמח אין תורה
אם אין תורה אין קמח.
פרקי אבות 3:21

Where there is no bread, there is no Torah;
Where there is no Torah, there is no bread.

Ethics of the Fathers 3:21

who desired to return to the fleshpots of Egypt; similarly, it is not only the French Revolution that began with equality and liberty and fraternity and ended with tyranny. Liberty is easy to lose as we hurry back to the comfort of the old and familiar fleshpots, especially those where someone else tells us what to do, where choosing and responsibility lie in other people's hands. Liberty is also easy to lose when, for the sake of the new order, "temporary" measures are taken that soon negate the freedom that was gained. The easiest route *out* of Egypt leads back *to* it or else forward into a new Egypt.

Instead, we are to turn aside to Sinai, where we are given the blueprint of a new order that calls for choice and responsibility rather than slavery to a new ideal—a new order that demands justice and mercy for others, not privileges for its members. We are to turn aside as Moses did years earlier, to see a wondrous site—a bush that was on fire and yet was not consumed, a symbol of the paradox of a set of commandments that frees rather than enslaves, a symbol of a revolution that burns with its own fiery convictions and yet consumes neither its adherents or others.

In order, then, not to lose the liberation of Passover and to prepare for Shavuot, it is important to count each day. Moreover, we are to mark the passage of this crucial time as a reminder that we should mark all of time's passage. As the psalmist says, "The span of our life is seventy years," or symbolically seven weeks.

PREPARING FOR SINAI

How do we prepare for this event? Since, according to tradition, we all stood at Sinai, how will we be ready this year when in the past we were not? The traditions about the Israelites at Sinai all stress their lack of readiness—in fact, a reluctance to be there altogether. First, the Israelites slept late the morning of the Revelation and had to be awakened by Moses. Then when God began to speak, they fled and said to Moses, "This is too much for us. You, Moses, speak to God and relay His word to us." One problematic midrash relates the tale of how God suspended Mount Sinai over the Israelites' heads and said, "Either you accept the Torah or here shall be your graves!" (An interesting projection on the part of the Israelites reflecting a total passivity in the face of the experience.)

Each of us must prepare in her or his own way for Sinai, so that we can still hear the voice that calls to us at every moment with God's words. For some, this preparation may involve the study of Torah, the content of Revelation. For others, it will involve meditating on what God's revealing Himself to us will be like and how to prepare so as not to flee. For beyond the giving of the Torah at Sinai was the moment when the divine and the human came into contact. How, then, can we strive to recapture that experience?

These are the questions that face us each day as we fulfill the simple ritual of counting from one to forty-nine. So simple a ritual, and yet it is so easy to forget a day, unaccustomed as we are to marking time's passage, seeing one day like another. The challenge is to remember what day it is, who we are, and how close we stand to Sinai. To completely forget even one day is to

If you toil in the Torah, then God has much reward to give you.
Ethics of the Fathers 4:12

הֲפֹךְ־בָּהּ
וַהֲפֹךְ־בָּהּ
דְּכֹלָּא־בָהּ.
פרקי אבות 5:25

Turn it and turn it over again, for every-
thing is in it.
Ethics of the Fathers 5:25

forfeit the opportunity to recite the *berakhah* of the omer, to become lost and
to wander from the path to Sinai onto the multitude of well-trodden paths
that lead back to Egypt.

OTHER HOLIDAYS OF THE OMER PERIOD

Three new commemorative days occur during the omer period: Yom ha-
Shoah—the Day of Remembrance of the Holocaust; Yom ha-Atzma'ut—
Israeli Independence Day; and Yom Yerushalayim—the day marking the
reunification of Jerusalem. The development of these days highlights both the
potentials and the problems of creating new holidays around recent events.

YOM HA-SHOAH:
DAY OF REMEMBRANCE OF THE HOLOCAUST

The twenty-seventh day of Nisan has been established by the government of Israel as the date to commemorate the Holocaust and its victims. The
ritual of this day is still in formation, partly because it was instituted by a
secular authority; the most traditional rabbinic authorities do not believe a
special day should be set aside for the Holocaust and therefore are opposed
to the observance of Yom ha-Shoah. In Israel, the day is observed by the
closing of all theaters and places of amusement, banks, schools, and most
businesses. There are a variety of memorial observances, as there are in the
United States.

Complicating the picture for Yom ha-Shoah are two American observances. The first is the annual Warsaw Ghetto Uprising Memorial in New York
City and other places, which takes place on April 19 or the nearest appropriate Sunday. This is usually marked by mass meetings with speeches by
survivors and public figures, readings of Holocaust accounts, and memorial
prayers such as kaddish and *eil maleh rahamim.* More recently a U.S. Holocaust
Commission was established by then-president Carter. Each year it holds a
ceremony in Washington, D.C., attended by the president and other dignitar-
ies. It has much the same basic format as the Warsaw Ghetto Memorial.

The date of Yom ha-Shoah has been a matter of controversy. Some traditional authorities have suggested other days to memorialize those killed in the
Holocaust. Some have suggested the fast day of the Tenth of Tevet (one of
the traditional fasts commemorating the events leading to the destruction of
the temple). Others have suggested Tisha be-Av, which commemorates not
only the destruction of both temples but also many other tragic events in
Jewish history, such as the expulsion of the Jews from Spain in 1492. Still
others have suggested dates related to events during the Holocaust. Nisan 27
was chosen by the Israeli Knesset, and this date has been the most widely
accepted ever since.

Why the Knesset chose the twenty-seventh of Nisan is not clear. One opinion (which is incorrect) is that this date marked the first liberation of a death camp. The most common explanation is that this day was chosen because of its relation to two other events. The first is the Warsaw Ghetto Uprising, which began during Pesah (April 19, 1943) and allegedly ended on Nisan 27 (yet active resistance continued for at least another week). Since a day in memory of the Holocaust during the holiday of Passover seemed inappropriate, a date later in Nisan was chosen. The second event is the founding of the State of Israel, which is commemorated a week later on the fifth of Iyyar with Yom ha-Atzma'ut—Israeli Independence Day.

In the minds of many Knesset members, the Holocaust and the founding of the state are linked on both a historical and philosophical level. The historical link is that this ultimate tragedy that befell the Jews of Europe prompted a sympathetic world opinion and the United Nations to support the creation of the state of Israel as a refuge for Jews. Similarly, the Holocaust convinced virtually every Jew, even those who until then had been indifferent or opposed to Zionism, that the founding of a state was necessary to prevent the recurrence of such a tragedy. On the philosophical level, the Holocaust exposed the problematic nature of the exile (or galut) and supported the case for Zionism. These events marked the end of the East European style of Judaism and the growth of a new kind of Jew, symbolized by the strong and independent sabra. Thus the transition between these two commemorative days is symbolic of a change in a mythic dimension marking the beginning of a new era for the Jewish people following the end of galut.

Kavvanot Both the Reform siddur *(Shaarei Tefillah—Gates of Prayer)* and the Conservative one (*Siddur Sim Shalom,* a prayer book for Shabbat, festivals and weekdays) contain material for Yom ha-Shoah. The Reform prayer book has a *ma'ariv* service interspersed with readings and liturgical interpolations appropriate for the day. The Conservative prayer book contains a unit of readings with some suggestions for their use. There is also a booklet entitled *Nightwords* by David Roskies (available from B'nai B'rith Hillel, 1640 Rhode Island Avenue N.W., Washington, D.C. 20036) that is a dramatized midrash-reading to be used as a ritual for Yom ha-Shoah. It requires thirty to forty people, who are assigned parts to read as they enter the room for the service. Rabbi Jules Harlow has suggested that the recital of selections from Psalms could replace the traditional evening service. (Reciting Psalms in memory of the dead is an old custom.) He also suggests assigning each person who wishes to participate the name of one of the 6 million (with any information known about him or her) to personalize the overwhelming horror of the event, which can otherwise be numbing.

Finally, Yom ha-Shoah might be the occasion for us to resurrect the medieval kabbalistic custom of *tzom shtikah*—a fast of silence, rather than a fast from eating. In face of the Holocaust, unsure of how we should respond or what we can say, the most appropriate response may be silence. In that silence, the questions raised by the Holocaust can be reflected upon. Then, too, an aura of silence creates an appropriate space in which to ponder the silence of the world and the silence of God during those awful years.

Such a fast would be in sharp contrast to the Days of Awe—especially Yom Kippur, when we recite an endless amount of words. The evening service might be chanted by one person while everyone else listens silently. However, since the Shoah raises questions concerning our traditional beliefs about God, it would be more appropriate not to read the daily liturgy, which affirms those traditional beliefs, but to create new liturgy that reflects this questioning. Until such liturgy exists, the reading of accounts of those who lived through the Holocaust might be appropriate, and would create a service that consisted of listening to readings followed by long periods of silence. Or the service could consist of listening to tapes and records of appropriate songs (e.g., "The Partisan's Song") or selections from the oral histories of survivors. One such record is Elie Wiesel's reading from his works (Spoken Arts).

This service would call upon us to spend the evening confronting the issues that the Holocaust raises for us. We would, like Job, try to hear God's voice out of the whirlwind, and, even after hearing it, respond in silence.

Besides the Book of Job, you may wish to draw from the following list of source materials (gathered by Rabbi Jonathan Porath):

BASIC LISTING OF MATERIALS

Brickman, Seymour. *On Teaching the Holocaust.* New York: Board of Jewish Education (426 W. 58th St., New York, N.Y. 10019), in cooperation with the American Zionist Foundation (AZYF, 515 Park Ave., New York, N.Y. 10022). Contains bibliography, "Eternal Light" radio scripts (1956–65), audiovisual materials listing.

Selected Bibliography of Program Resources. American Federation of Jewish Fighters, Camp Inmates and Nazi Victims, Inc., in cooperation with the AZYF. Contains bibliography, listing of exhibitions available, and survivors and fighters organizations in U.S. and Canada.

AVAILABLE SOURCES

Anthology of Holocaust Literature. Edited by Jacob Glatstein et al. Philadelphia: Jewish Publication Society, 1969.

Friedlander, Albert. *Out of the Whirlwind,* a reader of Holocaust literature. New York: Union of American Hebrew Congregations, 1968.

The Holocaust, a reader for educational programs for Yom ha-Shoah Vehagvurah, AZYF.

RELIGIOUS DIMENSION

Eliav, Mordechai. *Ani Ma'amin.* Jerusalem: Mosad Harav Kuk, 1969.

Oshry, Ephraim. *Mema'amakim.* 3 vols., New York, 1959, 1963, 1968.

Rosenbaum, Irving J. *The Holocaust and Halakhah.* New York: Ktav, 1976.

Zimmels, H. J. *The Echo of the Nazi Holocaust in Rabbinic Literature.* London: Marla, 1976.

AUDIOVISUALS AND EXHIBITIONS

Gestapo: A Simulation of the Holocaust, and *Holocaust: A Study in Values.* Alternatives in Religious Education (3945 S. Oneida St., Denver, Colo. 80237).

The Holocaust: 1933–1945. Anti-Defamation League (823 United Nations Plaza, New York, N.Y. 10017). A twenty-poster exhibition, each 23 × 29 inches, suitable for public display.

Medium. Jewish Media Service (15 E. 26th St., New York, N.Y. 10010), October 1974 issue entitled "East European and Soviet Jewry."

Resistance. Board of Jewish Education of New York and YIVO. A filmstrip with cassette and teaching materials.

Rise and Fall of Nazi Germany; Nazi Holocaust, series I and II, *Nuremberg War Crimes Trials.* Documentary Photo Aids (P.O. Box 956, Mt. Dora, Fla. 32757). Four picture reports suitable for an exhibition.

The Warsaw Ghetto in Pictures. YIVO (1048 Fifth Ave., New York, N.Y. 10028). An illustrated catalogue of 450 pictures.

OF SPECIAL NOTE

Likrat Shabbat. "We Remember the Holocaust." Bridgeport, Conn.: Prayer Book Press, 1973, p. 57. Responsive reading, suitable for synagogue use.

Siegel, Danny. *And God Braided Eve's Hair.* United Synagogue Youth (155 Fifth Ave., New York, N.Y.), 1976. Particularly section III, "When Your Arm Adds Up to 18" (pp. 35–54) and "Selig and the Judge," p. 48.

Also, mention should be made of three particularly useful bibliographies on the Holocaust:

The Holocaust: An Annotated Bibiliography. Compiled by the National Holocaust Remembrance Committee, Canadian Jewish Congress 1950. Dr. Penfield, Montreal, Quebec, Canada H3G 1C5, 1980.

The Holocaust: An Annotated Bibliography by Harry James Cargas. Published by Catholic Library Association (461 Lancaster Ave., Haverford, Pa. 19041), 1977.

A Selected and Annotated Resource List of Materials on the Holocaust. Prepared by the Holocaust Information Center of the Anti-Defamation League of B'nai B'rith (823 United Nations Plaza, New York, N.Y. 10017).

Derash I have long experienced a sense of discomfort with the present date and pattern of observance of Yom ha-Shoah. One difficulty in discussing the Holocaust lies in its emotional nature, even for those born after the event. Part of the reason we respond so powerfully to the Holocaust is that it affects our deepest beliefs as Jews. Thus one person maintains that the Holocaust must transform Judaism radically; another Jew maintains the Shoah is no different fundamentally from all the other persecutions that befell the Jewish people; a third may say it is no different from any particularly grievous tragedy that befalls humans, such as the death of a small child. Some believe not enough has been made of the Holocaust in Jewish education and life; others feel that the Holocaust has been unduly emphasized. It is thus with some trepidation that I approach the subject, trying to make clear my own viewpoint on the "meaning" of the Holocaust.

I do believe that Judaism must be different after the Holocaust. Yes, any death is a tragedy. And, yes, the Jews as a people suffered many holocausts. Yet the Shoah is different—partly because it happened in the twentieth

Comprehensive, comprehending, and compassionate, Terrence Des Pres's moving and life-affirming *Survivor* stands at the very top of my personal list of Holocaust literature. (Oxford University Press, paper, 1980.)

E.GE.

We must be different after the Holocaust, we *are* different, not because the event was unique but because it casts its shadow directly upon our lifetimes, and imposes responsibilities for the preservation of Jews and Judaism that we might otherwise have avoided. *Judaism,* however, need not be different; it is no more inadequate to comprehension of the Holocaust than to other tragedies, individual and collective, that have befallen our people and all others.

That is not to say we should not set aside a day to remember the Holocaust and its victims. We should, we must; not to remember would be as wrong as it is impossible. Two forms of remembrance seem especially appropriate to me. One, recollection of the lives of those killed, a focus on their culture, their faith, their commitments, so that we can "build a name" for them among ourselves by carrying on from where they left off. Teaching our children how European Jews lived is far more urgent than rehearsing the details of how they died. Second, we could honor their deaths with silence. Words—ideologies—played a principal role in accomplishing their destruction; words, ideas, images are a distraction, a comfort, to those of us who squirm uncomfortably as we remember. Let Yom Ha-Shoah also be a Day of Silence, enabling us to hear whatever the Holocaust, and the faith that survived it, have to teach us.

A.E.

century. The questions it raises about theology—about good and evil and God's role in the world—and the answers we are grappling toward are essentially twentieth-century phenomena reflecting the fact that we live in a secular and modern world. The question "How could God do this to me?" has been with us since Job, but how we ask and, even more, how we have begun to answer are very different today.

Thus, one of the things Yom ha-Shoah evokes is a reexamination of God and His relationship to us. It calls into question the traditional notions that the bad are punished and the good are rewarded, as well as the notion of a God who intervenes in the world. On its simplest level, if God does not intervene, then there is no justice in the world and one wonders, Who needs God? Or why pray? Alternatively, if God does answer and can act, then how could the Holocaust (and for that matter any death of an innocent) be explained?

Yom ha-Shoah therefore serves as a counterpoint to much of the tradition, including the festival cycle. It stands in sharp contrast, for example, to Passover with its message that not only did God redeem us in Egypt but that even though in every generation enemies will "rise against us, the Holy One will save us." Yom ha-Shoah causes us to wrestle with these questions and strive for new understanding of God and humans.

Because of Yom ha-Shoah's significance, I find deeply disturbing the juxtaposition of Yom ha-Shoah both with the Warsaw Ghetto and with Yom ha-Atzma'ut. Its connection with the Warsaw Ghetto Uprising seems to me to make us agree with those who would desecrate the memory of all the 6 million by emphasizing only those who engaged in armed resistance against the Nazis. It reflects a defensiveness about—and thus an acknowledgment of some truth in—the statements made by those who accuse the Jews of being led to slaughter as sheep. To emphasize the Warsaw Ghetto revolt is to accept those critics' field of discourse by trying to prove that some Jews did fight back. The Warsaw Ghetto should be remembered, but I am not willing to imply that its defenders were more heroic than any other of the 6 million, or, what is even worse, to imply even a subliminal embarrassment for those Jews who did not fight back.

The Connection with Israel Similarly, there is a highly disturbing tendency in Israel to see the Jews of the Exile as cringing figures who shuffle before the authority of the gentiles. Whatever truth there was in that imagery, it is not true enough to enshrine it in the familiar comparison of the old-world Jew who plays the role of victim of Yom ha-Shoah to the brave Israeli freedom fighter of Yom ha-Atzma'ut. This contrast is part of a more general tendency in Israel to negate the exile period and its achievements and, in its most extreme form, to hark all the way back to the biblical period as the last time that Jews were authentic or whole beings. Without minimizing the growth of a Jewish self-confidence since the founding of the state, it does not seem necessary, nor even desirable, to regard the Diaspora as basically a history that is best forgotten—something embarrassing, like an immigrant parent's foreign accent.

It is worth quoting Steven S. Schwarzschild's passionate and moving response:

Certainly the Jews in the Warsaw Ghetto had every human right to defend themselves and to fight back. The same is true of all the other military or paramilitary expressions of resistance and counterattack. Rightly do we honor their memories. But let us remember: in the first place, we lament to say that they, too, died—if survival is to be the yardstick of tactical or ethical worth, then we mourn to have to conclude that neither military resistance nor martyrdom availed. In the second place, it has been and is a terrible defamation of the third of the Jewish people that went to their deaths to claim or to imply that because they did not fight back they either did not resist or—mmmm mm (God forbid)—collaborated. To be *mentshen* in the midst of inhumanity, to sanctify the name of God while surrounded by a flood of heathenism, to study, teach, and pray in a world in which only murder, rape, and brutality reigned, to squeeze a precious drop of life through the sieve of all-consuming death, and finally to go to one's death in ranks of thousands because the world had turned into hell and no longer had a place for decent human beings—who will rise and have the forwardness of claiming that this was not, in its way, the greatest, the most admirable, the most heroic form of resistance—that the more than five million who did not, as it happens, resort to guns, knives, stones, and fire did not plant the banner of Israel, God, and humanity fluttering high on the battlefield of history? ["On the Theology of Survival," ACID, April 1973.]

E.GE.

The implications of the belief that the significance of the Holocaust is that it helped bring about the state of Israel are no less disturbing. It is blasphemous to suggest that the 6 million died so that the state could be created. Still, the placement of Yom ha-Shoah just before Yom ha-Atzma'ut implies the connection and its attendant rationalization of the Holocaust even if this is not stated explicitly. In response to this misuse of Yom ha-Shoah, I have come to believe that Yom ha-Shoah should have no connection with Yom ha-Atzma'ut nor be placed in any way that suggests such a connection. While historically there is some reason to link them, it is important for philosophical reasons to separate them.

Yom ha-Shoah in Heshvan I have tried to think of a better date and place in the calendar for Yom ha-Shoah. Neither the Fast of the Tenth of Tevet nor Tisha be-Av seems appropriate since the Shoah is different from past tragedies in Jewish history and should stand alone. Also, the theological context of both days is inappropriate since tradition holds that the temples were destroyed because of our sins. (Do we want to state that the 6 million died for their sins?) In my mind the most appropriate day is the sixteenth of Heshvan, which corresponds with November 10, 1938—Kristallnacht, the night of broken glass. Kristallnacht marks the outbreak of the Nazis' war against the Jews and seems an appropriate choice for Yom ha-Shoah.

Heshvan also seems appropriate, for it is the only month of the year without any commemorative days. The rabbis called it *marheshvan*—"bitter Heshvan." Heshvan-the-bitter is also, according to tradition, the time of the biblical flood when all humans and animals were destroyed except for those in Noah's ark. After the flood, God promised that He would never again destroy the world and placed a rainbow in the sky as a sign of that promise. Yet it is still within the power of human hands to destroy the world. The Nazis and their use of modern technology for killing are a warning of that possibility, as is the mushroom cloud of Hiroshima. Thus the imagery of the flood and the rebirth of life from the ark could serve as a background motif of Yom ha-Shoah.

The fact that Heshvan follows the month of Tishri, replete with its autumn holidays, would also make it appropriate. Sukkot is the end of the pilgrimage festival cycle, the end of the harvest, and marks the ingathering of resources before the oncoming winter. The fall of leaves and the barrenness of the world are again symbols of death as part of the cycle of nature, which in human hands could become a permanent state of affairs.

Then, too, Yom ha-Shoah stands in contradistinction to Yom Kippur. On Yom Kippur, we are judged by God as all of our imperfections are held up for minute examination. On Yom ha-Shoah, in effect, we question and judge God and reexamine our theology and our relationship to God.

Finally, Yom ha-Shoah would precede Hanukkah, which, while set in the dead of winter, actually marks the beginning of the end of winter as reflected by the ever-increasing light of the Hanukkah menorah. Heshvan is the darkest period of the year, the moment before any sign of life appears, a time of death and decay.

I applaud what you write on this. To see the establishment of the state of Israel as God's reward for the Holocaust is obscene, the highest defamation of God conceivable. Yet, the position of Yom ha-Atzma'ut following Yom ha-Shoah conforms to the Jewish theology of hope and survival that has carried us from biblical to contemporary times. The Book of Amos, for example, culminates eight chapters of doom with one of hope. As the classical rabbis put it, we place the catastrophes together first, then we place consolations after them. The state of Israel can hardly be the consummation of the Shoah; but it is the hope that a historical turn like the state of Israel holds out to us that enables us to continue to imagine the ultimate redemption. We ought to develop a more realistic theology regardless of when Yom ha-Shoah is commemorated.

E.Gr.

The multiplication of commemorative days of mourning has not, I think, gained widespread support among Jews through the ages. While our calendar is marked by a number of such dates, the energy of communal observance has been concentrated around Tisha be-Av, and this date has proved capable of receiving additions through not just centuries but millennia. There is, then, a strong case to be made for fixing Yom ha-Shoah on this date.

On the other hand, it is difficult to combine a long-remembered, hence muted pain with a recent, hence acute pain. From this perspective, I can feel the argument for a separate date for Yom ha-Shoah, at least in our particular period of history.

If a separate date is to be adopted, I am persuaded by the author's sensitive and thoughtful considerations that incline him to advocate the Heshvan/Kristallnacht date. And that "Rachel weeping for her children" is associated with this emotionally charged month makes it all the more appropriate for expressing the fresh pain and unhealed wounds of the Holocaust.

E.Ge.

One last image: According to tradition, the matriarch Rachel died during the month of Heshvan. Rachel is the only one of the patriarchs/matriarchs who is not buried in the Cave of Machpelah in Hebron. She was buried on the road to Bethlehem, where, in the words of Jeremiah, she weeps for her children suffering in exile as she lies alone by the roadside. "A cry is heard in Ramah—wailing, bitter weeping—Rachel weeping for her children. She refuses to be comforted for her children, who are gone" (Jer. 31:15). Rachel weeping provides a powerful metaphor from the tradition to weave into Yom ha-Shoah.

YOM HA-ATZMA'UT: ISRAELI INDEPENDENCE DAY

Since 1948, the miraculous return of the Jewish people to their homeland has been celebrated on the fifth of Iyyar, the Hebrew date of the founding of the state of Israel. In Israel the whole country celebrates with parties, performances, and, at times, military parades. After some years of uncertainty, the religious establishment has developed a full set of liturgical rituals. In America the celebration has also included concerts, films, parades, Israeli fairs, and other public events. (The Israel Day parade in New York takes place in May or June, not always near the fifth of Iyyar. For information, contact the American Zionist Youth Foundation.)

Traditions In Israel, Yom ha-Atzma'ut is preceded by Yom ha-Zikkaron—the day of remembering those who died fighting for the state. Public observances include lighting candles, visiting graves, reciting Psalms, and lighting a torch that burns for twenty-four hours. During the shaharit (morning liturgy) service, additions are often made to the regular liturgy. Following the kaddish after *aleinu,* a candle is lit in memory of the fallen soldiers, the ark is opened, and Psalm 9 is recited. This is followed by yizkor for the war dead, mourner's kaddish by relatives, and the *eil maleh rahamim* prayer. This addition to the regular liturgy is concluded with Psalm 144. At the end of the day, sirens are sounded and a few minutes of silence are observed as the whole country comes to a halt.

Then Yom ha-Atzma'ut begins, and the mood changes from sorrow to celebration. Over the years a number of synagogue rituals have developed, the most widely observed being those published by the Chief Rabbinate and by the Religious Kibbutz Movement/World Zionist Organization. A combined summary of these two rituals follows.

At night, introductory psalms such as Psalms 98 and 100 or Psalms 107, 97, and 98 are recited. *Ma'ariv* is chanted to the holiday *nusah* (melody). While some congregations recite Hallel at night, others do not. Psalm 126—*Shir ha-ma'alot*—is sung to the tune of "Hatikvah." A *seudat mitzvah* (festive meal)—with singing, lighting of candles, and even, according to some opinions, kiddush—is observed after *ma'ariv.* That evening and the next day, the greeting is *Moadim le-simhah* ("Have a happy festival") and the response is *Le-geulah sheleimah* ("Toward a complete redemption").

We often wonder whether God still speaks to us today. If we understand revelation as our own perception of God's hand in history, then the establishment of the state of Israel constitutes a magnificent act of God, and it entails a bold revelation: Keep the state of Israel and sustain it. We are privileged to live in the time when the voice of God speaks more clearly than at any time since Sinai. It is important with respect to holidays like this, Yom Yerushalayim, and Hanukkah, too, which commemorate military victories, that we celebrate not the triumph of our armies but the concern and effectiveness of our God.

E.GR.

One liturgical suggestion is to recite the opposite of the partial Hallel said on Rosh Hodesh and part of Passover, and thus say Psalms 115:1–11 and 116:1–11, leaving out 115:12–18 and 116:12–19. This would express the notion that the founding of the state is only a beginning; it remains to be finished.

Z.S.

The next morning during shaharit, the psalms added on Shabbat and holidays are recited (as is done on Hoshana Rabbah—see Sukkot, p. 136). The service leader begins the main part of the service with the chanting of *ha-eil* as on festivals. After the amidah, hallel is recited with a *berakhah* (some say it without). Some congregations take out the Torah and read three aliyot from Deuteronomy 7:12–8:18, followed by a haftarah of Isaiah 10:32–12:6. Then the prayer for the state is recited and the service is concluded as on weekdays. Some people recite Psalm 111 after the psalm of the day. Again there is a festive meal. Another popular custom is to walk at least a short distance (four *amot*) somewhere in the land of Israel where you have never walked before.

Additional Ideas for Services The Reform prayer book has a whole service especially written for Yom ha-Atzma'ut. The Conservative prayer book has an *al ha-nissim* prayer similar to those for Purim and Hanukkah to be added to the Amidah and to the Grace after Meals. It also contains a suggested Torah reading and more general readings/meditations on the themes of Zion and Israel. *Prayers and Readings for Israel Independence Day* by Rabbi Ben Zion Bokser (Hebrew Publishing Company, 1967) incorporates some of the elements of the liturgies created in Israel, but also includes the reading of Ezekiel's vision of the dry bones (Ezek. 37:1–14) and the reading of Israel's Declaration of Independence.

The tradition is a rich resource for creating your own service, especially by drawing upon the prophets and Book of Psalms. There is also a good deal of poetry about Israel, ranging from Yehuda ha-Levi to Hayyim Nahman Bialik to modern Israeli poets. A selected bibliography of resources collected by Rabbi Jonathan Porath follows:

GENERAL PROGRAMMING

Yom Ha'atzmaut: A Guide to Programming for Israel Independence Day. New York: American Zionist Federation. A superb programming guide including home, school, and community celebrations. Also Yom Yerushalayim materials.

Yom Ha'atzmaut—Israel's Independence Day—Projects, Ideas and Materials. A fine kit of materials including background readings, program materials, and additional scripts, audio aids, documents, and songs. A great deal of valuable material. Can be purchased from the Youth and Hechalutz Department, WZO, 515 Park Ave., New York, N.Y.

Yom Ha'atzmaut—Israel Independence Day—Program Materials. Edited by Jacob Perla, et. al. Department of Education and Culture, WZO (515 Park Ave.), 1970. A 336-page collection of program suggestions, prayers and readings, quotations from Zionist founding fathers, dramatic readings, and stories. A bit outdated but still a useful collection.

PRAYER MATERIALS

Seder L'yom Ha'atzmaut: Israel Independence Day Service. Edited by Rabbi Ezra Finkelstein, Israel Affairs Committee of the New York Metropolitan Region, United Synagogue, in cooperation with the RA, 1967. *The best compilation in English for the day.* Contains introductory psalms, *Hadlakat Neirot, Maariv* service with *Al Hanisim,* responsive reading from Ezekiel 37, reading, selections from Hallel, kiddush.

*And they shall beat their swords into plowshares, and their spears into pruning hooks;
Nation shall not lift up sword against nation, neither shall they learn war any more.*

Isaiah 2:4

My suggestion for readings would be selections from the Book of Deuteronomy, for it not only deals very subtly with the interplay between humanity *(adam),* land *(adamah),* and *eretz* (land, country, earth, *the* earth), but compels us to see our relation to the land of Israel as central to the meaning of Jewish existence.

Shema: Moses is speaking to the children of Israel, on the far side of the Jordan. He is trying to evoke for them the Life with a capital *L* that awaits them on the river's far bank, if only they will cross over, and begin to live it. He cannot describe that reality convincingly, because it has never existed before—*they* must create it. All he can do is awake them to the precious opportunity to bring that new reality into being, according to the direction of Torah.

We stand with those Israelites, on the river's far bank, facing the opportunity of building a new life in our land. The possibility that the vision of Deuteronomy will ever be more than a mere possibility seems as remote to us as it must have seemed to them. Yet the translation of words *(devarim)* into facts *(devarim)* that we are commanded to accomplish is, I believe, the task that defines us as Jews. We are meant to build just Jewish communities with God in their midst. Independence offers unparalleled opportunities for performing that task—and also, of course, unparalleled chances for failure. That is the privilege of our generation: Our words become far more serious when we are challenged to act on them, and live up to them; putting our words into practice, we may find them inadequate to the tasks at hand.

Israel, then, is a religious imperative, and statehood a blessing. We need to acknowledge both in our ritual calendar so as not to forget the mitzvot that renewed *atzma'ut* imposes upon us.

A.E.

Seder L'yom Ha'atzmaut: Prayer Service for Israel Independence Day. Mizrachi-Hapoel Hamizrachi, in cooperation with the Torah Education Department, WZO, 1977. An all-Hebrew collection (from the *Siddur Rinat Yisrael*) with Hallel and suggestions for religious observance.

Seder Tefillot L'yom Ha'atzmaut. Hakibbutz Hadati, Tel Aviv, 1969. The most extensive (100-page) seder for the day, containing a listing of *dinim uminhagim*—laws and customs and complete services for day. All-Hebrew, and difficult to obtain in the States.

AUDIOVISUAL MATERIALS

Alden Films (7820 20th Ave., Brooklyn, N.Y. 11214). A catalogue of ninety-three films on Israel, all available for a nominal charge.

Board of Jewish Education of New York, *David's City.* A slide set on Jerusalem, and additional educational materials.

Medium, Jewish Media Service, issue number 12, July 1976, "The Real Israel." A review of twenty-eight films on Israel. A very useful source.

OF SPECIAL INTEREST

"Anniversary Prayer for the State of Israel," *Likrat Shabbat,* p. 61. A responsive reading suitable for synagogue use.

Derash Looking at Yom ha-Atzma'ut, I am struck by its lack of unique rituals or celebrations. While this reflects in part how recent was the founding of the state, it also points to a failure by religious Jews to develop a theology concerning the significance of the rebirth of the state of Israel. Most religious Zionists, with a few notable exceptions such as Rav Kook, seem to have simply grafted some religious forms onto secular Zionist ideology. While a contemporary religious Jew might be distinguished from a secular Jew by the observance of kashrut or Shabbat, in regard to Israel they both give money, visit, and politically support the state in ways indistinguishable from each other. This is not to deny how important a component of our Jewish identity the relationship to Israel has become; it is rather to say that there is no religious expression of that importance.

There is a further related question that is especially pointed for Jews living outside of Israel: What is the relationship of the Diaspora to Israel? A common Zionist position negates the Diaspora and demands that all Jews make aliyah to Israel. Another widely held position states that Israel is the center and the Diaspora is the periphery that is aided by and aids that center.

Yet one could argue in favor of upholding the validity of the Diaspora while at the same time not negating the importance of Israel. Both Israel and the Diaspora have value and purpose, and in this view both are necessary to complement each other. For centuries Jewish life remained unbalanced with a Diaspora but no Israel. Now we should rejoice in the restoration of that balance, not try to unbalance the equation once more by removing the Diaspora.

Why are both necessary? The case for the Diaspora and Israel as two

contemporary centers can best be explained by utilizing the symbols of the two centers of religious experience and revelation in the Jewish tradition—Mount Sinai and Mount Moriah, or more simply Sinai and Jerusalem.

The Torah of Sinai is familiar to us as the way of life of our people during the 2,000 years of the Diaspora. It has been the daily preoccupation of millions of Jews. As such, it cannot be accidental that the revelation of this Torah took place outside of the land of Israel at Mount Sinai. Sinai is symbolized by the burning bush composed of the elements of fire and wood, which live together rather than consume each other. The bush represents a lowly people who suffer but nevertheless prevail and who at times transform the fire of torture to a blazing beacon of enlightenment.

Yet there is another Torah, a Torah yet-to-be envisioned for us by the prophets, as it says:

> It shall come to pass in the latter days that the mountain of the house of the Lord shall be established as the highest of mountains, and shall be raised up among the hills; and peoples shall flow to it, and many nations shall come and say: "Come, let us go up to the mountain of the Lord to the house of the God of Jacob; that He may teach us His ways and we may walk in His paths." *For out of Zion shall go forth the law, and the word of the Lord from Jerusalem. . . .* They shall beat their swords into plowshares and their spears into pruning hooks, nation shall not lift up sword against nation, neither shall they learn war any more; but they shall sit every person under his vine and under his fig tree, and none shall make them afraid; for the mouth of the Lord of hosts has spoken. [Mic. 4:1–4. See also Isa. 2:3 ff.]

This Torah of Jerusalem finds its symbols in the place itself—the site of the ancient temple of sacrifices, and the political capital of King David. Its symbols emphasize sovereignty and independence. It calls for the creation of a Jerusalem that will be "a house of prayer to all nations." While the prophets speak of this Torah coming only at the end of days, in our time with the restoration of the state, we must begin to create that Torah. For the Torah of Jerusalem grapples with the questions born of sovereignty, from sanitation to war and peace. If the Torah of Sinai showed us how to survive as a minority among other peoples, then the Torah of Jerusalem must teach us how to survive as a majority holding power over a minority.

We need both, for with only Israel and its Torah, it would be easy to make an idolatry of nationalism. We would end up reveling in earth, blood, and power. But with only the Torah of Sinai, we could continue to revel in abstractness and powerlessness, constructing worlds, as the Talmud does, made of oxen that fall into pits and gore each other. Together they balance one another, adding universalism to particularism, pragmatism to idealism, and the future to the past.

We need both Torot. For while we must make aliyah to Jerusalem and its Torah, we must continue to make aliyah to the Torah at Sinai by being called up to its reading in the synagogue.

We need to keep before us *both* of these verses:

> If I forget you, O Jerusalem, let my right hand be forgotten! Let my tongue cleave to the roof of my mouth.

Great is Torah.

Ethics of the Fathers 6:7

My child, do not forget My Torah, your heart should keep My commandments. Remember the Torah of Moses My servant which I commanded him laws and statutes at Mount Horeb [Sinai].

This model for religious Zionism need not be the only one, but as we explore more deeply what is the religious significance of Israel, then Yom ha-Atzma'ut will become the focus of these religious responses. The following are some suggestions:

On Yom ha-Atzma'ut we could make a point of eating foods associated with the land of Israel, perhaps featuring those made from milk and honey. People making a trip to Israel in the coming year could be seen as making an *aliyat ha-regel*—a pilgrimage—as was done during the pilgrimage festivals in the time of the temple. If so, what rituals could be developed for it? What offerings could be brought to Israel in the spirit of the offerings brought to the temple long ago? The rest of us might view those from our community going to Israel as our *shelihim*—messengers. *Terumot* and *ma'aserot* (the biblical tithes) could be adapted to our time, making financial support of Israel a religious imperative. If we regard Israel as the potential fulfillment of God's words that we are a "kingdom of priests," then the tithes to the *kohanim*— the priests of the Bible—become a gift for the entire kingdom of priests—that is, the state of Israel. Similarly, the *ma'aser sheni* (second tithe), which, in the Bible, was to be taken by the farmer to Jerusalem and there eaten himself (not given to the priests or Levites), could become a specific amount of money we set aside each year to enable each of us to make periodic journeys to Jerusalem.

As our religious perspective on Israel deepens, Yom ha-Atzma'ut will become more and more a reflection of a vision rather than the simple birthday of a nation.

YOM YERUSHALAYIM: JERUSALEM DAY

On the twenty-eighth of Iyyar, Yom Yerushalayim is celebrated—the day that commemorates the capture of Jerusalem during the Six-Day War. It is the most recent addition to the calendar and for the most part is observed only in Israel. Even in Israel there are those who do not observe it, out of opposition to the policies that have come about due to the capture of the West Bank. As of yet, there are no specific rituals, although services and study that stress the importance of Jerusalem would seem very appropriate.

Liturgical Customs Hallel is recited. Psalm 107 is recited following *aleinu*. *Sefirah* mourning customs are suspended.

SIVAN

The month of Sivan brings to a close the omer period, and at the end of its first week, we celebrate Shavuot. The first few days of Sivan are considered

---

Of late, as my connection to Israel has grown stronger, the meaning of the words of *Shir ha-ma'alot* has grown accordingly. I was stirred when Prime Minister Begin recited the psalm at the signing of the Camp David accords; I cannot help but see Israel as a precious example, precious evidence, of a fulfillment of our wildest dreams. Whether statehood marks "the beginning of the flowering of our redemption," as the chief rabbinate of Israel would have it, I do not know. May it only be so. But that the state is a wonder we should celebrate, a "reaping in joy" for which we need to give thanks, I have no doubt. The day can be used, in the Diaspora, to reflect on our responsibilities to the dream and the reality of Israel—including the mitzvah of living there.

A.E.

Some, myself included, find this a political rather than a religious holiday, a celebration that we have not earned because we have yet to deal justly with the aspirations of the tens of thousands of Jerusalemites whom we have conquered. Indeed, as currently observed in Israel, the day tends to justify and sanctify that conquest, as if it is manifest destiny that we reoccupy the city's sacred precincts, no matter how their inhabitants are treated. "Is this the fast that I have chosen?" I doubt it; the very name "Jerusalem" symbolizes so much in our tradition, bears so many messianic hopes, that to employ it in celebrating the spoils of victory seems sacrilegious.

A.E.

special. The first day, of course, is Rosh Hodesh, the minor holiday celebrating the beginning of each new month. The second of Sivan is known as *yom di-miyuhas* (the day of connection) because it connects Rosh Hodesh and the three days of preparation for Shavuot (as we shall see below). According to the Talmud, there is a deeper connection established on this day, for on this day God said, "You shall be to Me a kingdom of priests and a holy nation" (Exod. 19:6).

The next three days (Sivan 3, 4, and 5) are known as *sheloshet yimei hagbalah* (the three days of restriction), as God commanded: "Go unto the people, and sanctify them today and tomorrow, and let them wash their garments and be ready against the third day" (Exod. 19:10–11). (If you read the verse carefully, you will see only two days of preparation were commanded by God; why we have three will be more fully discussed in the next chapter, "Shavuot"). In remembrance of the Israelites' three-day preparation for Sinai, we, too, begin to ready ourselves for Shavuot three days before. Traditionally, the mourning practices of the omer period are ended with the beginning of these three days.

The Shabbat before Shavuot is called "Shabbat Kallah," the name given (in some traditions) to the Shabbat before any bride's wedding. As we shall see in the next chapter, there is Shavuot imagery that perceives Sinai as the marriage between God and Israel. On Erev Shavuot, it is customary to go to the mikveh—ritual bath—to purify ourselves just as the Israelites purified themselves before Sinai.

As the omer draws to a close, our steps lead us closer and closer to Sinai. We try to ready ourselves as best we can to stand before the mountain and hear the word of the Lord. Our preparation will determine whether we shall be afraid and once again tell Moses, "It is too much! *You* tell us what God is saying," or whether we shall pierce the fiery cloud surrounding the mountain and hear the voice that has something special to say to each living soul.

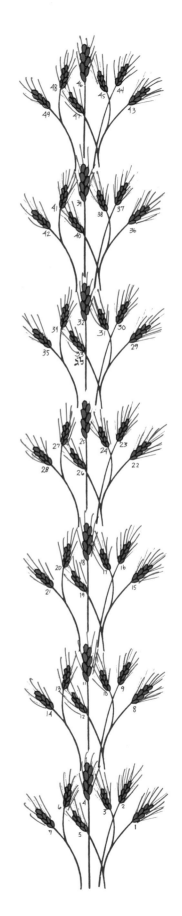

SHAVUOT
REVEALING THE TORAH

havuot (Pentecost, Feast of Weeks) occurs on the sixth day of Sivan (and on the seventh of Sivan for those observing two days in the Diaspora). It celebrates the giving of the Torah, God's gift to the Jewish people, which is the guide for how we are to live in this world. The Torah is the spelling out of the details of the Covenant that, while initiated by the events of the Exodus, is agreed upon and sealed at Sinai. Sinai is more than the receiving of the Torah—it is the experiencing of the Divine, an experience shared by all Jews of all time, for each of us was there and heard the Voice of Sinai. While theologians and scholars may debate what actually happened at Sinai, for the religious Jew Sinai is central to both belief and practice—to belief in a God who cares about this world and expects us to strive in our lives to practice what is good and just.

Yet if we look back at the history of Shavuot, we see a number of problems in associating it with the revelation at Sinai. The biblical references to Shavuot (e.g., Exod. 23:14–19; Lev. 23:9–22) regard it only as the feast of harvest *(hag ha-katzir)* or the day of the first fruits *(yom ha-bikkurim)*. Nowhere in the Bible is any link made between Sinai and Shavuot. Indeed, even the biblical account of the Revelation at Sinai does not connect it with Shavuot.

True, Shavuot is the only one of the three pilgrimages that has no historical connection within the Torah itself. Historical and comparative studies show that all three festivals—Pesah, Shavuot, and Sukkot—originated as nature rites and later took on a historical association with the Exodus and Wandering period. Being proximate in time to the Sinai revelation, Shavuot could hardly resist such a connection. The two themes of Shavuot—harvest and Revelation—come together most poignantly in the Book of Ruth, which we read on Shavuot. There the renewed fertility of the earth and the ensuing harvest parallel and anticipate the fulfillment that is delivered to the Israelite woman Naomi by her Moabite daughter-in-law, Ruth. Ruth inaugurates this process of fulfillment by embracing the Israelite Covenant: "Where you go," Ruth tells Naomi, "I go. Where you lodge, I lodge. Your people is my people, and your God is my God" (Ruth 1:16). We, too, embrace the Covenant again each year on Shavuot.

E.GR.

In fact, Shavuot provides only the clearest example of the transition, apparent in all three of the pilgrimage festivals, between the agricultural rituals celebrated by the farmers of ancient Israel and the historical events commemorated by their later descendants. In the case of Passover, the transition from spring planting rites to the celebration of the Exodus from Egypt is already quite thorough in the Bible itself. Only the omer offering and a few other hints in the wording of the sacrificial gifts for that time suggest that the full moon of the spring month was a time held sacred from time immemorial, and that the attachment of the Exodus to that day was not coincidental. Sukkot is described chiefly in agricultural terms in the Bible, as a fall full-moon harvest festival. Only a single biblical verse, "for I caused the children of Israel to dwell in *sukkot* when I brought them out of the Land of Egypt," indicates the beginning of a shift into the historical mode. In the case of Shavuot, the shift

THE BIBLICAL SHAVUOT

You shall count off seven weeks; start to count the seven weeks when the sickle is first put to the standing grain. Then you shall observe the Feast of Weeks for the Lord your God, offering your freewill contribution according as the Lord your God has blessed you. [Deut. 16:9–10]

From this passage we can see much about the nature of the biblical conception of Shavuot. For example, unlike other holidays, the date of Shavuot was a fluid one, dependent upon the counting of the omer, rather than fixed at a specific date—the sixth day of Sivan. Presumably when the calendar was still based on the actual witnessing of the new moon, Shavuot could have fallen anywhere from the fifth to the seventh of Sivan, depending on whether Nisan and Iyyar were full (thirty-day) months or not. Thus, even though Shavuot would always fall forty-nine days (seven weeks) after the harvesting of the omer, there was—and, as we shall see, remains to this day—an aura of fluidity about Shavuot. The name Shavuot itself means "weeks" (unlike Passover and Sukkot, whose names are intrinsically related to the holiday) and it was probably so named to reflect the nature of its dating.

Many scholars speculate that originally Shavuot had no connection with the Revelation at Sinai and was simply an agricultural festival. Indeed, in biblical times, Shavuot was a day marking the end of the grain harvest (which began with the bringing of the omer on Pesah), a one-day festival during which two loaves of leavened bread were brought to the temple as a concluding rite. As we have seen in the previous chapter, each of these rituals was both a thanksgiving to God, the provider of all foods, and a prayer for His blessing for a successful harvest.

Shavuot also marked the rite of a new agricultural season—the bringing of the first fruits of the land to the temple. Each farmer would bring his first fruits whenever they ripened—anytime during the period that began with Shavuot and ended with Sukkot (which, as we will see, is the holiday that marks the end of harvest and the agricultural year).

THE LATER DEVELOPMENT
OF THE HOLIDAY

The nature of Shavuot began to change following the destruction of the temple in A.D. 70. Without the temple, neither of the two agricultural rites of Shavuot could be observed. At some point in the rabbinic period, connections began to be made with the Revelation at Sinai, which, as the biblical text tells us, took place in the third month—that is, during Sivan (see Exod. 19:1). The exact date of Sinai is not given, and in fact there is a disagreement in the Talmud over whether the Revelation took place on the sixth or seventh of Sivan! Gradually Shavuot became intricately tied to the Revelation at Sinai, and its earlier origins faded from memory. Since the fixing of the calendar, Shavuot's date is always Sivan 6.

Still, even with a character of its own as the Day of Revelation, there are two tendencies within the tradition for understanding Shavuot: One is to see it as the concluding piece to Passover; the other is to see it as an independent festival. As a day commemorating the Revelation at Sinai, Shavuot would seem to be of a clearly independent nature. It is, after all, counted as one of the three pilgrimage festivals. Yet, beginning with the Targum (the Aramaic translation of the Bible, second century of the Christian Era), Shavuot is referred to in the rabbinic tradition as Atzeret. The word *atzeret* is used in the Bible with the festival Shemini Atzeret (see Numbers 29:35) and seems to mean "remain with Me [God] another day."

There is a sense therefore that an *atzeret* is the final part or completion of a festival. Thus Shavuot would be seen as the conclusion to the earlier holiday of Pesah as Shemini Atzeret is to Sukkot. On the other hand, both Shemini Atzeret and Shavuot are shown by the rabbis to be independent festivals in most ways. This is even more true of Shavuot, which commemorates one of the most important events in our history—if not *the* most important.

One strong connection between Pesah and Shavuot has already been touched upon in the previous chapter: The counting of the omer serves as a chain linking the two festivals. No other festivals are connected so emphati-

is entirely postbiblical, showing us that the biblical text represents but a single stage in the ongoing evolution of our sacred times, stretching from the most hidden reaches of antiquity on through into the as yet unknown future.

A.G.

How could the Talmud debate which day the Torah was given? A number of rabbinic scholars present a remarkable explanation for the different dates of Sinai. They claim that the Torah was in fact given on the seventh of Sivan! God had planned to give the Torah on the sixth of Sivan, but Moses, *on his own authority,* ordered the people to prepare an additional day, and God acquiesced in Moses' decision. Therefore, that year Shavuot and the actual giving of the Torah occurred on the fifty-first day of the omer, the seventh of Sivan. Ever since then, however, we observe Shavuot on its proper date —the fiftieth day of the omer count.

Rabbi Shlomo of Radomsk explained: "By adding an extra day in preparation for Sinai, Moses meant to teach us that even at an early stage of our acceptance of Torah, there can be no observance of the Torah without interpretation by the sages. Moses added one extra day on his own even though this meant delaying for a whole day the giving of the Torah."

M.S.

The Exodus leads to Sinai; tribute to Pharaoh gives way to tribute to God; our recollection of God's promises to Israel at Pesah is joined via the omer to our recollection of the fulfillment experienced by the Israelites in their land, as they offered the first fruits of our redemption.

A.E.

While the giving of the Torah is what God does on Shavuot, our role is to receive it. During the omer, we prepare by forming ourselves into vessels to receive the Torah. Each of us creates a receptacle made of our needs and questions. This process precipitates the drawing down out of a universe saturated with blessings just those things that your vessel requires. This is each person's Torah.

Z.S.

cally. The connections operate on a number of levels—from connecting the beginning and the end of the wheat harvest to marking the movement from Egypt to Sinai, to acknowledging the connection between liberation and Revelation.

Another interesting connection between Pesah and Shavuot is that Deuteronomy 26:5–8, which was said by Israelites bringing their first fruits to the temple, became the core text of the Passover Haggadah—*Arami oveid avi*—"My father was a wandering Aramean."

M.S.

TRADITIONS

Because of its original agricultural nature, Shavuot does not have any rituals equivalent to the sukkah of Sukkot or the seder of Passover. The agricultural rituals of Shavuot ceased with the destruction of the temple. On a more symbolic level, the Revelation at Sinai can be viewed as an experience so cosmic and mysterious that no ritual could encompass it, just as the Torah itself is so multifaceted that it eludes any attempt to delineate it. Like God, who cannot be described, His Torah cannot be limited by a specific ritual or symbol other than the Torah scroll itself.

Yet a number of customs have arisen for Shavuot, the oldest of which are the decorating of the synagogue and home with green plants, branches, and even trees, and the eating of dairy foods. Both are of obscure origin. The most common explanations for the floral motif are as follows:

- The area around the mountain of Sinai was green, according to the implication of "neither let the flocks and herds graze" (Exod. 34:3).
- According to one tradition, the day of judgment for trees is Shavuot. To focus our prayers for the trees, we put them in the synagogue.
- They are a remembrance of the decorations on the baskets of first fruits brought to the temple on Shavuot.
- They remind us of baby Moses in his basket on the Nile, which according to tradition was found on Shavuot.

One of the favorite flowers we use on Shavuot is the rose, chosen because of a play on words in Esther 8:14: "And the decree [*dat*] was proclaimed in Shushan." This verse is playfully reinterpreted to mean that the law was given with a rose *(shoshan)*. Therefore, one custom was to scatter spices and roses around the synagogue to create a beautiful fragrance, or, similarly, to give every congregant fresh myrtle to smell. These customs recall a midrash which states that the Israelites fainted from fear when God began to speak the Ten Commandments at Sinai and so God had to revive them with fragrant spices. Another midrash teaches us that as each commandment came forth from God, the entire world was filled with the fragrance of wondrous spices.

Theodor Gaster suggests parallels with other folk customs—especially the decorating of churches at Whitsun with trees. His suggestion is supported by the fact that the Goan of Vilna (the leading Talmudist of the eighteenth century) strenuously opposed the custom of decorating the synagogue with trees as an imitation of gentile practices.

Because of the symbol of roses, the folk art of papercutting associated with Shavuot was called *reizelekh* or *shoshanta* (both meaning roses), as well as *shevusolekh* from the word *Shavuot.* It was customary to decorate synagogues and homes with papercuts displaying complicated designs using flowers and trees as well as many other folk motifs.

The eating of dairy foods is also of uncertain origin, but is particularly notable because for most holidays there is a call for eating meat, which is regarded as an expensive and substantial fare and thus appropriate for a special occasion. The most common traditional explanation for this deviation is that when the Israelites received the laws of kashrut (keeping kosher) at Sinai, they realized that all their pots were not kosher and so ate uncooked dairy dishes instead. Another explanation is that by first eating dairy and later eating meat (thus two dishes), we recall the two loaves offered on Shavuot. Some people eat dairy foods with honey in them because the Torah is likened to milk and honey. "Honey and milk are under your tongue" (Song of Songs 4:11).

THE BOOK OF RUTH

Among Ashkenazic Jews, another custom that arose is the reading of the Book of Ruth. A number of reasons are given for this custom:

- The story is set at harvest time.
- Ruth's conversion to Judaism is analogous to our voluntary acceptance of the Torah and God's covenant at Sinai. We are taught, in fact, that the Israelites in the desert had the status of converts and hence underwent circumcision and ritual immersion.
- King David, according to tradition, was born and died on Shavuot. The Book of Ruth ends with the genealogy from Ruth down to King David.
- Reading Ruth means that the totality of the Torah is celebrated on Shavuot, for Ruth is part of the *ketuvim*—the writings that together with the Torah and the prophets compose the whole Bible.

Most commonly the Book of Ruth is read without a blessing during the morning services of Shavuot (on the second day for those observing two days of Shavuot).

TIKKUN LEIL SHAVUOT

A kabbalistic custom emanating from the mystics in Safed (sixteenth century) is to stay up the whole (first) night of Shavuot studying Torah. The tikkun—a set order of study—was composed of selections from the Bible, rabbinic literature, and even mystical literature such as the *Zohar.* In this fashion the kabbalists prepared for the momentous revelation of the following morning.

This practice of staying up all night is in stark contrast to that of the

For many years I have bemoaned the fact that Shavuot occurs at a nondescript phase of the moon. The *sixth* day of the lunar month? What kind of date is this for a nice, self-respecting Jewish holiday? After all, most others fall at either new moon or full moon, and both the other pilgrimage festivals, Pesah and Sukkot, are celebrated at the brilliance of full moon.

Recently, however, I have found some understanding of this apparent calendrical oversight, resulting in the separation of Shavuot from the usual natural lunar rhythms that fix holiday dates. If one wants emphatically to assert that a transcendent dimension has intersected the created order of natural events, how better than by assigning for the Festival of Divine Revelation a date that bears no connection with the obvious, visible, natural rhythms by which we ordinarily measure our lives? The very unnaturalness of this undistinguished lunar date bears the mark and message of the extraordinary event that we celebrate on this holiday. It is unmistakably by the more-than-natural that we have fixed this day for celebration!

E.GE.

A lovely midrash on the book notes that while its minor figures all treat their fellows justly, doing all that the law requires of them, the major characters (Ruth, Naomi, Boaz) are distinguished by their acts of *hesed*—loving kindness—which go beyond what is demanded. The rabbis, in having us read Ruth each Shavuot, thereby teach us something: that on the day when we celebrate reception of the laws of Torah, we need to remember that law is never enough. Certainly it will not bring the Messiah, whose lineage goes back to Ruth. For that, the world needs *hesed.*

A.E.

Israelites at Sinai, who according to tradition slept late that morning and had to be awakened by Moses. In atonement for this, Jews nowadays stay awake all night. The sense of preparation for Sinai is heightened by a mystical tradition holding that the skies open up during this night for a brief instant. At that very moment, we are told, God will favorably answer any prayer. The kabbalists also regard Shavuot as the wedding of God and Israel and of God's masculine and feminine parts. Therefore, we stay up all night to "decorate the bride." While the kabbalists instituted other *tikkunim* (for the seventh day of Pesah and for Hoshana Rabbah), this is the only one widely observed.

The traditional tikkun includes the study of small sections from each book of the Torah and Talmud, symbolically representing all of the central texts of Judaism.

A lesser-known custom is to recite the whole Book of Psalms by staying up late the second night of Shavuot. This is because of the tradition that King David, the author of the psalms, was born and died on Shavuot. Another custom is to read the Book of Psalms during the afternoon of the second day of Shavuot.

At sunrise the tikkun is ended and the morning services are recited. One custom is to ritually immerse yourself on the morning of Shavuot in remembrance of the three days of preparation observed by the Israelites in the desert. Purifying your body is a wonderful way to prepare to receive the Torah on the morning of Shavuot.

SERVICES

The morning service is the regular festival liturgy including Hallel. For those observing only one day of Shavuot, the Book of Ruth is read. The Torah reading is the section (Exod. 19 and 20) describing the Revelation at Sinai and includes the Ten Commandments. There is a widespread custom of standing when the Ten Commandments are read, both to emphasize their importance to us and, in some small way, to imitate the experience at Sinai when the Jews stood to receive God's revelation. (Some rabbinic authorities were opposed to standing, because they felt it was improper to emphasize one part of the Torah over another.)

On Shavuot the section of the Ten Commandments is read to a special *trop* (manner of chanting the Torah) called the *ta'am elyon,* which is a more dramatic way of reading. This *trop* also separates the verses by commandments rather than by their regular sentence structure.

Ashkenazic synagogues customarily chant a medieval piyyut (liturgical poem) entitled "Akdamut" to a special tune before the Torah reading on the first day of Shavuot. "Akdamut," written in Aramaic, praises God's glory and speaks of the messianic future; it is recited after someone is called for the first aliyah. Instead of "akdamut," Sephardic synagogues recite a piyyut called "azharot," which lists the 613 toraitic commandments. Yizkor is recited on the first or second day, depending on observance.

SHAVUOT AS MARRIAGE

One of the most beautiful images of Shavuot is that of the marriage between God (the groom) and Israel (the bride). Developing this image, Pesah is the period of God's courtship of Israel, and Shavuot celebrates the actual marriage. Sukkot, then, is the setting up of a *bayit ne'eman*—a household faithful to Judaism.

Even the midrash's problematic imagery of God holding the mountain of Sinai over the Israelites' heads while saying "Accept My Torah or else!" is transformed in this romantic symbolism as the mountain becomes a huppah —a wedding canopy for the marriage. According to this view, Moses smashes the tablets because they are God's ketubah—marriage contract—to Israel, and Moses, as messenger, chooses to smash them rather than deliver them to Israel and thereby complete the marriage of Israel and God. To complete the marriage would have meant that the Israelites, who were worshiping the golden calf, were in fact being unfaithful in their marriage.

The most concrete expression of this imagery is the Sephardic custom of writing a ketubah between God and the Jewish people. The language is adapted from the traditional ketubah and is read after the ark is opened and before the Torah scroll is removed for the Torah service. Selections from one text are as follows:

> Friday, the sixth of Sivan, the day appointed by the Lord for the revelation of the Torah to His beloved people. . . . The Invisible One came forth from Sinai, shone from Seir and appeared from Mount Paran unto all the kings of the earth, in the year 2448 since the creation of the world, the era by which we are accustomed to reckon in this land whose foundations were upheld by God, as it is written: "For He hath founded it upon the seas and established it upon the floods" (Psalms 24:2). The Bridegroom [God], Ruler of rulers, Prince of princes, Distinguished among the select, Whose mouth is pleasing and all of Whom is delightful, said unto the pious, lovely and virtuous maiden [the people of Israel] who won His favor above all women, who is beautiful as the moon, radiant as the sun, awesome as bannered hosts: Many days wilt thou be Mine and I will be thy Redeemer. Behold, I have sent thee golden precepts through the lawgiver Jekuthiel [Moses]. Be thou My mate according to the law of Moses and Israel, and I will honor, support, and maintain thee and be thy shelter and refuge in everlasting mercy. And I will set aside for thee, in lieu of thy virginal faithfulness, the life-giving Torah by which thou and thy children will live in health and tranquillity. This bride [Israel] consented and became His spouse. Thus an eternal covenant, binding them forever, was established between them. The Bridegroom then agreed to add to the above all future expositions of Scripture, including Sifra, Sifre, Aggadah, and Tosefta. He established the primacy of the 248 positive commandments which are incumbent upon all . . . and added to them the 365 negative commandments. The dowry that this bride brought from the house of her father consists of an understanding heart that understands, ears that hearken, and eyes that see. Thus the sum total of the contract and the dowry, with the addition of the positive and negative commandments, amounts to the following: "Revere God and observe His commandments; this applied to all mankind" (Ecclesiastes 12:13). The Bridegroom, desiring to confer privileges upon His peo-

The Ten Commandments

ple Israel and to transmit these valuable assets to them, took upon Himself the responsibility of this marriage contract, to be paid from the best portions of His property. . . .

All these conditions are valid and established forever and ever. The Bridegroom has given His oath to carry them out in favor of His people and to enable those that love Him to inherit substance. Thus the Lord has given His oath. The Bridegroom has followed the legal formality of symbolic delivery of this document, which is bigger than the earth and broader than the seas. Everything, then, is firm, clear, and established. . . .

I invoke heaven and earth as reliable witnesses.

May the Bridegroom rejoice with the bride whom He has taken as His lot and may the bride rejoice with the Husband of her youth while uttering words of praise.

RECENT CUSTOMS

Two customs have grown up recently in celebration of Shavuot, but both of them have roots in the past. Throughout Israel today, particularly in kibbutzim, there are various religious and secular celebrations of the first fruits of the season, which hark back to bringing the first fruits to the temple on Shavuot. Today's ceremonies are characterized by processions, and by dancing and singing in celebration of the bounty of the land. The first fruits are carried with elaborate ceremony and placed on a central dais.

The second custom is that of confirmation. Reform synagogues, in particular, hold confirmation ceremonies that mark the end of the Jewish school year. Confirmation is also viewed as indicating the beginning of adulthood for Jewish children of sixteen or seventeen. Originally it was instituted to replace the bar mitzvah ceremony, held at the age of thirteen, which seemed too early an age for a child to become a Jewish adult. Recently the bar mitzvah has, for the most part, come back into its own in the Reform movement, but confirmation is still observed. Others observe confirmation more simply as marking the end of the Jewish school year and as a graduation ceremony for high-school children.

The connection between confirmation and the acceptance of the covenant at Sinai is often made explicit in the texts written for these ceremonies. There is no standard confirmation text because it was felt that the students should create their own service. The enthusiasm and personal style of these ceremonies often make up for their lack of sophistication. Even though the practice of confirmation was originally copied from Christianity, it has resonances with a medieval Jewish custom, which also connected a child's education with Shavuot. On Shavuot, a young child would be brought to the classroom for the first time, and a number of rituals grew up around this event—mostly variations on the theme that learning should be a pleasant and rewarding experience. One custom was to cover the letters of the alphabet with honey or candy; as the child learned the first letters, he or she was allowed to lick off the honey or eat the candy, thus fulfilling the verse "How pleasing is Your word to my palate, sweeter than honey" (Ps. 119:103).

ISRU HAG

The day after Shavuot is known as Isru Hag. It is a day of minor rejoicing and a way of holding on to the holiday for a little longer. The Talmud states: "Whoever observes a continuation of the festival by eating and drinking, the Torah accounts it to him as if he had built the altar [in the temple] and offered sacrifice upon it as it is said: 'Bind the festival [Isru Hag] with cords unto the horns of the altar' " (Psalms 118:27). Thus, the days after Pesah and Sukkot/-Shemini Atzeret are also known as Isru Hag. Today, Isru Hag is observed only by the omission of Tahanun (a petitional prayer) in the synagogue liturgy and a prohibition on fasting. The Isru Hag of Shavuot was at one time particularly joyous because there were too many festival sacrifices to be offered on Shavuot itself, therefore many were offered on Isru Hag instead. This was less true of Sukkot and Pesah, each of which had a period of *hol ha-moed*—intermediate days—allowing more time for the offering of a festival sacrifice, which was incumbent on each pilgrim to Jerusalem.

KAVVANOT

Even if there is no ritualized re-creation of the event we are commemorating, as there is with Pesah and Sukkot, Shavuot calls upon us to remember the event and reaffirm our commitment to Torah and its study. It also urges us until the very last moment to prepare ourselves as though Sinai will occur again this very Shavuot. The self-preparation, which began during the omer and intensified during the month of Sivan, reaches even greater intensity during Shavuot, leading up to the reading of the Ten Commandments on Shavuot morning.

This up-to-the-last-minute preparation is embodied in the *tikkun leil shavuot*—the all-night study session created by the kabbalists. While there is a traditional text for study, many people study other texts as well. One variation of the traditional tikkun is a marathon of Torah study with different groups assigned in shifts to cover different times throughout both the night and day of Shavuot. This would be a fulfillment of the verse "Let not this Book of Torah cease from your lips, but recite it by day and by night . . . " (Josh. 1:8). More modestly, those who cannot or are not willing to stay up all night could spend most or all day engaged in the study of Torah, demonstrating that right after the Revelation of the morning we are eager to begin our Torah study. A good text might be Genesis 1:1 or the first Mishnah in the Talmud, as if to say that this Shavuot is the first one and therefore we begin our study at the beginning. It also expresses the realization that even the most basic texts are worthy of repeated study. According to one tradition, you have not really learned a text until you have gone over it one hundred times. In truth, we are all beginners in the study of Torah, with its unplumbable depths.

The group I'm involved in sets up a tikkun as follows: Four or five people

Some questions to ask while preparing for Sinai: What are my Ten Commandments—the ten absolute rules that I am willing to take on myself? What is my present level of skill in Torah study? What is the next level I want to achieve? What areas of Torah study do I want to focus on next year? What mitzvah did I especially try to fulfill last year? What new mitzvah will I concentrate on this year?

Z.S.

On our retreats we hold the tikkun on the second night because people come to the retreat after a long day of working and traveling and are too weary for a first-night tikkun.

One way to create a tikkun text is for each person to bring a passage that excited them during the past year, and then make copies of the texts and organize them in some manner. Each person thus brings bikkurim—the first fruits of the past year's study—as an offering on Shavuot.

Z.S.

When assigning the aliyot for Shavuot, ask the recipients to think about what problems are on their minds these days. Tell them to each roll the Torah to wherever they want, which will become their aliyot. More often than not, the Torah provides a strikingly illuminating response. After the aliyah, the person should meditate on his or her passage.

Z.S.

What do I need to ask God for at this Shavuot? Abraham Joshua Heschel wrote that the Torah is an answer, but we must rediscover the question. We are not interested in recovering the old questions. Rather, just as in the past we could ask the Torah questions relevant to our deepest concerns and expect an answer, so can we now. This is why each year we stand anew before the mountain of Sinai.

Z.S.

are asked to prepare "units." Most of these units are text-oriented, though one or two may be more open-ended. Frequently, the tikkun is organized thematically. One year, for example, each unit was oriented around one chapter of the Book of Ruth. Another year we studied the theme of messianism in material ranging from rabbinic texts to modern Israeli writers. The leader of each unit prepares enough material for about an hour, with food or physical-activity breaks following each unit. The tikkun begins at 11:00 P.M. and ends at sunrise. People are encouraged to nap during the evening before the tikkun and are discouraged from eating a heavy meal or drinking a lot of wine since both are soporific.

THE MORNING OF SHAVUOT

Because we should be eager to receive the Torah on the morning of Shavuot, even those who do not want to stay up all night could rise early for a sunrise shaharit service. A similar suggestion is to reverse the standard order of the morning service by having the Torah reading precede the shaharit service. Unlike every other Shabbat or festival, our desire to hear the Ten Commandments once again can be reflected in our giving precedence on this morning of Revelation to the Torah service over shaharit.

One custom observed by some services all during the year is particularly appropriate for Shavuot: Instead of only the service leader carrying the Torah scroll in procession around the synagogue, it is lovingly passed from one person to another until everyone has done so. The scroll is then placed on the reading table. For each of us to grasp the Torah at this moment on the morning of Shavuot is an expression of our willingness to accept the Torah and its covenant. For each of us to then pass it on is a symbol of the chain of tradition that stretches from Moses to each of us today.

DECORATING WITH TREES

Other Shavuot customs are concerned with enhancing our surroundings. A variation on the old custom of decorating the synagogue with flowers is to ask all the members to lend houseplants to the synagogue for Shavuot so that the synagogue will be filled with green. Another custom is to pass around spices during services to add to the fragrance of the plants. Since it is a festival the halakhah permits the burning of incense. Such practices appropriately recapture the bursting forth of growth at this time of the agricultural season and commemorate the colorful first-fruits ritual of temple times. On another level, trees evoke the image of the Torah as the *etz hayyim*—the tree of life. Banished from the Tree of Life in the Garden of Eden, we seem to have lost any opportunity for eternal life and have been condemned to our mortality. Yet, the Torah *is* "the Tree of Life for all who grasp it," for it is our means to attain eternity by being engaged with the Eternal One. Thus the growing plants and the fragrance of spices are meant to awaken us to growth both in the agricultural cycle and in our own lives.

DERASH

FROM PESAH THROUGH THE OMER TO SHAVUOT

The omer as the link between Pesah and Shavuot is marked by an interesting progression from its opening to its closing ritual. On the second night of Pesah, barley is harvested and the first sheaf is waved before the altar in the temple. On Shavuot, two loaves of bread are waved as an offering before the same altar. It cannot be coincidental that these two loaves of bread are to be hametz—leavened. We have seen in the discussion of Pesah that matzah was used as the meal offering all during the year, and in fact there existed a prohibition (see Lev. 2:11) against offering hametz on the altar *at any time.* And yet the two loaves of Shavuot are specifically to be leavened bread! (They are only waved before the altar, not burned on it, and hence their offering does not violate the prohibition.)

Philo, among others, sees this as a progression from the Pesah bread of poverty (matzah) to the bread of affluence (hametz) on Shavuot. This progression might also reflect the success of the harvest. Or perhaps the period of the omer can be seen as a gradual process of symbolically moving away from matzah and returning to hametz. The Torah of Sinai, with its regulations and its guidelines on how to live in this world, sets us free to eat hametz, which might otherwise corrupt us. With the Torah we do not need to be nourished by a special food, whether that food be the matzah of liberation or the manna of the desert. With the Torah as a guide to life, we can be part of this world, partaking of its delights, fully confident that the observance of the Torah will protect us from corruption by the hametz of life, which contains within its essence the power both to corrupt and to give pleasure. To symbolize all of this, we wave two loaves of hametz before the altar.

On another level, Shavuot as the commemoration of the experience of Sinai is a necessary completion of the experience of Passover. If Passover is a liberation, the question remains, a liberation toward what? Freedom does not lie in anarchy; rather it is found at Sinai. There, we enter into the service of God, the one Master who offers freedom as the underlying basis for choosing the Covenant. Because of God's insistence that we choose, we come to understand that unlike serving Pharaoh or any other human authority, serving God sets us free from servitude by placing us in contact with the Divine. To accept of our own will the covenant at Sinai enables us to face the world in freedom, even to eat of hametz and yet remain free. It teaches us to choose. Hence, the forty-nine days separating Pesah from Shavuot is the period in which we ready ourselves to freely choose the Covenant by saying yes to Sinai and its revelations.

"The Torah says: 'The tablets were the work of God and the writing was the writing of God, engraved upon the tablets' (Exodus 32:16). Read not *harut* meaning engraved but *herut* meaning freedom" (*Ethics of the Fathers—Pirkei Avot* 6:12).

Again, I must differ on the extent of freedom the Israelites had to accept or reject the Covenant. That the Revelation follows upon the Exodus is integral to God's plan. God created the world with purpose and intention. With the generation of the Flood, he saw that he could not expect all people to behave properly without the guidance of law; therefore, God instituted law and singled out one people, the seed of Abraham, to become the model of a people living by God's law. But in order to bind the entire people of Israel to the law, God had to obligate them, place them in his debt. Thus, he had them enslaved in Egypt so that he could liberate them, earn their profound gratitude, and saddle them with the Torah. Now the purpose of Creation could begin to be accomplished. It depends upon us.

E.Gr.

And how shall we teach this lesson to our children, when it is so antithetical to the message of American culture? How shall we teach that authority involves obedience, that creativity presupposes discipline, that selfhood requires bounds to what we may and may not be—in short, that we are not God, that we cannot dictate the terms of the Covenant, that our option is to accept it or not; and that, accepting it, we are blessed with all the Life there is? How shall we get this across, in the face of demands for "experience" and "expression" and "do your own thing" and self-assertiveness? They will call us authoritarian, or worse; and yet, without this linkage of liberation to obligation, Pesah to Shavuot, we cannot call ourselves Jews.

A.E.

While some psalms are indeed "responses to the revelation of God's presence," it is useful to recall that many psalms are vehicles for seeking out and finding the divine presence. "One thing I have asked of the Lord, it is it that I seek: that I may dwell in the house of the Lord all the days of my life; to envision the bounty of the Lord, and to visit in his palace" (Psalm 27:4). Reciting psalms may induce an intimate experience, a dialogue with God.

E.GR.

The golden-calf incident does show that the Sinai revelation did not have a lasting impact on the Israelites. We see that people cannot be transformed but must transform themselves. But we should not forget the greater lesson of the golden-calf episode. At first, God was enraged by the people's lack of trust in him. His ego was hurt and he wanted to annihilate them. Moses prayed on the people's behalf, and God relented. Human words can move God. Even more, God may threaten to punish us for our transgressions, but he knows we're only human; he has learned not to expect too much from us. Only after our misbehavior sinks us deeper and deeper into ruin does God punish—only when we have sunk too far without repenting, too far to be saved.

E.GR.

Of course there was coercion at Sinai. God is God, after all, and we are not. All the more reason to wonder at the wisdom of our ancestors, who got control of their *yetzer ha-ra,* suppressed their rage at not comprehending the God upon whom they depended, grasped the incredible uniqueness of the moment they were witnessing, and signed on the dotted line of a contract they had not yet been allowed to read. Thank God!

A.E.

KING DAVID AND SHAVUOT

Because tradition holds that King David was born and died on Shavuot, some people have the custom of reading the Book of Psalms, which is attributed to him. But the connection between the psalms and Shavuot is deeper than biography and legend. David's psalms reflect the mystical side of the Sinai experience, a side too often lost sight of in the preoccupation with Torah. Torah is only the more concrete dimension of the experience; the revelation of God, the divine being, is the spiritual/mystical one. The latter is in fact the basis of the former, since without the presence of God, the Torah no longer derives from an encounter with the Divine.

As later Judaism came to lay great stress on the mitzvot in all their detail, it became easy to think of Torah as a point system for collecting merit badges from the Great Scoutmaster in the sky. In such a system, it is easy to forget that the real purpose of the mitzvot is to help us "to become a kingdom of priests and a holy nation" and to maintain a covenant with the living God. Psalm after psalm speaks from the depth of David's human experience of his relationship with the Divine. The psalms are a response to the revelation of God's presence and seek to continue the interaction that occurred at Sinai between the Eternal and the human. To counterbalance a night of studying Torah, then, it is important to read the Book of Psalms and thereby remember why we were given the Torah and by whom.

THE CYCLE OF THE LAW

If we as a people stood at Sinai and heard the Voice that forever changed our lives, why do our lives seem so unchanged? Why do we feel as though we had never heard the Voice? Exactly these feelings are enacted in the biblical text itself when the very same Israelites who stood together at Sinai to receive the Torah were forty days later steeped in the sin it designates as the worst—that of worshiping an idol, the golden calf. If there is a climb up from Pesah to Shavuot, a climb out of the depths of *mitzrayim*—Egypt—to the heights of the experience at Sinai, then after Sinai a descent begins that ends in the incident of the golden calf.

How could those who stood at Sinai come to worship the golden calf? Is the answer simply that after the awesome events of Sinai a return to reality set in?

As Sinai faded, the people settled into the routines of their former lives, and the experience became lost in shadows as the former slaves began to worry anew: Where is God? Where is Moses? The Israelites needed reassurance; they needed a concrete god, and so they created the golden calf.

Then, too, perhaps Sinai in the end did not change them. The idea that God lifted the mountain of Sinai and held it over the Israelites, saying "If you accept My Torah, well and good; if not, then here will be your grave" is in stark contrast to the picture of the Israelites eagerly responding to God by saying, "We will act and we will obey." Somehow we know intuitively that, mountain or no mountain over our heads, there was a measure of coercion at Sinai. The very experience of God's revelation was awesome and terrifying enough for the people to call out to Moses, "No more! *You* tell us what God wants to convey." Thus they did not accept the Covenant with a full and confident heart but rather were overwhelmed by the fearsome grandeur of the moment.

Perhaps there is a moment when, in finally confronting and understanding truth, we childishly expect that we ourselves, and indeed the whole world, will be transformed. But the Israelites, after the Revelation, remained what and where they were. And so, feeling that perhaps they had not really been transformed at all, they slipped easily into their old ways learned in Egypt. They created the golden calf forty days after Shavuot, on the seventeenth of Tammuz. As we shall see, this cycle of the law will continue both in the rest of the festivals of the year and in history.

The Voice of Sinai Still Calls

On Pesah, by means of the seder and its rituals, we strive to reexperience and not just remember the slavery and redemption. We state in the Haggadah that *all of us,* not just our ancestors, were slaves and now all of us are redeemed. On Shavuot, we remember the tradition that states that all of us were present at the Revelation at Sinai. Yet on Shavuot we do not really try to reexperience or reenact the Sinai Revelation. Why? Shouldn't we try to make ourselves feel once again the voice of the Lord amid the thunder and lightning?

The reason we don't is that Shavuot is different from Passover, for Sinai is a continuous event. It is not accidental that originally no date was given for the Revelation at Sinai, for the voice of the Lord constantly speaks to us. The Revelation continues to occur as the Torah unfolds before us, *if* we pay attention to it. Thus Sinai needs fulfillment, not reexperiencing; enactment, not reenactment. Our task is to hear anew and then renew the Torah each day. Therefore Shavuot, for symbolic reasons, does not have a date fixed in time on the sixth of Sivan, for perhaps it occurred on the seventh of Sivan or the eighth. Perhaps Sinai is today. It is impossible to circumscribe the giving of the Torah to one day. *Any* time a person studies Torah with devotion and holiness is a *zeman matan torah*—the moment of the giving of the Torah. As the rabbis said, "Anything any student in any age will say was already given to Moses at Sinai": This means anything we add to the Torah is considered original as if it was part of what was then transmitted to Moses. Revelation of the Torah began at Sinai and has never ceased.

Yet to hear the Voice is difficult and can be sustained for only a brief time. Therefore, the tradition tells us, only the Ten Commandments, not the whole Torah, was heard at Sinai. Or, according to another tradition, only the first two commandments. Or perhaps, according to a third tradition, only the first word, *anokhi*—"I am." Or perhaps just the first letter of the first word, the *aleph*—the mystery of the sound of a silent letter. The moment of revelation

Anokhi—*I am.*

Why was the first word *anokhi* rather than the more usual *ani?* One further rabbinic suggestion: this word resembled an Egyptian word with which the weary and wary slaves were familiar (cf. ankh, the Egyptian symbol of enduring life); hence they were able to hear it.

E.GE.

By comparing revelation to "consciousness-raising" we incur the danger of explaining revelation solely as a process that we ourselves undergo. But it is important to remember that revelation is at least an interaction between events in the world and our perception or understanding of those events as the behavior of God. For this reason, in teaching revelation I have compared revelation to two models, each of which is necessary to make an approximate analogy. On the one hand, revelation is like a special light, illuminating that which we by ourselves could not see before. On the other, it is like music, reaching us from an outside source but moving us to respond and react.

E.GR.

Why did God insist that Moses warn the people not to go up on the mountain itself? By implication it teaches us that a mystical union with God is impossible. Although there are momentary encounters with the Divine, Sinai being the classic one for the Jewish people, they are temporary. As human beings, we must return to our humanity, to the world; we cannot dwell in Sinai, the mountain we are not even allowed to ascend. We do not go up to Sinai, Sinai/the Divine comes down to us, as it says: "The Lord came down upon Mount Sinai, on the top of the mountain. . . . " (Exod. 19:20). The working out of Sinai, the living in its aftereffects, takes place here in an imperfect world that calls out for perfection.

M.S.

is always brief; thus Shavuot lasts only one day and not the full week of Pesah and Sukkot.

Yet amid the thunder and lightning, the blaring of horns and dense smoke of our lives, the Voice can still be heard calling to us.

THE SINAI EXPERIENCE

What happened at Sinai has provided the basis for Jewish theology and provoked many interpretations. It is at Sinai that the Covenant is finally sealed and accepted as an agreement binding on both parties. It is here that the Torah is given to us as a guide for life.

According to traditional doctrine, all of the Torah was revealed at Sinai —both the written (the Five Books of Moses) and the oral (later to be written down as the Talmud). By emphasizing that at Sinai we were given the Torah in its entirety by God, this doctrine allows little room for changing laws that are of divine origin. Yet even traditionalists disagree over whether specific parts of the tradition were part of this revelation or not.

At the other end of the spectrum are those who do not believe God revealed the Torah as we have it at Sinai. Accepting the basic premises of biblical criticism, they view the Torah text as a document created from a number of sources over centuries by the Jewish people in response to what they thought to be divine will. Only those parts which reflect that will—such as the laws of morality—are Divine. Other parts are rooted in the ideas and ethics of people of that time—for example, the institution of slavery—and are to be disregarded as we progress to higher ethical understanding. In this view, it is the right and even the duty of each rabbi and Jew to define those practices and beliefs that he or she will accept as binding. What happened at Sinai can be viewed in a number of ways from this perspective, ranging from seeing it as a mythic event symbolic of the human encounter with the Divine, to some form of actual revelation, the content of which is either not known or perhaps limited to the Ten Commandments.

Between the view of a whole Torah given once and for all time at Sinai and a Torah that is of human origin and thus constantly changing with each new generation, there is a range of views. Some, while accepting biblical criticism, still maintain that the Torah was given at Sinai, but believe that the Torah was given *through* Moses—that is, they emphasize the human element of Sinai. How the Revelation was heard, written down, and transmitted affect the divine nature of the text by allowing the human element to mix with the divine. Therefore, the law can change if it can be shown that it is based on human mistakes (e.g., the wording of the text is corrupt because of scribal errors) or is rooted in the culture of the time. Still others emphasize that the Torah was written by humans who were divinely inspired. Therefore the claim can be made that revelation began at Sinai and continues even to our day. Finally, some people believe that God did reveal His presence at Sinai but had no specific message. The Torah is divinely inspired then only in the sense that its authors wrote the text in reaction to the encounter with God.

For us today, Sinai can perhaps be best compared to the phenomenon of "consciousness-raising" in two respects. First, there is consciousness-raising in the sense of a heightened perception and understanding that goes beyond our everyday cognition, a consciousness that comes from the encounter with the Divine. This is the spiritual/mystical component of revelation, for it makes us aware of the invisible Other.

Second, Sinai "raises consciousness" in the way the phrase is used in the women's movement—i.e., as a radical change in self-perception and also in our perception of the world. Even as the first sense of consciousness—that is, the experience of the Divine—becomes a vaguer and vaguer memory, the second sense of consciousness grows more distinct. After Sinai, we begin to work out in ethical terms what this new world view means. Concepts of justice and mercy, of doing what is right before the Lord, infuse us when we reexperience Sinai. Thus we try to lead our lives differently than we did before. This second response to Sinai and its consciousness-raising is embodied in the text of the Torah. The mitzvot are the concrete ways the Jewish people have reacted to the revelation of Sinai. Micah encapsulates these two aspects of Sinai in the verse "What the Lord requires of you: only to do justice and to love goodness and to walk humbly with your God." We need to act in the world of justice and injustice and feel the presence of God as our fellow traveler to fully respond to the Voice of Sinai.

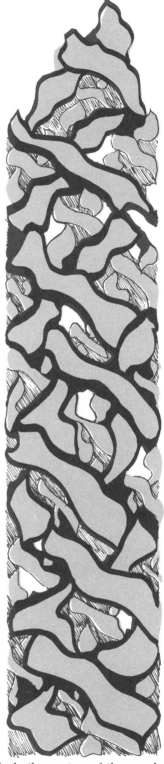

Aleph: the mystery of the sound of a silent letter.

שם השכינה שכנה לך והיצרך פתח למול שעריˑשחק שעריך

Then the Presence abides in you, there your Maker opened your gates to face the gates of heaven.
from "Tzion ha-Lo Tishali" by Judah ha-Levi

THE THREE WEEKS

THE DARK TIME

The months of Tammuz and Av are the low point of the cycle, marked by commemorations of tragedies that befell the Jewish people in several ages of their history. The most important is the destruction of the first and second temples, both on the ninth of Av. The second destruction not only brought to an end the temple service but also marked the end of Jewish sovereignty and the beginning of galut—Exile—which was the Jewish fate until only a few decades ago, when the founding of the state of Israel marked the beginning of a new period of Jewish sovereignty.

Beginning with the seventeenth of Tammuz and culminating with Tisha be-Av is a period of mourning for both temples. This period, referred to as the Three Weeks, begins and ends with fast days, and in general is marked by customs of grief.

There are four fasts in the Jewish calendar that mark the destruction of the temple, Jerusalem, and the independent Jewish state in ancient times. They are referred to by the prophet Zechariah (8:19) as "the fast of the fourth month, and the fast of the fifth, and the fast of the seventh, and the fast of the tenth." Counting the months beginning with the first month, Nisan, Zechariah refers respectively to the fast of the seventeenth of Tammuz (fourth month); the ninth of Av (fifth month); Tzom Gedaliah—the Fast of

There is a danger posed by the Three Weeks with its list of catastrophes that befell the Jewish people one generation after another. The danger is a paranoia that declares that everyone else in the world is wrong and therefore their fate is of little concern to us. Instead, we should generalize from our experience and become involved in the universal. At a time when the sun is burning hot, we must mark Hiroshima Day, not retreat into a bleak vision of our place in the world. The teshuvah for the Three Weeks is to examine how we have distorted the particular. In the midst of remembering our history, we must reclaim as well our role as planetary citizens.

Z.S.

Jewish tradition is far more subtle than contemporary Zionist propagandists or their opponents in the Diaspora would have us believe. It speaks of galut both as *metaphysical* exile, which we suffer as human beings, upon the earth, in an unredeemed world; and of *political* exile, which we suffer as Jews when we are scattered among the nations and so are unable to build our nation or develop our culture with full independence and integrity. At Tisha be-Av, we mourn the death of possibilities bound up in life upon the Land and focus on a sacred Center especially blessed with God's presence. We acknowledge the tragic limitations placed on our endeavors by conditions of dependence upon other peoples and their cultures, however rich our opportunities among them might be. Finally—and uniquely in our generation—we combine regret over what might have been with resolution that it yet might be, a silent prayer that we will not make the same mistakes, and that history will therefore treat us more kindly. Observance of Tisha be-Av in Jerusalem is a privileged fast indeed.

A.E.

Gedaliah—on Tishri 3 (seventh month); and the tenth of Tevet (tenth month). (Actually the Fast of Tammuz probably took place in Zechariah's time not on the seventeenth but on the ninth of Tammuz, which was the date the Babylonians breached the walls.) The latter two fasts will be treated in their appropriate places in the festival cycle, though they have much in common in terms of observance.

TISHA BE-AV AFTER 1948

Since the founding of the state, there are those who question the continued observance of the four fasts commemorating the destruction of the temple and the loss of sovereignty. They claim that to continue to fast as before is to ignore the reality of the founding of the state. In this regard they believe that the verse from Zechariah (8:19) that speaks of the four fasts becoming days of rejoicing refers to the actual practice of second-temple times, not to a messianic future. If the Jews of the Second Commonwealth ceased to observe these fast days, they argue, then so should we. This position was strengthened after the Six-Day War, when the old city of Jerusalem was captured, including the Western Wall of the Temple.

Those who disagree with this view include traditionalists who point out that the temple has not been rebuilt and the Messiah and complete redemption have still not arrived, and others who claim it is still important to memorialize these past events. A small but growing number of Jews continue to observe Tisha be-Av but ignore the three minor fasts. In this way, they express the belief that our situation is different after the founding of the state and yet we are still in a state of exile and thus should continue to read the Book of Lamentations on Tisha be-Av. To them, galut exists and we are part of it. Narrowly defined, *galut* can mean being outside of the state or land of Israel; but under a broader definition, it means being in a state of spiritual alienation that afflicts all Jews *whether in Israel or America* and in reality all people as long as we live in an imperfect world.

TRADITION

This period begins with the Fast of the Seventeenth of Tammuz. The tradition ascribes a number of catastrophes to that day, most notably the breaching of the walls of Jerusalem by the Romans (A.D. 70) and the incident of the golden calf at Sinai. Other catastrophes include the cessation of the daily sacrifice at the temple during the siege of Jerusalem, and the burning of a Torah scroll and the erection of an idol in the temple by Apostomos. These two events have puzzled historians as to when they actually took place. It is not clear which siege of Jerusalem is referred to in the first event, or who is Apostomos in the second. Speculations for each event range from the

Maccabean period (second century B.C.) up to the destruction of the second temple.

The seventeenth of Tammuz is a minor fast day—that is, fasting is required only from sunrise to sunset and the only prohibition pertains to eating and drinking; the other fasting rituals associated with the major fast days of Yom Kippur and Tisha be-Av are not observed. There is no prohibition against work as there is with such festivals as Pesah. Other than fasting, the day is marked by a number of minor additions to the Amidah of the daily liturgy.

THE THREE WEEKS

During the period of mourning known as the Three Weeks (also known as *bein ha-metzarim*—"between the straits"), no weddings or other joyous celebrations are held, particularly those involving instrumental music. Some people do not cut their hair. The blessing of *she-he-heyanu,* which is an expression of joy recited over new fruit or new clothes (see "Rosh ha-Shanah," p. 103), is avoided during the Three Weeks.

The mourning customs become more pronounced with the first day of the month of Av. During this period, known as the Nine Days, no meat or wine is consumed except for Shabbat meals. Authorities of the last few centuries have prohibited haircutting, shaving, bathing, swimming, washing clothes, or wearing freshly laundered clothes. More generally, activities that bring joy are avoided, such as going to movies, painting a room in your house, or sewing new clothes. On the Shabbatot of the Three Weeks, special haftarot are read relating to the themes of destruction and retribution. The Shabbat before Tisha be-Av is known as Shabbat Hazon after the first word of the haftarah from Isaiah 1:1–27.

TISHA BE-AV

The ninth of Av stands out from the other three fasts related to the destruction of the temples. Tisha be-Av is so important because it marks the day when both temples were destroyed—the first temple by the Babylonians in 586 B.C. and the second temple by the Romans in A.D. 70. It is a major fast day and therefore bears some resemblance to the only other one in the Jewish calendar, Yom Kippur.

The fast begins at sundown and continues until sundown. The midrash states that God marked the ninth of Av as a day of catastrophe because of the incident of the spies in the desert. Moses sent spies to the land of Canaan, and they returned with a report emphasizing the impossibility of conquering the Promised Land because of the strength of its inhabitants. The people on hearing the spies' report began to weep and complain about being taken out of Egypt. God declared, "You wept without cause, I will therefore make this day an eternal day of mourning for you." God then ordained the later de-

There is a practical reason for phasing out certain of the minor fasts, aside from loss of the significance they once had. Now that we have added observances to the calendar—Yom ha-Shoah, Yom ha-Atzma'ut, and more—we need to drop those that mean little to us, lest we fill the calendar up with holidays. If too many days are special, what's special about special days?

E.GR.

Scarce are they planted, scarce are they sown,
scarce has their stock taken root in the earth;
When He blows upon them, they wither, and
the whirlwind takes them away as stubble.

Isaiah 40:24

All the catastrophic events that have been identified with the ninth of Av did not, of course, really occur on that day. But it is the mythic power of this day of national hurt that has attracted, so to speak, so many of the disasters that have befallen the Jews. Indeed, many communities have included the Shoah, too, in their Tisha be-Av mourning simply because that catastrophe is the most overwhelming and inscrutable to contemporary Jews and because Tisha be-Av has always served as the day for commemorating disasters. Unfortunately, including the Shoah results in obscuring the other, earlier events and distorting the theological nature of Tisha be-Av. Now that Yom ha-Shoah and other occasions have been instituted for confronting the horror and tragedy of the Shoah, it is becoming increasingly feasible to use Tisha be-Av as a day of mourning the exiles of our people and the exile of God and us from one another. We cannot do that in the context of the Shoah, for we do not know how to relate to God with respect to the Shoah. The Shoah manifests not the presence but the absence of God.

E.GR.

Two recent catastrophes that occurred during the heat of summer are the atomic bombings of Hiroshima, August 6, 1945, and of Nagasaki, August 9, 1945. Given a date in our religious calendar so receiving of human tragedy, should not these monumental events from the same season of the year be included?

For more than twenty years, my own personal and communal observance of Tisha be-Av has included an interweaving of verses from Lamentations with some selections from Arata Osada's *Children of the A Bomb* (reissued by Harper & Row in 1982 as *Children of Hiroshima*). The Japanese schoolchildren's pained recollections of those fateful days of Av 1945 are deeply moving and, I think, an indispensable addition to our contemporary Tisha be-Av liturgy.

E.GE.

struction of the temple on that day and condemned the generation who had left Egypt to wander forty years in the desert and ultimately to death because they were unworthy of entering the promised land. Other catastrophes associated with Tisha be-Av are the fall of Beitar ending the Bar Kochba rebellion (A.D. 135) and the expulsion of the Jews from England (1290) and from Spain (1492).

Tisha be-Av is marked by strict mourning practices and the reading of the Book of Lamentations. It is preceded by a meal called the *seudah ha-mafseket* ("the meal that interrupts"—that is, differentiates between a regular day and the fast day). It is usually a modest meal. Some people eat food that is customarily provided for mourners—hard-boiled eggs and lentils. An old custom was to put ashes in the food.

During Tisha be-Av, as on Yom Kippur, the following are forbidden: eating, drinking, bathing, anointing with oil/perfume, wearing leather shoes, and sexual intercourse. Unique to Tisha be-Av is a prohibition against the study of Torah, since studying Torah is a joyous activity. All that is permitted to be studied is the Book of Job, the parts of Jeremiah that describe the destruction of Jerusalem, and the sections of the Talmud that deal with the destruction, such as the chapter *ve-eilu migalhin* from Moed Katan. (Some Sephardim recite the Book of Job during Tisha be-Av.) Even though working is not forbidden, we are encouraged by the tradition to minimize the amount of work we do this day.

The synagogue service begins after sundown with ma'ariv, followed by the reading of the Book of Lamentations. It is customary to sit on the floor or on low benches during the reading, which is again analogous to mourning customs. Only a few lights or candles are left on in the synagogue. The ark curtain *(parokhet)* is removed. The ma'ariv service is recited in hushed tones and Lamentations is chanted to its own special melody. At the end of Lamentations, the next-to-last verse is repeated by everyone so that the book will end on a hopeful note: "Turn us unto You, O Lord, and we shall be turned, renew our days as of old." Following Lamentations, a series of piyyutim— liturgical poems—are recited. These prayers, known as kinot, describe the destruction of the temple and the sins of the Jewish people. The last one is entitled "Eli Tzion" and is sung to a well-known melody. After the reading of Lamentations and the recital of kinot, a full kaddish without the line beginning *titkabeil* is recited. This kaddish is the same as that recited in the house of mourners. Also, Lamentations 3:8 states that God shuts out our prayers. This stands in opposition to the sentiment of *titkabeil,* which states that God accepts our prayers. This kaddish without *titkabeil* is also recited in shaharit.

While many people do not wear shoes all day long on Tisha be-Av, others refrain from doing so only during services. It is forbidden to exchange greetings on Tisha be-Av, though you should respond if someone says hello to you.

The next morning, tallit and tefillin are not worn. This is another sign of mourning, because a mourner before the funeral does not put on tallit and tefillin. The Torah is read, and the congregants sit on the floor and recite kinot. Some have the custom of reciting the phrase *Barukh dayan emet—*

"Praised be the true judge"—when called for an aliyah. (This phrase is traditionally recited upon hearing of a death.) The haftarah is from Jeremiah 8:13–9:23 and is chanted to the melody of Lamentations (except the last two verses, which are chanted to the regular haftarah melody). In some synagogues, Lamentations is read again in the morning.

There is a tradition that the Messiah will be born on Tisha be-Av—an image akin to the phoenix rising from its ashes. Thus out of destruction is born the ultimate redemption. This change of mood from despair to hope is reflected in a number of customs. One old custom is to sweep your house out in the afternoon as a preparation for the Messiah if he or she should come. For the same reason, in some communities women adorn themselves in the afternoon. At minhah, the full kaddish is recited, including the line stating that God accepts our pleas *(titkabeil).* Finally, the addition of the *naheim* paragraph in the minhah service introduces the theme of *nehamah*—comfort—and the paragraph itself looks hopefully to the future redemption. Also at minhah, tallit and tefillin are worn, the Torah is read again, and *aneinu* is added to the amidah.

At the end of Tisha be-Av, some people recite the poem "Tzion ha-Lo Tishali" by Judah ha-Levi, which speaks eloquently of Israel and the galut. Tisha be-Av brings the Three Weeks to an end.

TU BE-AV

One of the more minor holidays of the festival cycle is Tu be-Av (the fifteenth of Av). What it celebrates is unclear, but a statement found in the Talmud says, "There are no days as festive to Israel as those of Yom Kippur and the fifteenth of Av. The daughters of Israel used to dress in white and go out to the fields to dance and young men would follow after them" (*Ta'anit* 4:8).

This strange statement has been interpreted in various ways. One opinion is that the afternoons of Yom Kippur and Tu be-Av (following the ninth of Av) are periods of forgiveness. Thus one traditional belief is that on Tu be-Av, in the fortieth year of wandering in the desert, the Israelites were forgiven for the sins of the spies and the people. The last 15,000 Israelites still alive from the desert generation were spared from death and allowed to enter the promised land. Since by tradition the decree condemning all the Israelites to die in the desert was issued on Tisha be-Av so many years before, its commutation on Tu be-Av, a week later in the calendar, is striking.

Other opinions state that Tu be-Av ended the prohibition on an Israelite woman marrying a man from a different tribe if she had inherited land from her father (there being no male heirs). This prohibition was established in regard to the case of the daughters of Tzelofhad (Num. 27:14). The problem was that if a woman of the tribe of Gad married a man from the tribe of Reuben, the land would have shifted from the inheritance of one tribe (Gad) to another (Reuben). To prevent this, such marriages were prohibited until the conquest of Canaan was completed and all the inheritances were properly

In blazing anger He has cut down all the might of Israel;
He has withdrawn His right hand in the presence of the foe;
He has ravaged Jacob like flaming fire, consuming on all sides.

Lamentations 2:3

divided; only then did the Israelites feel secure enough to remove this prohibition. A further prohibition on marrying involved the tribe of Benjamin at a certain time in Israelite history, because of that tribe's role in the incident of the concubine of Giv'ah (see Judg. 21). Both prohibitions were suspended on Tu be-Av. In time Tu be-Av was observed as a day of courting, in which young women took the lead.

Tu be-Av and Bar Kochba Another important tradition concerning Tu be-Av stems from the defeat of the Bar Kochba revolt. After the fall of Beitar (on Tisha be-Av in A.D. 135), the Romans, as a punishment for the revolt and as a warning for the future, would not allow the Jews to bury their dead. This was a terrible desecration of the thousands of dead. The next Roman emperor rescinded this decree three years later on Tu be-Av and allowed the burial of the remains. This event was so important to contemporary Jews that the fourth *berakhah* of the Grace after Meals *(ha-tov ve-ha-meitiv),* expressing thanks to God, was composed in response to it and added to the liturgy.

The fifteenth of Av (which falls on the full moon as do most Jewish holidays) also marked the last day for bringing wood offerings to the temple altar for that year. And the prohibition against planting crops during the sabbatical year began with the fifteenth of Av, a month and a half before the actual beginning of the sabbatical year on the following Rosh ha-Shanah.

There is a custom of adding to the fixed time you have set aside for Torah study beginning with the fifteenth of Av and continuing through the winter by studying at night as well as by day.

Beginning with Tu be-Av, some people end their letters "May you be inscribed for a good year!"

One scholar speculates that Tu be-Av was originally a midsummer festival—hence the tradition of dancing and courting. In fact, he speculates that originally Tisha be-Av was just a fast day initiating the week before this midsummer festival. Festivals in many cultures are preceded by periods of mourning. This would explain why it was decided to fast on Tisha be-Av even though historical evidence suggests the temples were burned on the tenth of Av.

Contemporary Tu be-Av Today, Tu be-Av is marked only by the omission of Tahanun in the daily liturgy. Yet Tu be-Av can serve as a transition from the mourning of Tisha be-Av to the renewal of Elul and the New Year. For those who wish to recover some sense of the day, the following are some suggestions:

- Have a good time. Go on a picnic, hike in the woods, lie in the sun, swim in a lake. . . . Try to recapture the colors of the year—especially the nourishing greens of flora and the blues of water, in contrast to the blackness and parched quality of Tisha be-Av. Notice the spectrum of colors and even the spectrum within one color—for example, the infinite variety of shades of green in a stand of trees.
- Rediscover love. Plug into the courting traditions of the day by rediscovering the love between God and humans and its earthly counterpart,

Alas! Lonely sits the city once great with people!
She that was great among nations is become like a widow. . . .
Lamentations 1:1

the love between people. Try to refresh old loves and remove estrangements. Also do something that you love—for example, see a fine movie or reread a favorite book.

BEYOND THE THREE WEEKS

Following Tisha be-Av, we begin to experience the sense of comforting that is embodied in the rabbinic name for the month itself: Menahem Av— Av the Comforter. There are seven weeks of prophetic consolation in special haftarot, beginning with Shabbat Nahamu with its haftarah that begins *Nahamu nahamu ami*—"Comfort you oh comfort you My People" (Isaiah 40:1). These Shabbatot move us from the gloom of the Three Weeks into the month of Elul.

Elul, the month before Rosh ha-Shanah, is marked by the beginning preparations for the coming Days of Awe. We begin to reflect on the past year drawing to a close and the new year soon to begin. There is a custom of blowing the shofar each morning as a herald of Rosh ha-Shanah, in which the sound of the shofar plays a central role. We begin to wish each other a Happy New Year. At the end of the month, selihot—penitential prayers—are recited in the middle of the night.

DERASH

At first glance, this part of the festival cycle seems out of step with the cycle of our personal lives. For most of us, summer is a time of ease and enjoyment of the outdoors. The natural cycle is marked by the continued growth of spring plantings. But our history, with its mythic dimensions, forcefully reminds us that there can be another kind of summer, one whose heat is a consuming furnace rather than beneficent warmth.

Anyone who has spent a summer in Israel can more easily understand how the Three Weeks is in fact in consonance with the natural cycle. There the afternoon sun seems to bleach all the color from the landscape. Movement slows or comes to a halt in the afternoon—for even if the sun is no hotter than in the United States, it seems to beat down unrelentingly on the land's inhabitants. One can easily become parched and debilitated just from spending a few hours outdoors. No longer are the prevalent colors the greens of spring that decorated the synagogue on Shavuot; rather, the colors are a blazing white of sun on stone and the contrasting deep blacks of shade. Thus in Israel it is easy to call up images of a burning temple and a desolate land.

This aura of desolation reflects the fall from the heady moments of Egypt and Sinai. No sooner is the unique experience of the revelation at Sinai over than Moses and God disappear for forty days. Feeling lost, the people turn to a golden calf (on the seventeenth of Tammuz). The air is filled with a sense of loss and abandonment: the people abandoned by God, God abandoned by

I was wondering when you would bring up the full moon. In ancient times, the full moon provided extra light, and hence extra security to people who lived in a far greater state of nature than most of us do. It was a natural time for holding a celebration, and most of the Jewish festivals were established during the better-lighted period, when the "smaller lamp" of heaven (Gen. 1:-16) was in full force. It is, I think, true that we cannot fully enjoy and celebrate anything when we are anxious and insecure. The scheduling of the holidays midmonth enhances our ability to celebrate them.

E.GR.

Comfort you, oh comfort you My people, says your God. Bid Jerusalem take heart. . . .

Isaiah 40:1–2

His people, each longing for the other, each eager to renew the covenant of Shavuot, the trust of that night of the Exodus when we faithfully went off into the desert with only God to sustain us. No rain, no sustenance, no wave offerings, no joy. Illusions or ideals seem to have melted under the fiery rays of the summer sun with no sheltering wings to protect us. Tisha be-Av erases the last innocence and brings home the difficulty of living by the covenant, for the covenant means being chosen for strife, anger, and even destruction and persecution as well as love. No longer a mountain suspended over our heads (as at Sinai), nor as yet a sukkah of our own construction, we cringe in the heat of the day, and even find solace in the blackness of three long weeks of night and nightmare. We sit as mourners on Tisha be-Av, first remembering and then bewailing what could have been.

FROM THE SEVENTEENTH OF TAMMUZ TO TISHA BE-AV AND BEYOND

The two worst sins of the desert are attributed by tradition to these two days respectively: the golden-calf incident on the seventeenth of Tammuz and the incident of the spies on Tisha be-Av. The first incident, only forty days after the Revelation at Sinai, shows how quickly the people forgot the Sinai experience in seeking a tangible image to worship. The second incident occurred in the second year of the Exodus. Because they believed the spies' report that they could not defeat the inhabitants of Canaan, God condemned that whole generation to die in the desert; only their children would enter the promised land. These rejections of God and of Eretz Yisrael can be regarded as prophetic of the later historical experience when the Jewish people were exiled from both God and the land.

The rest of Jewish history is an attempt to work our way back. According to tradition, the Israelites received final forgiveness for the golden-calf incident when Moses came down from Mount Sinai at the end of the third period of forty days. That day was the tenth of Tishri—Yom Kippur.

Just as Yom Kippur brings forgiveness for the golden-calf incident of the seventeenth of Tammuz, so the minor holiday Tu be-Av (according to one tradition) brings forgiveness for the spies incident of Tisha be-Av. It marks, in fact, the end of the forty years of wandering and immediately precedes the entrance to the promised land. No longer abandoned in the desert, we, as part of the mythic dimension of Judaism, can end our aimless wandering and finally move onward.

Tu be-Av provides a contrast of joyous celebration following the ever-deepening gloom and mourning of the Three Weeks. Coming seven days after Tisha be-Av, Tu be-Av symbolically serves as the end of the *shiv'ah*—the seven days of mourning for the dead. Just as the mourner ends *shiv'ah* on the morning of the seventh day, so may we cast off the blackness of despair and go out of our house of mourning wearing white and dancing and courting in the fields as did the maidens of old in Israel.

Destruction and rebuilding are recurring underlying themes of the festival cycle, for we are meant to create a *mishkan* or sanctuary in our lives. As God states: "Let them make for Me a sanctuary and I will dwell in their midst" (Exod. 25:8). If Tisha be-Av marks the failure in the attempt to build such a sanctuary, the failure to construct our lives as though creating a human sanctuary for God, then we quickly move to try once again, beginning with Yom Kippur when we have readied our own selves to be dwelling places for God, to begin to create spaces where God can dwell in our midst.

M.S.

From Tu be-Av we are ready to move on to Elul, a prelude to the High Holiday season with its themes of renewal and return. In fact, the period of Elul embodies a process of courtship between us and God. This theme of courtship is captured in the traditional belief that the Hebrew letters of the word *Elul* are an abbreviation for the phrase *Ani le-dodi ve-dodi li*—"I am my beloved's, and my beloved is mine," referring to God and Israel. Estranged from each other during the Three Weeks, Israel and God rediscover each other beginning with Tu be-Av and initiate the slow and at times painful process of becoming lovers again. This process climaxes with Yom Kippur, when we are forgiven for that original breach of faith, the incident of the golden calf, which began this whole process of mourning and renewing on the seventeenth of Tammuz.

Truly the Lord has comforted Zion, comforted all her ruins;
He has made her wilderness like Eden, her desert like the Garden of the
  Lord.
Take us back, O Lord, to Yourself, and let us come back;
Renew our days as of old!

Isaiah 51:3; Lamentations 5:21

ROSH HA-SHANAH
RETURNING ANEW

The High Holidays are the second major cycle of festivals in the Jewish year. In its narrowest sense, the cycle is composed of Rosh ha-Shanah (the first two days of the month of Tishri), observed for two days both in Israel and the Diaspora (except by Reform Jews, who observe it for one day), and Yom Kippur (Tishri 10). Whatever the original origin of these festivals—a subject of much debate among scholars—they are today a celebration of the beginning of the new year and a striving for atonement of our misdeeds of the past year. Both elements, reflected respectively in Rosh ha-Shanah as the New Year and Yom Kippur as the Day of Atonement, are present in this period, though over time the themes of repentance, judgment and atonement of Yom Kippur have become predominant. The days between these two festivals have also become part of the cycle, as have the days following and the month of Elul preceding them. In Hebrew this cycle is called *yamim noraim*—Days of Awe—which more truly captures the mood of this period than the phrase High Holidays or even High Holy Days.

This period is devoted to a careful examination of who we are in an attempt to become cognizant of the ways we have failed—failed others, failed our own selves, and failed God. This introspection is meant to lead to regret and remorse for the harm we have done, to attempts at restitution when

It's about time we dropped the anglicized, Christian-sounding names for Rosh ha-Shanah and Yom Kippur, High Holy Days or High Holidays, and reverted to the Jewish name, *yamim noraim*—Awesome Days, or Days of Awe. Days of anxiety, trepidation, humility, soul-searching. These are the connotations we want. We do not want a Jewish ritual equivalent of going to the opera. (Because that's what we have, it reinforces those Jews who, for example, instead of wearing the traditional kittel or white robe, don the sort of dress they would wear to attend the opera. Nor does an operatic cantor help remedy this misperception.)

E.Gr.

With honey from the rock will I satisfy you.

וּמִצּוּר דְּבַשׁ אַשְׂבִּיעֶךָ:

Ps. 19

possible, and to turning away from our past selves to better selves who will act differently in the coming new year. We are each meant to be a new and improved version, not just the same old self one year older and deeper in debt.

This process of inner change is a difficult one, hence the rabbis began it well in advance of Yom Kippur so as to leave plenty of time to accomplish it. During the month of Elul, we begin to examine our lives and our relationships. Then comes Rosh ha-Shanah with its blasts of the shofar meant to awaken our slumbering souls to time's passage and to what we have done and, more important, what we could do with our lives. The new year gives us a chance to reshape our lives in our better image by reminding us of our humanity and our relationship to the Divine. All this preparation is training every day to be ready for the spiritual marathon of Yom Kippur—the day on which we almost ceaselessly pray for forgiveness and renewal. The tradition uses the image of a contest—a life-and-death one, for the imagery of the Yom Kippur liturgy is that each of us is judged as to "who shall live and who shall die" in the coming year. Whether we literally believe in the imagery of Yom Kippur as the Day of Judgment or see it as only symbolic, those images confront us with our mortality and warn us that the time for teshuvah is *now*. This process of teshuvah—repentance—will hopefully culminate in forgiveness—our forgiving those who hurt us; others forgiving us; and finally God forgiving us. It is literally a process of atonement that allows us to become at-one with God and with the rest of humanity.

THE NEW YEAR

In fact the Bible's silence about the fall New Year and its celebration is hardly accidental. Celebrations of this festival were so frought with pagan associations that the rather puritanical biblical authors probably opposed the festival altogether, much as later rabbis fought against *tashlikh* and kapparot as containing too much of the pagan or magical for their comfort. Only in the Talmud does Rosh ha-Shanah emerge as a major Jewish festival, showing that the folk, then as later, did not always listen to their more purist religious leaders. It is likely that especially the first Diaspora Jews, those of Babylonia, did much to support the acceptance of this festival, and gave it a legacy that is in many ways reminiscent of the ancient Babylonian New Year. The central themes of the coronation of God as King and the Book of Life are both found in the religions that preceded rabbinic Judaism in that region.

A.G.

In the seventh month, on the first day of the month, you shall observe complete rest, a sacred occasion commemorated with loud blasts. [Lev. 23:32]

Rosh ha-Shanah is referred to in the Torah as Yom Teruah—the Day of Sounding the Shofar—or Yom ha-Zikkaron—the Day of Remembering. It was not called Rosh ha-Shanah—the New Year—until Talmudic times. While it is clear from the verse above that this was a festival day in the Bible, the nature of the festival is unclear. The notion of Rosh ha-Shanah as the New Year may have come later. In the tradition, Rosh ha-Shanah as the New Year is tied to the creation of the world. Thus in the Talmud there is a debate as to whether the world was created in Nisan (the month when Passover falls) or in Tishri. This reflects a more general divergence of practice found throughout the ancient world, where some people's new year began in the spring (Nisan) and others' in the fall (Tishri). The Talmud settles the argument by saying, "You're both right," there being four new years in the Jewish calendar. Nisan 1 is the New Year day for kings (the date used for determining how many years a king has ruled) and months (Nisan is the first month); Elul 1 is the new year for tithing of animals; Shevat 15 (Tu Bishvat) is the new year for the trees; and Tishri 1 is the new year for years and marks the anniversary of the creation of the world.

Biblical scholars speculate that Rosh ha-Shanah's origin lies in ancient Near Eastern divine coronation festivals, some of which took place in the fall. If this is true, then it is not surprising that God as King is the central motif of the Rosh ha-Shanah liturgy.

The focal place for our observance of Rosh ha-Shanah is the synagogue rather than the home. The synagogue services are very long, exceeded by only those of Yom Kippur. The liturgy's main theme is that of God as King— *melekh,* the One who created the world and continues to renew His creation. The themes of God as King and Rosh ha-Shanah as the birthday of the world are intertwined with those stating that this is a period of repentance, that God is in the process of judging all living things. The traditional *nusah*—the musical rendition for the High Holiday services—conveys the solemnity of the period. Each of the services has its own variation in the music for the High Holidays. There is even a different musical rendition of the *trop*—cantillation —for the Torah readings of Rosh ha-Shanah and Yom Kippur.

TRADITIONS

TRADITIONS FOR ELUL

The whole month of Elul is a process of preparing ourselves for the coming High Holy Days. The shofar is blown after every morning service. One traditional belief is that Moses told the Israelites to do so throughout Elul to remind themselves of the sin of the golden calf while he was up on Mount Sinai receiving the second set of tablets. Perhaps we continue to blow the shofar today to remind ourselves of the golden calf and of how quickly the transition from the heights of Revelation to the depths of idolatry can take place. Psalm 27, which begins with the verse "The Lord is my light and my salvation," is also recited at the end of the morning and evening liturgy.

During Elul we begin to wish each other in person and in writing *shanah tovah*—a good New Year. Many people visit the graves of their parents and of others who are important to them. This custom probably originated in the hope that they would intercede on our behalf with God during this period of judgment. Today, it also expresses a desire to remember the past at a time of transition when we move from the old year to the new. We are not recalling only our misdeeds of the past year, but also important memories of parents and others who deeply affected our lives. Some synagogues arrange for public memorial services at the cemetery. For the Shabbatot of Elul, special haftarot with themes of consolation are read.

The end of Elul is marked by selihot—special penitential prayers—recited during the week before Rosh ha-Shanah. It has become customary to begin selihot at twelve o'clock the Saturday night before Rosh ha-Shanah. In many synagogues, the cantor and/or choir will give a foretaste of the High Holiday services. Some synagogues have study sessions preceding the selihot services. Every day after that until Rosh ha-Shanah, selihot is said just before sunrise

Elul is a time not only for introspection but of inspection. Your state of being should be checked out by professionals—physician, mental-health specialist—and by those important to you —spouse and friends.

Z.S.

Rabbi Shneur Zalman of Liadi said that during Elul the thirteen midot— attributes of mercy—are shining. While this is also true on Yom Kippur, the difference is that during Elul the King is on the road; therefore, you are more comfortable addressing the King if He stops at your house. By Yom Kippur, the King has returned to His palace, and even though the thirteen attributes of mercy are still shining, you feel intimidated in approaching the palace without even knowing how to get past the palace guards.

Z.S.

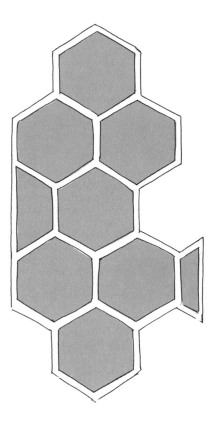

Why are the attributes of mercy so important? Each year we do teshuvah and each year we do not seem to change for the better. The power to overcome old habits comes from the thirteen attributes, which are in effect a Jewish mantra aiding you to overcome what you believe is your inexorable karma (fate).

Z.S.

The practice of *hatarat nedarim* is an important part of the process of teshuvah. First, choose a *bet din*—a court of three—or at least one person, a partner, who will answer honestly the questions: What do you see when you look at me? What did you see me do this year that I should regret?

According to halakhah, any custom you do three or more times becomes like a *neder*—a solemn personal oath. This *neder* quality is true of all habits and relationships. Begin the process of *hatarat nedarim* by listing all the things to which you are bound: I am bound to my spouse, my social image, my religion, etc. Your partner or *bet din* answers, *"Mutarim lakh"*—"It is permitted to you"—that is, you are released from your oaths.

Between Rosh ha-Shanah and Yom Kippur, you should try to be aware of all the things that bind you. Those to which you were bound only because you did not understand that this was so can be discarded. The more difficult bindings involve chasing your blind spots. What are the mistakes you keep making over and over again?

Before neilah, you end this process by stating, "This I do want to be bound to, that I do not," etc. You must look at what are your karmic debts. What will you owe if you give up that commitment? To whom will you owe it? Together with your partner (for whom you will act reciprocally), going through the cataloging of all your vows and then reaccepting some is a way to accomplish the task of teshuvah.

Z.S.

Most of the biblical contexts make it clear that the shofar was sounded primarily to announce the beginning of the special day, especially the new moon: "Sound on the new moon the shofar, at the darkening of the moon,

or early in the morning. The selihot service is composed of prayers asking for forgiveness. The central prayer, repeated a number of times, is that of the thirteen merciful attributes of God (taken from Exod. 34:6–7). The day before Rosh ha-Shanah marks an intensification of the preparations, reflected in an extra-long selihot service. In traditional circles, men go to the mikveh—the ritual bath. The *parokhet*—ark cover—and the cover of the reading table are changed for white ones that will be used throughout the High Holidays, white being a symbol of atonement and purity.

A practice called *hatarat nedarim* is observed in traditional circles. This involves one person asking three others to serve as a *bet din*—a court from whom he asks absolution for any unfulfilled vows from the past year. Usually each of the four takes a turn asking the other three to serve as a *bet din*. While there is a ritualistic formula found in prayer books for these proceedings, any unfulfilled vow that a person remembers is specifically mentioned.

A GUIDE TO GREETINGS

During the month of Elul, the traditional greetings are *Shanah tovah* ("A good year"); or *Le-shanah tovah tikatevu* ("May you be inscribed for a good year [in the Book of Life]"; or *Le-shanah tovah u-metukah tikateivu* ("May you be inscribed for a good and sweet year"); or—less common—*Ketivah tovah* ("A good inscription [in the Book of Life]."

The appropriate response: *Gam le-mar* or *Gam lekha* (fem.-*lakh)*—"The same to you."

Between Rosh ha-Shanah and Yom Kippur, some people add to the above: *Le-shanah tovah tikkateivu ve-tehateimu* ("May you be inscribed and sealed for a good life"). Others use these greetings only through the first night of Rosh ha-Shanah; after that, it would be indelicate to suggest that a person is not already inscribed in the Book of Life, for on Rosh ha-Shanah all the righteous are so inscribed—only those whose records are closely balanced between good and bad have their fate postponed until Yom Kippur.

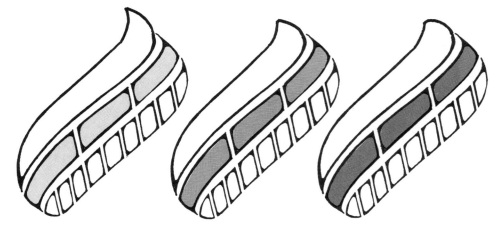

On Yom Kippur (and until Hoshana Rabbah) the greeting is *Gemar hatimah tovah* ("A good final sealing [to you]!") or *Hatima tovah* ("A sealing for good!").

TRADITIONS FOR ROSH ha-SHANAH

The Shofar The blowing of the shofar is the only special biblical ritual for Rosh ha-Shanah. The symbolism of the shofar is not made explicit in the Torah. Whether it is meant to arouse our slumbering souls or as a clarion call to war against the worst part of our natures, the primitive sound of the shofar blast stirs something deep within us. There is a sense of expectation in the silence before the shofar sound, followed by unease evoked by the various blasts. Part of its sense of mystery lies in the interplay of the silence, the piercing sound, and the hum of people praying. On its most basic level, the shofar can be seen to express what we cannot find the right words to say. The blasts are the wordless cries of the people of Israel. The shofar is the instrument that sends those cries of pain and longing hurtling across the vast distance toward the Other.

There are three shofar sounds: *tekiah*—one long blast; *shevarim*—three short blasts; and *teru'ah*—nine staccato blasts. The Torah does not state explicitly how many shofar blasts are required, but the rabbis (based on a complicated exegesis of Lev. 25:9 and 23:24, and Num. 29:1) derive the necessity to have three blasts of *teru'ah* preceded by and followed by *tekiah*. The only question for the rabbis is what constitutes a *teru'ah*. One opinion is that it should sound like groaning (our *shevarim* sound); another is that it should sound like sobbing (what we call *teru'ah*); and a third opinion is that it should sound like both together (our *shevarim teru'ah*). Therefore, we have the pattern of *tekiah teru'ah tekiah, tekiah shevarim tekiah, tekiah shevarim teru'ah tekiah* to cover all possibilities.

The shofar blowing takes place at a number of times during the Rosh ha-Shanah service. One set occurs right after the Torah reading (this set is called *de-miyushav*—"while sitting," since at one time you were allowed to sit during these blasts). According to one tradition, this was the point in the

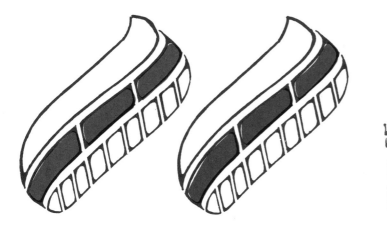

תְּקִיעָה
שְׁבָרִים
תְּרוּעָה

the day of our festival; for it is a statute for Israel, a ruling of the God of Jacob" (Psalm 81:4–5). Rosh ha-Shanah is the seventh, and thus a special, new moon. Two of the shofar's other associations in the Torah make it appropriate to Rosh ha-Shanah. The shofar heralds the nearing of God at the Sinai revelation (Exod. 19). On Rosh ha-Shanah we turn ourselves back toward the ways of God that the Torah teaches. In addition, the shofar is sounded, significantly, on Yom ha-Kippurim, the tenth day of the seventh month, to announce the Jubilee Year, the fiftieth year, in which land, estates, and freedom that people had lost in the forty-nine (7 × 7) preceding years will be restored: "Declare independence in the land for all its inhabitants" (Lev. 25:10). Rosh ha-Shanah promises a new lease on life, a shot at redemption, to all those who are moved by the sounding of the shofar to do teshuvah.

E.GR.

Make a shofar—Plan 1:
Go to a slaughterhouse and obtain a ram's horn. Boil it for three to five hours until you can remove the cartilage. Heat sand to 300°–500° and let the horn sit and sit and sit in the sand. Using insulated gloves, pick up the horn and bend it little by little until the fibers stretch. You have to straighten it out enough so that you can drill a hole to form a mouthpiece. When you have the shape you want, plunge the horn into cold water. Drill a hole for the mouthpiece until you reach the hollow part of the shofar.

Make a shofar—Plan 2:
Have the whole congregation, not just one person, call out the shofar blasts during Rosh ha-Shanah services, then have anyone with a shofar sound it. Let the congregation continue to call the sounds in Hebrew or in English: blast, break, shatter, and blast. At the end of Yom Kippur, let the shofar begin and then let all the congregation join in with the traditional words chanted out loud.

Z.S.

Rabbi Yehuda Aryeh Leib of Ger suggests that Rosh ha-Shanah refers to the state of being prior to the differentiation of the divine emanation into distinguishable parts (a play on Rosh ha-

Shanah as words meaning "prior to differentiation"). It is with this original state of being, formless, immaterial, and the original source of all created being, that we reestablish contact on Rosh ha-Shanah, assisted by the wordless sounds of the shofar.

Words represent the division of sound into discrete, significative units; pure sound, undifferentiated, connects directly with the undifferentiated Source of all being. On Rosh ha-Shanah, when the vitality of the world is reconnected with its Source, undivided and undifferentiated, the comparable sounds of the shofar serve uniquely to effect this reconnection.

E.Ge.

Rabbi Isaiah Horowitz, author of *The Two Tablets of the Covenant,* an important moralistic work of the seventeenth century, takes special note of the fact that each series of shofar blasts begins and ends with a *tekiah,* a whole note, surrounding a *shevarim* or *teru-'ah,* a broken note. This is the theme of Rosh ha-Shanah, he writes. We were whole, we became broken, but we shall be whole again. We were whole, broken, even shattered into the fragments of the *teru'ah,* but we shall yet be whole again!

A.G.

On the first day we read of individuals blessed with new or continued life (Ishmael and Hannah); on the second we read of new or continued life for the people Israel (the patriarch Isaac and the nation as a whole, which, in Jeremiah's words, "found favor in the wilderness"—just like Hagar). The interrelations among the four readings are staggeringly complex; appropriately for these days, we are left pondering the relation of one generation to another, the transmission of faith, and the grace of new beginnings. The readings also contribute to the peculiar mood of Rosh ha-Shanah: a mixture of joy and solemnity not experienced at any other moment of the Jewish year.

A.E.

It is no accident that most of the first day's Torah reading is devoted to the story of Hagar and Ishmael and not only to that of Sarah and Isaac. Rosh

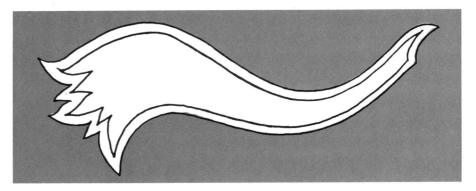

service when the shofar was originally blown, until an incident occurred in which the ruling government thought this was a call to rebellion and sent in its troops. The rabbis therefore moved the shofar blowing to later in the day (when it would be clearer that no rebellion was planned), but the first set was subsequently reinstituted.

Another set is blown during the repetition of the musaf amidah at the end of each of the central *berakhot* of that amidah. There are a number of variations on the exact order of blowing as well as the placement of some additional shofar blowings near the end of the service. These latter blasts are needed to achieve the customary 100 shofar blasts each day of Rosh ha-Shanah.

The mitzvah of the shofar is to hear the shofar being blown, not to actually blow it yourself, hence the blessing "to hear the sound of the shofar." Because it might lead to a violation of Shabbat laws (through carrying), the rabbis decreed that when Rosh ha-Shanah falls on Shabbat, the shofar should not be sounded. Most synagogues follow this practice, which means that during those years when the first day of Rosh ha-Shanah falls on Shabbat, the shofar is not blown until the second day.

The Liturgy The traditional liturgy for this festival has many additions that express the themes of judgment and repentance. One of the most famous is the *unetaneh tokef* hymn, written, according to legend, by a rabbi in the Middle Ages who was tortured for refusing to convert to Christianity. Before dying he composed this hymn, which vividly describes all humans passing before God, Who decides who shall live and who shall die. Another recurrent image is that of the Book of Life. According to tradition, there is a Book of Life and a Book of Death and each person's name is written down in one of these books. On Rosh ha-Shanah, all the righteous are written in the Book of Life and all of the wicked in the Book of Death, but all those who are neither righteous nor wicked have until Yom Kippur to repent before their fate is sealed. The liturgy is replete with requests to be chosen for life.

The Torah readings for Rosh ha-Shanah are the birth of Isaac on the first day and the binding of Isaac—the *akedah*—on the second. The haftarot are the birth of Samuel from the Book of Judges on the first day and a selection from Jeremiah, including a vision of the deliverance of the people of Israel from exile, on the second. The themes of birth after barrenness, deliverance after exile, and rescue from sacrifice are boldly delineated by these readings and

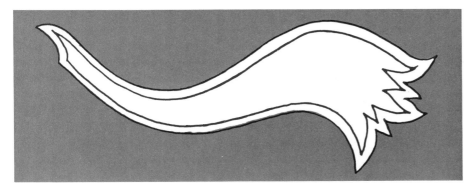

add a positive note to the day. The theme of the birth of children also reminds us that Rosh ha-Shanah marks the birthday of the world. And the story of the *akedah,* demonstrating our ancestors' supreme love for God, ties in with our appeal to God to rescue us from death.

The amidah of musaf—the additional service—is unique to Rosh ha-Shanah. While the regular Amidah of the morning service (as with the Amidah of all other festivals) has one central *berakhah* related to the festival, the musaf Amidah of Rosh ha-Shanah has three central *berakhot.* The first *berakhah* is *malkhuyot,* which talks of God's kingship. The second is *zikhronot,* which talks of God's remembering the past. The third is *shofarot,* which connects the shofar with important events of the past, such as Sinai, and *the* important event of the future—the messianic end of days. At each the shofar was or will be sounded. Each of these *berakhot* is centered around ten verses, three from the Pentateuch, three from the Writings, three from the Prophets, and finally one from the Torah again.

These three *berakhot* have been interpreted in many ways, but the most common is that they reflect three cardinal principles of Judaism:

1. the acceptance of God as King of the universe
2. the acknowledgment that God intervenes in the world to punish the wicked and reward the good
3. the recognition that God revealed Himself and the Torah at Sinai and/or will fully reveal Himself again to bring about the end of days

Two other deviations from the standard festival liturgy should be mentioned. First, there are a number of additions to the Amidah (in all the services of the day) that are meant to emphasize God's kingship and to request that God remember us for life and write our names in the Book of Life. Second, there is no hallel on Rosh ha-Shanah even though it is a festival. The most common explanation is found in the following midrash: The heavenly angels ask why Israel is not reciting Hallel. God says, "Is it possible that a king sits on the judgment seat with the books of life and death open before him and Israel will sing praise?!"

Other Customs Outside of the synagogue, there are few customs unique to Rosh ha-Shanah. Candles are lit and kiddush is said as on all holidays. There are a number of food customs associated with Rosh ha-Shanah, the most

ha-Shanah is the most universal of Jewish holidays; on it we celebrate God as father and creator of all the world, not of Israel alone. He is loving father of Ishmael, the "non-Jew" and the sinner, as much as He is of Isaac, the righteous offspring of righteous parents. As He hears the cry of the child Ishmael *ba-asher hu sham*—where he is—so He hears our cries, wherever we may be, as far as we think we are from Him.

A.G.

Another theme may also be discerned in the Torah readings, the mythical "two faces" of the parents. On the one hand, how solicitous of Isaac is his protecting father, Abraham; on the other hand, how terrifyingly he wields the knife! And accompanying Sarah's compassion and concern for Isaac is her ruthlessness toward Ishmael. For both matriarch and patriarch, the two aspects, the nurturing and the devouring, the protective and the destructive, are clearly portrayed.

Might this be subtly connected with verse 10 from Psalm 27, recited daily during Elul? "For though my father and my mother have forsaken me, the Lord will take me up."

E.Ge.

Malkhuyot: There are many places where habits or people rather than God are king. There are certain people in whose presence I cannot be myself. They have the power to flatten out my heart. This is the issue of *malkhuyot.*

Zikhronot: The issue of *zikhronot* is that there are memories I cannot let go of even though they are no longer appropriate. Having placed certain resentments in my memory bank, I have difficulty removing them.

Shofarot: This has to do with *shipur* (from the same root as shofar) *ma-asekha*—improve your deeds. I must examine the issues in my life to discover which changes are necessary, because without them my life is too terrible to live. Unless *I* write myself into the Book of Life, I am certainly not going to live for another year. I must renew my will to live. Each of us must try to write a page in the Book of Life, consisting of what we desire in the coming year.

Z.S.

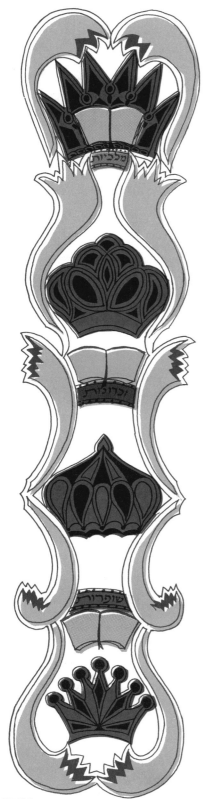

Malkhuyot

prevalent being the dipping of apples in honey. As an expression of a desire for a sweet year, apples or other foods—e.g., hallah—are dipped in honey at the beginning of meals on Rosh ha-Shanah. The phrase "May it be Your will to renew us for a year that is good and sweet" is recited. We also do not put salt on our hallot even though this is customary on Shabbat, because we want the sweet taste of honey, not a salty taste. It is also customary to eat round hallot rather than the oval or rectangular ones. This is because the former look like crowns—either the crown of God's kingship or the crowns with which God traditionally rewards the people of Israel if they are righteous. There is a related old tradition of making hallot in the shape of ladders (we will be exalted or brought low) or birds "Like the birds that fly, even so will the Lord of Hosts shield Jerusalem, shielding and saving, protecting and rescuing. Then the children of Israel shall return to Him . . ." (Isa. 31:5–6).

Other food customs are to eat foods that in similar ways also express wishes for the new year—e.g., eating the head of a fish since we would rather be a head than a tail. Obversely, we do not eat nuts, because the Hebrew letters of the word—*egoz*—have a numerical equivalent to the Hebrew word for sin. At the beginning of the second evening meal of Rosh ha-Shanah, it is customary to eat a "funny fruit," which means any fruit we have not eaten in a long time, such as casaba melon, kiwi . . . This has to do with the question of reciting the *she-he-heyanu* blessing on the second night, which is explained in the following discussion of why Rosh ha-Shanah is celebrated for two days even in Israel.

Tashlikh. On Rosh ha-Shanah afternoon of the first day, it is customary to go to a flowing body of water (a river, lake, or ocean rather than a pond) and symbolically cast our sins away by throwing bread crumbs into the water. This ceremony is accompanied by reciting Micah 7:18–20, Psalms 118:5–9, and Psalms 33 and 130. The verse "You will cast [*tashlikh*] your sins into the depths of the sea" (Mic. 7:19) is cited as support for this custom. *Tashlikh* has been opposed by a number of rabbinic scholars who are afraid the symbolism will be taken too literally and people will believe they can rid themselves of sin through this ceremony rather than through the arduous process of repentance. Despite this opposition, *tashlikh* is still widely observed. If the first day falls on Shabbat, Ashkenazim postpone *tashlikh* until the afternoon of the second day.

The second day of Rosh ha-Shanah is basically the same as the first, with some different poetical passages in the liturgy.

Why Is Rosh ha-Shanah Two Days? Unlike other festivals that are celebrated in the Diaspora for two days because of uncertainty about the calendar, Rosh ha-Shanah is the only holiday celebrated for two days in Israel. The reason is the same as with all the other festivals—that is, the uncertainty involved in a calendar that depended on when the new moon was promulgated by the rabbinic court in Jerusalem. The problem of Rosh ha-Shanah is heightened by the fact that it falls on Rosh Hodesh—the new moon itself; therefore, even in Jerusalem, it would have been difficult to let everyone know in time that the New Year had begun. To solve this problem, a two-day Rosh ha-Shanah was practiced even in Israel. (NOTE: Once the calendar was set, people in Israel observed only one day until the early Middle Ages, when the practice was changed back to observing two days.)

Creating a two-day Rosh ha-Shanah was also intended to strengthen observance of each day; in the rabbinic view, the two days are regarded as a *yoma arikhta*—one long day. In this way, the holiness of both days was fixed. Because Rosh ha-Shanah is "one long day," there is some question whether or not to say *she-he-heyanu,* the blessing expressing gratitude for special occasions, on the second day. To get around this problem, a custom arose on the second night to eat a new fruit or wear a new garment which of themselves require a *she-he-heyanu* and when you light candles or make kiddush to have these in mind. (But if you do not have a new garment, fruit etc., you should still say the *she-he-heyanu).*

The Ten Days of Repentance   The days between Rosh ha-Shanah and Yom Kippur are seen as part of the High Holiday process called *aseret yemei teshuvah*—the ten days of repentance. This is the period when those of us who are not utterly wicked or entirely righteous can still repent and be sealed into the Book of Life. The Talmud advises:

> A man should always consider himself evenly balanced, i.e., half sinful and half righteous. If he performs one mitzvah, happy is he, for he has tilted the scales toward righteousness. If he commits one sin, woe unto him, for he has tilted the scale toward sinfulness.
> Rabbi Elazar the son of Simon said: "Inasmuch as the world is judged in accordance with the majority of *its* deeds, and the individual is judged in accordance with the majority of *his* deeds, if he performs one mitzvah, happy is he, for he has tipped his scales and the scales of the world toward merit. If he commits one sin, woe unto him, for he has tipped the scales toward sinfulness for himself and for the world." [*Kiddushin* 40a–b]

Thus this is a period of heightening tension: Like Atlas, we bear our fate and even the fate of the world increasingly on our shoulders.

In terms of ritual, it is marked by maintaining the changes in the liturgy —particularly the Amidah, plus a few additional ones—that express a desire to be inscribed in the Book of Life during these days of judgment. The prayer *avinu malkeinu* is recited after the shaharit and minhah Amidah. Selihot are recited each morning.

THREE SPECIAL DAYS

TZOM GEDALIAH

This is a minor fast day that falls on the day after Rosh ha-Shanah (Tishri 3). It commemorates the assassination of Gedaliah, the last governor of Judea. Following the destruction of the first temple (586 B.C.), the Babylonians appointed Gedaliah governor over the remaining Jews. His death marked the end of any remnant of Jewish sovereignty and led to the further dispersal of the Jewish people (see Jeremiah 41–42). It is one of the four fast days concern-

What's that about not eating nuts because of gematria? By my calculation, *egoz* (nut) is seventeen whereas *chet* (sin) is eighteen. Hmm. Do you have another explanation at hand? If not, back to the almonds! [Editor's note: You add one for the word itself, an old gematria trick!]

E.GE.

Throwing away untreated sewage is polluting. Before throwing your sins in the water, neutralize them by asking: Have I learned my lesson? Otherwise, they will just come back to you in your food and water.

Z.S.

Gedaliah, supporter of Jeremiah and widely respected in the Jewish community, was a "neutralist" and cooperated with Babylonia rather than joining the pro-Egyptian faction. The assassination of this decent man by the superpatriots and zealots of his day is of sufficient contemporary significance that we should make some effort to expand its commemoration in our day.

E.GE.

I cannot profess the sort of grief over Gedaliah that would incline me to fast on the anniversary of his assassination. On the other hand, to observe a minor fast following Rosh ha-Shanah can contribute significantly to the process of teshuvah. First, the intensity of Rosh ha-Shanah, the dramatic opening of the Ten Days of Teshuvah, does not simply dissipate on the day after. The fast sustains our attention on the spiritual process at hand. Second, the minor fast anticipates the great fast of Yom Kippur, the most awesome day only a week ahead, by which time we should have achieved a readiness to change.

E.GR.

While the Shabbat ha-Gadol sermon was lengthy because of the details of Passover law to be explained, the sermon on Shabbat Shuvah was to serve as a *hit'orerut li-teshuvah*—an impassioned call for repentance. It was offered amid tears and wailing, and was so delivered as to wring dread and compassion from the most stonelike heart. The East European versions of the prayer book were filled with Yiddish commentaries, accessible in their meaning to both men and women who could not understand the words of the Hebrew liturgy. The prayer books for the ten days of penitence are filled with parables and simple homilies about people who were led astray by their vices, were punished for their sins, and returned to God in contrition and tears.

A.G.

Mystical tradition views the process of change as a struggle between the two passions of which we all are made: *yetzer ha-tov* (the passion for good) and *yetzer ha-ra* (the passion for bad). We are each created as a combination of these two human forces. When we dedicate ourselves and adhere to God, the passion for good prevails; when we do not, the passion for bad can. Thus, the process of repentance can be achieved best not by searching around willy-nilly in the cluttered attics of our personalities but rather by committing ourselves more fully to the shining beam of Torah, the way of God.

E.GR.

ing the destruction of the temple (for more details see "The Three Weeks," p. 85). Outside of traditional circles, it is not widely observed.

SHABBAT SHUVAH

The Shabbat between Rosh ha-Shanah and Yom Kippur is known as Shabbat Shuvah—the Sabbath of Turning—after the haftarah, which begins *Shuvah yisrael*—"Return O Israel to the Lord, your God" (Hosea 14:2). It is often called Shabbat Teshuvah—Sabbath of Repentance—as well. Besides its special haftarah, Shabbat Shuvah is marked in some synagogues by a traditionally lengthy discourse about repentance. In Eastern Europe, rabbis spoke only twice a year in the synagogue—on Shabbat Shuvah and on Shabbat ha-Gadol before Pesah. Perhaps they tried to make up for the rest of the year by giving exceptionally long sermons. The Shabbat Shuvah sermon was often given in the afternoon rather than the morning.

EREV YOM KIPPUR

This third special day will be discussed in the Yom Kippur chapter.

KAVVANOT

The period before Rosh ha-Shanah, and the festival itself, should be a time of reviewing the past year and trying to renew ourselves by a struggle with the negative aspects of our personalities. This is a very personal effort for which each individual must find her or his own way. Some of us will find that creating a structure is the best way to engage in this attempt at change. This could be done by a conscious review of the year, beginning with last Rosh ha-Shanah, or it could involve a careful examination of the many sides of our personalities. Others of us may find a more spontaneous and less conscious effort more effective. But each of us should become aware of the approaching Days of Awe and make a commitment to change.

Although the process is predominantly an inward and personal one, it does have a social dimension. As the tradition states: On Yom Kippur, we can achieve atonement for sins between God and us, but for sins between us and our fellow humans, Yom Kippur offers no atonement. For those sins, we must ask forgiveness from all the people we have wronged. We must try to repair the damage and pain we have caused during the past year. Being social creatures, our relations with other people affect the deepest reaches of our characters. Thus we cannot improve our inner lives without improving our behavior to those around us.

Therefore, this is a good time for group introspection as a means of examining how members of a group relate to each other. Communities of all kinds—*havurot* (small religious fellowships), synagogues, even families—

should be especially concerned with ways to effect reconciliations among members for hurts large and small. Also a new year brings the possibility of changes in the way groups act programatically as well as interpersonally. This time of year is fitting for groups to critique their activities of last year and ask questions about their direction in the coming year. Does the group want to reemphasize old goals not fully realized or change focus? Does it want to add new programs, etc.? An Elul/beginning-of-the-year retreat is a good vehicle to accomplish an examination of the past year as well as plan for the future, thus infusing new energy into groups that have been dormant over the summer. A retreat can also help integrate new members.

COMMUNAL RITUALS

There are a number of contemporary communal rituals that relate to the process of repentance or to the welcoming of a new year. Instead of, or in addition to, the major selihot service on the Saturday night before Rosh ha-Shanah, a group might want to gather for study and prayer. One group, Havurat Shalom, used to have its own selihot service in a Quaker style. Everyone would sit silently in a dimly lit room. When a person was ready to speak, she or he would reflect on the past year or express hopes for the coming year. Time was left for everyone to speak, though it was not incumbent upon anyone to speak. The service would end with a melody or the chanting of the High Holiday musaf kaddish.

On Rosh ha-Shanah itself, a group/*havurah* might want to gather for a communal meal that includes the traditional apples and honey. At that time or during services (if the group has its own), a communal blessing could take place. Traditionally, the *kohanim* (priests) would bless the people on Rosh ha-Shanah. A contemporary version goes as follows: Members stand in a circle with a hand on the head of the person next to them. Everyone recites in unison the priestly blessing of *yevarekhekha*—"May the Lord bless you and keep you. May the Lord make His face shine upon you and be gracious to you. May the Lord lift up His countenance to you and grant you peace" (Num. 6:24–26).

The *tashlikh* ceremony is both a pleasant relief from all the sitting at services and an opportunity for creative liturgy. Depending on local circumstances, it can be a nice social occasion to see friends who attended different services, or a striking ceremony of a small crowd standing on a deserted beach. The traditional service is brief and there is room for additional liturgy using water both as a symbol of birth and as a means of purification/cleansing.

STUDY

A major form of preparation for the High Holy Days is study. It can be done individually or by a group. Texts could include the liturgy or the Torah portions, especially those of Rosh ha-Shanah. Both the Book of Jonah (read

The process of individual teshuvah (repentance—literally, turning around) is so demanding and requires such concentration that I don't see how we can achieve reconciliation within the groups to which we belong at the same time. Group renewal and mending should be done, but it is so easy to deflect personal teshuvah that we might do best not to find justification for it by including corporate teshuvah in Rosh ha-Shanah. Alternatively, were we to adopt a more frequent process of personal teshuvah all year round, on each Shabbat or even Rosh Hodesh, for example, we might with greater equanimity devote Rosh ha-Shanah to our corporate teshuvah.

E.GR.

For ten years now, those of us in the Alternate Religious Community of Marblehead, a "living-room synagogue" group of six families, have combined several of these elements for our Second Morning Rosh ha-Shanah ceremonies. Assembling at Plum Island (a nature preserve on the Atlantic Ocean) half an hour before sunrise, we watch attentively as the eastern horizon constantly and wondrously changes color prior to the sun's appearance. The shofar is first sounded at that moment when the sun emerges from the ocean, and the sense of creation reenacted is quite awesome.

The remainder of the service includes material from the traditional Rosh ha-Shanah liturgy, readings reflecting beginnings, contemporary folk music that expresses such themes, various personal sharings, a potluck *yontefdik* breakfast-on-the-beach, sometimes a birthday cake with candle for this "birthday of the world," and a *tashlikh* ceremony later in the morning.

Needless to say, we are weather-vulnerable, with both the service and the breakfast subject to abbreviation. But just as creation is daily renewed and annually celebrated by Rosh ha-Shanah, whatever the weather, we also gather in community to greet, with the primordial sound of the shofar, the pristine emergence of the sun from the waters this day.

E.GE.

on Yom Kippur) and the Book of Job grapple with High Holy Day themes. A good guide to the liturgy is *Justice and Mercy* by Max Arzt (New York: Holt, Rinehart, 1963). The book *Days of Awe* by S. Y. Agnon (New York: Schocken, 1948) is a good collection of source material on all aspects of the High Holy Days. Study about teshuvah/change, whether with material found in Jewish sources or modern psychological ones, is another area of possibility. Two traditional Jewish views, one medieval and the other modern, are "The Laws of Teshuvah" in *The Code of Jewish Law* by Maimonides (there are various English editions) and *On Repentance* by Joseph Soloveitchik (Jerusalem: Oroth Publishing House, 1980).

CRAFTS

It is customary to wish acquaintances a happy New Year both in person and by cards through the mail. A craft project for individuals or groups is to make their own High Holiday cards, using linoleum blocks, papercut designs that are then photocopied, etc. Another alternative to commercial cards is to have a photograph or drawing of your choice or creation professionally reproduced to create your own card. One family uses a fairly simple printed postcard that they then fill with an update on what all their family members have been doing during the past year as a way to keep in touch with friends all over the country.

DERASH

TWO NEW YEARS

Why are there two beginnings to the year? How can Nisan be the first of all months, and yet Rosh ha-Shanah—the New Year—occur in the seventh month, Tishri? The presence of two new years is not accidental; rather it grows out of a notion underlying the Jewish calendar, the notion of two kinds of time—historical and cyclic.

Historical time is a constant linear movement in an upward direction and is centered upon progress and development. It is time created by humans and set arbitrarily. It is found in clocks with their minute and second hands and in calendars discarded at the end of last year. The unchanging sun is its symbol.

Cyclical time is circular and consists of recurring patterns. It is established by nature and is found in the four seasons. Its symbol is the moon with its phases.

Both kinds of time are found in the Jewish calendar with its two new years. At Rosh ha-Shanah, we commemorate the new year of creation, when our successes and failures are tallied in the account books of heaven. As we mark another year's passage, an evaluation of our progress is made by our-

I don't concede the boundary line you draw between two types of sacred time—historical/progressive time and cyclic/recurrent time. With each year, every festival finds us at an advanced stage of our own growth and catalyzes our continued growth. I prefer to see the progressive and the cyclic as two components of the same movement. Our sacred time resembles a helix, coiling around and around in an upward crest. Each season we come back to the same place on the curve, but we are at the next-higher level. We never run in place, but we do run up a spiraling ramp, like the one in the Guggenheim Museum, able to look down at last year and forward to next year at each curve on the journey.

E.GR.

selves and by God. As a people linked with God, our ups and downs in history are not viewed as accidental; our fate is tied into the morality of our deeds, thus how we act helps create history.

At Nisan we commemorate Pesah and note the coming of spring. Thus, Nisan marks the beginning of the timeless natural cycle—spring, summer, fall, and winter. It also marks the beginning of the pilgrimage festival cycle of Pesah, Shavuot, and Sukkot. These three festivals of cyclic time beckon us to confront the three great themes of liberation, revelation, and exile/ redemption each and every year no matter where we are at that moment in our own life cycles.

Both cyclic and historical time are necessary. We need the process of self-evaluation called forth by historical time to rouse us to change and thus foster creation and progress. Without that, it would be easy to become increasingly sedentary both spiritually and physically as our lives passed us by. With only cyclic time, each season comes to resemble its predecessor; nothing seems to change. On the other hand, we need cyclic time to give us perspective on the dangers of constantly seeking progress due to an unbridled devotion to the movement of historical time. Cyclic time comes to balance ''Progress is our most important product'' with ''There is nothing new under heaven.'' It teaches us how to flow with time, not to struggle against it as though it were an enemy. Particularly in our day, the sense of cyclic time is a necessary balance to the pressures in our society to succeed. If historical time teaches us that to be alive is to move, cyclic times teaches us that sometimes to wait in place is more important than moving on. Each is needed, both Tishri and Nisan, Rosh ha-Shanah and Pesah.

The Jewish calendar is basically cyclic in its dependence on the moon. However, it is adjusted at regular intervals to keep the festivals in their proper seasons—e.g., Pesah in the spring. The workings of the calendar with its lunar/solar complexity reflect the mixture of both kinds of time throughout the year. Pesah is cyclic, but it is also historical, for the Exodus was seen by the tradition as a verifiable event. Similarly, though Rosh ha-Shanah is historical, it partakes of cyclical time as well by being an annual occurrence. Thus both kinds of time are often present, and together make up the mythic dimension of Judaism. For both kinds of time occur here in the real world and yet also occur out of time. Judaism is not concerned with the question of when—When did the Exodus occur or even when will the new year begin? Its concern is with the meaning of those events and with the importance of time and its cycles. Together historical and cyclical time lift us out of the present into a mythic time where the Exodus still happens and the world is created anew each day. Both kinds of time, at moments merged and at moments separated, are required guides for us as time-travelers through life.

HAYOM HARAT HA-OLAM—
TODAY IS THE BIRTHDAY OF THE WORLD

Rosh ha-Shanah as the birthday of the world recalls for us God's creation of the world in the beginning of time. Strikingly, the Torah reading for Rosh

Zikhronot

I'm sure I'm reading too much into this, but there is a profound philosophical truth to the rabbinic insight that the world does not begin until the sixth day of Creation and the appearance on that day of the human being. So far as we know, there would be no world, nor God, without the perception of the world by human minds—one might go so far as to say by my human mind. Theoretically, God and the rest of the world might have existed, but like the famous falling tree in the forest that makes no sound without an ear to hear it, without a human mind to perceive God and the world, who would know? God certainly can only be recognized by human beings—God depends on us for that much, at least.

E.Gr.

The three sections—*malkhuyot, zikhronot,* and *shofarot*—follow a logical progression. The first proclaims Him Creator and King; as author of the universe, He is the one of absolute power, bringing life and death, awesome and holy. Emphasized here is the majesty of His kingdom, along with the promise that His true rule will one day be perceived by all. The God of *malkhuyot* remains distant, however, enshrined in a holiness that seems far beyond our reach. *Zikhronot* stands over against all that awesome kingship; indeed, He may be King and ruler, but He is one who *cares.* He remembered Noah, the one who was left alone in the hour of God's greatest wrath. So He remembered Israel in Egypt, the righteous in their trials, and the life of each individual human being. The awesome King has entered into a covenant with humanity (again, through Noah, not with Israel alone), a covenant that promises He will take cognizance of each individual human life, of every human cry. *Shofarot* then tells us of the *acts* of God: He who rules and remembers also *does.* He has given us the gift of revealing Himself at Sinai, and He will reveal His mighty hand yet again, at the end of time. These three sections of the liturgy should be read as a single unit, a summation of world history as seen from the perspective of Israel's faith.

A.G.

ha-Shanah is not the story of creation (Gen. 1:1) but rather the birth of Isaac, and the haftarah concerns the birth of Samuel—both tales of long-desired births to barren women. In fact, there is a tradition that Rosh ha-Shanah is *not* the day the world was created. *Pesikta Rabbati,* an early rabbinic midrashic work, states that the world was created on the twenty-fifth of Elul. Rosh ha-Shanah then is the sixth day of creation, the day on which humans were created. For the beginning of humanity marks the real beginning of creation. It is the beginning of history and most of all the beginning of the relationship between the human and the divine. Rosh ha-Shanah thus affirms the importance of human life, even of one single birth, as the equivalence of God's creating the world. By stressing life, it calls upon us to examine the quality of our lives as we prepare for Yom Kippur—the day when life is to be judged.

SARAH, A SYMBOL OF ROSH HA-SHANAH

On the first day of Rosh ha-Shanah, we read the story of Sarah giving birth to Isaac and demanding the banishment of Hagar and Ishmael. For us the image of Sarah may be even more important than that of Abraham, the perfect man of faith, who (as we read on the second day of Rosh ha-Shanah) is even ready to sacrifice his beloved son. Sarah in this tale emerges as a skeptic.

When three men visited Abraham, they asked him:

"Where is your wife Sarah?" And he replied, "There, in the tent." Then one said, "I will return to you when life is due, and your wife Sarah shall have a son!" Sarah was listening at the entrance of the tent, which was behind him . . . And Sarah laughed to herself, saying, "Now that I am withered, am I to have enjoyment—with my husband so old?" [Gen. 18:9, 10, 12]

Unlike Abraham, to whom God spoke directly, Sarah stood behind the tent flap and heard God's words only indirectly. She laughed at the absurdity of the promise of a child. Even when the promise came true, she mocked as if to say, Why wait ninety years to let me give birth? Why wait until after so many have died to bring redemption? Why not have redemption at the beginning of days, not the end of days? Sarah laughed skeptically even at the moment of fulfillment, naming her son Isaac, which means laughter.

Sarah deeply believed in God and yet was skeptical. We, too, believe but can hear God's voice only from behind the curtain. Not for us the pious faith of an Abraham marching with a knife held high for his Lord. We are more human—both skeptical and believing. We are Sarah.

ON THE THEMES OF MALKHUYOT/ ZIKHRONOT/SHOFAROT

The three major themes of the Rosh ha-Shanah musaf are most frequently spoken of as reflecting three important aspects of God and theology. The first, *malkhuyot*—sovereignty—proclaims God's sovereignty over the world and humanity. The second, *zikhronot*—remembrance—tells us that God cares about the world and remembers all our deeds, both the good and the bad. The third, *shofarot,* reminds us of the revelation of God at Sinai and of the final redemption still to come. Together they "describe" a god who is omniscient and omnipotent and who is actively involved in this world on a continuing basis.

These three aspects are also part of our lives, for we are created *be-tzelem elohim*—in the image of God. We are to reflect in our lives aspects of the Divine, or as the rabbinic principle states: You should be merciful just as He is merciful, you should be just, etc. Looking at these three themes in this manner gives us a different perspective. *Malkhuyot* focuses on control—control over others and over ourselves. *Zikhronot* has to do with memory and thought. Remembering is what the covenant is based on, for we are to remember what God did for us in Egypt and elsewhere. Remembering, too, is what all human relationships are based on, for without memory of past events and feelings, there is no way to deepen emotional attachments; each meeting becomes the first; whether for love or hate, no one has any more meaning to you than anyone else. *Shofarot,* the third, has to do with sound and thus with communication and speech.

Appropriately for Rosh ha-Shanah, these three themes are reflected in the three creation stories at the beginning of Genesis—that is, the Garden, the Flood, and the Tower of Babel.

For the story of the tree in the Garden is a story of controls—of self-control and of curbing desire. Both God and humans learn from the Garden that there is no self-control without tasting of knowledge; without even partial understanding of who we are and the consequences of our deeds, there is no motivation to curb desire. Both learn that self-control will be difficult for humans.

The second creation story is that of the Flood, which is quoted in the liturgy of *zikhronot* as follows: "Remember us as You remembered Noah in love, graciously saving him when You released the flood to destroy all creatures because of their evil deeds. . . ." The liturgy continues with a quotation (Gen. 8:1) from the Noah story. God *remembers* Noah and saves him. Later God remembers the people of Israel in Egypt and decides to redeem them. It is out of memory, out of cognition, that God acts, that God saves, and that God establishes or reestablishes relationships with humans.

We, too, are meant to remember the Noahs amid the floodwater and reach out to save them. We are to remember and emphasize the good in others in order to relate to them, not focus on their faults. We are also meant to remember the past and not live only in the present. Remembering the past gives us a proper sense of our place in the universe and, even more important, makes us cognizant of a future that we must be engaged in creating.

The third creation story is that of the Tower of Babel, in which we learn the power of speech and its danger. Today, we remain confounded by the diversity of languages, but even more by the difficulty of really communicating rather than just speaking.

Self-control, thinking/remembering, and speech are what make us human. To realize our full potential, we must strive with each of these aspects of our humanity, which in themselves are only reflections of the Divine.

Shofarot

YOM KIPPUR
DAY OF AT-ONE-MENT

Yom Kippur falls on the tenth of Tishri and brings to a close the ten days of repentance begun with Rosh ha-Shanah. In temple times, Yom Kippur was a day of elaborate cultic rituals to effect the atonement of the people. On this day, God's special name was pronounced by the high priest before the assembled masses in the temple courtyards. Yom Kippur has continued to be the day of atonement, though its setting has shifted from the temple to the synagogue, where we spend almost the whole day in prayer. To aid in focusing our minds on this task of repentance and atonement, we are told to afflict our bodies through fasting and other forms of abstinence. We are meant to feel that the natural course of our existence is suspended on this day while our lives, or at least the quality of our lives, hang in the balance. We are to face what a permanent suspension of existence—death—would be like, and thus to learn how to better embrace life.

Even more exclusively than on Rosh ha-Shanah, Yom Kippur's ritual is located in the synagogue. The day is structured around its services, which are five in number—one more than is usual for a Shabbat or festival. They are:

Kol Nidrei   the evening service named after its opening prayer
Shaharit   the morning service

Yom Kippur is no longer a day of repentance in its primary focus. Rather, it is a day of atonement, a day when those who have failed at repentance—and which of us has not?—may cast themselves upon God's mercies and ask that He act for them. Until this final day of the season of repentance, all is up to us; it is we who are given the burden of changing our ways. Now, seeing that we have not been able to do so fully, we turn to God and ask that He be the one to act, that He offer kapparah, a cleansing of the slate and an opportunity to begin again, even to us sinners who have not been able to work our own way out of the quagmire of our tangled lives.

A.G.

111

Musaf	the additional service, which includes the martyrology and the *avodah*—a description of the temple service
Minhah	the afternoon service, including a reading of the Book of Jonah
Neilah	the service that is unique in the liturgical calendar and concludes Yom Kippur

Besides the services, Yom Kippur is also marked by a series of five restrictions, or afflictions, regarded by the rabbis as commanded by the Torah: (1) no eating or drinking; (2) no bathing; (3) no anointing of the body with oil; (4) no wearing of leather shoes; (5) no sexual relations. All of these activities were considered physically pleasurable. To go barefoot or wear nonleather shoes was believed by the rabbis to be much less comfortable than wearing leather shoes.

As the most solemn day of the year, Yom Kippur is treated more like Shabbat than like a festival with respect to the laws prohibiting work. Therefore, carrying, using fire, and cooking are not permitted on Yom Kippur (unlike other festivals), for the day is called *shabbat shabbaton*—a sabbath of complete rest (see Lev. 23:32).

TRADITIONS

EREV YOM KIPPUR

Preparation for Yom Kippur begins the day before, which is a time with its own special qualities. The Talmud (*Yoma* 8lb) states that just as it is a mitzvah to fast on the tenth of Tishri (Yom Kippur), so is it a mitzvah to eat on the ninth. This is derived from the following verse:

> It shall be a sabbath of complete rest for you, and you shall practice self-denial; on the ninth day of the month at evening, from evening to evening, you shall observe this your sabbath. [Lev. 23:32]

Apparently the rabbis sought to make this day partially festive, reflecting their confidence that we shall be forgiven on Yom Kippur. Therefore, the selihot service is shortened and *avinu malkeinu* is omitted.

An old custom is kapparot (atonements), a form of scapegoat ceremony that involved taking a rooster or hen and twirling it around your head while reciting a prayer asking that this chicken be killed in your stead. The chicken was then slaughtered and given to the poor (who presumably could make use of your sins, if not the food). This ceremony evoked much rabbinic opposition, especially to its magical overtones (e.g., a white rooster was recommended as particularly efficacious for kapparot). It still survives, though most of those who observe it today have substituted money in a handkerchief for a chicken.

Viddui Minhah is said early in the afternoon to leave enough time for the final meal. In minhah, the viddui (confessional), which is recited during every service on Yom Kippur, is said. The usual reason given for saying it here is that in case you choke on a chicken bone and die during the meal, you will at least have died after seeking forgiveness for your sins. In traditional synagogues many *pushkas*—charity containers—are displayed for a variety of causes since "tzedakah [charity] can avert the evil decree." Also, of course, any Jewish holiday is seen by tradition as a time to remind Jews of those less fortunate.

Some people observe the custom of going to the mikveh—the ritual bath —to purify themselves before Yom Kippur. There are a number of old ascetic customs that have fallen into disuse. The most prevalent was *malkut*—flogging. Based on the biblical punishment for a variety of misdeeds, this flagellation was performed near the door of the synagogue. The person would lie down wearing his coat, and another would hit him (not very hard) three times while reciting Psalm 78:38, which has thirteen words; $13 \times 3 = 39$, the correct number for flogging in rabbinic tradition.

Seudah ha-mafseket After minhah, the *seudah ha-mafseket*—the last meal before the fast—is eaten. It is customary to wish people a *tzom kal*—easy fast. Because of a rabbinic interpretation of a verse, we are told to add on to the tenth of Tishri some time from Erev Yom Kippur and thus begin the fast early.

Beside the holiday candles (with the regular blessing and *she-he-heyanu),* a special memorial light that will burn all during Yom Kippur is lit in memory of deceased parents. The table should be covered with a holiday tablecloth. It is an old custom for women to wear white and for men to wear kittels as symbols of purity on Yom Kippur.

Just before leaving for services, it is customary to bless your children as is done traditionally on Friday nights. Additional prayers expressing wishes for the children in the coming year are appropriate.

YOM KIPPUR SERVICES

Kol Nidrei The evening service begins with one of the most famous passages in our liturgy—Kol Nidrei. Chanted dramatically by the service leader, it proclaims null and void those vows and promises that we may make and fail to fulfill in the coming year. Thus, we begin Yom Kippur with a recognition that our best intentions can go astray. Kol Nidrei, written in Aramaic, is a legal formula, and a number of legal customs therefore surround its recital. To form a court of three people, a person holding a Torah scroll stands on either side of the service leader. To formalize the declaration, it is repeated three times. Since it is a "legal procedure," it should be chanted while it is still daytime, so Kol Nidrei is chanted *before* sundown.

Sephardim have a slightly different text, which nullifies unfulfilled vows made during the past year rather than for the coming year. Both versions are problematic legally, but Kol Nidrei's power comes from its introductory moment and stirring chant rather than from the actual meaning of the words.

Even though traditionally a tallit is not worn for ma'ariv, on Yom Kippur a tallit is put on before Kol Nidrei and is worn not only for the evening service but for all the services on Yom Kippur. Similarly, those who wear a kittel—white robe—don it now before Kol Nidrei and wear it during all the Yom Kippur services. Some people who wear shoes on Yom Kippur will remove them during services in deference to the traditional prohibition on leather.

Ma'ariv Following Kol Nidrei is the ma'ariv service, which is similar to all evening services but is chanted to the special High Holiday melody for evening services. Each of the High Holiday services has its own special melody. These melodies are most distinguishable in the way the kaddish before the *barekhu* (shaharit) or the amidah (ma'ariv, musaf, minhah, neilah) is chanted. The phrase following *shema yisrael*—that is, *barukh shem kavod malkhuto*—is chanted out loud. During the rest of the year, it is said silently. The ma'ariv amidah, including the viddui or confessional, is followed by a section of selihot—penitential prayers. The viddui is repeated near the end of the selihot and is composed of two parts. The shorter, *ashamnu,* an alphabetical acrostic, is a listing of general sins; the longer, *al heit,* is a more specific listing of sins. The viddui is recited in all the other services of Yom Kippur, both in the silent amidah and in the repetition of the amidah. The confessional is in the first-person plural because even though each of us is asking atonement for his or her own sins, it is important to feel part of and responsible for the whole community of Israel. The prayer *avinu malkeinu* is recited at the end of ma'ariv and at the end of the amidah of each service (except minhah) on Yom Kippur.

Shaharit The morning service is basically similar to that of festivals, with the addition of a number of piyyutim, especially in the repetition of the amidah. The Torah reading describes the service in the temple. It is followed by the haftarah of Isaiah (57:14–58:16), which denounces those who fast out of rote ritual, for what God really desires is justice and mercy. The Torah

A possible reason why, on Yom Kippur, we are privileged to proclaim aloud this truth-not-yet-realized: On this day, in singular concentration, our own lives reflect more fully the Divine Dominion *(malkhuto)* over us; our awareness of this truth is high; and so these words, proclaimed aloud, are not so hollow as they might, at other times, be.

E.Ge.

On a day filled to overflowing with prayers that God "remember us to life," it is especially significant that we recite yizkor prayers, the *avodah* service, and the martyrology. In the first we ask God to remember those without whom we could not have been, or been as worthy of remembrance as we are. It is as if, through our remembrance of them, God remembers, just as many of God's mercies are given to us to give to each other, and revealed by God only through us. The lesson of the *avodah* service, I think, is that our lives would possess only the barest of meanings if we had to invent such meanings as we went along. How fortunate that our acts are not of our own authorship, that we can remember them. "Happy was the eye that saw these things"—that is, the person who learned the art of begging forgiveness up close—from the high priest in the temple. "May the memory of these things be our pardon"—for we rest secure in the knowledge that the acts of atonement we perform are not of our own devising.

In the martyrology, however, we remember that some acts should never have occurred, and so remind God, as it were, that He has often failed to remember His own mercies. We recall this precisely at the moment when His memory is of the utmost importance to us; and, emboldened by this recollection, we ask God to forgive all our failures to remember, reminding Him of ancestors who *did* remember, even when *He* did not. "Remember us," therefore, "unto life."

A.E.

שערי לב טוב   שערי כפרה   שערי ישועה

reading has a unique number of aliyot, six, which is one more than festivals but one less than the seven of Shabbat.

Yizkor. The memorial prayer for the dead is usually recited after the Torah reading, though some congregations have moved it to later in the afternoon. Originally yizkor was said only on Yom Kippur, but later it came to be included in all the major festivals. Many Sephardim do not say yizkor. In some synagogues those who have living parents leave the sanctuary while the prayer is being recited. Others insist that this is a remnant of the superstition of the evil eye and encourage everyone to remain for yizkor.

Musaf Unlike the special amidah of Rosh ha-Shanah, the amidah of Yom Kippur has only seven blessings. However, because of all the additions to the repetition, it is the longest service of the year. Two of its unique features are the *avodah* service and the martyrology. The *avodah* is a detailed recounting of the temple service on Yom Kippur. The service involved sacrifices and various cultic acts, as well as a series of confessions by the high priest on behalf of the priests and all of Israel. This elaborate ceremony was climaxed by the selection of one goat, the goat for *azazael* (meaning uncertain), which was taken to the desert and killed. This ritual, involving the original scapegoat, was to bring atonement for Israel's sins. The service was also highlighted by the high priest's entry into the holy-of-holies section of the temple. Entry into the holy of holies was only permitted on Yom Kippur and only to the high priest. The rabbis placed the *avodah* in the musaf service so that by commemorating it we might receive the atonement that the actual ritual was to have brought about.

While the high priest made confession (he did it three times), he would recite the *shem ha-meforash*—that is, he would pronounce the tetragrammaton, which we never pronounce today; in fact, we no longer know how it is meant to be pronounced. Upon hearing God's special name, the people would prostrate themselves completely. While prostration was a common form of obeisance in ancient times, we perform it only on Rosh ha-Shanah and Yom

As scholars have often noted, there is a basic difference between the orientation of the biblical Yom ha-Kippurim and Yom Kippur after the destruction of the temples. In biblical times, Yom Kippur served the function of cleansing the sanctuary, the abode of God, of any impurity, or ritual pollution, that might have penetrated the priestly system of controlling that which enters the sanctuary. Accidentally, or without the knowledge of the priests, violations of the Torah's code of holiness might accumulate to a dangerous level. Too much pollution will render the sanctuary defiled and push the divine presence away. So, whether it really is needed or not, once a year, on Yom Kippur, the sanctuary is purified lest the buildup of pollution become too serious.

Our Yom Kippur focuses on the behavior of the individual in his or her personal life and on the interaction of the community of Jews. Nevertheless, the motivation behind the biblical Yom Kippur is worth holding in mind. We must scrutinize our own lives carefully at least once each year so that we do not allow unwanted behavior to become so rigid that it will be too difficult to undo. We must repair the wounds we have inflicted before they develop into permanent ones. We must recharge our communities with a devotion to God and the holy lest we lose all sight of our purpose.

E.Gr.

In some not-so-traditional temples, people other than officiants also prostrate themselves, encouraged by the leaders of the service to join in this affecting ceremony. Moving to the grandeur of the awesome *alenu* melody for this day, with eyes closed, one drops to the knees at *va-a-nach-nu kor-im,* stretches forward at *u-mish-tai-cha-vim,* and places the forehead itself to the ground at *u-mo-dim,* remaining prostrate until the cantor, after some pause, resumes with *lif-ne melekh,* etc. At that point, either assisted by others or on one's own, one slowly rises and again opens the eyes.

It would be difficult to describe the inner effects of this act of prostration, but I do urge the reader to allow him/-herself the experience of this ancient

Jewish prayer posture—especially if one is already acquainted with or drawn to asanas (particular body postures in Hindu prayer). I can hardly overstate the power of this bodily position to evoke a sense of reverence and humility before the Divine. In the Bible we often read of prostration as an almost instinctive response to the sense of divine presence; in our day, by reverse dynamic, this same act of prostration may help us sense the divine presence.

E.Ge.

What have the laws of forbidden sexual relations to do with Yom Kippur? Well, among the many natural forces that move our lives are the sexual ones. On Yom Kippur we try, through fasting and other abstinence, to put such drives out of our minds and devote our attentions to our spiritual beings alone. As Yom Kippur wears on, the afternoon Torah reading reminds us to keep the lid on our physical passions and keep our minds on the demanding process of teshuvah. The Torah reading deals with the first issue; the haftarah—the Book of Jonah—deals with the second, teshuvah.

E.Gr.

Jonah is the great document of human change, and as such is given a central place in the Yom Kippur liturgy. As the day draws to a close and we feel near despair at our failure to achieve transformation, Jonah and the people of Nineveh are brought forth to tell us not to lose heart, that change is always possible, that all human lives can be given new beginnings.

The book documents two changes: that of the Ninevites and that of the prophet himself. The repentance of the Ninevites is of the more conventional kind: Warned of their destruction, they take the message to heart and return to God. But the book's deeper message may be the tale of Jonah himself, the hardened cynic who does not believe that their repentance will be real. He flees his task because he does not believe in people, does not believe that there will be an authentic change of heart. He is left without compassion, embittered by the ease with which God has let His sinners off the hook. Only

Kippur in memory of the temple service. (During the rest of the year, we just bow from the waist—for example, at *barekhu* or in the amidah.) It is done once on Rosh ha-Shanah (during the *aleinu* in the musaf amidah) and four times on Yom Kippur (at each retelling of the high priest's confession and at *aleinu*). In traditional synagogues, many people prostrate themselves by first dropping to their knees and then stretching their bodies so that their heads nearly touch the ground. In others, only the service leader and/or rabbi perform this prostration ritual. The *avodah* ends with the prayer of the high priest for the welfare of the people, which he uttered as he emerged from the holy of holies. *Martyrology.* Following the *avodah* is the martyrology section, which describes how many famous talmudic sages were cruelly martyred by the Romans during the reign of Hadrian. (While the text tells their fate as though they were all killed at the same time, in fact the killings took place over a period of time.) It is speculated that this section is recited on Yom Kippur to ask God to have mercy on Israel because of the ultimate sacrifice in God's honor made by these sages. One midrash states that God allowed the sages to be killed as a punishment for the sin of Joseph's ten brothers, who sold him into slavery—according to one tradition, on Yom Kippur. The martyrology text was composed after the Crusades and was an attempt to place the martyrdom of Jews of their own time in a larger context of martyrdom. The ten sages served as a model for them and for Jews of many other generations as well who faced death for their beliefs. Recently, some congregations and prayer books have revised the martyrology by adding to it material related to the Holocaust.

Musaf does not end with *aleinu* or any of the usual concluding hymns, for the day of Yom Kippur is marked by continuous services. However, many congregations take a break between musaf and minhah.

Minhah The minhah service is the shortest of the day. Its most distinctive features are not liturgical but rather its Torah and prophetic reading. Unlike other festivals, but like Shabbat, the Torah is read at minhah. The reading from Leviticus 18 talks about forbidden sexual relations. Why this is read is puzzling, and a couple of suggestions have been made:

1. On Yom Kippur, we must be especially careful in this area.
2. It reflects a strange tradition mentioned in the Talmud (*Mishnah Ta'anit* 4:8), which says that the fifteenth of Av (see p. 89) and Yom Kippur were the merriest days of the year, for young women would dress in white and go out in the fields to dance, and young men would come and choose brides.

Apparently, at one time the solemn mood of Yom Kippur ended with the temple ritual early in the afternoon, and the assumed forgiveness and absolution of the people was celebrated through dance and courtship. To remind people not to be carried away during the dancing, this Torah reading was chosen. Despite all these reasons, some have suggested that a more appropriate reading for Yom Kippur would be Leviticus 19:1–18, which speaks of being just and loving your neighbor.

Even on Shabbat there is no haftarah at minhah, but on Yom Kippur we read the Book of Jonah. Why Jonah is read has evoked many explanations, such as the following:

1. Here is an example of a whole city with no particular relationship to God who repent their evil ways and are forgiven. What better example of successful repentance and its consequence could be found!
2. A message Jonah does not comprehend until the very last line of the book is that God cares compassionately for all living things and prefers repentance to destruction. God's compassion is meant to be a model for us to copy.
3. Jonah shows us that we can not flee the service of God.

Neilah The concluding service of Yom Kippur takes its name and imagery from the symbol of the closing of the gates of heaven. Originally it may have referred to the closing of the temple gates. This imagery of time running out recurs throughout the service. For example, the liturgy is changed from *zakhreinu le-hayyim* to *hotmeinu le-hayyim*—from "remember us" to "seal us"—in the Book of Life. By custom the ark is left open beginning with the repetition of the Amidah to the end of neilah as a sign that we are trying to reach God with our prayers. Therefore, many people stand throughout neilah. (Most synagogues announce that those who do not feel up to standing should know it is permissible to be seated.) The viddui is shortened by the elimination of the *al heit* section as part of the sense of urgency as we approach the end of the service and the end of the day. Neilah concludes dramatically with the responsive recitation of the Shema, *barukh shem* (three times), and the phrase "The Lord is God" (seven times), followed by kaddish and then the final shofar blast.

The shofar, which is the central symbol of the High Holidays, marks the definitive end to the day and to the whole period. It evokes the feeling of a successful passage from sin to repentance, from death to life. Some commentators say it is blown as a reminder of the great shofar blast of the Jubilee year, which was blown every fifty years on Yom Kippur announcing the freedom of slaves and the reversion of all land to its original owners. The symbol of the Jubilee with its emphasis on being free and of everyone starting over again with the same amount of land (see Lev. 25:8–10) is most appropriate to the themes of repentance and of a new year of Yom Kippur and Rosh ha-Shanah.

After Yom Kippur, traditional synagogues recite ma'ariv and havdalah. Some have taken to blowing the shofar after ma'ariv to keep everyone there and prevent a noisy stampede for the exits while a faithful few recite ma'ariv. There is a custom of beginning the first few steps of building your sukkah, thus linking the festival of Sukkot to Yom Kippur.

the incident of the gourd, a simple thing of nature that he has come to love, reminds him that God's mercies know no bounds, and tells us that every human heart will sooner or later find that which calls it forth to open.

A.G.

No, Jonah had known all along that the Lord is compassionate toward all his creatures. He tells us in chapter 4, verse 2: "This was in fact my thinking when I was still in my land [at the beginning of the story]; for this reason I proceeded to flee to Tarshish: For I know that you are a God compassionate and kindly, patient and gracious, who is sorry for [doing] evil." Jonah understands God's nature well enough—but he disagrees with it! He has no compassion in him. He believes in strict, unmitigated justice. Whether Jonah becomes convinced of God's case at the end of the book is not the story's concern. The story ends without divulging Jonah's reaction because it is not so important how Jonah responds. It is crucial how we, the audience, respond. The ending of the tale is in our hands.

E.Gr.

This biblical attempt to maintain a stable, decentralized, smallholders base of society, with limits set to massive accumulations of wealth at the expense of a minimum subsistence base for each family unit, speaks challengingly to our own society. One could do worse than to spend some time during one of the Yom Kippur afternoon "intermissions" to explore what this might mean for our society. A helpful adjunct to the exploration might be E. F. Schumacher's *Small Is Beautiful* (Harper & Row paperback, 1975).

E.Ge.

KAVVANOT

The main preparation for Yom Kippur is to keep in mind what the day is about—teshuvah. We should approach Yom Kippur as the end of a long process of introspection leading to change. We should have already begun a turning away from our old ways and a turning toward God, a turning toward the other people in our lives, and, most important, a turning toward our true selves. Amid the imagery of doom, judgment, and sin, it is important to remember that Yom Kippur is not just a turning away from the negative but is a positive turning as well. This process should have begun in Elul and continued at a faster pace through Rosh ha-Shanah and the ten days of repentance. Yom Kippur's purpose is to give us a sense that time is running out. Yom Kippur stands at the end of the race, urging us on to make even greater efforts to cross the finish line before either time or our strength (commitment) runs out.

As such, some people have found it useful to see the Yom Kippur experience as a brush with our own mortality—with death. Hence we wear a white kittel, a robe that will serve as our shroud one day, and we abstain from those routine physical activities that keep us alive—eating and drinking. On this day, we confront that which we spend most of our lives denying—that we shall die and be no more. Yom Kippur awakens us to lead our lives more fully because we come face-to-face with and thus must acknowledge our own mortality.

Another image of Yom Kippur is that of making a journey, an experience we share with our fellow travelers—that is, the others we will be praying with during the next twenty-four hours. Some people like to begin this journey through time, if not space, with a prayer for a successful journey, adapted from the prayer traditionally recited before making long journeys:

> May it be Your will, Lord our God and God of our ancestors, to lead us in safety and to direct our steps in safety, to guide us to our desired destination in joy and peace and to bring us home in peace. Save us from all dangers and accidents, and from all afflictions that threaten our world. May You and all who we may meet look upon us with kindness, favor and mercy. Listen to our plea for You are God who hears prayers and pleas. Praised are You, O Lord, who listens to prayer. [The Hebrew text can be found in a traditional prayer book.]

Each of us will engage in this process in ways best suited for us. Since on Yom Kippur we do not atone for sins between us and our fellow humans, we should try to obtain forgiveness before the holiday from all those we might have hurt in the past year. This process of reconciliation has found a ritualized form in a prayer that recently some *havurot* have begun to recite at the end of the Kol Nidrei service. (A Hebrew version can be found on p. 350 of *Machzor for Rosh ha-Shanah and Yom Kippur,* edited by Jules Harlow, New York Rabbinical Assembly, 1972.)

> I hereby forgive all who have hurt me, all who have done me wrong, whether deliberately or by accident, whether by word or by deed. May no one be

punished on my account. As I forgive and pardon fully those who have done me wrong, may those whom I have harmed forgive and pardon me, whether I acted deliberately or by accident, whether by word or deed. I am now ready to fulfill the commandment of "to love my neighbor as myself."

Each person remains seated until he or she feels ready to recite the above, then quietly leaves the room. Whether placed in a ritual context or not, the mitzvah of loving your neighbor must be confronted on this day.

THE IMPLICATIONS OF TESHUVAH

Yom Kippur is supposed to lead from thought to deed—from looking at ourselves to transforming the way we act. The haftarah of Yom Kippur is a striking statement of the larger importance of the day and warns us against the danger of thinking that all this praying in and of itself is enough. Instead in the haftarah God quotes our words and answers us:

"Why, when we fasted, did You not see? When we starved our bodies, did You pay no heed?" Because on your fast day you see to your business and oppress all your laborers! Because you fast in strife and contention, and you strike with a wicked fist! Your fasting today is not such as to make your voice heard on high. Is such the fast I desire, a day for men to starve their bodies? Is it bowing the head like a bullrush and lying in sackcloth and ashes? Do you call that a fast, a day when the Lord is favorable? No, this is the fast I desire: To unlock the fetters of wickedness, and untie the cords of the yoke to let the oppressed go free; to break off every yoke. It is to share your bread with the hungry, and to take the wretched poor into your home; when you see the naked, to clothe him, and not to ignore your own kin [Isa. 58:3–7].

Personal change is to lead us to work for social justice in the world, not to an ascetic withdrawal from the impurities of the world. Projects in support of tzedakah and social justice should be given extra attention at this time of year.

Within the lengthy liturgy, there is much room for "new" prayers, meditations, intentions that individuals or groups may want to add. Many people have added to the martyrology section of musaf, which speaks of Rabbi Akiva and other rabbinic martyrs of long ago, and more-recent material that focuses particularly on the Holocaust. Another place for creative interpretation is also found in musaf, in the *avodah* section. The *avodah* recounts the elaborate temple ritual for Yom Kippur. Recently, some people have tried to recapture some sense of the drama of the day by using more accessible descriptions taken from the Mishnah's description of the ritual rather than from the traditional medieval piyyut with its difficult Hebrew.

Some groups gather to study if there is a break between services in the afternoon of Yom Kippur. The study is related to the themes of Yom Kippur. Alternatively, some groups gather to study after a break following Kol Nidrei. Since Kol Nidrei is over relatively early, there is a whole evening during which it is hard to find something appropriate to do. A study session fills the time with a worthwhile activity.

I don't see how we can become reconciled with our friends by means of liturgy. We cannot be forgiven without apologizing and asking for forgiveness; we cannot forgive until we are addressed. We must be bold enough to speak to those whom we have wronged, whether they know it or not, and we must perform the ofttimes humiliating and cathartic act of seeking forgiveness. The liturgy can provide a stimulus, but it cannot serve in lieu of a person-to-person dialogue. That is the wisdom of beginning the Ten Days of Teshuvah with Rosh ha-Shanah and following it with seven days for human interaction before Yom Kippur.

E.GR.

Before Yom Kippur began in our community, we handed out four different sets of blank cards, each set a different color. Each became one of the *al heit* confessionals recited on Yom Kippur. The one for Kol Nidrei/ma'ariv focused on sins of a person against his or her own self; the second, for shaharit, focused on those between a person and God; those of musaf on sins against a fellow human; and those of minhah on sins against the universe/nature. People wrote down sins that they had committed in the past year on the appropriate cards without signing their names. The cards were shuffled and each person received one. We stood in a circle and read them. Knowing these were real, not some standard list of the prayer book, made these *al heit* powerful experiences.

Z.S.

For the process of teshuvah, make a complete inventory of yourself: Who is in your inner audience? On your board of directors? What kind of parts are you playing? What would you like to play? What are your "rats" à la *1984*? What are your masculine traits? What are your feminine?, etc.

Z.S.

One model for an approach to Yom Kippur services is the description of the cleansing of the sanctuary found in Leviticus 16. Thus: Ma'ariv becomes the cleansing of the will (the *sefirah* of *keter*). Shaharit is the cleansing of the mind (*hokhmah, binah, da'at*), while musaf is the cleansing of the heart (*hesed, gevurah, tiferet*). Minhah is the cleansing of functions *(netzah, hod, yesod)*, while neilah concludes with the *sefirah* of *malkhut* that involves completion.

                                        Z.S.

One may also augment the story by reading other literature that draws its inspiration from Jonah. At least every other year, and sometimes annually, I ask a member of our temple who reads effectively aloud to read Father Mapple's deeply moving sermon from Reb Hayim Melville's *Moby Dick* (chapters 8 and 9). Another year the selection may be Hayim Greenberg's "Go to Nineveh," or Ernst Simon's "Meditation"; but always I return to Melville, and never does the sermon fail to stir me. In this adaptation as in so many others, both the message and the drama of Jonah retain their freshness and vitality.

                                        E.GE.

For those confined to an indoor service, an alternative is to make sure that no artificial illumination lights the sanctuary from minhah onward. The total dependence on natural light makes all of us keenly aware of the fading of the day, and the sharing of the deepening dusk is a tenderly touching communal experience.

A further advantage: As darkness falls, not even cantor or rabbi can see the text, so the service must end by a reasonable hour.

                                        E.GE.

ENDING THE DAY

As Yom Kippur draws to a close, we have the short service of minhah, distinguished by the reading of the Book of Jonah. The story of Jonah lends itself both to study and to retelling for children (and adults). The dramatic last service, neilah, focuses on the image of the gates of heaven closing, presenting us with our very last chance to do teshuvah. To highlight this theme of the day ending, one group recently held its neilah services on the roof of its building so that the setting sun served as a backdrop to the words of the liturgy.

Another custom is to go outside after havdalah to perform the ritual of blessing the moon. In traditional circles, Jews go outside near the beginning of every month and bless the moon in a ritual found in any traditional prayer book. One part of the ritual is saying *"Shalom aleikhem"*—"Peace unto you"— to three people, who are to respond with *"Aleikhem shalom"*—"For you, peace." The Jewish people have often been compared to the moon, which waxes and wanes and waxes again. According to a midrash, the moon will be restored to a splendor equal to the sun's in the end of days. Because this ritual asks for blessings on the people Israel and for the final redemption, it is a particularly appropriate way for a group to end the experience of spending twenty-four hours in prayer together.

FOODS AND CRAFTS

Yom Kippur is necessarily lacking in both foods and craft projects. However, Yom Kippur is preceded and followed by meals that are affected by their relationship to it. The *seudah ha-mafseket,* which precedes Yom Kippur, is a full meal and in traditional circles is usually similar to a Friday night meal—soup and chicken, etc. To help with the fasting, it is advisable to drink a lot of liquids on the day before Yom Kippur. For those who drink a lot of caffeine, it is a good idea to begin gradually cutting down during the week before Yom Kippur. This will prevent symptoms of caffeine withdrawal on Yom Kippur, such as headaches and other unwelcome afflictions.

The post–Yom Kippur break-the-fast meal should be made up of foods very different from those of the pre–Yom Kippur meal. They should be light and not very spicy so as to give your shrunken stomach time to get used to regular eating. The break-fast is a good way for a group to end the Yom Kippur experience together.

DERASH

TURNING TOWARD TESHUVAH

Yom Kippur is a day of physical abstinence for the purpose of spiritual toil. We do not eat, drink, or make love. Some people wear a kittel, a white

robe that is also used as a shroud at traditional funerals. On Yom Kippur, we
are meant to feel the touch of death, for death cuts through all the defenses
and illusions we have carefully created around our own mortality. The whole
world is suspended in judgment on Yom Kippur—who shall live and who
shall die. Over and over, the liturgy stresses our frailty, our failings, our
worthlessness. All our egotism is stripped away. We stand before the one who
sees all and are forced to confront our innermost selves. Yom Kippur is a true
mirror that reflects back to us what we really are. It is as though, like the first
humans, we have eaten of the Tree of Knowledge and *know* that we are guilty
and naked and thus are embarrassed. On Yom Kippur, everything is clear,
everything is black and white, morally speaking, with no shading of colors.
The masks, disguises, clothes are all gone and only you and your Creator
remain. Thus, the first step in the process of teshuvah is to recognize without
illusions who we are.

We are then ready to begin the struggle to purge those traits we do not
like in ourselves and revitalize our souls for the new year. Feeling regret for
the past, we commit ourselves to change—to do teshuvah. *Teshuvah* is usually
translated as repentance, and the process certainly contains the component
of repenting what was done in the past. But the word also means turning or
returning, for the process involves a turning back to God.

On Yom Kippur, we recognize our aloneness and seek to repair our relationships to others. Central to this is our relationship to God. God says to us,
"Turn toward me and I will turn toward you." We ask that our days be
renewed as of old *(Hadesh yameinu ke-kedem).* Literally, this means "Make our
days new as of old"—a paradox that captures the sense of a reconnection to
the way we were or at least the way we should be. We try to make the old
new, not to discard it. We go back to go forward. By repairing the breach
between ourselves and the Divine Other, we can also begin to repair the many
breaches between ourselves and the myriads of people with whom we have
relationships.

Yom Kippur calls for profound reexamination of our self-definition and
our relationship to the rest of the world. The tradition recognizes the difficulty of this process and sets aside the day of Yom Kippur specifically and
this whole period more generally to force us to focus on a subject we prefer
to avoid. All of us are like Jonah, ready to flee to some exotic Tarshish rather
than face the reality of who we are and, even more threatening, the possibility
that we could become different.

Ironically, Jonah is the only successful prophet in the whole Bible, the
only one whom people listen to and who causes them to actually change their
ways. Yet it is his knowledge that he will succeed, not doubts about a possible
failure, that causes Jonah to flee. Jonah is not afraid that the people of
Nineveh will dismiss him as a quack; rather, he knows that they will repent.
As he says: "O Lord! Isn't this just what I said when I was still in my own
country? That is why I fled beforehand to Tarshish. For I know that You are
a compassionate and gracious God. . . . Please, Lord, take my life, for I would
rather die than live."

Rather than face that possibility, he flees. To the end, Jonah resists any

sense of responsibility for the fate of the world or his own fate. Jonah lacks compassion for the people of the city, a compassion found in everyone else in the story, including the sailors, who are extremely reluctant to throw Jonah overboard. Lacking compassion for others, he lacks compassion for himself. Fearing teshuvah and change in others, he fears change in himself and flees the truth, only to find it at least for a moment in the dark depths of the whale.

Rosh ha-Shanah and Yom Kippur together affirm the chance for positive change; for no matter how old or routine, there is hope for new birth and new ways. Each year these days ask us, "Which shall it be, Tarshish or Nineveh? Darkness or light? Death or life?"

THE NEW BEFORE THE OLD

Why does Yom Kippur follow Rosh ha-Shanah? Should it not be the other way around—first a settling of accounts for the previous year and then a celebration of a new year with its promise of change and its potential for betterment? Is it not necessary to clear away the old, to repent for the past, before we can really welcome the new?

The hope for a *new* year must precede a systematic review of the old, for it shakes us awake to the possibility of renewal. The new year calls on us to join in the struggle to transform ourselves. The shofar blasts are meant to arouse our slothful selves to the new possibilities that await us. Once conscious of the new year and what it offers, we are ready to look back at our past. Conscious that life can be as sweet as apples dipped in honey, that the barren woman can bear fruit even in old age, and that the descending knife can be halted in midair, we approach Yom Kippur with the hope for growth and change and with full consciousness of our failures in the past year.

A MEDITATION ON WORDS FOR YOM KIPPUR

On Yom Kippur, the day when we need the help of the shofar to pierce all the barriers between us and heaven, we are very much alone. We receive no outside help in communicating. There are just ourselves and a constant flow of the words of prayer.

Words are important in the tradition. The world itself was created by God through the power of the word. We begin Yom Kippur with Kol Nidrei, proclaiming all our vows are naught. Like lovers making up only to know the futility of it all for they will quarrel again, we begin by declaring that all New Year resolutions will be broken.

Since the Tower of Babel, God and humans have been searching to recapture that one language in which people could express themselves so clearly that everyone else and God could instantly comprehend them. We have been trying to recapture a time when our purpose was clear—a time when we almost reached the heavens using a structure of language. Only this time, God would no longer be afraid but eager for us to come close.

On Yom Kippur, we use speech in an effort to create a new world for ourselves, thus imitating God who created this world through the use of the word. We echo His words: In the beginning, there was void and chaos and darkness covering the abyss, and God *said,* "Let there be light." And there was light.

We strive again and again to find the right words, sounds, inflections, and movements. We chant Kol Nidrei, declaring our vows nullified, in a manner that says we are of the utmost seriousness. If the words say the opposite of what we mean, it is due only to the inadequacy of our language.

On this day, let us be like Moses, heavy of tongue, who had to struggle over each sound. On this day when we shall say more words than on any other day in the year, we strive to find one sentence, phrase, word, or letter that will begin here on earth and reach to the heavens.

With longing I read that "the descending knife can be halted in midair." Would that the same were true of missiles! That it is not should surely be remarked, with musing on the possible consequences thereof!

E.GE.

Open for us the gates of
light, blessing, joy, knowledge, splendor, confession, merit, compassion,
purity, salvation, atonement, kindness, forgiveness, solace, pardon, as-
sistance, sustenance, righteousness, uprightness, healing, peace, and re-
pentance.

A season is set for everything, a time for every experience under heaven. Eccl. 9:7

A time for planting and a time for plucking that which is planted

Go, eat your bread in gladness and drink your wine in joy.

בָּרוּךְ אַתָּה יהוה
אֱלֹהֵינוּ מֶלֶךְ הָעוֹלָם
אֲשֶׁר קִדְּשָׁנוּ בְּמִצְוֹתָיו
וְצִוָּנוּ לֵישֵׁב בַּסֻּכָּה.

SUKKOT
CREATING SHELTER

Sukkot, usually translated as Tabernacles or the Festival of Booths, occurs for seven days, from Tishri 15 to 21. There is therefore a quick transition from the High Holidays, with their somber mood of repentance and judgment, to a holiday of rejoicing and celebration for which we are commanded to build a hut (sukkah; plural sukkot) and make it our home.

Sukkot is the third pilgrimage festival. It continues the story of the Israelites, which began with the Exodus from Egypt (Passover) and the giving of the Torah at Sinai (Shavuot) and now ends with the wandering in the desert. Thus while Sukkot has some connections to the High Holiday period preceding it, it is more intrinsically a part of the other major festival cycle of Passover, Shavuot and Sukkot.

Like the other pilgrimage festivals, Sukkot has an agricultural element. It marks the time of the harvest, of the final ingathering of produce before the oncoming winter. Hence, it is also called *hag-ha-asif*—the festival of ingathering. As it is written: "You shall celebrate the festival of ingathering, at the end of the year, when you gather in your labors out of the field" (Exod. 23:16). Some scholars maintain that the practice of living in huts comes from this agricultural background rather than from the wandering in the desert. During harvests, the workers would live in temporary huts in the fields. These scholars argue that our sukkot with their leafy roofs bear a greater resemblance to these harvesters' huts than to the dwellings of desert nomads.

Whether this theory is correct or not, both elements, the agricultural and the mythic/historical, play important roles in the makeup of the festival.

Another basic motif of Sukkot is that of joy. Sukkot is called *zeman simhateinu*—the season of our rejoicing. Whether this is because we have successfully completed the harvest or because we have finished the process of repentance of the Days of Awe, we are meant to have a sense of fulfillment and security.

In biblical times, Sukkot was the most important festival of all; in fact, it was referred to simply as *ha-hag*—"the festival" (e.g., 1 Kings 12:32). Pilgrims would come from all over Israel up to Jerusalem to observe the colorful and elaborate temple rites, which included a large number of sacrifices each day (see Num. 29). As *the* holiday of the biblical period, Sukkot was chosen for the consecration of the temple by Solomon (1 Kings 8). It was also the occasion every seven years for the ceremony of *hak'heil*—the public reading of the Torah before the whole people (Deut. 31:10–13). Sukkot is *the* festival of the future, too—for in the messianic period, all the nations will come up to Jerusalem and celebrate Sukkot (Zech. 14:16).

There are three mitzvot (commandments) concerning Sukkot found in the Torah: (1) living in the sukkah, (2) gathering together the four species, and (3) rejoicing during the holiday. Other rituals/customs include the reciting of the hoshana prayers while making circuits in the synagogue; reading the Book of Ecclesiastes; inviting *ushpizin*—symbolic guests—to the sukkah; and finally the special rituals involved with Hoshana Rabbah, the seventh day of Sukkot. (While often thought of as part of Sukkot, the holidays of Shemini Atzeret and Simhat Torah are basically independent festivals and will be discussed in the next chapter.)

TRADITIONS

THE SUKKAH

"You shall live in huts seven days; all citizens of Israel shall live in huts, in order that future generations may know that I made the Israelite people live in huts when I brought them out of the land of Egypt, I the Lord your God. [Lev. 23:42, 43]

The most important ritual of Sukkot (hence the name) is living in a sukkah. The sukkah is a temporary structure usually constructed of four walls and covered with a roof of tree branches. We eat in the sukkah and some people sleep in it as well. The sukkah is constructed before the holiday, usually between Yom Kippur and Sukkot, and is used for the first time on Sukkot Eve.

The basic concepts affecting the nature of and laws about the sukkah reflect the holiday's historical and agricultural background:

- The sukkah must be a temporary structure, not a permanent one. This is to remind us of the portability of the huts in the desert as the Israelites wandered from place to place for forty years. It also stresses one of the themes of the holiday—the impermanence of our lives.
- On the other hand, we are to treat the sukkah as our home during the holiday. The rabbinic principle for this is the verse "You shall live" (Lev. 23:42), which is taken to mean that we shall live in the same manner as we ordinarily live. Hence the rabbis said, "All the seven days [of Sukkot] one should make his sukkah his permanent abode, and his house his temporary abode. In what manner? If he has beautiful vessels, he should bring them into the sukkah; beautiful couches, he should bring them into the sukkah . . . he should eat and drink and pass his leisure in the sukkah; he should also engage in rabbinic study in the sukkah" (*Sukkah* 28b).
- The roof (*skhakh*: literally, covering) is the key element in the makeup of the sukkah. Most halakhic discussions about whether a particular sukkah is "kosher" or not focus on the issue of the *skhakh*. It, too, must be of a temporary nature, and it must be made of organic material— specifically, something that has grown and subsequently been detached from the ground. Branches (especially evergreens), lathing, and bamboo poles are the most frequently used materials. There should be enough *skhakh* to ensure more shade than sun in the sukkah, but not so much as to prevent us from seeing the stars at night.
- The holiday of Sukkot is associated with beauty, and therefore we put creative effort into decorating the sukkah. The Talmud suggests hanging "handmade carpets and tapestries, nuts, almonds, peaches, pomegranates, branches of grape, vines, [decanters of] oil, fine meal, wreaths of ears of corn" (*Betzah* 30b). Standard decorations include paper chains, crepe paper, fruit, Indian corn, and gourds as well as pictures of Jerusalem and the prayer for *ushpizin* (see below).

Using the Sukkah Today, we use the sukkah mostly for eating. There is a special obligation to do so on the first night. On that night, even if it is raining, we try to eat a token meal by reciting kiddush over wine and the blessing of *motzi* for bread.

We are encouraged to study, read, and talk in the sukkah, but only if it can be done comfortably. There is a general principle that you should rejoice in the sukkah, not suffer in it. Because sleeping in the sukkah could be unpleasant if not unbearable, especially in the Northern Hemisphere, many rabbis declared that it was no longer required. Similarly, if you cannot concentrate on your study while in the sukkah, you are free to study elsewhere.

Even with regard to eating in the sukkah, the rabbis exempted us if it is raining. In fact, the tradition denounces those who continue to eat in the sukkah in the rain. "Whoever is exempt from eating in the sukkah and does not go out from the sukkah, does not receive a reward [for fulfilling a mitzvah] and is nothing but an ignoramus" (*Shulhan Arukh*). If this person recites the blessing for the sukkah, it is considered a *berakhah le-vatalah*—the taking

Sukkot—the last of the three pilgrimage festivals—is in a way the paradigm for the Jewish festivals as a whole. Precisely as the Jewish calendar enables us to impose rich meaning upon bare time, so that we are blessed with Tishri instead of a mere September, so Sukkot commands us to construct Jewish space—which, whatever our surroundings, for eight days becomes a world. The Israelites, in their wilderness wanderings, built the tabernacle; we, in our dispersions in the unredeemed world, construct the sukkah, and try to fill it with only good things. At Pesah we set the seder table so that the symbols we placed on it could remind us of why we put them there. At Shavuot we *did* nothing, but, like Israel at Sinai, simply strained to hear the words of the living God. At Sukkot we build, because the only way to have order in a wilderness is to construct it there—which is also, of course, the only way that we, God's partners, can bring (His) meaning to life in the world.

A.E.

If you, as we, grow sweet corn and-/or popcorn, the cornstalks make fine *skhakh* also. And if you don't grow them, try to locate a nearby farm where you can go to cut some cornstalks for your sukkah. Besides their contribution to the sukkah, the stalks will also entice you to the country, a fine preparation for this agriculture-based festival.

E.Ge.

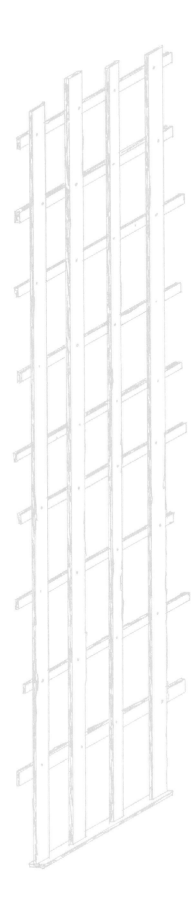

of God's name in vain, which is forbidden. You are exempt from eating in the sukkah if it is raining enough to make you feel uncomfortable or, in the rabbis' terms, if it will spoil the soup. Once you enter the house because it is raining, you are not obligated to return to the sukkah for that meal even if the rain stops.

Thus the mitzvah to especially rejoice on Sukkot gives rise to an unusual attitude in the rabbis. Whereas they will often make exemptions to various other laws but encourage people to go beyond the letter of the law and perform the mitzvah anyway, their attitude is the opposite in regard to the sukkah. The rabbis are saying that you *must* leave the sukkah if it is raining. In this way, they try to ensure that the sukkah will be seen as a symbol of joy, not as a burden. Similarly, the RaMA states that if on Shabbat the light in your sukkah blows out and you have a light on in your house, you should eat there (unless you can eat in a neighbor's sukkah without great difficulty); it is more important to enjoy Shabbat and the holiday than to eat in the sukkah and curse the darkness. This ruling gives an even broader sense to what is exemptive discomfort and stresses again the importance of enjoying the sukkah.

THE RITUAL

On the first night of Sukkot, we light candles in the sukkah and recite:

> Praised are you, Lord our God, Ruler of the universe, who has sanctified us through His commandments, commanding us to kindle the festival lights.

Then we recite the *she-he-heyanu* blessing:

> Praised are you, Lord our God, Ruler of the universe, for keeping us in life, for sustaining us, and for helping us reach this moment.

If the candles are in danger of being blown out, then someone other than the person who lit them carries them into the house. (For the candlelighter, the holiday and all its restrictions began with the lighting of the candles. Therefore, someone else should carry the candles.)

Unlike the practice for Shabbat candlelighting, we first say the *berakhah* and then light the candles.

After evening services, or in general when you are ready to eat, the festival kiddush is recited over wine. Then the blessing for the Sukkah is recited:

> Praised are you, Lord our God, Ruler of the universe, who has sanctified us through His commandments, commanding us to live in the sukkah.

This is followed by the *she-he-heyanu* blessing (unless you recited it earlier at candlelighting). By saying the *she-he-heyanu* blessing last, we make it refer to both the first day of the festival and the first use of the sukkah.

For those who observe the second day of yom tov, the same procedure is followed except that the *she-he-heyanu* precedes the blessing for the sukkah.

Traditionally this is followed by a ritual washing of hands and by the *motzi* over bread. It is customary to have two loaves of bread for the meal just as on Shabbat.

During the rest of the week, the pattern generally agreed upon is *motzi* followed by the blessing for the sukkah.

Anyone who forgets to say the blessing can do so as long as he or she is still eating. It is customary to recite the blessing only when eating a meal, whether in a neighbor's sukkah or your own; not if you are just visiting.

USHPIZIN

There is a custom of inviting *ushpizin*—symbolic guests—each day to join us in the sukkah. These honorary guests are Abraham, Isaac, Jacob, Joseph, Moses, Aaron, and David. One is invited each day. This custom was popularized by the kabbalists of Safed, who composed the short formula that is recited. For the kabbalists, each guest represented one of the *sefirot*—the spheres that make up the universe—in the kabbalistic system. By inviting them, they were adding a different mystical significance to each day.

Recently some people have invited the matriarchs and other important women of the Bible to also be *ushpizin* in the sukkah. One list includes Sarah, Rachel, Rebecca, Leah, Miriam, Abigail, and Esther.

Sephardim set aside an ornate chair for the honored guest and recite, "This is the chair of the *ushpizin.*"

There is another connection between the *ushpizin* and Sukkot. All of the *ushpizin* were wanderers or exiles: Abraham left his father's house to go to Israel; all three patriarchs wandered in the land of Canaan, dealing with the rulers from a position of disadvantage; Jacob fled to Laban; Joseph was exiled from his family; Moses fled Egypt for Midian and later, together with Aaron, led the people for forty years wandering in the desert; and David fled from Saul. The theme of wandering and homelessness symbolized by the temporariness of the sukkah is reflected in the lives of the *ushpizin.*

THE FOUR SPECIES

The other important mitzvah is that of the *arba minim*—the four species —also called the lulav and etrog (palm branch and citron).

> On the first day you shall take the product of goodly trees, branches of palm trees, boughs of leafy trees, and willows of the brook, and you shall rejoice before the Lord your God seven days. [Lev. 23:40]

"The product of goodly trees" is interpreted by the rabbis to refer specifically to an etrog (citron), and the "branches of palm trees," "boughs of leafy trees," and "willows of the brook" have been interpreted as a lulav (palm branch), *hadasim* (myrtle), and *aravot* (willows), respectively.

The four species emphasize the agricultural nature of Sukkot. Just as the farmer harvests his crops, so we gather four kinds of growing things and use them to praise God for the bounty He has provided us.

In extending the invitation to the *ushpizin,* the Aramaic formula reportedly used by Rabbi Isaac Luria can be intoned to wonderful effect:

Ú-lu ush-pí-zin i-lá-in ka-dí-shin!
Ú-lu a-vá-han i-lá-in ka-dí-shin!
Té-vu ush-pí-zin i-lá-in, té-vu!
Té-vu ush-pí-zin m'hem-nú-ta, té-vu!

(Enter, exalted, sacred guests!
Enter, exalted, sacred ancestors!
Be seated, exalted guests!
Be seated, faithful guests!)

Emanating from the small, foliage-covered hut, with the candlelight flickering, the leaves rustling, and moonlight filtering through from above, this invitation to the ancestral spirits may receive more of a response than one could imagine by the bright light of day.

E.GE.

Treat each *ushpizin* as a real presence in the sukkah. Set aside a chair for him or her. Try to see the world through the eyes of an Abraham or Rachel. What idols would Abraham smash today? Ponder each of these figures and their characteristics. If you are in a group, ask each person to have a conversation with the *ushpizin* for the day and then discuss the different Isaacs and Miriams that emerge from those conversations. A different list of female *ushpizin* attuned to the *sefirot* is Miriam, Leah, Hannah, Rebecca, Sarah, Tamar, and Rachel.

Z.S.

Gaster points out that the four species have parallels to other harvest/agricultural festivals; in particular he compares the lulav to the Maypole.

M.S.

The emphasis on the number 4 at Sukkot seems especially appropriate for a festival so rooted in the earth. The four winds, the four directions, and the four seasons are all reminders of how related to the growth cycle is the number 4.

E.Ge.

Rabbi Yehuda Aryeh Leib of Ger points out that in gematria, lulav (68) equals in numerical value *hayim* (68)—life. No wonder there is such vitality transmitted by this symbol!

E.Ge.

The reason the etrog is held upside down has to do with the halakhah concerning *berakhot.* A *berakhah* is supposed to be recited immediately preceding the fulfillment of the commandment. Some of the rabbis felt it would be too long a delay to say the blessing, pick up the four species from the table, and shake them. On the other hand, if you were first to pick up the four species and then recite the *berakhah,* you might have already fulfilled the commandment before reciting the blessing. Thus they devised this procedure in which you first pick up the four species but hold the etrog upside down so that you have not fulfilled the commandment. You then recite the blessing and immediately turn the etrog right side up and thus fulfill the mitzvah.

M.S.

In ancient times, the four species were used in the temple each day of Sukkot. Outside of the temple, they were used only on the first day of Sukkot. After the second temple was destroyed (A.D. 70), only on the first day was the taking of the four species still considered a biblical commandment. Yet the rabbis instructed that the taking of the four species be performed the rest of the days of Sukkot as a remembrance of the temple (except on Shabbat, lest someone carry them to the synagogue).

Using the Four Species The basic commandment of the four species consists of holding them in your hand and then shaking them. The four species are also used at two points in the morning service: during hallel and during hoshanot (explained below).

The four species more specifically consist of a long palm branch that has a holder made of palm leaves. In the holder on your left side, you place two willows *(aravot)* and on the right side you place three myrtles *(hadasim).* The citron (etrog) is not attached with the other three species. (See p. 223, "Buying the Four Species," for more details.)

The attention paid to the aesthetic dimension during this holiday pertains to the four species as well as to the sukkah. The concept of *hiddur mitzvah*—beautifying the commandments—means that we should obtain the most beautiful example of each species, especially of the etrog. According to halakhah, a dried-up specimen of any of the four species is *pasul*—invalid for fulfilling the mitzvah. As the rabbis quoted when rejecting a dried-out lulav, "The dead shall not praise you" (Ps. 115:17). Thus you will often see people examining one etrog after another with a magnifying glass until they find the perfect one. This desire for beautifying the mitzvah, as with all good things, can be carried too far. People have been known to spend exorbitant sums for their etrogim. To prevent the exploitation and competition that is fostered, a few rabbis and Hasidic *rebbeim* annually set a maximum price to be paid for an etrog.

The Ritual. The procedure for reciting the *berakhah* is as follows:

1. While standing, pick up the lulav with its attached willows and myrtle in your right hand. Hold the lulav so that its spine is toward you. (The spine is the long green stem that runs the length of the lulav. The yellower and flatter side is the back of the lulav. The side that rises in ridges has the spine in the center.)
2. Pick up the etrog in your left hand with its tip *(pitom)* pointing down. If you have an etrog that comes naturally without a *pitom,* look for the top of the fruit (the narrower end, as in a pear) and turn the etrog upside down. Hold the etrog next to the lulav.
3. Recite the blessing:

Praised are you, Lord our God, Ruler of the universe, who has sanctified us through His commandments commanding us concerning the waving of the palm branch.

On the first day only, then recite *she-he-heyanu:*

Praised are you, Lord our God, Ruler of the universe, for keeping us in life, for sustaining us, and for helping us reach this moment.

4. Turn the etrog right side up and shake the lulav.

The blessing can be recited at home. It is customary to perform it in the sukkah, thus combining the two symbols of the holiday. Many say it in the morning service right before hallel.

Some Sephardim simply recite the blessing and then pick up the lulav and etrog.

The Number Four In the rabbinic tradition, interpretations of the lulav and etrog are linked to the number four, and thus the four species have led to a variety of typologies.

One well-known interpretation sees the four species as symbolic of four types of Jews. The etrog has taste and fragrance and so stands for those Jews who possess learning and good deeds. The palm tree has taste but not fragrance, like Jews who possess learning but not good deeds. The myrtle has fragrance and not taste, like Jews who possess good deeds but not learning. The willow has neither, just as there are Jews who are neither good nor learned. God declares that to destroy the last group is impossible, so instead let them all be tied together and they will atone for each other.

Another interpretation views the four species as symbolic of a person. The lulav stands for the spine of a person, the myrtle the eyes, the willow the mouth, and the etrog the heart. Through the four species, we express our desire to praise and worship God with our vital parts.

Another interpretation states that the four species bespeak land and settledness, fruit and fertility, in contrast to the sukkah, which bespeaks wandering and rootlessness, dryness and sand.

A mystical interpretation begins with the obvious masculine imagery in the lulav and the feminine breast imagery in the etrog. The four species are seen as conduits of the divine flow into the world, each representing one of the four letters of God's special name, with the lulav as the letter *vav,* which is the main channel for that flow. There is a striving for union, out of which comes blessing. On this level, the desire for the perfect etrog takes on further significance.

The Four Species in Folk Tradition Two of the four species have additional symbolism attached to them.

According to one tradition, the etrog, not the apple, is the fruit eaten by Eve and Adam in the Garden of Eden. Only the etrog tree has wood and fruit that are good to taste (see Gen. 3:6). Perhaps because of this tradition, the etrog in Jewish folk medicine is seen as useful for facilitating births. The pains of childbirth were Eve's "punishment" for eating the fruit in the Garden. This tradition appears already in the Talmud (*Menahot* 27a), which also suggests that pregnant women eat the etrog in order to have "fragrant" children. There arose a custom for women to bite the *pitom* off the etrog after services on Hoshana Rabbah (when the etrog's ritual use was finished). In this way the women were demonstrating that, unlike Eve, they had resisted the temptation

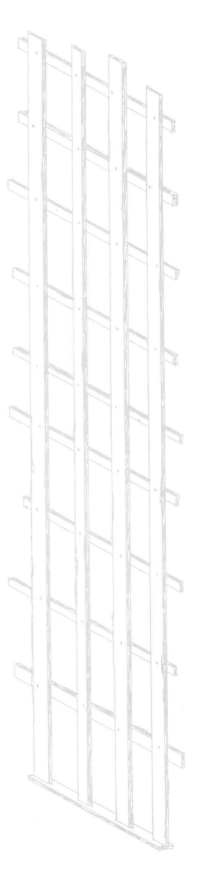

The *pitom* is, of course, the remains of the blossom, once fragrant and beautiful but now quite dried and shriveled, within which the fruit first began to form. When fresh and young, neither human eyes nor honeybees could resist its beauty; now, old and shriveled, it seems an unnecessary residue, perhaps even a distasteful reminder of the ravages of time.

How considerate, then, to insist that the *pitom,* although desiccated, be included in the joyous celebration using the fruit to which it gave birth! A touching instance of *Al tashlikhenu l'et zikna* —"Cast us not off in old age."

Interesting, also, that the *pitom,* which might be construed as the shriveled remnant of the womb, is by folk tradition especially connected with the women of the community.

E.GE.

We become the wielders of magic when we shake the four species in all directions. On one level, we are dispersing the bad winds that cause a disastrous agricultural season (too little or too much rain). On another level, we are extending God to *eyn sof*—the place of infinity. This is a primitive act with many layers of symbolism, the most obvious being the joining of a phallus (lulav) with a womb/cervix (etrog). In the language of the kabbalistic *sefirot,* the three myrtles are *hesed, gevurah,* and *tiferet;* the two *aravot* are *netzah* and *hod;* the lulav is *yesod;* the etrog is *malkhut.* The meaning of the ritual is so important that even those worshipers without the four species should stretch themselves in the six directions in order to make manifest the rule of the Holy One.

Z.S.

to eat the etrog until it was no longer needed for Sukkot. (Great custom!) The *pitom* on the etrog was placed under the pillow of or near a woman in difficult labor to ameliorate the pain.

Myrtle *(hadasim)* has many associations with festivities, especially weddings. It was used in bridal processions and to make wreaths for the heads of bridegrooms, and is still used by some people for the spices used in havdalah (marking the end of Shabbat). It also has some connection with the messianic theme of Sukkot as it appears in that context in Isaiah describing the return to Zion:

> Yes, you shall leave in joy and be led home secure. Before you, mount and hill shall shout aloud; and all the trees of the field shall clap their hands. Instead of the briar, a cypress shall rise; instead of the nettle, a myrtle shall rise. These shall stand as a testimony to the Lord, as an everlasting sign that shall not perish. [Isa. 55:12–13]

Caring for the Four Species The four species are used each day of Sukkot (except on Shabbat). The blessing is recited, they are shaken during hallel, and carried as we circle the synagogue during the daily hoshanot. The four species require some care to remain fresh for the whole holiday. Many keep the *hadasim* and *aravot* (still in their holder—you will tear off the bottom leaves if you try to take them out) in the refrigerator wrapped in a damp towel and/or in aluminum foil. Some people put the lulav and myrtles and willows in a plastic bag with a little water in it and then tie the bag shut. Since the willows tend to dry out, it is best to buy them as close to the holiday as possible. The RaMA mentions people buying new *aravot* each day, but almost no one goes to that length anymore. The lulav and etrog will not dry up during the holiday. To prevent the etrog from being damaged, etrog holders have existed as a form of Jewish folk art for centuries. These boxlike structures have been made from all kinds of material ranging from wood to pottery to silver. If you do not have a special etrog holder, keep the etrog wrapped up in the soft packing material in the box it came in.

Hallel As mentioned, many precede the hallel service with the recital of the *berakhah* for lulav. During Sukkot, hallel is recited every day right after the morning amidah. When certain of its verses are recited, we hold the lulav and etrog and shake it in all directions. There are different customs, but the most common pattern is as follows: twice in the first *hodu ladonai* (Ps. 118:1); twice in *ana hoshi'ah* (Ps. 118:25); twice in the last *hodu ladonai* (Ps. 118:29)— six times in all.

The four species are shaken in the following way. You point the lulav in front of you (to the east) and shake it three times. Each time the motion of shaking should be followed by a drawing in to you—that is, you stretch your hands out, shake the lulav, and pull them back; stretch out, shake, and pull back; etc. Now you repeat the same motion three times to your right (south), over your shoulder (west), left (north), up above you, and finally lower it below you (bend over a little bit; the lulav is not pointed down).

Joseph Karo considers the shaking of the lulav in hallel the central component of the commandment. The RaMA points out that while there is a customary way to shake it, you have fulfilled the mitzvah by performing this ritual in any fashion.

Hoshanot Each day of Sukkot, the hoshanot are recited during the morning service. These are hymns that begin with the words *hosha na* ("save us"), hence the name. One is recited each day as a circuit is made of the synagogue. Hoshanot recall the procession in the temple, which was done around the altar. Today the Torah replaces the altar.

The procedure is as follows: After the musaf service (in some traditions, after hallel), the ark is opened. A Torah scroll is taken out and held on the *bimah.* The ark is left open. The service leader takes a lulav and etrog and begins chanting the hoshana service. The congregation repeats each line responsively. Those who have a lulav and etrog form a procession behind the leader and follow as he or she circles the synagogue (some say even those without lulav and etrog should join the procession). The leader and congregation continue to recite the day's hoshana. The procession circles only once and then there is a closing hymn. People return to their places. The Torah is returned and the ark is closed.

The contents of the hoshanot are connected with the days of the week, therefore the order changes according to the day of the week on which the festival begins. On Shabbat there is no procession (there was none in the temple); the ark is opened, but the Torah is not taken out. The hoshana of *am netzurah* is always recited on Shabbat. An individual praying alone recites the hoshanot prayer while holding the four species, but does not circle.

HOL HA-MOED—THE INTERMEDIATE DAYS

Both Passover and Sukkot have intermediate days that follow the first days of the festival. These days are characterized by the particular customs of the festival—e.g., eating matzah for Passover, eating in the sukkah for Sukkot. They do not have the character of full-fledged festivals in that there are no biblical prohibitions against work and travel. In traditional circles, some restrictions are observed. Some people do not work, or they perform only essential work. Others do not write. (A complete exposition in English of the *most* traditional attitude can be found in *Chol ha-Moed* by Dovid Zucker (Lakewood, N.J.: Halacha Publications, 1981). There are also changes in the daily liturgy to reflect the character of this period as a semifestival, such as the recital of hallel. There is a Torah reading of four aliyot each day. This again reflects its "intermediate" status between the three aliyot of the weekly Monday/Thursday morning readings and the five aliyot of a festival day.

Passover begins and ends with full festival days, while Sukkot has a slightly different pattern. Because Shemini Atzeret immediately follows Sukkot, Sukkot does not have a final festival day. Thus in the Diaspora the pattern is as follows:

As the circle of people carrying the four species makes its way around the synagogue, other people should stand in the middle creating new hoshanot reflecting contemporary needs, such as "Save us from nuclear war," "Save the whales . . ."—to each of which the circle responds, "Hoshana." Also, special attention should be paid to the fifth and sixth paragraphs of hoshana in the traditional service. These could be seen as ecological hoshanas because they mention such things as saving the ground from curse, cattle from sterility, etc.

Z.S.

Hoshanot should really be done around the borders of our homes, our institutions, and our neighborhoods as a means of praying for protection for those spaces.

Z.S.

1st day	2d day		3d	4th	5th	6th	7th		8th & 9th	
festival			intermediate days				Hoshana Rabbah		Shemini Atzeret & Simhat Torah	

In Israel the pattern is the following:

1st day	2d	3d	4th	5th	6th	7th	8th
festival		intermediate days				Hoshana Rabbah	Shemini Atzeret & Simhat Torah

The seventh day of Sukkot (which should have been the full festive day) is slightly different in character from the other intermediate days, as we shall see below.

During the intermediate days of Sukkot, we continue to eat all our meals in the sukkah while reciting the blessing for the sukkah. (Kiddush and *she-he-heyanu* are recited only on full festivals.) There is, as mentioned, the custom of inviting one of the *ushpizin* each day to the sukkah. We also recite the blessing *al netilat lulav* and shake the lulav each day. The complete hallel is recited each morning during services (and we shake the lulav at the appropriate places).

The Torah reading of four aliyot consists of a description of the daily sacrifices for Sukkot. On Shabbat we have seven aliyot and the reading is Exodus 33:12–34:36. The haftarah on Shabbat is Ezekiel 31:18–39:16, which talks of the climactic war of the final days, thus expressing the messianic theme of Sukkot.

Reading of Kohelet Ashkenazic Jews read the Book of Kohelet—Ecclesiastes —on Shabbat *hol ha-moed* (the Sabbath that occurs during the intermediate days of the holidays). The most common explanation is that Ecclesiastes' message that worldly possessions are vain and transitory accords with Sukkot's message that the material possessions in our houses are not real security. See, for instance, chapter 2:4: "I multiplied my possessions. I built myself houses and I planted vineyards. But all is nought." In a peculiar way, Ecclesiastes' theme of eat, drink, and get pleasure (since everything else is vanity) also corresponds to the theme of joy during Sukkot.

Some argue that there is no clear connection between Kohelet and Sukkot. They speculate that since Kohelet was the only one of the five biblical books known as *megillot* that was not initially incorporated into the liturgy, it was assigned to Sukkot, the one pilgrimage festival without a *megillah*. The connections of Esther to Purim, Song of Songs to Passover, Ruth to Shavuot, and Lamentations to Tisha be-Av are much clearer.

Kohelet is attributed by the rabbis to King Solomon, as is the Song of Songs. They explain the contrast between the ecstatic love of the latter and the cynicism and despair of the former by claiming that Solomon wrote one while young and the other in old age. It can be said then that we begin the year with the Song of Songs and the hope of Passover, of freedom, and of spring—of life reborn and renewed; and that we end the year with Sukkot

---

The book resonates with the themes and imagery of Sukkot even in small ways. A constant refrain of the book is about things being done *tahat ha-shemesh*—under the sun—including the verse stating that there is nothing new under the sun. The phrase *under the sun* evokes the image of the open roof of the sukkah.

M.S.

The match between the Book of Kohelet and the festival of Sukkot is hardly less odd than the fit between the philosophy of Kohelet and the theology of the rest of the Bible. While the Bible generally conceives of a God immanent and caring, Kohelet envisions a God remote and cold, governing the world through a mechanism of arbitrary fate. Yet the ironic pairing of Kohelet and Sukkot does serve to highlight certain aspects of the holiday. Kohelet envisions the world running in cycles, and Sukkot falls near the beginning of the New Year, if one calculates from Tishri, and at the time of the year's final harvest. Kohelet does speak of a time of harvesting, and a time of rejoicing, too. In fact, Sukkot, *zeman simhateinu*—the season of our rejoicing—is the most apt time for reading the only book in the Bible that ostensibly praises pleasure for its own sake.

E.GR.

and Ecclesiastes—with the oncoming winter, with death in nature, with the wandering in the desert, with our hopes for redemption once again unfulfilled. Yet we also end the year with the promise that the redemption will come, and with the hope of God's sheltering promise. We know we must continue as best we can with the Torah as our guide. As the Book of Ecclesiastes (12:13) concludes, "The sum of the matter, when all is said and done: Revere God and observe His commandments."

Simhat Beit ha-Sho'eivah During Sukkot in temple times, there was a ritual performed daily connected with the sacrificial cult. This was *nisukh ha-mayim*—the libation of water. In general, many sacrifices in the temple were accompanied by a wine libation, but during Sukkot this additional libation was performed. The ritual became elaborated into a colorful and joyous, even riotous, celebration called *simhat beit ha-sho'eivah*—"the rejoicing at the place of the water-drawing." This ceremony took place every day except for the first festival day and Shabbat. The Talmud (in *Sukkah* 51a–b) describes this ceremony in detail, including a portrait of venerable sages juggling lighted torches and performing somersaults as part of the celebration. The Talmud states, "He who has not seen the rejoicing at the place of the water-drawing has never seen rejoicing in his life."

With the destruction of the temple, the ceremony has for the most part disappeared, though there are some, particularly Hasidim, who continue to celebrate *simhat beit ha-sho'eivah* with dancing and singing and general celebrating. Often they recite the fifteen *Shir ha-ma'alot* psalms (Ps. 120–134) as was done in the temple.

It seems a pity that the ceremony has almost disappeared, and there may be ways in which we can reclaim elements of it, especially those relating to water and agricultural growth.

Three or four times in recent years I've been involved with groups that have played out at least part of the ceremony. Rhythmic movements while holding the willow branches, simulations of the sound of wind and rain, songs appropriate to the occasion (e.g., Shlomo Carlebach's "Ru-ah"), circular movements around something growing, a ritual pouring of water upon a newly planted tree or shrub, rain liturgies from the traditional prayer book, midrashim relating to water, adaptations from other ancient Middle Eastern rain ceremonials, compatible material from Native American traditions—all of these and more can be appropriately combined into a fresh and enlivening expression of our renewed appreciation of water.

E.GE.

HOSHANA RABBAH

Hoshana Rabbah (literally, the Great Hosanna or the numerous hosannas) is the seventh day of Sukkot. As we have just noted, Hoshana Rabbah should have been a full festival day but is not, because of Shemini Atzeret, which follows it. However, it has some special rituals and customs that make the day more like a full festival day than any of the intermediate days.

The most important of these rituals are (1) the circling of the synagogue seven times instead of once while carrying the four species and reciting the hoshana prayers and (2) the beating of the willows.

The hoshanot are performed like those of the other days of Sukkot except that many or all of the Torah scrolls are taken from the ark. One tradition is to take out seven Torah scrolls and return one to the ark with each circuit. Another custom is to carry a separate bunch of *aravot* (willows) that will be beaten on the floor. A less common practice is blowing the shofar at the end of each circuit.

The Beating of Aravot In temple times, branches were struck against the ground near the altar. This ritual probably symbolized a casting away of sins and is the reason that Hoshana Rabbah is still known as the *final* day of judgment. Today this ritual comes at the end of hoshanot and involves beating a bunch of willows against a chair or the ground. Authorities disagree as to whether the willows are taken from the lulav or must be a separate bunch, though the latter is the most widespread custom. No blessing is said during this ritual. After the verse *kol mevasseir mevasseir ve-omeir,* the willows are beaten five times. Some shake the willows, as with the four species, before striking them.

This ritual is a very important one to the rabbis, so much so that it was held to supersede the Shabbat laws. Indeed, the rabbis of the fourth century of the Christian Era set our calendar so that Hoshana Rabbah would never fall on Shabbat, though Yom Kippur, the most solemn fast day, was allowed to do so. (Since the destruction of the temple, beating the *aravot* is only a rabbinic commandment.)

According to some authorities, Hoshana Rabbah marks the conclusion of the High Holiday period. There is a tradition that harsh judgments can still be changed before Hoshana Rabbah—that the final seal is not put on the Books of Life and Death until then. Therefore, the morning service on Hoshana Rabbah is a solemn one.

In keeping with the penitential undertone of the day, in some synagogues the leader of the service wears a kittel as on Rosh ha-Shanah and Yom Kippur. The service itself differs in that the psalms said only on Shabbat and yom tov are added by Ashkenazim to the introductory portion of the service. Also, the melodies of yom tov are used for parts of the service. One tradition calls for lighting many candles in the synagogue as on Yom Kippur, and/or to use a few Yom Kippur melodies during the service.

It is traditional to wear your good clothes on Hoshana Rabbah. This is the only time Hasidim do so other than on a yom tov or Shabbat. If you wish to observe a Hasidic synagogue during a major holiday, this is a good time to do so since you will not offend them by violating the rules against travel, which do not apply to Hoshana Rabbah.

Hoshana Rabbah Customs Among some people, a festive meal customarily follows the morning service. The meal features nuts, *kreplah* with meat, and carrots cut into rings (the shape being a sign of wealth). People wish each other *pikta tava*—literally, a good note, but meaning a good writ of judgment. This is based on the *Zohar* (*Tsav* 31b): "The seventh day of the festival is the close of the judgment of the world, and writs of judgment issue from the sovereign."

One custom is to stay up the whole night of Hoshana Rabbah to recite and study a text called *tikkun leil hoshana rabbah.* This practice was prominent in kabbalistic circles and is similar to the tikkun of Shavuot but not widely practiced. Its purpose was to make sure that you finished Deuteronomy before the Torah reading was completed on Simhat Torah. For the kabbalists, the tikkun was an attempt to "unite" the night and day through Torah and prayer. Some connect this tikkun to King David, the *ushpizin* for the day, who is reputed to have remained awake every night (except for a short nap). There are a number of different tikkun practices. One is to study the Book of Deuteronomy until midnight and the psalms thereafter, with the blowing of

The tikkun of Hoshana Rabbah could focus on the dialogue between Deuteronomy (which is finished on Simhat Torah) and Kohelet. Deuteronomy states that nature is the reflection of the moral; thus if you obey the commandments, rain will fall. Kohelet states that nature is nature—that is, the same thing happens to both the righteous and the wicked. To Kohelet, the world runs on cycles—a time to build and a time to tear down. While traditional Judaism stresses the outlook of Deuteronomy, a dialogue between Kohelet and Deuteronomy is necessary, particularly given the theological issues raised by the Holocaust.

Z.S.

the shofar at the end of each of the five books of psalms. Some also recite "the thirteen attributes" of the selihot prayers of the High Holy Days, or, as on Shavuot, ritually bathe at dawn.

According to an old legend, if you see your shadow without a head on the eve of Hoshana Rabbah, you will die in the coming year. If your shadow has a head, you will live. The *Shulhan Arukh* mentions this belief but, because it is difficult to perceive the omen correctly, tries to dissuade people from practicing magic, recommending that it is "better to be pure than to search out the future."

The afternoon of Hoshana Rabbah is the winding down of Sukkot. Some people visit the sukkah one last time and recite the following prayer: "May it be that we merit to dwell in the sukkah made of Leviathan."

God said to Abraham: "I am one, and you are one. I will give your children one day for atonement—Hoshana Rabbah." God said to Abraham: "If Rosh ha-Shanah does not atone, then Yom Kippur will; if Yom Kippur does not, then let Hoshana Rabbah."

M.S.

According to legend, God will make a sukkah out of the body of the leviathan at the end of days and will place the righteous there. The leviathan is a mythical beast of enormous dimension who will be killed by God at the end of days.

M.S.

KAVVANOT

Next to Pesah, Sukkot requires the greatest amount of physical preparation. The tradition encourages us to begin to build a sukkah on the evening at the end of Yom Kippur. It is a good idea to build it earlier rather than later in case you are missing a necessary part or there is a torrential downpour the day you planned to build it.

A sukkah can be as simple or elaborate as your needs and tastes require. City dwellers often call forth remarkable ingenuity. You have only to walk the streets of a section like Williamsburg in Brooklyn to be amazed how a sukkah can be squeezed into a tiny spot, such as putting it on the stoop of a townhouse while still leaving room to get in the front door. In certain neighborhoods, people take tours of sukkot, especially those of Hasidic rebbes who have large and sometimes ornate ones. (Some decorations are bizarre as well, such as blinking Christmas tree lights!) One recent fad in sukkah building is store-type awnings that can be unrolled to cover your sukkah when it's not in use.

If this is your first sukkah, talk with other people about theirs and then decide which kind you want. For the less adventuresome, there are some prefab sukkot that are relatively simple to put together. But whatever kind you choose, it is important to build it yourself so as to experience firsthand the underlying themes of shelter and home.

Sukkot come in many varieties, but are basically walls attached to a frame. The walls are commonly made of canvas or other cloth, or paneling (a hodge-podge of odd panels can be purchased cheaply), quarter-inch plywood, or whatever wood is lying around. The frame is usually made of wood, but some are made of metal piping that can be screwed together. (On these frames, it is simplest to make walls of canvas. Use a grommet maker to create holes, then attach the canvas to the frame with either rope or strong shower-curtain hooks.) The possibilities for construction are limitless. I grew up with a sukkah whose walls were made of screen doors that slid between upper and lower tracks; each track was made from a wood base with two pieces of

One aspect of sukkah-decorating that receives all too little attention is that of lighting. How illuminate the sukkah for night use in a manner appropriate both to the structure itself and to the themes of the holiday? After much experimenting, our family has hit upon a "fixture" that seems ideal in every respect: the Yaakov Lantern.

What is a Yaakov Lantern? A bright orange pumpkin, hollowed out and carved with appropriate motifs—small Stars of David for the eyes, an elongated Star of David for the nose, and the usual friendly or fearsome jagged mouth. On the side opposite the face, we carve a large Star of David; into the pumpkin we insert either a regular candle or a votive candle in a hobnail glass container. And there it is—a bright, good-natured symbol of the harvest, a windproof container for the yom tov candles, an object of delight made by all the family, and a splendid combination of Jewish and American motifs.

And if you grow your own pumpkin in the garden, even better!

E.GE.

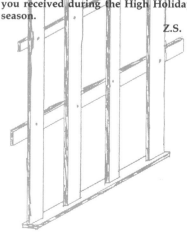

molding to hold the doors in place. (For more of the halakhic details regarding the sukkah, see p. 220.)

It is worthwhile to check with your local parks department as a possible source of *skhakh.* They may be doing tree pruning for the fall and be glad to allow you to come to the site and collect as much *skhakh* as you need.

The following is a complete sukkah plan taken from *The First Jewish Catalog.*

The easiest way to build a sukkah is with cement blocks, 2 × 4 standards, and improvised walls. . . . If you can use the back wall of a house or garage as one of the walls, do so. Stack 3 cement blocks in each corner and insert 7-foot 2 × 4's into the air holes of the blocks. Connect the 2 × 4's with 1 × 2's across the middle and the top. Stretch cloth (or nail 1/4-inch plywood, if you can afford it) over the frame and one wall is complete. One wall can serve as the entrance if covered with cloth on a wire track. Place some 1 × 1's running in both directions on the roof and cover that with rushes or pine boughs. A sample sukkah might be a 7-foot cube, for which the following materials would be necessary:

12 cement blocks	cloth drape for entrance
4 pieces of 2" × 2" × 7 1/2'	wall
7 pieces of 1" × 2" × 7 1/2'	nails
8 pieces of 1" × 1" × 8'	binding twine
enough cloth or plywood to	greens for roofing
cover 3 walls	

You might want the challenge of not using nails, and binding with rope at all joints. It can be done, and a fine binding is a beautiful thing to see.*

You might find it less onerous to build a sukkah with the help of one or more friends. You can ask people who will want to eat in it during the week to join in the mitzvah of building it, or ask a neighbor with whom you can exchange labor.

The most fun, of course, is decorating the sukkah. Since there are no rules or even strong traditions, the possibilities are limitless. A sukkah-decorating get-together where everyone makes decorations that can later be used in individual sukkot helps expand each person's or family's repertoire.

One custom that has become widespread in America is the synagogue sukkah, which serves two purposes: as a sukkah for those people who cannot build their own, and as a place for the congregants to have kiddush after services. Building and decorating a communal sukkah, in the manner of an

Decorate the sukkah with the cards you received during the High Holiday season.

Z.S.

*Richard Siegel, Michael Strassfeld, and Sharon Strassfeld, eds. and comps., *The First Jewish Catalog* (Philadelphia: Jewish Publication Society of America, 1973), pp. 129–130.

old-fashioned barn raising, is the best substitute for building your own. Synagogue sukkot also facilitate communal meals since they are usually much larger than private ones.

HOSPITALITY

Sukkot is a week full of opportunities for inviting and being invited. In some communities, after morning services the first day(s), people go from sukkah to sukkah "making kiddush"—that is, having at least wine and cake. Instead of a formal lunch at any one place, during the course of the afternoon they visit many sukkot in their neighborhoods.

Sukkot is also a holiday of hospitality in its most basic sense. As mentioned, there is a tradition of inviting *ushpizin*—honorary guests—to your sukkah. This custom is related to the important concern of giving shelter to the homeless and food to the poor. As with the Passover seder, we are encouraged to invite the poor to be our real guests in the sukkah. We are also encouraged to invite those acquaintances who do not have a sukkah to join us so they can fulfill the mitzvah of using one.

SUKKAH ACTIVITIES

You might give some thought to preparing a text or reading that lends itself to meditation, so that each night/day of eating in the sukkah has a different feel or focus. Any story with seven or eight parts will do—for example, "The Seven Beggars" by Rabbi Nachman (also appropriate to the theme of hospitality). Others may want to study and discuss the *ushpizin* for that day, such as Abraham and Sarah the first day. Another suggestion for study is the Book of Ecclesiastes, which is read during Sukkot. Others may choose to recite as a kavvanah one of the following psalms, which touch on the themes of God's sheltering presence: Psalms 27, 31, 34, 36, 57, 63, and 91.

Alternatively, one can simply reflect upon the various themes of the holiday, such as the symbolism of the sukkah, the meaning of shelter and of home and homelessness, the symbolism of the period of wandering in the desert, the importance of hospitality, the significance of the harvest or of the beginning and end of the year, the symbolism of the four species, etc. Because of the emphasis on joy during Sukkot, there is a tradition of singing during meals in the sukkah.

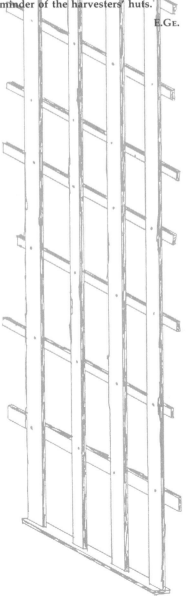

A very nice way to combine the nomadic and agricultural motifs is by constructing the walls of brightly dyed madras cloths firmly pinned to the supporting structure of the sukkah. The walls thus remind one of nomadic tents while the foliage on top serves as a reminder of the harvesters' huts.

E. GE.

SUKKOT AS HARVEST FESTIVAL

The other central rituals focus around food and harvest, especially the mitzvah of taking the four species. The four species and the other rituals, such as hoshanot or the beating of the willows, may seem more foreign to us than some of the symbolic interpretations of a sukkah. However, no matter how far we have come from any connection with the agricultural cycle, it is important to remember our dependence on food that is sown, nurtured, and finally harvested. In our society, it is hard not to take food for granted. If there is a drought in Florida or California, it only signifies higher prices for vegetables, not famine. Would this were true for the large part of the world that borders on starvation! We should all remember the human dependence on a successful agriculture year, and thus the joy that a bumper harvest brings.

Similarly, it is important to grasp the significance of rainfall and thus the awe with which prayers and rituals for rain are approached. Only a few years ago, the northeastern states faced a critical water shortage necessitating contingency plans for water rationing. Both famine and drought are closer than any of us would like to think. These rituals put us in touch with the fertility cycle of the land, from which most of us are so distant.

It is perhaps for these reasons that the rituals of the four species and hoshanot and the beating of the willows can stir deep feelings within us. There is something spectacular about a synagogue filled with green trees (lulav) rustling without a wind, the sound of willows being beaten against chairs, the chant of hoshana. In the liturgy, we should focus on the imagery of trees and growth as well as on shelter and sheltering.

FIRE/WATER AND CIRCLES

Areas for ritual creativity include some form of *simhat beit ha-sho'eivah*—the ritual that accompanied the special water libation in the temple during Sukkot. As we have seen, this ritual was accompanied by joyous merrymaking. It also involved the use of both fire and water, two seemingly antagonistic elements. All of which may suggest a new ritual for *simhat beit ha-sho'eivah,* one that would also serve as a focus for a group activity during the midweek.

The week itself includes an element of movement, as if with each day of hoshanot circuits we wind ourselves up a little bit, climaxing with the seven circuits of Hoshana Rabbah. We remain wound up through the following day(s) of Shemini Atzeret/Simhat Torah when we let loose with a joyful

embrace of the Torah, and we wind ourselves down with seven more circuits (the hakkafot of Simhat Torah) before this holiday period comes to an end.

CRAFTS/FOODS

Building and decorating the sukkah and making a box for an etrog are the major crafts of the holiday.

Surprisingly, there is no food that is widely linked with the holiday. Since meals are carried from the kitchen to the sukkah, the most common Sukkot dishes are lukewarm soup with a dash of rainwater, and solid foods garnished with pine needles from the roof. However, a number of traditions tie Sukkot to the food-related activities of other holidays. One tradition calls for saving the lulav or the willows to light the fire to bake matzot for Pesah or to burn the hametz. A similar tradition is to save the lulav and use its leaves instead of a feather for the ritual search for hametz (bedikat hametz) that takes place on the night before Passover. Another tradition is to collect as many etrogim as you can and make etrog jelly to be eaten on the holiday of Tu Bishvat, which centers around trees and their fruit.

DERASH

A TALMUDIC DEBATE: WHAT IS A SUKKAH?

Unlike Passover and Shavuot, the other pilgrimage festivals, Sukkot does not commemorate a specific event but a period of time. The religious significance of God's freeing us from slavery in Egypt or giving us the Torah at Sinai is immediately evident, but why are we commanded to remember the desert period through the observance of Sukkot? What is its religious significance?

An argument in the Talmud presents two answers. There is a disagreement between Rabbi Eliezer and Rabbi Akiva about the interpretation of the following verse:

> You shall live in huts seven days . . . in order that future generations may know that I made the Israelite people live in sukkot when I brought them out of the land of Egypt, I the Lord your God. [Lev. 23:43]

What are these sukkot of the desert? Rabbi Akiva interprets the verse literally—that is, they are huts. Rabbi Eliezer, however, says that the sukkot of the verse refer to the clouds of glory that accompanied the Israelites in the desert. Why would Rabbi Eliezer depart from the literal meaning of the verse? What are the clouds of glory?

> The Lord went before them in a pillar of cloud by day, to guide them along the way, and in a pillar of fire by night, to give them light, that they might travel day and night. [Exod. 13:21]

According to tradition, these clouds not only led the way but also leveled the path by removing steep hills and valleys. One tradition states that there were seven clouds—one on each of four sides, one above to protect the Israelites from the rain and sun, one below to kill scorpions, and the seventh to lead the way and level the ground. Most of all, the cloud was a sign representing God's presence, or was even His actual presence, for it says:

> The cloud covered the Tent of Meeting, and the Presence of the Lord filled the Tabernacle. Moses could not enter the Tent of Meeting, because the cloud had settled upon it and the Presence of the Lord filled the Tabernacle. [Exod. 40:34–35]

For Rabbi Eliezer, the desert period then is marked by God's sheltering presence, and by His sustaining the Israelites with food and water. God turned the desert into a garden—in fact, into *the* garden. Just as in Eden, everything was provided. The Israelites, like Adam and Eve, did not have to work for their sustenance; rather, the heavens rained down manna, the miraculous food of which there is always just enough. Thus the newly freed slaves, unused to responsibility for their lives, can be seen as newborns unable to care for themselves. As infants, they demand instant gratification. Their complaints are those of someone who fears being abandoned, no matter how many times they have been reassured or saved. It is out of this need that they create the golden calf: "Come, make us a god who shall go before us, for that man Moses, who brought us from the land of Egypt—we do not know what has happened to him" (Exod. 32:1). These complaints are like the whining of a child asking for more reassurance and sustenance.

The former slaves still remain slaves in their hearts, unable to make decisions, to provide for themselves, to act independently, to take on responsibility—and yet, despite all their complaints to God and to Moses, they remain deeply in love with their leader and with their Parent.

God remembers a generation that trusted in Him and was willing to leave Egypt to follow Him into a desert. We are to remember when a home and a land were just a promise made by an invisible God. We are to remember what it was like to be wanderers in a wasteland; a time when we dwelt in huts and followed God's cloud and felt His sheltering presence.

On Sukkot, we leave our solid homes of fifty-one weeks a year and go out to live in temporary, porous, shaky structures. Therein lies the importance of the *skhakh,* for the sukkah walls may be similar to the walls of our homes, but the *skhakh* is different—it is open to the heavens, open to God's sheltering presence. It is under the wings of the Shekhinah (God) that we can find real security, real shelter, not in our homes, no matter how strong or elaborate they are.

Skhakh is simultaneously a sign of our vulnerability to the vicissitudes of the world and also of the reassuring shelter of the Holy One who once lead a people into the desert and out again. Sukkot gives us the strength to live the rest of the year by reminding us of God's presence and concern.

Rabbi Akiva's View   Rabbi Akiva sees the desert generation as an unworthy people who desired to return to the fleshpots of Egypt and therefore were ultimately condemned to die in the desert without ever reaching the promised land. In a second disagreement with Rabbi Eliezer (*Sanhedrin* 110b), he declares that this is one of the few generations of which it can be said that they have no portion in the world to come. This attitude of Akiva's is all the more striking because of his frequent expressions of love for the people of Israel. Thus for Akiva it is the sukkah itself, not the generation of the desert, that should be remembered.

What then is a sukkah? It is a shaky, temporary dwelling that we create and to which we move for one week a year, leaving our solid homes where we have spent so much time creating a place of warmth and comfort, a place that is our shelter against the world.

Our homes are where we surround ourselves with nostalgic mementos, with acquisitions that are trinkets of the trades we have made in our lives. We fill the space with things we cherish or collect and we decorate it with reflections of our worldly success. We have windows to see out, but those windows, like our doors, lock the external world out. Here is our refuge from the chaos of that outside world. This is our castle, where we can pull up the drawbridge at times of darkness. We are in control. Here we return each day to eat and sleep, to talk, to love, and to share.

The tension between the two perceptions of the wilderness generation—that it was mutinous, that it was meritorious—is not at all a contradiction but a reality about being human. The man and the woman in the Garden of Eden first asserted their humanity, the power to express their own will in conflict with the divine will, when they violated God's commandment to lay off the Tree of Knowing. By eating of that tree, the man and woman became more "like God, knowing good and evil" (Gen. 3:5). Although God might see us as his slaves (Lev. 25:42), we still accept the Torah according to our own will. Were we not human, expressing our own sentiments and having the liberty to rebel against God's will, God could derive little satisfaction from our embrace of His Torah. Israel in the wilderness is both attractive to God and independent and spunky. Israel is God's lover, not his whore. When Israel acts up, God gets hostile, then warms up and forgives.

E.GR.

Why then do we move out of this place, this carefully constructed safety zone all of whose inhabitants (i.e., family) are our most trustworthy allies? Why do we move into a dwelling that cannot keep out the external world, nor be permanent, nor provide the key sheltering component of a house—a roof over our heads?

The sukkah makes us realize what sheltering is all about. It makes us confront the danger that lies within our homes, for there is a kind of idolatry lurking in the closets and cabinets and amid the furniture. We must shatter that idolatry and learn not to rely solely on the works of our hands. We must learn not to trust in the size or strength of our homes, nor in how filled they are with precious things. These are as broken reeds that can be swept away in a moment of ill fortune. The home is not where real security lies.

How then are we to create a spiritual shelter for ourselves in this world? The tradition tries to answer by pointing out the construction of the sukkah.

First of all, it is to have walls that are secure enough to stand up in a normal wind but not in a raging storm, and are not so high that they are permanent and that their shadow blocks out all sunlight. There is a fine line between a shelter that helps protect us and a shelter that walls us off. It is not only in Poe's "Cask of Amontillado" that people are walled up alive; the castle can be besieged and its drawbridge permanently raised, thereby becoming a prison that keeps its inhabitants locked in. Walls are necessary but should not be so high nor so unbreachable that nothing can ever break through. They are not meant to stand up in gale-force winds. Sometimes they may sway or flap with the wind. Other times they may collapse and have to be built again. No one can protect his or her spirit from all of life's contingencies; to try to do so is to establish a scenario for a fall with no potential for rising again.

Second, the shelter must be portable, as was the sukkah in the desert and, for that matter, the *mishkan*—the sanctuary in the desert—as well. We must be able to carry a sense of shelter with us wherever we go; to become too rooted in one place makes us inflexible.

Moreover, a shelter should not be just a refuge to run to in time of trouble or to rest in at night. We must take the security of the shelter with us when we go into the outside world in our everyday lives. We need it not just for self-protection but for a deep sense of security that frees us to relate to others. Without it, we carry a suit of armor that encumbers our encounters on the road, for all others remain objects of suspicion or envy, and we are always poised to retreat or strike first, on the lookout for dungeons and dragons that may not exist.

Most important of all, the shelter should have an open roof, one through which you can see the stars and heaven. It must be open to the Other and in this way serve as a model to being open to many others. Yet its openness is also to give us a sense of enclosure, for to be enclosed is to be vulnerable and related. Security comes from trust, not strength, and thus shelter is an expression of love. Hence the image of finding shelter under the wings of the Shekhinah just as a mother bird shelters her children.

Perhaps then Rabbi Eliezer and Rabbi Akiva are looking at the same object from two different perspectives. Rabbi Eliezer sees the necessity to remember a special time, at the beginning of the Jewish people's relationship to God, when we were fed and sheltered by the Holy One. It was a period of their courtship, when God and Israel learned to live with one another amid the deserts of this world. Sukkot is to remind us of that time and urges us to recapture the sense of God's sheltering presence, of the One who rained down manna. We are to trust even when the manna does not come but cold rain falls instead. Faith in God, which is a shaky shelter for many of us, is the best we have in this unpredictable world. Rabbi Eliezer sees us as wanderers who need the feeling of that sheltering presence.

Rabbi Akiva, on the other hand, is concerned that we are too secure in our shelters and need to recapture some of the sense of insecurity that comes from being wanderers. It is not the importance of shelter but its problematic nature that is his focus. We are to reexamine our shelters to gain a different appreciation of them. Sukkot comes to teach us how to build a proper shelter, one that is open to the elements—human and other—rather than a total self-enclosure that too easily becomes a sealed vacuum.

From Yom Kippur to Sukkot

On Sukkot there is a transformation from the stern judge of Yom Kippur to the sheltering mother of Sukkot. For Sukkot marks a new beginning. On Yom Kippur, we are forgiven for all our past misdeeds, for all the ways we failed God and our fellow human beings. After Yom Kippur, we start at the beginning, with a clean slate, as though we were newborns. Sukkot celebrates our newfound trust in each other, and it recalls the good days of old when Israel and God discovered each other, when each of us first experienced love and trust. That is why Sukkot is celebrated with such joy, for though it is also the end of the year with its final harvest, Sukkot is at the same time the beginning of the new year following the atonement process of the High Holy Days. We rejoice in that trust, and we feel secure as we build the model, the sukkah, of what true shelter is.

Not coincidentally, this same time period marks the beginning of the construction of God's sukkah, of the *mishkan*—the sanctuary in the desert. According to tradition, Moses again ascended Mount Sinai for forty days and nights to receive the second set of tablets and descended on Yom Kippur carrying them as a sign of God's forgiveness of Israel for the sin of the golden calf and as a symbol of the lasting covenant between God and Israel. The following day Moses relayed God's instructions for building the *mishkan*—a dwelling place. Material for this portable structure was collected during the days before Sukkot, and work was begun on it.

Why was the *mishkan* built? The Torah says, "Let them make me a sanctuary that I may dwell among them" (Exod. 25:8). To establish the relationship between God and Israel, God would dwell amid the people. Once the *mishkan* was constructed, it was placed in the center of the Israelite camp surrounded

Every year the Holy One sends a new name for Himself into the world. The high priest calls out that name on Yom Kippur, but it still requires four days to descend (one day for each letter of the name). This explains the tradition that the beginning of Sukkot is considered the first day for reckoning sins for the new year, for the preceding four days are a period between the old and new years. On Sukkot, by shaking the four species and eating in the sukkah (the gematria of *sukkah* and *adonai*, y'h'v'h, are both ninety-one), we draw down into the world the new name of God.

Z.S.

I find the midrashic analogy between our sukkah and God's *mishkan* to be problematic. The sukkah is stationary yet impermanent; the *mishkan* is portable yet stable. The sukkah reminds us of our dependence on God; the *mishkan* reflects not God's need of us, but, as with the sukkah, our need of God's presence. The sukkah is a place for us to sojourn; the *mishkan* is a locus for God's presence to dwell in a hospitable environment. As long as the Israelites maintain a holy environment, God will continue to dwell in their midst. The sukkah is open to all who may enter, but the *mishkan* shields the compartment of God from the public area where the people bring their offerings. The *mishkan* at once represents the intimacy of God and Israel and the separateness of the divine and the human. Two more differences: The sukkah is individual; the *mishkan* is communal. The sukkah entails a festival rite once a year; the *mishkan* is the focus of worship all year round.

E.GR.

For some years now I have, during Sukkot, walked through and around our lower garden, our upper garden, the blueberry patch, the strawberry planting, the fruit trees, the hayfield, the nut trees, etc. Carrying lulav and etrog, I stop at the corners of the various sections. I hold the lulav and etrog as prescribed by tradition, wave them ceremonially in the four directions of the winds, then up and down to form, as it were, the axis of a four-directional sphere. The ordered waving, while rooted in the ground of this place where I stand, points limitlessly outward. Following its pointing, I find myself aware anew of my connection with a vastness unrealized at ordinary moments.

This is the Lord's doing;
It is marvelous in our eyes. [Psalm 118:23]

E.GE.

by the twelve tribes. This building of the *mishkan* serves as a model for the sukkah. Each year, in imitation, we create a sanctuary for ourselves in this same period between Yom Kippur and Sukkot. It is to be a place of openness and hospitality, where God can dwell, where *ushpizin*—guests symbolic and real—are made welcome.

ON GATHERING AND CIRCLING: THE FOUR SPECIES

As we shake the lulav and etrog in the six directions, we acknowledge God's surrounding presence. By shaking it forward and then drawing it back, we are drawing into ourselves God's presence. It also suggests a gathering in of our resources before the coming winter. Winter is a period of sterility and is cold and deathlike. The month of Heshvan that follows, having no holidays or even fast days, suggests the withdrawal and distance of God. It is two months to Hanukkah with its first glimmers of light.

The motif of gathering in and encircling is a constant refrain of Sukkot. We surround ourselves with the walls of the sukkah. We remind ourselves of how God encircled the Israelites in the desert with the clouds of glory. We shake the lulav in all directions. We circle the synagogue carrying the lulav and etrog while reciting hoshanot. We climax the holiday with Hoshana Rabbah, circling seven times. The motif of circling continues on Simhat Torah with the seven circuits of the Torah around the synagogue. We are creating circles, which have traditionally signified a magically protected inner space. But there is no magic circle here; rather, there is the interaction between ourselves and our material resources and between ourselves and our God. We take the four species to represent the former; we shake them to represent the latter. Equipped with both, we can enter with confidence and joy the new/old year that lies in the months ahead.

GALUT AND REDEMPTION

An important underlying theme of Sukkot is its messianic and universalistic character. Coming at the end of the agricultural year and the end of the pilgrimage cycle, Sukkot marks the end of a passage of time. It thereby anticipates the messianic end of days for all people. During Sukkot a total of seventy sacrifices were brought into the temple, corresponding to the tradition's count of the number of nations in the world. In the days to come, all nations will go up to Jerusalem on Sukkot to worship God, as it is written:

And it shall come to pass that everyone that is left of all the nations that came against Jerusalem shall go up from year to year to worship the King, the Lord of Hosts, and to keep the feast of tabernacles. [Zech. 14:16]

This vision of universal brotherhood is reflected in the sukkah, whose door and roof are open to all. The sukkah, in turn, evokes a vision of God's sukkah as a house of prayer for all nations. In that future, God will spread a *sukkat shalom*—a sheltering cover made of peace and harmony. Even as we remember the desert period of old, having reached the end of time, we eagerly await the redemption, the crossing over into the promised land.

And yet the sukkah, while evoking the image of God sheltering us in the future, raises another, opposing image: The sukkah as a temporary structure open to the winds of autumn cannot help but remind us of the Jewish people's experience of the last 2000 years of exile and wandering. Are we not the prototypical alien—the wandering Jew? Are not the forty years in the desert —the period Sukkot commemorates—the archetype of our 2000 years of wandering?

The sukkah, then, evokes opposing sets of images: rootlessness and home, wandering and return, exposure and shelter. Just as matzah is both slave bread and free bread, the sukkah stands for the contradictory realities of our lives.

From exile to eternity and back again—this, too, is contained in the four walls of the sukkah.

A FINAL WORD

The tradition understands the need for a house as protection against the elements, and even more the need for security, for being settled in one place. It understands the acquiring of possessions and does not condemn it unless done in a way that contradicts other values, such as tzedakah—charity. It is not an ascetic life that we are supposed to live, but a full life open to the potential within ourselves and others. Sukkot is a reminder not to become entombed in our homes, a reminder of a different kind of shelter made of openness and faith. It is a reminder of the time long ago when we followed the Lord into the desert, and painfully learned the meaning of trust. It is to remind us of all these things, so that for the other weeks of the year, our homes are different, our sheltering is different, and our relationships to God and other people are different. As it is written: "For seven days you shall dwell in the sukkah."

On the other hand, quite touching and laudatory is the treatment of the Rechabites (Jer. 35) who do dwell year-round in tents and engage in no form of settled agriculture. The tribute to their nomadic faithfulness suggests that at some level of the psyche there is admiration and respect for "living in the sukkah all year round."

E.GE.

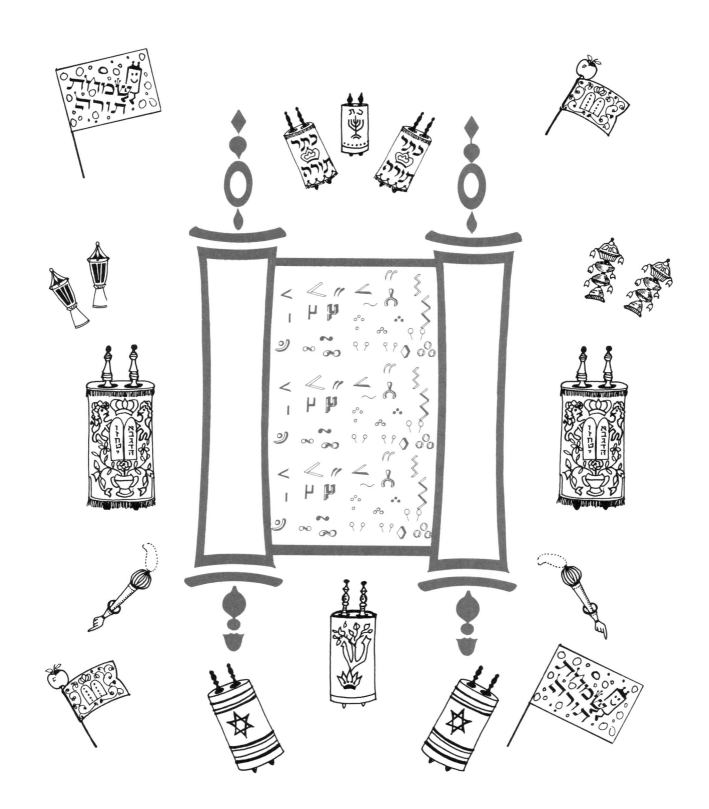

SHEMINI ATZERET/ SIMHAT TORAH

REVELING WITH THE TORAH

 mmediately following the last day of Sukkot (Ho-shana Rabbah) is Shemini Atzeret—the Eighth day of Assembly (Tishri 22, 23). "On the eighth day you shall hold a solemn gathering [*atzeret*]; you shall not work at your occupations" (Num. 29:35). The rabbis interpreted this verse to mean that God asks all those who made a pilgrimage for Sukkot to tarry (*atzeret,* from the root "to hold back") with Him one additional day. Its biblical character then is vague, seemingly just an additional day following Sukkot for the pilgrims to remain in Jerusalem. This indistinctness led to much discussion over whether Shemini Atzeret is the end of Sukkot or a completely independent festival. In general, the rabbis concluded that Shemini Atzeret is an independent festival despite the lack of its own characteristic rituals. Therefore, in the amidah we call the day Shemini Atzeret, not Sukkot.

If we look at the festival cycle, Shemini Atzeret seems analogous to Shavuot, which as we have seen was called by the rabbis *atzeret.* Just as in certain ways Shavuot (a one-day festival) is the conclusion to Pesah (a seven-day festival), so Shemini Atzeret (a one-day festival) is the conclusion to Sukkot (a seven-day festival). According to one midrash, Shemini Atzeret should have taken place fifty days after Sukkot, just as Shavuot follows Pesah. However, Shemini Atzeret would then have fallen in the midst of the rainy season, a difficult time for pilgrims to travel to Jerusalem. Therefore, God ordained that Shemini Atzeret immediately follow Sukkot.

149

There are other analogies between Shemini Atzeret and Shavuot. Just as Shavuot is lacking in specific rituals, so, too, is Shemini Atzeret. Both begin with only temple and agriculturally related rituals. With the destruction of the temple, Shavuot successfully made the transition to a historical festival commemorating the revelation at Sinai. Shemini Atzeret at first consisted only of *tefillat geshem,* the prayer for a bountiful rainfall in the coming winter months. Because it was not directly tied to the temple, the prayer for rain remained Shemini Atzeret's sole distinct ritual. However, beginning around the tenth century, Shemini Atzeret (actually the second day of Shemini Atzeret), as Shavuot had earlier, began to take on the character of a festival of Torah. The connection to Torah was not based on a historical event such as Sinai, but rather on the synagogue liturgy. At this time of year, the end of the Book of Deuteronomy was read in the synagogue, completing the reading of the whole Torah. On the Shabbat after Shemini Atzeret, the cycle was begun again with the reading of Genesis 1:1. To celebrate the completion of the cycle, the holiday of Simhat Torah was developed.

One reason Simhat Torah was a later development than the change in the nature of Shavuot was that until the early Middle Ages there was more than one cycle with regard to the reading of the Torah. Another widespread cycle was the triennial one, in which the reading of the Torah took three years and ended before Pesah. When the annual reading cycle became predominant, the festival of Simhat Torah quickly developed.

Thus, in those places where two days of festivals are observed, the eighth day remains Shemini Atzeret and the ninth is Simhat Torah. In Israel and wherever only one day of festivals is observed, all the rituals of both days take place on Shemini Atzeret, which is also Simhat Torah. (For the sake of clarity, however, the rituals for each will be described separately in this chapter.)

The joyous character of Simhat Torah and its rituals surrounding the ending and beginning of the Torah reading cycle have overwhelmed the virtually ritualless Shemini Atzeret, so that in our day the biblically ordained holiday has taken second place in many people's minds to Simhat Torah, which did not originate until the Middle Ages (and which falls on the rabbinically ordained second day of yom tov wherever two days are observed). The hakkafot of Simhat Torah Eve have become one of the most widely celebrated rituals of the Jewish festival cycle. The fact that both of the major pilgrimage festivals, Pesah and Sukkot, end in holidays celebrating Torah signifies the importance Judaism places on it.

TRADITIONS

SHEMINI ATZERET

Shemini Atzeret is a full festival day marked by the usual rituals of kiddush, candlelighting, etc., and by the prohibition on working. It is referred to as Shemini Hag ha-Atzeret in the kiddush and the amidah. The blessing *she-he-heyanu* is recited at candlelighting and/or at kiddush. The lulav and etrog are not used ritually on Shemini Atzeret; and though kiddush is recited in the sukkah, both in the evening and morning, the blessing *leisheiv ba-sukkah* is omitted. (In Israel, most people do not use the sukkah on Shemini Atzeret since it is clearly *not* Sukkot.)

During the musaf service, we recite *tefillat geshem,* the prayer for rain. It is analogous to the prayer for dew recited at the beginning of Passover. Each marks a transition point in the agricultural year in Israel. We pray for rain on Shemini Atzeret because the rainy season (winter) is coming. However, we wait until the end of Sukkot to pray for rain, because we desire good weather for sitting in the sukkah. According to tradition, the world is judged at this time for how much rain will fall during the year. Thus, throughout Sukkot we hint at our desire for rain through such rituals as *simhat beit ha-sho'eivah*—the water libation practiced in the temple—and the four species, particularly the willow, which represents the association of plant growth and water. Beginning with musaf, we recite in the second *berakhah* of the amidah the phrase *mashiv ha-ruah u-morid ha-gashem,* which praises God as the one "who brings forth the winds and brings down the rain." During the reader's repetition, a piyyut elaborating on our desire for rain is recited. The melody for this piyyut has echoes of the High Holiday ones. In some congregations, the service leader wears a kittel—a white robe—as on the High Holidays. Both of these customs are meant to convey the importance of rainfall for the planting season to come. We continue to recite *mashiv ha-ruah* in every amidah until Passover.

Other than the prayer for rain, Shemini Atzeret is marked by the recital of yizkor—the memorial prayer for the dead. This is customarily said on the last day of a festival (e.g., the last day of Passover). However, Shemini Atzeret is regarded in this respect as the last day of Sukkot even in those communities where the ninth day is celebrated.

Some communities, especially Hasidic ones, anticipate Simhat Torah by performing hakkafot—circling with the Torah scrolls the night of Shemini Atzeret. Some even read from the Torah.

SIMHAT TORAH

The rituals of Simhat Torah revolve around the completion and the beginning again of the cycle of Torah readings. The completion is marked by hakkafot—circlings—that are similar in form to the hoshana ritual of Sukkot. In many places these hakkafot are accompanied by much singing and dancing in honor of the Torah. The late development of this holiday is reflected in the statement of an early-twentieth-century halakhic authority that some synagogues have three circlings and others seven. Today, the custom is to have seven hakkafot, followed at night by the reading of the last section of Deuteronomy, but not the final verses (which are read next morning).

The celebration of Simhat Torah begins at nightfall with ma'ariv. After

Unlike other second days of yom tov (e.g., the second seder), there is no duplication of ritual. The prayer for rain is recited only on the eighth day, and the celebrating with the Torah only on the ninth (except for some Hasidic groups). Even on the ninth, however, the day is referred to as Shemini Hag ha-Atzeret in the liturgy, as Simhat Torah has no source in the Bible.

M.S.

the amidah, the hakkafot are begun with the recital of *attah hareita*—a series of verses praising God and Torah. Each verse is read by the service leader and then repeated by the congregation, in some congregations more than once. The ark is opened upon recital of the verse *Vayhi binsoa ha-aron*—"It came to pass whenever the ark . . . "

After reciting *attah hareita,* all the Torah scrolls are removed from the ark. (Some congregations do not leave the ark empty; they put either a lighted candle, symbolic of Torah as a light, or a Bible inside.) It is considered an honor to carry a Torah scroll during a hakkafah, and even more of an honor to lead the procession. In traditional synagogues, all *kohanim* and *levi'im*—priests and Levites—are honored first, followed by scholars and philanthropists, longtime members of the synagogue, etc. Usually, by the end of the evening, everyone will have gotten a chance to carry the Torah during the hakkafot.

The service leader or someone so honored circles the synagogue while holding a Torah and reciting responsively with the congregation a short prayer reminiscent of the hoshana prayers of Sukkot. In the hakkafot the refrain is *Hoshi'ah na*—"O Lord, save us." The other people holding the Torah scrolls follow behind the leader as he or she circles the synagogue. It is customary for the rest of the congregation to kiss the Torah scrolls as they pass. As a sign of respect for the holiness of the Torah, this is done by touching a siddur or scarf to the Torah and then bringing it to your lips rather than using your hand. Simhat Torah is the only time in the year when some traditional synagogues allow women to enter the men's section in order to be able to touch the Torah scrolls; otherwise, women line the *mehitzah*—the partition between the male and female sections—and reach over to kiss the passing Torah scrolls. Customarily, the *bimah*—the central platform from which the Torah is read—becomes the focus of the circling.

After the procession of Torah bearers has circled the *bimah* or the synagogue one time, the leader breaks out in a joyous song and all the congregation joins in singing and dancing. Those without Torah scrolls may join the procession or form circles of dancers with one or more Torah scrolls at their centers. The dancing goes on spontaneously, the groups changing as one ends and another begins. From overhead, these circles look like reproducing amoebas. As they tire, those holding the Torah scrolls pass them on. The frenzy —or merely enthusiasm, as the case may be—will vary widely from place to place. Certain synagogues acquire the reputation of being good places to celebrate Simhat Torah. In some, Israeli folk dances are substituted for the less familiar Hasidic ones, but all Simhat Torah celebrations take their style from that of Hasidim, who lose themselves in ecstatic fervor in honoring the Torah.

Instead of our building campaigns and membership drives, synagogues in Eastern Europe would raise their yearly operating expenses through the sale by auction of various honors—for example, receiving an aliyah on the High Holidays or other special occasions. The recital of *attah hareita* was one of these occasions. Sometimes the person who bid the most was then expected to give the actual honor of reading the verse to the rabbi or another distinguished person. In other communities, that person would honor his friends by giving them one verse to recite. It was customary to give to a *kohein* the verse "May Your priests be clothed in righteousness." There was even a custom of auctioning off all the special Torah portions of the year at this time, such as those beginning with the verses Gen. 27:28, 48:16; and Num. 6:24, 25:5. (Gen. 48:16 was supposed to be useful in saving you from being drafted into the Russian army.)

M.S.

עָנֵנוּ בְּיוֹם קָרְאֵנוּ   עָנֵנוּ בְּיוֹם קָרְאֵנוּ

After a while the first hakkafah is called to a halt (there is no set time) and the Torah scrolls are given to other people. A new procession is formed that circles the synagogue while the congregation responsively recites some more lines of the *Hoshi'ah na* prayer. Then more dancing, then the third hakkafah . . . and on into the night.

Children are especially encouraged to participate in the simhah—joy—of the evening. It is customary to hand out flags supposedly reminiscent of the tribal flags under which the Israelites marched in the desert. Another custom is to put an apple on top of the flagstaff, or an apple with a hole carved out for a lighted candle—again, to evoke images of Torah as light.

After the seventh and last hakkafah, all the Torahs except one are returned to the ark. The service leader takes the remaining Torah and recites responsively with the congregation the rest of the service for taking out the Torah (Shema, *ehad eloheinu, gaddelu*). Reading the Torah at night is unique to Simhat Torah, and since there is no real halakhic basis for it, customs vary widely as to what is read. In some places the section that happens to be open is read. More often, three aliyot are read from the last portion (though not the last verses) of the Torah *(ve-zot ha-berakhah).* Then the Torah is returned and the service is concluded.

The Morning The morning service is the usual holiday one, with its own amidah and hallel. After hallel, there are hakkafot as on the night before, though usually less spirited. After the hakkafot, three Torah scrolls are left out. In the first we read five aliyot from *ve-zot ha-berakhah* (Deut. 33:1–26). Since the custom is for everyone to be honored with an aliyah on Simhat Torah, this section is read over and over again. To facilitate this, large congregations will divide into smaller groups, each with its own Torah. Other congregations will call up more than one person at a time.

After everyone receives an aliyah, there occurs a special aliyah called *kol ha-ne'arim*—"all the children." For the only time in the year, children are given an aliyah. A tallit is spread like a canopy over their heads and they say the blessings along with an adult who accompanies them. After the second blessing, the congregation recites Genesis 48:16: "The angel who has redeemed me from all evil, bless the youths; and let my name be named on them, and the name of my fathers Abraham and Isaac; and let them grow into a multitude in the midst of the earth."

This is followed by the last verses of Deuteronomy (33:27–34:12). The person honored with this aliyah is called the *hatan torah*—"groom of the Torah." This aliyah, if not auctioned, is given to someone the community especially desires to honor. As that person is called up, a special piyyut is traditionally recited in praise of the Torah. After this aliyah, the beginning of Genesis (1:1–2:3) is read from the second Torah scroll. The person honored with this aliyah is called the *hatan bereshit*—"groom of Genesis"—and is also someone the community wishes to honor. Again a special piyyut is recited. As the first chapter of Genesis is read, the congregation recites for each day of creation *Vayhi erev vayhi bokeir*—"There was evening and there was morning"—which is then repeated by the reader. At the sixth day, the congregation continues from "There was evening" and reads out loud the verses about the seventh day, which are then repeated by the reader. In some places a tallit is spread like a canopy over the *hatan torah* and *hatan bereshit.*

The *hagbah*—lifting of the Torah scroll—is done in a special fashion. The person crosses her or his hands so that the scroll when lifted is reversed—that is, the writing is facing the congregation. This is done to symbolize turning the Torah back to its beginning—to Genesis. It also evokes the expression found in *Ethics of the Fathers:* "Turn it [the Torah] over and over, for everything is in it." (It is also a practical measure since all the weight is on the left-hand roller.) The maftir (Num. 29:35–30:1) is then read from the third Torah scroll, and the haftarah is the first chapter of Joshua, which begins appropriately: "Now it came to pass after the death of Moses . . . "

In some synagogues it is customary to allow some good-natured fooling around during the musaf, particularly by children, who tie the fringes of tallitot together or throw water on the service leader when she or he recites *mashiv ha-ruah*—"who brings forth wind and brings down rain." The service leader or others may sing melodies from other holidays or secular sources.

Immediately after Shemini Atzeret/Simhat Torah is Isru Hag, more fully described in the Shavuot chapter (p. 77). The following Shabbat is Shabbat Bereshit, when we read the whole portion of Genesis 1:1 and begin the weekly portion cycle. It is customary to stop studying *Ethics of the Fathers* on Shabbat afternoons after minhah and, beginning with this Shabbat, to recite Psalm 104, which describes the creation of this world, and the fifteen "Songs of Ascent" psalms (Ps. 120–134).

A phrase *(ve-tain tal u-matar)* asking for rain is added to the ninth blessing of the daily amidah beginning with December sixth. While we praise God as the bringer of rain *(mashiv ha-ruah u-morid ha-gashem)* beginning with the prayer for rain recited on Shemini Atzeret, in the Diaspora we wait until December 6 (the fifth in a leap year) before reciting this petition. This date is calculated as being sixty days after *tekufat Tishri.* (The calendar is divided into four *tekufot*—seasons.) In Israel, this phrase is added to the amidah beginning with the seventh of Heshvan.

M.S.

The connection on Shemini Atzeret of water with birth is a natural one. The full harvest completed, we look forward to the fertility of spring and the renewal of the series of harvests from spring to fall. It is the imminent early and later rains that prepare the ground for the rebirth in spring in the land of Israel. More basically, we renew the reading of the Torah at this time of year, returning to the story of Creation, in which God fashioned the world, as in human birth, out of a dark, watery mass.

E.GR.

KAVVANOT

While the focus today for celebrating is Simhat Torah, groups nevertheless may want to develop the theme of water for services on Shemini Atzeret. This theme evokes a number of images, ranging from rainfall and growth to water as birth. It is striking as the year comes to an end and we enter the "death" of winter that Shemini Atzeret brings out the imagery of birth. It is out of water that life comes, that the world is re-created after Noah's flood, that each baby emerges from its mother's womb upon the breaking of her waters. Thus water is needed both for continued survival and for prosperity, but it is also a symbol of rebirth, of a purifying process. In the winter months following our purification during the High Holy Days, the earth is purified, the rains wash away the old, renewing the earth for its rebirth in spring. Thus, just as the old is dying, the cycle of life continues with new birth.

Simhat Torah is a grand celebration of the Jewish people's relationship to Torah, not just a time of unadulterated revelry. In this it differs from Purim, which, at least in the common view, is a liberation from all restraints. Too often Simhat Torah and Purim are confused because people regard them the same way, forgetting that there are different kinds of joy. The wild revelry of Purim, when we are so drunk as not to know the difference between Haman and Mordechai, is different from the rejoicing for the Torah, no matter how enthusiastic or ecstatic it may be. The rejoicing on Simhat Torah is an expression of our love for and joy in the Torah.

This expression of joyful love for Torah also distinguishes Simhat Torah from Shavuot, which also commemorates the Jewish people's relationship to Torah. Shavuot marks the establishment of the Covenant and of the acceptance by Israel of the *ol mitzvot*—the yoke of the commandments. It commemorates the moment and experience of revelation at Sinai. Shavuot's tone is both serious in acknowledgment of the consequences of agreeing to the Covenant and joyful in our gratitude for being given the Torah. Our relationship to Torah on Shavuot is expressed through study. On Simhat Torah, there is no sense of this awe at the experience of Revelation—in fact, the focus is not on God giving us the Torah but on the Torah itself as the beloved companion in our lives. As with a bride and a groom dancing with each other at their wedding, on Simhat Torah we desire to hold the Torah in our arms and dance the night away.

A CELEBRATION FOR ALL

In the recent past, Simhat Torah has become very much a holiday for children (along with Purim), perhaps because adults have become embarrassed about expressing enthusiastic joy in public. This relegation of Simhat Torah to the children may also reflect our attitude toward Torah—a more distant and ambivalent attitude than that of our ancestors. Yet, even with all of our ambivalences and knowledge of critical biblical scholarship, we should still be able to rejoice in the Torah one day of the year, just as we can rejoice at times in all the relationships in our lives (with spouse, children, friends) despite our ambivalences about those relationships. For those who believe that in some fashion the Torah is "a tree of life to those who grasp it," grasping it on Simhat Torah becomes essential.

Also, it is important, in and of itself, to be more "childlike" at times and thus to lose *one* self and find another through the pounding dances and boisterous singing of the hakkafot of Simhat Torah. The dancing calls upon us to throw ourselves completely into rejoicing with the Torah. It is a time of dropping our defenses to express joy when for most of us letting go takes place only at times of tragedy. To be able to express a fullness in relationship to Torah on this night will help us to express unmitigated love at other moments and in other relationships. To dance like Zorba is a challenge to us all.

Many people cease to study Torah, or Bible stories, when they are young, so they have appreciated the Bible only on a child's level, if at all. But the Bible is adult literature, dealing in a profound and often exquisite way with the most mature human concerns: the meaning of life; the nature of what is good; the conflict between the urge to live and the fact of death; the place of interpersonal relations in the larger scheme of the world; the dangers and attractions of nature; and much more. It abounds in pathos as much as in moralizing. The Bible is mostly wasted on children. Simhat Torah should develop into a stimulus to mature Jews to reconsider the study of Torah, or at least to take Torah seriously. What are all those lawyers, teachers, doctors, accountants, and the rest of them dancing with a Torah for anyway? Critical Bible study may shed new light on the complex historical and cultural forces that produced and shaped the Bible, but it also enables us to see the many levels of serious themes in which the Bible deals. More than ever are we capable of penetrating to deeper reaches of the biblical psyche.

E.GR.

In the process of doing teshuvah, it is not sufficient to regret certain ways of behaving and desire to act differently. To be able to carry out that resolution to change, you need a repertoire from which to draw the appropriate actions. Thus, if you are having problems in the area of *gevurah*—strength—and your response is an either/or one of either losing your temper or being a total patsy, you need to learn how to act in the whole range of responses between those two extremes. This repertoire can be learned by dancing through the seven hakkafot, which can provide you with seven modalities for behavior.

One way to focus on these seven forms is to divide everyone into seven groups. Each group is assigned a hakkafah that is associated with a day of the week and a kabbalistic *sefirah*—that is, *hesed*/Sunday, *gevurah*/Monday. . . . Each group is to develop a dance and music appropriate for that hakkafah—for example, for *netzah* a dance with army precision; for *malkhut* a dance with music of a college processional, etc.

Pamela Faith Lerman describes a piece of the *gevurah* hakkafah:

Gevurah—I will stop at nothing. I will come forth with short bursts of energy. . . . This group used the image of strength as it combined with each of the other six *sefirot* and sang or chanted appropriate songs for each dance. . . . For *gevurah she-bi-gevurah*, there was a presenting dance of the group in a circle. When they began *hesed she-bi-gevurah*, the *gevurah* group entered the center of the circle of the group of *hesed*, as a symbol of entering into the heart and forming *tiferet*, which is actually compassion, beauty, and strength all in one. *Gevurah* dancers faced *hesed* dancers, and circled around with individual partners holding hands, dancing to Beethoven's Ninth Symphony.

                                Z.S.

Attah hareita can also be done in the following fashion: One person takes a Torah scroll and recites a verse from *attah hareita* that they can really swear to. They then call another person, who takes the Torah and recites her or his verse. Another person follows, with each person standing next to the preceding person, and thus they build a circle for the hakkafot.

                                Z.S.

The Hakkafot While stressing the importance of adult participation, it is also a wonderful time for children to sing and dance, to be carried on shoulders, to carry flags or miniature Torahs in an atmosphere where energy and noise are welcome rather than discouraged. In fact, the more people—both children and adults—who join in the Simhat Torah celebration, the better it will be.

The evening requires little planning, for the dancing should be more spontaneous than structured. That is why Hasidic dancing, which consists basically of circle dances with no real steps to learn, is best suited for the evening. It calls for a great deal of energy but not necessarily grace or agility. The accompanying songs (some without words) are sung over and over and over again as the dancers circle. Its very simplicity and repetitiveness allow the participants to focus on the joy of rejoicing with the Torah rather than on their two left feet.

Those in charge of the hakkafot should pay attention to the ebb and flow of energy during the evening. There is a temptation to dance for so long at the first hakkafot that people become tired and, by the seventh and climactic hakkafah, the dancing rapidly peters out. Thus, it is necessary for someone to decide when to end one hakkafah and go on to the next. To allow people to catch their breath, it is useful to slow down a fast song for a short while and then speed it up again. For longer breaks, a responsively sung song with a number of verses allows for relaxing while singing. Traditional for Simhat Torah are "Mi-pi-eil, Mi-pi-eil" and "Aderet ve-Emunah," but others are also appropriate. For an even longer break, after the fourth or fifth hakkafah a short *devar torah*—talk about a subject relevant to the holiday—might be useful.

Various attempts have been made to differentiate between the seven hakkafot. Some have tried to do so based on the seven kabbalistic *sefirot* and thus do a hakkafah characterized by the attribute of mercy, etc. Others have used a broad theme—Torah, Israel, etc.—as a motif for each hakkafah and have used the theme as a kavvanah for each hakkafah. Songs for that hakkafah may be linked to the theme. Some synagogues have given the honor of carrying the Torah scrolls for each hakkafah to a different group in the community or synagogue, such as old members, children, first-time holders of a Torah scroll, etc. Other synagogues do something similar with the introductory verses of *attah hareita*, giving them out one verse at a time to a variety of people in the room—e.g., all left-handed people, all Ph.D.'s, all those who wish they had Ph.D.'s, etc. The categories are for the most part humorous, and people can be included in more than one category. Those in the chosen category rise and chant the verse and everyone else repeats after them. Another contemporary custom, particularly for smaller groups, is to each take a turn reciting a verse until the verses are over or until everyone has had a chance. Simhat Torah is meant to be very participatory, and whatever can be done to encourage people to join in rather than remain bystanders should be tried.

Recently, some services have included a silent hakkafah or at least a silent circling of the synagogue in honor of and to highlight the plight of Soviet

Jews. Simhat Torah is one of the most important Jewish holidays in Russia (if not *the* most important), as many Jews gather in Moscow and elsewhere to proclaim their Jewishness.

Finally, a suggestion about setting: It is better to have a space that is tight than one that is too big. Simhat Torah is meant to be noisy, not decorous, and the reverberations of stamping feet and loudly singing voices should not get lost in a cavernous hall. Some of the best Simhat Torah celebrations take place in very small Hasidic synagogues where there is barely room to move, but where the intensity of the experience is allowed to build up, not dissipate. Although holding Simhat Torah outside in the streets sounds romantic, it is only for very large crowds and even then something is lost by being in a wide open space.

In the morning once again there are hakkafot, but usually of a more subdued nature. Much of the morning focuses on the Torah readings, which include the finishing of Deuteronomy and the beginning of Genesis. The mood of joy and playfulness continues throughout the morning services. One contemporary custom worthy of mention is to unroll the Torah scroll the whole way while it is held by the congregants in a large circle. In this way we are completely surrounded by the Torah as its end and its beginning are brought into touch with each other.

DERASH

THE END OF TIME

We have seen that there are two kinds of time—historical time, which marks progress, and cyclic time, which is marked by recurring patterns (see p. 106). Historical time is centered in the High Holiday festival cycle. Cyclic time is found in the three pilgrimage festivals. Sukkot is the end of the pilgrimage cycle, and yet, by its placement in the year, also brings to a close the High Holiday cycle. Seemingly, then, Sukkot comes at the end of both kinds of time.

Redemption is Sukkot's theme and as such it answers the great question of Yom Kippur: Are we forgiven? Yet Sukkot only *promises* redemption and thus reflects an underlying uncertainty that bespeaks a cruel reality. Since redemption still has not come, Sukkot continues to signify our status as wanderers lost in the desert. Despite Rosh ha-Shanah and Yom Kippur, most of us are still far away from each other and the Other. Despite the liberation of Pesah and the revelation of Shavuot, we do not end the pilgrimage festival cycle by entering the Promised Land; we are left wandering as the Promised Land eludes our grasp. On Sukkot, we rejoice with our lulav and etrog, imbued with a sense of relief, security, and joy now that the penitential days are over, and yet we sit in our sukkot, those temporary dwellings, open to the winds of time—both kinds of time.

When unrolling the Sefer Torah, go from person to person and read a section from where they are holding the parchment. This becomes their revelation for that year.

Z.S.

The ketubah is an alimony arrangement that the groom presents to the bride at the time of their marriage. Accordingly, I think it not an apt symbol of the covenantal bond between God and Israel that is formulated by the Torah. Unlike the ketubah, which provides for dissolution, the Torah furnishes us with a failproof plan for leading our lives in harmony with God. The ideal of living by Torah is that whatever we do, we will act in unison with God in such a way that there will be no perceptible difference between what we do and what God is doing. God is behaving through us.

E.GR.

If Sukkot brings both cycles to a close, it does so by looking toward the end of time and the final redemption. Sukkot's haftarah, from the prophet Zechariah, describes how in the future all the nations will go up to Jerusalem in peace to worship the Lord on the holiday of Sukkot.

To understand Shemini Atzeret and Simhat Torah, we must go back a bit. The seven days of Passover are followed by the forty-nine (7 × 7) of the omer, climaxing with the fiftieth day of Shavuot. Thus liberation is linked with revelation and the giving of the Torah. The experience of receiving the Torah is awesome. It is characterized by boundaries set around the mountain and a sound so terrible that the people flee. The mountain looms threateningly over their heads. There are no joyful outbursts at Sinai, only fear and anticipation. The experience concludes with the people's acceptance of the Torah and the Covenant.

Shemini Atzeret and Simhat Torah are preceded by Sukkot, again seven days followed by one day, but here there is no intervening period as there is between Pesah and Shavuot. Shemini Atzeret is the eighth day—that is, the day after seven. Seven, being a perfect number in Judaism, signifies a complete unit of time—each week ends with the seventh day, Shabbat. Thus, the eighth day is the day after time. It is the end of both kinds of time. It is thus not just the promise of redemption but the actual moment of it. God said, "Remain with me [atzeret] an extra day," a time beyond time.

Shemini Atzeret is a taste of the messianic, of the time when Torah, the Holy One, and Israel will be one. This comes to a climax with Simhat Torah. Instead of circling around the Torah scrolls as we did on Sukkot, during hoshanot we circle with the Torah scrolls. We take the connecting link between us and God—our ketubah, as it were—and circle around an apparently empty space that is filled with the One who fills everything.

Simhat Torah celebrates a Torah of joy, a Torah without restrictions or sense of burden. We circle God seven times with the Torah and then no more. There is no eighth circling. We read from the last portion of the Torah just before we enter the promised land, but leave the last few verses unread—the Torah unfinished. It is a magical moment when all that exists are God and Torah and ourselves. We throw ourselves into endless circles of dancing and become time lost.

But this moment must pass. Time does continue, and therefore the unity is broken. The sun rises and historical time, briefly halted, begins again.

Cyclic time begins as well, for we start again the Torah reading cycle. There is no end to Torah; after Deuteronomy, we immediately begin Genesis as part of a constantly renewing cycle.

We also read the first chapter of the Book of Joshua, which shows that even after the Torah there is still something else. The Torah did not end last night. There is more to hear, for not only does the Torah cycle begin again, the Torah itself enters historical time beginning with the Book of Joshua.

Then, too, the Book of Joshua is the fulfillment of the dream of entering the promised land. It tells us that last night was no illusion, that the moment of redemption is always at hand.

> Now it came to pass after the death of Moses the servant of the Lord that the Lord spoke to Joshua the son of Nun, Moses' minister, saying: "Moses My servant is dead; now therefore arise, go over this Jordan, you, and all this people, unto the land which I do give to them, even to the Children of Israel. . . . Only be strong and very courageous, to observe to do according to all the law, which Moses My servant commanded you; turn not from it to the right hand or to the left, that you may have good success whithersoever you go. This book of the law shall not depart out of your mouth, but you shall mediate therein day and night, that you may observe to do according to all that is written therein. . . ." [Josh. 1:1, 2, 7, 8]

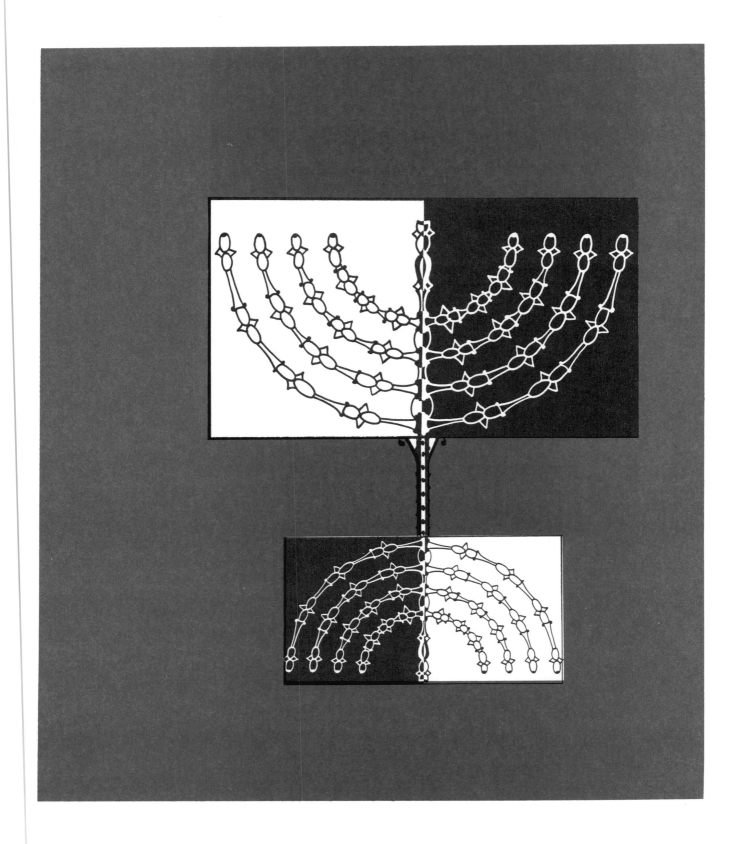

HANUKKAH
INCREASING THE LIGHT

ai hanukkah?—"What is Hanukkah?"—asks the Talmud. Upon reflection, this is a strange question for the rabbis of the Talmud to be asking. Did they not know what the holiday of Hanukkah commemorated? Did they not themselves ordain Hanukkah as an eight-day celebration beginning with the twenty-fifth of Kislev?

All of us are aware to some degree of the story of Hanukkah, of the victory of the brave Maccabees against the Greeks and of the miracle of the cruse of oil that burned for eight days instead of one. Yet upon closer examination, the early history of the holiday of Hanukkah is not clear, and the story is not so simple.

The common version is worth a brief review before we examine its sources in detail. In the fourth century B.C., Alexander the Great with his Greek armies conquered the Near East including Israel. After his death, his empire split apart. The land of Israel, after a period of struggle, came under the control of the Seleucid dynasty, which ruled the region of Syria. In the year 167 B.C., the king Antiochus Epiphanes decided to force all the peoples under his rule to hellenize. The practice of Jewish rituals such as the Sabbath and circumcision was outlawed. The worship of Greek gods and the sacrifice of pigs replaced the traditional worship in the temple. Some Jews eagerly flocked to

There is a prevalent confusion concerning who is the enemy of the Maccabees—the Greeks or the Syrians? Much of Jewish tradition (for example, the *al ha-nissim* prayer) refers to the enemy as *yavan*—Greek. The reality is both are true, for Antiochus and his soldiers were hellenized Syrians. Over 150 years before the Maccabees, Alexander the Great had conquered all of the Near East, and he and his successors tried to hellenize their conquered lands to help unify their empires. Soon after Alexander's death, his empire split into a number of parts. One part was the Seleucid empire, which controlled Syria and much of the adjoining areas. Thus, while the enemy soldiers were really Syrians, not Greeks, they had, to varying degrees, become hellenized. Part of the struggle was in fact a struggle between Hellenism and its values and Judaism and its values.

M.S.

the gymnasium, symbol of the Greek emphasis on the beauty and strength of the body. Others resisted Hellenism and died as martyrs.

One day the Greeks came to the village of Modi'in and set up an altar. They commanded the Jews to bring a pig as a sacrifice to show obedience to Antiochus's decree. Mattathias, an old priest, was so enraged when he saw a Jew about to do so that he killed him. He and his five sons then fought the Greek detachment, retreated to the mountains, and began a guerrilla war against the Greeks and their Jewish allies. Before he died of old age, Mattathias passed on the leadership to his son Judah the Maccabee. Judah led his forces against a series of armies sent by Antiochus, and through superior strategy and bravery he defeated them all. Finally, he and his followers liberated Jerusalem and reclaimed the temple from its defilement by the Greeks. They could find only one small cruse of oil, enough to last one day, but when they lit the temple menorah with it, a miracle occurred and the menorah burned for eight days. Since then we celebrate Hanukkah to remember the Maccabees and their successful fight for independence against the Greeks, and most of all the miracle of the oil.

Hanukkah is the most historically documented of the Jewish holidays. We have early sources for the story in the First and Second Books of the Maccabees and in the works of Josephus. We have somewhat later accounts in the Talmud and other rabbinic literature. There is even a medieval work called *Megillat Antiochus—The Scroll of Antiochus*—which is modeled after the biblical Book of Esther. The problem we face is that in none of these accounts do we find the story as outlined above and as it is popularly known. Let us examine each of these accounts and speculate on why this is true.

WHERE IS THE MIRACLE?

The earliest versions are found in the First Book of Maccabees and the Second Book of Maccabees. While these books tell the history of the Maccabees, they did not become part of the Hebrew Bible. They were preserved by the church and can be found in collections of Apocrypha literature. Thus Hanukkah is the only major holiday that has no basis in the Bible.

The story found in the First and Second Books of the Maccabees (with some variations between the two books) is fairly similar to the traditional story outlined above except for one major exception—there is no mention of the cruse of oil nor of the miracle. While both books mention the cleansing and rededicating of the temple and even briefly mention the relighting of the lamps in the temple, nothing is said of the miracle. Hanukkah is instituted specifically for *eight* days not because of the miracle of the menorah but because it is modeled after the holiday of Sukkot, which the Maccabees could not observe while they were still fugitives in the mountains of Judea.

In the next account we have, that of Josephus, the Jewish historian of the first century of the Christian Era, there is again no mention of the miracle, but he does call the holiday "Lights."

As for rabbinic sources, we would expect to find the laws for the candle-lighting in the Mishnah (the early collection of rabbinic material). In fact, we might expect a whole tractate devoted to Hanukkah as there is to Purim (the tractate *Megillah*). Instead we find virtual silence in the Mishnah about Hanukkah. Only in the Gemara (the later rabbinic material that together with the Mishnah makes up the Talmud) do we find our long-lost miracle of Hanukkah. In the tractate *Shabbat* 21b, the Gemara asks, "What is Hanukkah?" and answers by saying that the Greeks defiled the temple, and when the Hasmonaeans (another name for the Maccabees and their descendants) defeated them, they found only one cruse of oil with its seal unbroken. It contained enough oil for only one day, but a miracle happened and the menorah burned for eight days.

It should be pointed out that the Talmud's account pays scant attention to the military victory of the Maccabees and focuses instead on the miracle of the oil. Scholars speculate that the differences in these texts reflect the history of the festival. At first Hanukkah was celebrated as a reminder of the victory of the Maccabees. It also marked the rededication (*hanukkah* means dedication) of the temple. Only later did the miracle of the oil come to dominate the military victory. This shift in focus can perhaps be attributed to the subsequent history of the Hasmonaeans. The Hasmonaean dynasty, with the passage of time, became hellenized and, more important, some of them opposed and even persecuted the rabbis. This dark later history superseded the brief bright period of their beginning. This may explain the Mishnah's silence about Hanukkah. Others speculate that in Mishnaic times, the rabbis, living under Roman rule, may have felt obliged to censor a story of a successful revolt by a small number of Jews against a powerful enemy. The Mishnah was composed after the disastrous revolts of A.D. 70 (when the second temple was destroyed) and of A.D. 135 (the Bar Kochba rebellion). Both to appease the Romans and to discourage Jews from being inspired by the Maccabees, the Mishnah may have minimized the military significance of Hanukkah.

Finally, one can speculate that because the independence of the Hasmonaean state lasted less than a hundred years, the importance of the Maccabees' victory diminished as time went on, until it seemed like a relatively brief moment in the history of Israel. Other dates in the Jewish calendar from that period also subsequently passed into obscurity—for example, the day of Judah's victory over the general Nicanor was celebrated on Adar 13 (which later became the Fast of Esther). To ensure Hanukkah's lasting importance, then, the tradition decided to emphasize its spiritual meaning and its symbol —the menorah.

In spite of this ambiguous history, Hanukkah remained popular and the rabbis established rules for the lighting of the candles. While these commemorated the miracle of the oil, the tale of the Maccabees never completely disappeared from Hanukkah. Thus we also recite the *al ha-nissim* prayer in the amidah and the Grace after Meals—*birkat ha-mazon*—which stresses the military victory and only mentions lighting the temple menorah in passing, without any reference to the miracle.

The most frequent translation of "Hanukkah" is "dedication"—that is, we remember the rededication of the temple. According to some traditions, the Maccabees built a new altar and/or menorah since the old ones were profaned by the Syrians and thus Hanukkah marks the dedication specifically of these objects in the temple. Some commentators play on the Hebrew word by dividing it in half: *hanu/kkah* (hnv/kh) —that is, they rested *(hanu)* on the twenty-fifth day (the numerical value of the letters of *k* and *h* equal twenty-five). The Maccabees ceased fighting on the twenty-fifth of Kislev, and thus Hanukkah marks their victory over the Syrians.

M.S.

Elias Bickerman's *The Maccabees* (New York: Schocken Books, 1947) offers a succinct portrayal of yet another instance of zealotry becoming self-defeating, as Judah and his brothers, erstwhile liberators, quickly become oppressors of their people. Once mobilized, fanaticism is not easily checked.

E.GE.

Another speculation attributes the de-emphasis to the Mishnah's author, Rabbi Judah ha-Nasi. He was of Davidic descent and may have regarded the Hasmonaeans, who were of priestly descent, as usurping the role of the secular ruler, which by tradition was reserved for the Davidic line.

M.S.

HANUKKAH'S CHANGING ROLE

Hanukkah as a holiday continued to change and develop. During the Middle Ages, the focus of Hanukkah remained on the miracle of the oil, though stories of the bravery of the Maccabees were well known. While First and Second Maccabees, as well as Josephus, were unknown to most Jews, these stories were recorded in various midrashim or collections of folk tales or in *Megillat Antiochus.* Some communities read *The Scroll of Antiochus* during Hanukkah. Strangely, this scroll, which does speak both of the miracle and of the victory, downplays Judah's role and instead makes his brother Jonathan the chief hero. *Megillat Antiochus* can be found in some prayer books— for example, *Ha-Siddur ha-Shalem (Daily Prayer Book)* by Philip Birnbaum (New York: Hebrew Publishing Co., 1949), which has an English translation.

Another important focus during the Middle Ages was the religious martyrdom of the story. All the accounts speak of Jews who preferred to die rather than submit to Antiochus's decree. The Second Book of Maccabees in particular has many such accounts. One tells of Eleazar, a scribe in his nineties, who refused to eat pork and died by torture. The most famous is that of Hannah and her seven sons. Each son is asked by the king to eat pork (or in some versions to bow to an idol), and each refuses. After proclaiming his faith in God, each is horribly put to death. Even the seventh and youngest refuses and both he and Hannah die. This story (and that of Eleazar) with some variations also appears in rabbinic literature (*Gittin* 57b, *Lamentations Rabbah* 1:16:50). These martyrs have served as models to Jews under persecution throughout the ages, but particularly to the Jews of the Middle Ages.

In America, Hanukkah has been influenced by the celebration of Christmas. While a tradition of giving Hanukkah gelt—money—is an old one, the proximity to Christmas has made gift giving an intrinsic part of the holiday. In general, the attempt to create a Jewish equivalent to Christmas has given Hanukkah more significance in the festival cycle than it has had in the past. Indeed, in most American Jewish families, Hanukkah is much more important than the biblical holidays of Sukkot and Shavuot.

In the state of Israel, the nationalist and military aspects of the festival have once again come to play a central role. The heroic struggle of the Maccabees against a larger foe is, of course, much in keeping with Israel's

self-image. Celebrations are held in Modi'in, the hometown of the Macca-bees, and torches of freedom are carried by runners from there to all parts of Israel and even by plane to other countries.

And so the answer to the simple question *Mai hanukkah?*—What is Hanuk-kah?—has continued to be like the flickering flame of the menorah. The flame never looks the same from one instant to the next, but at its core it remains unchanged.

A FINAL HISTORICAL NOTE

Scholars have questioned the role of Antiochus in the traditional account of Hanukkah. Many find it hard to believe that Antiochus instituted the persecution described in the story. They maintain that there was only a veneer of Hellenism in the Near East in the second century B.C. Moreover, they conjecture that, being a polytheist, Antiochus would not have cared that the Jews continued to worship their god, since there were already many gods in his pantheon. These scholars maintain that the villains of the story are Jewish hellenizers—namely, a group of Jewish aristocrats who wished to form a Greek polis or city-state, perhaps to be called Antioch of Jerusalem. Eager for the economic and social opportunities such a position would give them, they established a gymnasium (a sports and educational center), changed their names from, say, Joshua to Jason, and took on other trappings of Helle-nism. According to the Book of Maccabees, they went so far as to undergo a painful operation to simulate a reversal of their circumcision.

When segments of the people opposed these hellenizers, they called upon their powerful supporter, Antiochus, to back them up with Syrian troops. A bitter civil war ensued, with the Syrian troops supporting the Hellenistic faction. As the war progressed, the Maccabees extended the Jewish cause from religious to national freedom. The story of the Hasmonaeans (as their dynasty is called) is that of the gradual development of a Jewish state based on their military might and on the weakness of the Syrian empire, whose rival factions they played against each other to their own advantage. The Has-monaean kings themselves became hellenized over a period of time, however,

The fact that different Jewish com-munities have found various meanings in Hanukkah drives home the truth about all religious rituals: They thrive only when they mean something to people, when they externalize deeply felt concerns. Often, when we are at-tached to a ritual, we will infuse it with special meaning or manifest some la-tent significance in it. In other cases a ritual may fall out of use for lack of contemporary impact. Yet, the Jews have had the wisdom to keep even un-derutilized rituals on the books. As cir-cumstances change, we may rediscover their power at some time later on.

E.Gr.

Some symbols are so primary that purported "meanings" can only prove inadequate. Light in the dead of winter, victory when it had seemed improbable, more than enough when there had been far too little, few against many, the freedom to *be*—these are the essence, and the stories built around them only so much adornment—and therefore alterable.

A.E.

and opposed the rabbis. In the end the Hasmonaean line was killed off by Herod, who rose to power under the Romans and whose story of insane jealousy toward all descendants of the Hasmonaeans is recorded by Josephus.

It should also be noted that it was not Judah's victory and dedication of the temple that brought independence. Judah died in battle well before the end of the struggle. Judea was still under Syrian rule, and a Syrian garrison would remain in Jerusalem for years to come. The subsequent Hasmonaean kings would bring independence. Yet on Hanukkah, we do not commemorate the later history of the Hasmonaeans, nor the brevity of the period of independence they won. Instead we remember the victory of the original few Jews against the many Syrians, the weak against the strong, and we rejoice in a people who were freed from religious persecution and who successfully resisted assimilation.

TRADITIONS

LIGHTING HANUKKAH CANDLES

The major ritual associated with Hanukkah is the lighting of the menorah. (Like the holiday itself, the ritual is rabbinically ordained.) The menorah is lighted each night of Hanukkah after sundown. One light is added each night until we light eight on the last night of Hanukkah. The purpose of the ritual is *pirsum ha-nes*—to make known the miracle of Hanukkah. Originally the menorah was lighted outside near the doorstep so that all passersby could see it. It is still customary to place the menorah in the window so that passersby can see the lights, though some people regard the *pirsum* today as being for the members of the household and therefore the menorah can be placed wherever the family gathers. While the tradition prefers the use of oil, particularly olive oil, to remind us of the menorah in the temple, most people today use candles. Lighting only one menorah fulfills the commandment, but it has become customary among Ashkenazim for each person in a household to light his or her own menorah.

Make wicks for your oil menorah using the lint from the lint trap of your dryer.

Z.S.

The Menorah In ancient times, the menorah often was composed of eight individual lamps, not one candelabrum. Most menorahs (also called *hanukiyyot*) have spaces for eight candles (or oil and wicks). They are placed in a straight line and on the same level to ensure that the viewer can readily see how many candles are burning and therefore what night of Hanukkah it is. The basic rule of menorahs is that the number of candles remain distinct; thus even certain circular menorahs are permitted. On many menorahs the shammash (the candle used for lighting the other candles) is therefore placed higher or to one side to differentiate it from the other candles. There are menorahs in all kinds of shapes and patterns (see for example the article on Hanukkah lamps in the *Encyclopaedia Judaica*). Some authorities advise against using an unglazed clay menorah, which could become dirty after one use and could not be used again for the second night. Recently the question of electric menorahs has arisen. Most halakhic opinion is against their use on aesthetic grounds as well as because electricity is not analogous to kindling oil. Electric menorahs can be used in places where a flame is prohibited, such as hospitals.

The lighting procedure is as follows:

The correct number of candles are placed in the menorah beginning at your right. Each subsequent night you add one candle, starting at the right and moving left. After the candles are set, you light the shammash, the helper candle, which usually has a distinct place on the menorah apart from the other candles. Before lighting the candles, the following blessings are recited:

> Praised are you, Lord our God, Ruler of the universe, who has sanctified our lives through His commandments, commanding us to kindle the Hanukkah lights.
> Praised are you, Lord our God, Ruler of the universe, who performed miracles for our ancestors, in those days, in this season.

On the first night we recite *she-he-heyanu:*

> Praised are you, Lord our God, Ruler of the universe, for giving us life, for sustaining us, and for helping us to reach this moment.

Then use the shammash to light the candle. After the first night, begin the lighting with the candle that has been added. Thus you always begin on the left and end on the right—the opposite of the way you place the candles in the menorah. (NOTE: The mitzvah is fulfilled whether you light the menorah left to right or right to left, but the above is the customary method.)

If the menorah is on a windowsill, many people reverse the menorah after lighting it so that people in the street will see the candles in the right position. After the lighting is completed, some people recite the *ha-neirot hallalu* paragraph:

> We kindle these lights to commemorate the miracles, wonders, triumphs and victories which You performed through Your holy priests for our ancestors in those days, in this season. These lights are sacred for all eight days of Hanukkah. It is forbidden to make any use of them except to look at them in order to praise Your great name for Your miracles, wonders and triumphs.

While customs vary, most people after the candlelighting sing "Ma'oz tzur," a hymn composed in the thirteenth century. The most common melody for it is believed to have been borrowed from fifteenth-to-sixteenth-century German Protestant church music.

After singing "Ma'oz tzur" and other Hanukkah songs, gifts are exchanged. The custom of giving children Hanukkah gelt is an old one. Recently, as Hanukkah has had to compete with Christmas, the giving of gifts has played an increasing role in Hanukkah. (In Israel, elaborate gift giving is not widely practiced.)

It is also an old custom to play games, the most popular being dreidel (*sevivon* in modern Hebrew). Though the rabbis of the Middle Ages opposed

To demonstrate that the purpose of lighting the menorah is to proclaim the miracle *(pirsum ha-nes),* we are not allowed to gain any other benefit from the light. Therefore it is forbidden to read by the light of the menorah. In order to prevent accidental use of the light of the menorah, we light the shammash (helper). If you do read in a room illuminated solely by the menorah, it can thus be claimed that you are using the light of the shammash candle, not the light of the menorah itself. This is one reason why many menorahs have the shammash placed higher than the other candles. Sephardim have the custom of lighting an additional lamp or light, not just one shammash candle. Today when we use electric lights for illumination, the role of the shammash is less important (since it is clear that lighting candles or oil is unusual), yet the custom is still followed. The shammash is also used to light the Hanukkah candles rather than lighting one candle with another.

M.S.

On that evening when Rosh Hodesh and Hanukkah coincide, some special observance seems appropriate, and three or four times I've participated in the following ceremony.

First of all, construct a Rosh Hodesh torch. This is accomplished by cutting a four- or five-foot branch of a tree, trimming off all foliage and shoots, then winding around the tip of one end some shredded flax (the protective, fibrous wrapping for the etrog) and covering it with a small square of linen, which is then tied around the tip of the pole. Just before using, soak for ten or fifteen minutes in olive oil, then let drain.

Next, construct seven more such torches and place them out of doors shortly before the time you'll be lighting the Hanukkah lights. Ideal for placement and support is a snowbank into which you thrust the poles (wicking up, of course). Lacking snow, prepare small holes in advance with a pry bar, a sounding bar, or other sharp tool, then arrange the torches securely.

During the Rosh Hodesh ceremony, light the Rosh Hodesh torch; use it in the Rosh Hodesh ceremonial, then let it serve as the shammash for lighting the Hanukkah torches as you shift to singing the traditional Hanukkah blessings and songs.

If you happen to have many people available, you might make as many as ten Rosh Hodesh torches, Tevet being the tenth month in the Hebrew calendar. In such circumstances, you'll enjoy a more elaborate Rosh Hodesh ritual. Either way, the effect of torches blazing out of doors is quite splendid, and most appropriate both to Rosh Hodesh and to Hanukkah.

E.GE.

The significance of the number eight is clearly related to the tradition that the Maccabees cleaned, purified, and rededicated the temple. In the Torah, dedications take place on the eighth day: Firstborn animals are consecrated to God on the eighth day after their birth; Hebrew boys are circumcised on the eighth day after birth. Before a sanctuary can be rededicated, it must undergo a seven-day period of purification. The actual Hanukkah, or dedication, takes place on the eighth day then.

E.GR.

playing games of chance, they permitted them during the long nights of Hanukkah. The dreidel is a top with a different Hebrew letter inscribed on each of its four sides—*nun, gimel, heh, shin.* They form an acronym for the phrase *Neis gadol hayah sham*—"A great miracle happened there." (In Israel the letter *shin* is replaced by a *peh* for the word *poh*—"A great miracle happened here.")

Each player has or is given a stake for playing the game. This can be anything from coins (usually pennies) to walnuts. To begin the game, each player puts one coin in the "pot" (if only a few people are playing, you may want to put two coins in). Then the players take turns spinning the dreidel and following its instructions: The letter *nun* means neither win or lose; *gimel* means you take the whole pot; *heh* means you take half the pot (rounding to the highest number in case of fractions); *shin* means you put one coin in the pot.

It is also fun to try spinning the dreidel upside down (the dreidel, not you!) or to see how many you can keep spinning at one time. Another dreidel game is to try to knock down other spinning dreidels.

It is customary to eat foods fried in oil, such as potato latkes (Ashkenazim) or *sufganiyot*—a type of doughnut (Sephardim)—to remind us of the miracle of the oil.

OTHER CUSTOMS AND LAWS

While there are no prescribed festive meals (such as the seudah on Purim), many people have parties or invite friends over to light candles, eat, exchange gifts, and play dreidel. (Sephardim, particularly, arrange communal meals during Hanukkah, especially for children.) Another custom is to bring together people who have had arguments for a meal of reconciliation. Some families add a special extra course to make Hanukkah meals more festive.

The prayer *al ha-nissim* is recited in the amidah during all eight days of Hanukkah and in *birkat ha-mazon*—the Grace after Meals. The complete hallel is recited every morning during shaharit. Many end the shaharit service with Psalm 30 (said after Psalm 104 on Rosh Hodesh). Some Sephardim read *Megillat Antiochus* in the synagogue, most commonly at minhah on Shabbat. In Tunisia, Rosh Hodesh Tevet is known as the New Moon of the Daughters and there is a tradition whereby parents and spouses give gifts to wives and daughters.

Zot Hanukkah The last day of Hanukkah is considered by some people to have a special significance as the culmination of the holiday, the day when the menorah burns the most brightly. It is called Zot Hanukkah—literally, "This is Hanukkah"—because these are the opening words of the Torah reading. According to one tradition, Zot Hanukkah means "This is the essence of Hanukkah." This is connected to the role the number eight plays in the tradition. The number seven is the perfect number, the number of completion and fullness. The week and Shabbat, the sabbatical years, the omer

(7×7) all reflect the importance of the number seven. Eight is seven plus one—that is, one beyond the number of completion. If seven marks the limits of time by marking the limits of the week, then eight is beyond time. Eight signifies the eternal. Just as Shemini Atzeret is a special day when God asked His people to stay one more day with Him, so the eighth day of Hanukkah is the essence of Hanukkah and a reminder of the Light that is ever present in this world. (Hasidim and others have special meals and celebrations on this day.)

The Menorah in the Synagogue   There is an old custom of lighting the menorah in the synagogue before ma'ariv in order to proclaim the miracle. The synagogue is seen as a *mikdash me'at*—a miniature temple. Therefore we light the menorah and place it near the southern wall of the synagogue where the menorah stood in the temple. Even though it is merely a custom, the blessings are recited; however, lighting the menorah in the synagogue does not fulfill the mitzvah and the person who does so should light the menorah at home with the blessings. Some synagogues light the menorah in the morning as well, but no blessing is recited. There is no evident source for this latter custom; however, just as with electric menorahs in public buildings, both practices serve to make known the miracle.

Women and Hanukkah   Rabbi Joshua ben Levi stated, "Women are obligated to light the Hanukkah menorah for they took part in the miracle" (*Shabbat* 23a).

How is this so? Two sets of stories are told:

In the first, the Syrian governor demanded that Jewish brides be first given to him on their wedding nights. When the daughter of the high priest finished her wedding ceremony, she tore off her clothes and stood naked before all the guests, whereupon her brothers became enraged with her and wanted to kill her. She said, "Over my nakedness you become angry, but over what the governor will do to me you remain silent." Roused to fury, her brothers went to the governor and killed him. Thus the revolt started.

In the second, the Syrians were besieging a city and the Jews had no hope for a successful defense. Then a woman named Judith left the city and entered the Syrian camp. The Syrian general desired her, and that night Judith prepared a feast for him, including many cheeses to make him thirsty. He drank wine until he fell asleep, and Judith then beheaded him. When the Syrians discovered their general dead and saw the Jews bearing his head aloft while advancing to the attack, they fled.

The latter tale is based on the Book of Judith, which, like the Book of Maccabees, is found in the Apocrypha. The Book of Judith is set in the Babylonian period and seems to have no connection with Hanukkah. How it came to be connected is unclear, but medieval Hebrew versions of the story place it in the context of the Hasmonaean revolt. In some of these variations, Judith's name is changed. Recent scholarship explains the connection of Judith and Hanukkah by dating the writing of the book to the Maccabean period. The story is used to explain the custom of eating cheese on Hanukkah.

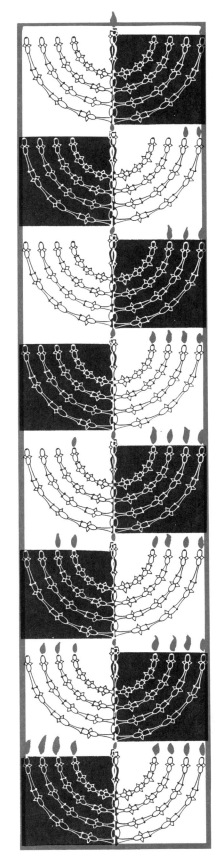

The prominent role of women in the resistance to Antiochus's decrees is also reflected in the story of Hannah and her seven sons. It also explains the custom that women should not have to do any work while the candles are burning. Some carry this honor further, saying that women should not work during Hanukkah or at least not during the first and last days. One tradition is to dedicate the eighth day to women and read the Book of Judith.

The Tenth of Tevet Shortly after Hanukkah comes the Fast of the Tenth of Tevet, one of the four fast days commemorating the destruction of one or both of the temples. The Tenth of Tevet marks the beginning of the siege of Jerusalem by Nebuchadnezzar and the Babylonians, which led to the destruction of the first temple. It is a minor fast that begins at sunrise and includes additions to the liturgy as well as a special Torah reading. It is still observed in traditional circles. For more on the four fasts, see page 85.

Shovavim Tat During a year when the extra month of Adar was added to the calendar, there was an old tradition of fasting on the Thursdays of the Torah portions referred to as ShOVaVIM TaT, an acronym made up of their initial letters: *Shemot, Va-era, Bo, Be-shallah, Yitro, Mishpatim, Terumah,* and *Tetzaveh* (the first eight portions of the Book of Exodus). The most common explanation for this fast was that the time between Monday/Thursday/Monday fasts that follow Passover and Sukkot was too great in a leap year, hence these days of fasting and reciting selihot were needed. This custom is no longer widely observed.

KAVVANOT

The celebration of Hanukkah focuses on the lighting of the menorah. It is a special time for families and friends to spend together singing, playing, giving gifts, telling stories, and meditating on the meaning of Hanukkah.

While there are a number of traditional prayers and songs recited after the candlelighting, alternative suggestions include Psalm 30 (traditional among Sephardim) and Psalm 44:2–9. Or you can develop your own reading, using the collection of biblical verses that follows. These can be read all in one night or divided among the eight nights.

On the first night:

The earth was unformed and void, with darkness over the surface of the deep. . . . God said, "Let there be light"; and there was light. God saw that the light was good, and God separated the light from the darkness. God called the light Day, and the darkness He called Night. . . .

God said, "Let there be lights in the expanse of the sky to separate day from night; they shall serve as signs for the set times—the days and the years; and they shall serve as lights in the expanse of the sky to shine upon the earth." And it was so. God made the two great lights, the greater light to dominate the day and the lesser light to dominate the night, and the stars. And God set them in the expanse of the sky to shine upon the earth, to dominate the day and the night, and to separate light from darkness. And God saw that this was good. [Gen. 1:2–5; 14–18]

On the second night:

Woe to those who call evil good and good evil; who present darkness as light and light as darkness; who present bitter as sweet and sweet as bitter!

Woe to those who are so wise—in their own opinion;
So clever—in their own judgment!

Woe to those who are so heroic—as drinkers of wine, and so valiant—as mixers of drink!

Who vindicate him who is in the wrong in return for a bribe, and withhold vindication from him who is right.

Assuredly, as straw is consumed by a tongue of fire and hay shrivels as it burns, their stock shall become like rot, and their buds shall blow away like dust.

For they have rejected the instruction of the Lord of Hosts, spurned the word of the Holy One of Israel. [Isa. 5:20–24]

On the third night:

They have eyes, but cannot see; ears, but cannot hear.

They are rebels against the light; they are strangers to its ways, and do not stay in its path.

For darkness is morning to all of them; for they are friends with the terrors of darkness.

Indeed the light of the wicked fails; the flame of his fire does not shine.

The light in his tent darkens; his lamp fails him.

They grope without light in the darkness; He makes them wander as if drunk.

And I will banish them from the sound of mirth and gladness, the voice of bridegroom and bride, and the sound of the handmill and the light of the lamp.

All the lights that shine in the sky I will darken above you; and I will bring darkness upon your land—declares the Lord God.

Listen, you who are deaf; you blind ones; look up and see! [Ps. 115:5–6; Job 24:13, 17; Job 18:5–6; 12:25; Jer. 25:10; Ezek. 32:8; Isa. 42:18]

On the fourth night:

Thus said God the Lord, who created the heavens and stretched them out, who spread out the earth and what it brings forth, who gave breath to the people upon it and life to those who walk thereon:

I the Lord, in My grace, have summoned you, and I have taken you by the hand. I created you, and appointed you a covenant-people, a light to the nations—

Opening eyes deprived of light, rescuing prisoners from confinement, from the dungeon those who sit in darkness.

I form light and create darkness, I make peace and create woe—

I the Lord do all these things.

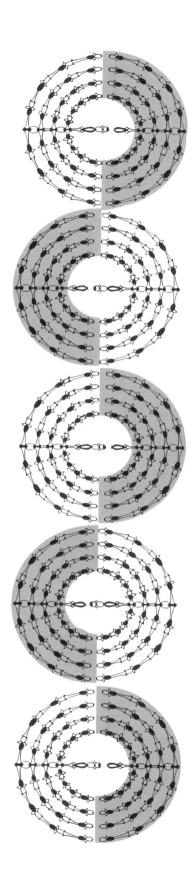

I will lead the blind by a road they did not know, and I will make them walk
by paths they never knew. I will turn darkness before them into light, rough
places into level ground. These are promises—I will keep them without fail.
[Isa. 42:5–7; 45:7; 42:16]

On the fifth night:

Look at me, answer me, O Lord, my God!
Give light to my eyes lest I sleep the sleep of death.
Darkness is not dark for You; night is as light as day; darkness and light are
the same.
Now therefore, O our God, listen to the prayer of Your servant, and to his
supplications, and cause Your face to shine upon Your sanctuary that is
desolate, for the Lord's sake.
Send forth Your light and Your truth; they will lead me; they will bring me
to Your holy mountain, to Your dwelling-place.
With You is the fountain of life; by Your light do we see light.
It is You who light my lamp; the Lord, my God, light up my darkness.
The soul of a human is the lamp of the Lord, searching all the innermost parts.
For You have saved me from death, my foot from stumbling, that I may walk
before God in the light of life.
Truly, God does all these things, two, three times to a person, to bring him
back from the Pit, that he may bask in the light of life. [Ps. 13:4; 139:12;
Dan. 9:17; Ps. 43:3; 36:10; 18:29; Prov. 20:27; Ps. 56:14; Job 33:29–30]

On the sixth night:

The Lord is my light and my help whom shall I fear?
Bless the Lord, O my soul; O Lord, my God, You are very great;
You are clothed in glory and majesty, wrapped in a robe of light;
You spread the heavens like a tent cloth.
Your word is a lamp to my feet, a light for my path.
The precepts of the Lord are just, rejoicing in His heart, the instruction of the
Lord is lucid, giving light to my eyes.
For the commandment is a lamp, and the Torah is a light.
Enlighten our eyes in Your Torah, attach our heart to Your commandments,
unite our heart to love and revere Your name. [Ps. 27:1; 104:1–2; 119:105;
19:9; Prov. 6:23; traditional prayer book]

On the seventh night:

For the path of the righteous is as the light of dawn, that shines brighter and
brighter until full day.
Light is sown for the righteous, radiance for the upright.
O you righteous, rejoice in the Lord and acclaim His holy name.
The people that walked in darkness have seen a brilliant light; on those who
dwelt in a land of gloom light has dawned.
For all the Israelites enjoyed light in their dwellings.
Arise, shine, for your light has dawned; the Presence of the Lord has shone
upon you!
O House of Jacob! Come, let us walk by the light of the Lord. [Prov. 4:18; Ps.
97:11–12; Isa. 9:1; Exod. 10:23; Isa. 60:1; 2:5]

On the eighth night:

Behold, there will come a time!
And the light of the moon shall become like the light of the sun, and the light
of the sun shall become sevenfold, like the light of the seven days, when
the Lord binds up His people's wounds and heals the injuries it has suffered.

In that day, there shall be neither sunlight nor cold moonlight but there shall
be a continuous day, of neither day nor night, and there shall be light at
evening time.

No longer shall you need the sun for light by day nor the shining of the moon
for radiance by night; for the Lord shall be your light everlasting, your God
shall be your glory.
Your sun shall set no more, your moon no more withdraw; for the Lord shall
be a light to you forever.

Cause a new light to shine upon Zion and soon may all of us be worthy to
enjoy its light. [Isa. 30:26; Zech. 14:6–7; Isa. 60:19–20; traditional prayer
book]

GIFTS

In preparing for Hanukkah, it is important to consider how you want to
handle giving presents to your children as much as what those presents will
be. You will need to decide, for example, whether one large gift or eight
smaller gifts will be your family practice. To balance the acquisitiveness
surrounding presents, one friend asks his child to choose one of his toys to
be donated to the poor during Hanukkah. Gift making, whether done by
children for each other or for adults (and vice versa), adds a special dimension
to gift exchanging. Both the issues of gifts and the overwhelming visual
bombardment of Christmas may require some discussion with your children.
At some point, children can be made to understand that Hanukkah is not in
competition with Christmas. Hanukkah, after all, is a relatively minor holiday
in the Jewish festival cycle. If it is celebrated as part of the larger cycle, then
its observance will seem natural to children and the issue of Christmas will
be less problematic.

There is no way to be "evenhanded"
in the treatment of Hanukkah and
Christmas in, say, public schools, without blowing the importance of Hanukkah all out of proportion. I see no reason that Hanukkah should become
more significant than Shavuot, for example. An alternative is to increase our
involvement in the other Jewish festivals and find better roles and treats for
our children in them. We can't compete
with the tinsel of Christmas, but we can
enhance the celebration of our own
many festivals.

E.GR.

GAMES AND OTHER PASTIMES

Besides dreidel games, another custom is to transform a regular deck of
cards into a Maccabean deck using gummed labels. The eight candles of
Hanukkah, dreidels (as nines), and latkes (as tens) become the number cards;
jacks become Judah, queens Judith, and kings Antiochus. Even simpler, blank
decks of cards are available at stores that sell teacher resource materials. Part
of the fun is drawing your own cards, which can be used to play any regular
card game. We play a version of crazy eights except big fat Antiochus is wild.

The dreidel can also be used like an
I-Ching. The four sides equal yes, no,
undecided, and later. You can even play
human dreidel: A person spins with
eyes closed until he/she staggers to one
side.

Z.S.

Some wonderful introductory or accompanying reflections are to be found in Gaston Bachelard's *Psychoanalysis of Fire* (Boston: Beacon Press, 1964).

E.GE.

Storytelling is traditionally associated with Hanukkah. Editions of Josephus and the Book of the Maccabees (in the Apocrypha) are readily available. Recently, the Rabbinical Assembly (Conservative) published *Megillat Hanukkah* edited by Rabbi A. Chiel, which contains a Hebrew version and English translation of most of the First Book of the Maccabees. Modern stories are also appropriate, such as a recently published collection of eight tales by Isaac Bashevis Singer. Or each person can be assigned a night on which to tell or read a story that relates to the themes of Hanukkah.

As mentioned, there is an old custom of women not working while the Hanukkah candles are burning. Indeed, one tradition holds that no one works while Hanukkah candles are burning. To devote the half-hour or so after the lighting to celebrating together or contemplating the ever-changing light of the menorah is an appropriate way to enhance the fulfillment of this mitzvah.

DERASH

THE MIRACLE OF LIGHTS

Traditionally, Hanukkah celebrates not a victory but a miracle. Although God may be present in all events, we sense God's presence in only those events in which there is an element of awe, an element pointing to the hand of God. For the Jewish people, the significance of the victory of the few and the weak is that it raises our consciousness of God. Because it is the hoped-for but unexpected help of God that we have celebrated, another miracle was added to the major one, the potency of one cask of oil to burn for eight nights instead of only one. Lest Hanukkah be overmilitarized, we should be cautious about describing what it is that we celebrate: the agency of God not only in our lives but in our history. For the Jews, history trails in the tracks of God.

E.GR.

A favorite rabbinic question concerning Hanukkah is, What is the miracle of the first day, since there was enough oil in the cruse to burn for that day? Many commentators provide answers—in fact, one rabbinic work has collected 100 answers to this burning (pun intended) question. One popular response is that the miracle on the first day was the victory or the dedication of the temple. Another is that, miraculously, no oil was consumed even by the first morning.

To my mind, the answer that comes closest to the meaning of Hanukkah is that the miracle the first day was the deep faith that it took to light the menorah, knowing there was not enough oil for eight days. That same faith led the Maccabees to revolt against impossible odds, to strike like hammers and scatter sparks of revolt in the hills of Judea. They believed they would prevail "not by strength, nor by power, but through My spirit—says the Lord." This faith allowed them to light the menorah, and it is this faith that made it burn for eight days. It is the miracle of faith despite darkness, and of belief in the growth of light in the depths of winter.

HANUKKAH AND THE TEMPLE

One place where the two strands of Hanukkah—the military victory and the miracle of the oil—come together is in the dedication of the temple. The dedication of the temple marks both the climax of the war and the miracle of the oil that occurred there. When we light our menorahs, we should remind ourselves of the temple of old.

The role of the temple has resonances with Sukkot, the holiday that focuses, as we have seen, on shelter and dwellings and touches on the building of God's dwelling—the sanctuary *(mishkan)* in the desert. Not surprisingly, there are a number of links between Sukkot and Hanukkah, the most important of which is found in the Second Book of Maccabees:

> They celebrated it for eight days with rejoicing in the manner of the Feast of Tabernacles, mindful of how but a little while before at the festival of Tabernacles they had been wandering about like wild beasts in the mountain caves. That is why, bearing thyrsi and graceful branches and also palm leaves, they offered up hymns to Him . . . . [2 Macc. 10:6–7]

Thus Hanukkah was observed by the Maccabees as a second Sukkot (somewhat like Pesah Sheni, see p. 36), borrowing from Sukkot the use of the four species and celebrating it for eight days.

While some of the customs, such as the four species, are no longer observed during Hanukkah, we still recite hallel every day of Hanukkah just as we do on Sukkot. This is striking because hallel is not recited on Purim, the other rabbinically ordained festival. Even on Passover, which is biblically ordained, after the first day(s) only a partial hallel is recited. As if to complete this connection between Hanukkah and the temple and Sukkot, there is a midrash stating that they began work on the *mishkan* on Sukkot and finished it on Hanukkah.

DEDICATING OUR TEMPLES

Metaphorically, Hanukkah is a time of dedication and renewal. The old altars, which have become impure, are torn down and new ones are built. It is a time of rededication to the service of God. Our menorah has replaced that of the temple, and we have replaced the Levites and priests. We are to be God's priests, but Hanukkah teaches us that our service is not restricted to the temple; for the Maccabees were priests and showed that in a war for religious freedom, it is the priests who are the generals and the leaders. The struggle to light the menorah of religious freedom is an unending one.

Hanukkah is also a development of Sukkot; for if on Sukkot we build a dwelling, then on Hanukkah we fill the inside with "furniture." In the sanctuary in the desert, there were three utensils: an altar for incense, a table for the show breads, and the menorah. We, too, must fill our homes with an altar, a table, and a menorah. What mixture of incense shall we offer on the altar? How will our deeds, words, thoughts, and emotions smell when combined as the offering of our souls before the Lord? And how will our table appear? Will it be laden with the fruits and breads of our hard labors? Will the food be offered to others? Will it be food that nourishes or chokes, that offers love or subtle poison (pollutants)?

But it is the menorah that is the key. Of all the utensils of the temple, only the menorah is commemorated, for the menorah is the light that illuminates the dwelling. What is the quality of that light? Does it provide only light or does it illuminate? The traditions of Hanukkah teach (1) that any kind of oil,

Every now and then I find myself wondering what might have been if the light and vegetation motifs of Hanukkah had early coalesced around those green branches described in 2 Maccabees rather than around clay or cast menorahs. Might our present menorah, rather than being an abstract or stylized tree of light (one way of viewing it), have been an actual illuminated tree?

And if that beckoning, twinkling, brightly lighted, fragrant tree had been ours, would Christian children have grown up wishing that they might have a Hanukkah tree?

E.Ge.

According to the tradition, the menorah in the temple illuminated the whole world. Therefore King Solomon built the temple's windows wide on the inside and narrow on the outside (the opposite of medieval castles, which tried to capture as much outside sunlight as possible), for the temple's windows did not convey light into the temple but rather were a source of light to the outside world. This is the light of our menorah.

M.S.

not necessarily the most pure, can be used to light a menorah, if lighted with the right intention; (2) that the light is not meant to be read by, rather it is to serve as light; (3) that one small cruse of pure olive oil can miraculously light up everything—it can shine forth and light not only the house but, more important, the outside world as well. The dwelling is to be a source of light, not its container.

THE MEANING OF THE MIRACLE

Why was the miracle of the menorah necessary? Wouldn't the military victory have been enough?

Notwithstanding the necessity to take up arms, you must know when to put them down. Too many wars are lost in their victories, too many revolutionaries forget why they fought. At times it is necessary to fight, but "not by strength, nor by power, says the Lord." It is the spirit that must be the ultimate victor; if not, the enemy will have won, for you will become like him. It is not pacifism advocated here, but the miracle of the menorah. To have fought and yet be able to cleanse the temple, to rededicate it, to relight the menorah, this is victory. Victory is to be free, not to triumph.

HANUKKAH AND WINTER

Hanukkah has associations older than the Maccabees' story. Some scholars argue that Hanukkah originally was linked with the winter solstice (the shortest day of the year). Others disagree, pointing out that the winter solstice only occasionally falls during Hanukkah, which, like all Jewish holidays, is determined by the lunar calendar. Be that as it may, there is a traditional link between Hanukkah, the festival of lights, and the darkness of winter, as reflected in the following passage from the tractate *Avodah Zara* 8a:

> When Adam saw the day getting gradually shorter, he said: "Woe is me, perhaps because I have sinned, the world around me is being darkened and returning to its state of chaos and confusion; this then is the kind of death to which I have been sentenced from Heaven!" So he began keeping an eight-day fast. But as he observed the winter equinox and noted the day getting increasingly longer he said : "This is the world's course," and he set forth to keep an eight-day festivity.

MAI HANUKKAH?

By lighting the menorah, we ignite the flame in our souls, the spark that cannot be extinguished, that will burn not for eight days but for eternity. We place the menorah in our windows to be visible to those passing by, just as our inner light must shine against the darkness of evil and indifference and must kindle the spirits of our fellow humans. The menorah reminds us of the

And who furnish a better example of this than the Hasmonaeans? Which is why the rabbis retained the holiday, shifted its focus to the miracle of the oil, and informally transmitted a legend of what was, or should have been but was not, sustained. Had the Maccabees' initial purity of motive been long-lasting, there would have been a little less darkness for the lights of Hanukkah to illumine.

A.E.

If "pacificism" means anything, it means struggling for human freedom and dignity by a method that renounces violence ("might" and "power") and mobilizes other forces found within each human being as well as among human beings. Nonviolence, a force born from truth and love, soul-force: Are these terms really so far from Zechariah's discussion of the *means* to an end—

"Not by my might, nor by my power, but by my spirit, saith the Lord of hosts"?

Isaiah, too, knew of such power distinct from violence: "For thus said the Lord God, the Holy One of Israel: In sitting still and rest shall ye be saved, in quietness and in confidence shall be your strength. . . ." (Isa. 30:15).

Josephus reports in detail two successful applications of Jewish nonviolent resistance—to Pontius Pilate and Caius Caligula, neither noted for being Mr. Nice Guy of the ancient world.

We live in an age when the traditional human reliance on might and power is at the point of self-negation. We also live in an age that has seen nonviolent freedom fighters such as Mohandas Gandhi in India and Martin Luther King, Jr., in the U.S. take what were thought to be religious ideals of miracle that no matter how dark life may be, there remains a source of light deep inside us. The light in our souls reflects and refracts the light from the One who is all brightness. This light can accompany us on our way and illumine the darkest path. We need not walk through life's paths stumbling over obstacles as though we were blind. The plague of darkness is all around us, but the light is there for those who continue to fan it into flame.

This is why the light of the menorah is holy and is not to be used for worldly things. Its light is not for reading, nor for counting money, but for seeing into the soul. The Bnei Yissacher (a nineteenth-century Hasidic rebbe) says that on Hanukkah we are given part of the *or ha-ganuz*—the primordial light, which has been hidden away since Creation and is preserved for the righteous in the world to come. With this light, you could see from one end of the earth to the other. With this light, we are not allowed to kindle mundane lights; we can kindle only other holy lights—the souls within each of us.

Being kindled by the Hanukkah lights, we are ready for Hanukkah—the dedication of the temple/God's dwelling place. We are ready to replace the altar that is profaned with new stone and we are ready to answer the question *Mai hanukkah?*—What is Hanukkah?—by saying, *"Zot hanukkah"*—*"This* is Hanukkah."

Rabbi Jose said: "I was long perplexed by this verse: 'And you shall grope at noonday as the blind gropes in darkness [Deut. 28:29].' Now what difference does it make to a blind man whether it is dark or light? Once I was walking on a pitch black night when I saw a blind man walking with a torch in his hands. I asked him: 'Why do you carry the torch?' He replied: 'As long as the torch is in my hand, people can see me and aid me' " (*Megillah* 24b).

merely individual validity and apply them with enormous effectiveness to societal situations. Scholars such as Gene Sharp have only begun to understand these phenomena, and we as a species have only begun to assimilate their significance for our future.

In such circumstances, these words of the prophets and the message of the menorah deserve to be taken seriously and not so casually dismissed.

E.Ge.

Light gives of itself freely, filling all available space. It does not seek anything in return; it asks not whether you are friend or foe. It gives of itself and is not thereby diminished.

M.S.

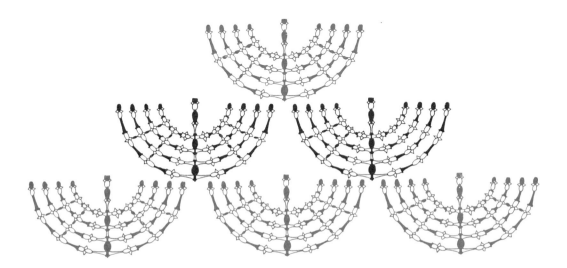

TU BISHVAT
TASTING OF THE TREE

Tu Bishvat (the fifteenth day of the month of Shevat)—the New Year for the Trees—dates back to talmudic times. It is one of the four "new years" of the Jewish calendar—Rosh ha-Shanah and Nisan (the first month) being the two most prominent. (The first of Elul is the new year in regard to tithing animals.) The Talmud regards Tu Bishvat as the new year with respect to certain agricultural laws related to tithing. With the passage of time, it became a minor festival rather than just an event in the Jewish calendar.

What exactly happens on this date to make it a "new year"? The rabbis' most common explanation is that the fruit of the trees begins to form. The majority of the winter rain has fallen by now, and the sap in the trees has risen. There is a debate in the Talmud (*Rosh ha-Shanah* 14a) over whether this change in nature should be marked on the first day of Shevat or the fifteenth. In any case, Tu Bishvat was seen as a harbinger of spring.

After the exile of the Jews from Israel, Tu Bishvat also became a day on which to commemorate our connection to Eretz Yisrael. During much of Jewish history, the only observance of this day was the practice of eating fruit associated with the land of Israel. A tradition based on Deuteronomy 8:8 holds that there are five fruits and two grains associated with it as "a land of wheat and barley, of vines, figs and pomegranates, a land of olive trees and

Why should the Jewish calendar have an arbor day? If Judaism is essentially a religion and its calendar a schedule of sacred times and spiritual celebrations, a day for tree planting seems less than venerable.

Not entirely. Although all events may have a spiritual side, some are more like civil or national holidays, the rites of a nation living on its land. We Jews are not only a religious community; we are a nation. We have a land, always in our minds if not beneath our feet. We have celebrations of our nationhood, such as Yom ha-Atzma'ut. And we have celebrations of our land and its capacity for growing things, such as Tu Bishvat.

E.Gr.

179

honey." (The honey referred to in the verse is date honey rather than bee honey.) Almonds were also given a prominent place in Tu Bishvat meals since the almond trees were believed to be the first to blossom of all trees in Israel. Though not mentioned in the verse from Deuteronomy, *bokser*—carob or St. John's bread—was the most popular fruit to use, since it could survive the long trip from Israel to Jewish communities in Europe, North Africa, etc.

In the twentieth century, because of the growth of Zionism and then the founding of the state of Israel, the association of Tu Bishvat with the land of Israel has gained even more significance. In Israel the day is celebrated with elaborate tree-planting ceremonies held by schoolchildren. In the Diaspora, children and adults give money to the Jewish National Fund (currently five dollars a tree) to plant trees in Israel.

Tu Bishvat is also viewed by the tradition as having the same meaning for trees as Rosh ha-Shanah does for humans—that is, as a new year and a day of judgment. According to this tradition, on Tu Bishvat God decides how bountiful the fruits of the trees will be in the coming year.

A KABBALISTIC VIEW

The kabbalists carried this relationship of Tu Bishvat and Rosh ha-Shanah a step further. For them, trees were a symbol of humans, as it says: "For a human is like the tree of the field" (Deut. 20:19). In line with their general concern for *tikkun olam*—spiritually repairing the world—the kabbalists regarded eating a variety of fruits on Tu Bishvat as a way of improving our spiritual selves. More specifically, they believed that eating fruit was a way of expiating the first sin—eating the fruit of the Tree of Knowledge in the Garden of Eden. Similarly, trees were symbolic of *the* tree—the Tree of Life, which carries divine goodness and blessing into the world. To encourage this flow and to effect *tikkun olam*, the kabbalists of Safed (sixteenth century) created a Tu Bishvat seder loosely modeled after the Passover seder. It involved drinking four cups of wine and eating many different fruits while reciting appropriate verses. (This will be more fully explained below.)

TRADITIONS

THE TU BISHVAT SEDER

The basic concept behind the ritual is to increase the flow of God's emanations/blessings into the world. By eating the various kinds of fruits with the proper intention, we aid in the refructification of our world from the divine Tree of Life. The ritual is found in the text *Peri Etz Hadar (The Fruit of the Goodly Tree)* and involves eating three groupings of ten kinds of fruits and nuts and

The kabbalists called it *ha-hu ita-na-la-na ra-ba u-ta-ki-fa*—"the great and mighty Tree" in which is food for all (*Zohar* III 58a), and *i-la-na had rav-r'va i-la-a ta-ki-fa*, "a mighty and wonderous celestial tree" which supplies nourishment to beings above and below (*Zohar* II 58b). Clearly one has here the Hebrew version of the Cosmic Tree, our very own Yggdrasil, as it were!

E.GE.

Just how is eating connected with the Tree of Life? If the question crossed your mind, worry no more—the kabbalists have it all figured out.

How many teeth has the adult human? Thirty-two. And how many times does the word *Elohim* (God) occur in the Creation account in Genesis? Thirty-two. Thus mastication using the thirty-two teeth, done with full awareness, connects directly with Creation and its continuation.

E.GE.

drinking four cups of wine. The number ten represents the ten *sefirot* (emanations) through which the divine flow comes into this world. Each of the three groupings represents a level of creation.

According to kabbalah, there are four worlds or levels of creation: *azilut* (emanation), *beriah* (creation), *yetzirah* (formation), and *assiyah* (action—our world of physical reality). The world of *azilut* is purely spiritual and cannot be symbolized in any concrete way. The world of *beriah* is symbolized by ten fruits that have neither pits on the inside nor shells on the outside—that is, they are totally edible: grapes, figs, apples, etrogim (citrons), lemons, pears, raspberries, blueberries, carobs, and quinces. (Seeds are considered edible in this system.) The world of *yetzirah* has pits inside, but the outside can be eaten. Its ten fruits are olives, dates, cherries, jujubes, persimmons, apricots, peaches, loquats, plums, and hackberries. The world of *assiyah* has an outside shell that must be discarded, and an inside that can be eaten. Its ten fruits and nuts are pomegranates, walnuts, almonds, pine nuts, chestnuts, hazelnuts, coconuts, Brazil nuts, pistachios, and pecans. The symbolism, in brief, is as follows: Those parts that can be eaten represent holiness; the inedible parts —that is, the pits—represent the impure; and the shells serve as protection for the fragile holiness inside.

The ritual itself consists of eating a combination of the above fruits and nuts as well as others not on the list in the course of drinking four cups of wine. Each fruit is accompanied by an appropriate verse from the Bible or a quotation from the Talmud. The sequence of fruits and nuts varies from one version of the seder to another. Each of the four cups is filled before each sequence of fruit, but is drunk only at the end of the sequence. The first cup is filled with white wine; thereafter red wine is mixed with the white. The fourth cup is basically red wine with a few drops of white wine mixed in. The white wine represents nature as dormant, while the red wine represents nature in bloom. An English version of the traditional seder is available, called *Tu Bishvat: A Mystical Seder for the New Year of Trees,* edited by Yehoshua Bergman, Diaspora Yeshiva, Mt. Zion, P.O. Box 6426, Jerusalem, Israel.

OTHER CUSTOMS

There is a Hasidic custom of praying on Tu Bishvat for a beautiful etrog —citron—to be used for the following Sukkot. Another custom linking these two holidays has already been mentioned in the Sukkot chapter—that is, making jam from the etrogim of Sukkot and eating it on Tu Bishvat. Sukkot as the harvest festival bears witness to how the trees were judged on the previous Tu Bishvat.

It is customary to make fruity, nutty, and Israeli-type dishes for this day. Another custom is to donate ninety-one cents or dollars to tzedakah since "charity averts the evil decree." Because Tu Bishvat is the day of judgment for the trees, we give ninety-one, which is the numerical value of the Hebrew letters that make up the word *ilan*—tree.

The categories of fruits may symbolize three kinds of interpersonal situations also. Entering an unfriendly or anxiety-producing atmosphere, one is guarded, externally armored, as it were: The shell is on the outside, like the fruits of *assiyah*.

In friendlier surroundings, but superficial or entered with some reservations, there is more interpersonal contact and exchange, even some degree of affable sharing, but the very private self remains surrounded by the inner shell, like the fruits of *yetzirah*.

In certain special situations of deep trust and intimacy, however, the inner self is revealed and shared with another; at this moment of I-Thou there is no inner shell, like the fruits of *beriah*.

At several Tu Bishvat seders in recent years, we have spent time reflecting individually on interpersonal situations during the preceding year that exemplified each of these categories, and each time most of us present have been nourished by the discoveries we've made.

E.GE.

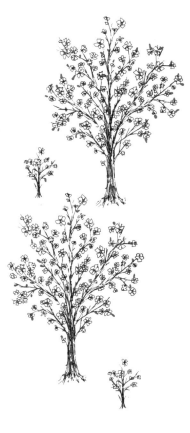

It is also customary in some synagogues to make Shabbat Shirah an occasion for a cantorial concert or special presentation of new songs for the congregation. Although the Jewish calendar abounds in melodies for all seasons of the ritual year, Shabbat Shirah is an apt time for enriching the Sabbath or everyday repertoire of song.

E.GR.

What a lovely custom, and how appropriate for a holiday celebrating the renewal of the Cosmic Tree. After all, birds have the good sense to inhabit trees and the good grace to surround them with song. And so we humans, graceless though we be at times, on this occasion have the grace to invite the birds to eat with us in celebration of our beloved tree.

E.GE.

SHABBAT SHIRAH

Around the time of Tu Bishvat, there occurs the special Shabbat called Shabbat Shirah—the Sabbath of Song/Praise. It marks the week of the Torah portion *Be-shallah* (Exod. 13:17–17:16), which includes the song of praises to God recited by the Israelites after the Egyptians drowned in the Red Sea. In some synagogues, the song (Exod. 15:1 ff.) is chanted to a special *trop*—cantillation. The crossing of the sea is celebrated as a great miracle and as the final step of the Exodus from Egypt. Therefore, the song at the sea has become particularly associated with thanksgiving and praise.

Another custom of the day is to feed birds. This is also related to the Torah portion. Moses told the people to collect a double portion of manna on Fridays because no manna would fall on Shabbat. Some troublemakers decided to make Moses look like a liar by spreading manna around on the ground late Friday afternoon so that when the people awoke the next morning it would look like manna had indeed fallen. However, the birds foiled the plan by eating all the manna lying on the ground. As a reward for this good deed, we feed the birds on this day. Some also claim that we feed them on Shabbat Shirah because their singing is a constant praise of God.

FROM TU BISHVAT TO PURIM

It is only a month from Tu Bishvat to the merrymaking of Purim. The Purim spirit begins to be invoked on the first of Adar, when we are supposed to increase our joyousness in preparation for the holiday.

The seventh of Adar is the anniversary of the death of Moses. Pious Jews fasted on this day in the Middle Ages. The day also became a special one for the members of *hevrot kaddisha*—burial societies—which would often hold their annual dinner on this date. Since God buried Moses, it was a reflection on the honor of these societies, who were also involved in the holy task of burial, for this to be a special day.

ARBA PARSHIYYOT: THE FOUR PORTIONS

On the Shabbatot preceding and following Purim, there are four special Torah readings called the *arba parshiyyot*. These portions are read in addition to the weekly portion. Their themes are related to the festival cycle at this time of year, and each Shabbat is named after the special portion.

Shekalim (Exod. 30:11–16), which is read on Shabbat Shekalim, the Shabbat closest to Rosh Hodesh Adar, describes how each Israelite had to donate a half-shekel to the Jerusalem Temple for a fund to buy animals for the daily sacrifices. Messengers were sent out on the first of Adar to collect the half-shekel for a new fund.

Zakhor (Deut. 25:17–19), which is read on Shabbat Zakhor, the Shabbat immediately preceding Purim, recounts how the people of Amalek attacked the Israelites in the desert. This portion is probably read because Haman the Agagite, according to tradition, was a direct descendant of Agag, the king of the Amalekites (see 1 Sam. 15:9 ff.).

Parah (Num. 19:1–22) is read after Purim on Shabbat Parah. It describes the ritual of purification involving the red heifer. Since everyone needed to be pure in order to sacrifice the Pesah offering, this was a time when those who had been defiled by contact with a corpse would undergo the purification rite of the red heifer.

Ha-Hodesh (Exod. 12:1–20) is read on Shabbat ha-Hodesh, the Shabbat before (or, if they coincide, on) Rosh Hodesh Nisan. This reading proclaims that the month of Nisan "shall be the first of all months," and goes on to describe the ritual of Passover.

These four portions help us to prepare for both Purim and Pesah by reminding us of their imminent approach.

KAVVANOT

The existing traditions for Tu Bishvat can be elaborated on to further enhance this festival. Tu Bishvat has continued to be a time to reflect upon our connection to the land of Israel. For some it has also become a time to reflect more broadly on our connection to land and nature throughout the world. These concerns can be manifested in the tradition of giving money to plant trees in Israel, by becoming involved in an ecological project in your neighborhood, or by carefully examining the trees in your backyard for any necessary care. All of these acts are meant to remind us of an aspect of our environment that we often take for granted.

Those of us who cannot actually plant a tree, whether here or in Israel, might want to substitute an indoor garden. This is especially useful in providing children with a sense of the natural growth cycle. A variety of seeds can be planted, one favorite being parsley, which can be "harvested" for use at the Passover seder. Another is alfalfa sprouts, which are easy to grow and ready to eat in a few days.

Recently, a number of people have adapted the kabbalistic seder to other uses. Some emphasize those fruits associated with the land of Israel both in the Bible and in modern times: for example, Jaffa oranges. They retain the verses alluding to these fruits and add other verses about the beauty of the land, thus creating a seder that highlights our relationship to Israel. Others use the seder to acknowledge our indebtedness to nature, by adding appropriate verses and other relevant material. Still others focus on the various fruits as symbolic allusions to our relationship to God, making use of scripture such as Song of Songs 2:2–3: "Like an apple tree . . . so is my beloved among the youths." (Song of Songs, as described in the Passover chapter, is traditionally read as referring to the love between the people of Israel and God.) Similarly, grapes are an allusion to the people of Israel, based on Hosea 9:10. Another version of this seder emphasizes *human* qualities—e.g., figs represent peace

Tu Bishvat should make us aware of and thankful for the trees around us. Go into your backyard and thank the trees that give off oxygen and provide shade for your house. Blow a shofar for your trees.

Z.S.

A good custom is to germinate something for the New Year of the Trees. One suggestion is to keep etrog pits in the freezer until a week before Tu Bishvat, then put them in moist cotton. They will begin to sprout in a short while.

Z.S.

At our Tu Bishvat seders, we regularly follow each of the four cups of wine with the song "V'hitifu" (Amos 9:13). Though Amos is not usually thought of as lyricist for a drinking song, with both sap and spirits rising he serves admirably in this role!

E.GE.

and prosperity ("But they shall sit every person under his vine and fig tree and none shall make them afraid"—Mic. 4:4); the carob stands for humility; and so forth. The Jewish National Fund (42 East 69th Street, New York, N.Y. 10021) has some material for a seder as well as much material for Tu Bishvat generally.

DERASH

SECOND SINAI

Deuteronomy 1:3 states that Moses' last great speech, comprised of the Book of Deuteronomy, began on the first day of Shevat. Since tradition ascribes Moses' death to the seventh of Adar, the whole Book of Deuteronomy *(Devarim)* must have been "given" between Shevat 1 and Adar 7. The book itself, as its English name implies, is a recapitulation of the earlier sections of the Torah. Thus this period was seen in some traditions as a second giving of the Torah, somewhat analogous to Shavuot. Both the book and the period of the year embody a notion that there is a second chance to hear and then accept the Torah.

This period is a moving forward to the greeting and accepting of the Torah, which, according to one tradition, was really only freely accepted by the Jewish people on Purim, a week after this period ends (Adar 14). Yet the period also harks back to the past. Shevat 1 becomes a kind of Shavuot; Shabbat Shirah recalls the crossing of the sea; and Purim as a moment of redemption brings to mind the first redemption of Pesah. Echoes upon echoes reverberate in this period. Yet, as much as these days seem to reflect the earlier festivals, they are also more human in that reflection, culminating in both a redemption and Torah giving brought about by human effort as related in the Purim story.

In the middle of this period (as in the middle of the Garden) stands the Torah as *etz hayyim*—the Tree of Eternal Life, whose fruits we eat on Tu Bishvat, and whose fruits sustain us all the days of our lives.

TU BISHVAT AND THE GARDEN OF EDEN

Once Honi was walking along the road when he saw a man planting a carob tree. Honi asked, "How long before it will bear fruit?" The man answered, "Seventy years." Honi asked, "Are you sure that you will be alive in seventy years to eat from its fruit?" The man answered, "I found this world filled with carob trees. Just as my ancestor planted for me, so shall I plant for my children" *(Ta'anit* 23a).

This tale reflects the image of trees as a symbol of eternity, for they live beyond the lifetime of a single human generation. At the same time, the tale

---

Interesting, in this connection, are the words of Cedric Wright:

Consider the life of trees.
Aside from the axe, what trees acquire from man is inconsiderable.
What man may acquire from trees is immeasurable.
From their mute forms there flows a poise, in silence, a lovely sound and motion in response to wind.
What peace comes to those aware of the voice and bearing of trees!
Trees do not scream for attention.
A tree, a rock, has no pretense, only a real growth out of itself, in close communion with the universal spirit.
A tree retains a deep serenity.
It establishes in the earth not only its root system but also those roots of its beauty and its unknown consciousness.
Sometimes one may sense a glisten of that consciousness, and with such perspective, feel that man is not necessarily the highest form of life. [*Words of the Earth,* 1960]

E.GE.

Although not so messianic as to promise a return to the original situation of Eden, certain works have, for me, pointed to possibilities for living now in ways that reduce the gap between the Garden and ourselves. Chief among these is Helen and Scott Nearing's *Living the Good Life* (Schocken), now being reissued with *Continuing the Good Life* and *The Maple Sugar Book* in a special centennial edition to celebrate Scott's 100th birthday. These books are as practical and inspiring a guide for reconnecting with Eden as one is likely to find in this age.

E.GE.

shows that, for humans, children are our trees, our means of achieving eternity. Thus this story closes the circle, as parents give the gift of trees to their children.

On Tu Bishvat, we return to the place of our first encounter with trees —the Garden of Eden. We enter once again into harmony with nature as we were in the Garden. The antagonism between humans and nature is set aside. In Genesis, for eating of the Tree of Knowledge, God punishes us: "Cursed be the ground because of you; by toil shall you eat of it all the days of your life; thorns and thistles shall it sprout for you. But your food shall be the grasses of the field; by the sweat of your brow shall you get bread to eat, until you return to the ground—for from it you were taken. For dust you are, and to dust shall you return" (Gen. 3:17–19). We were driven from the Garden, driven from a symbiotic relationship with nature into one of bitter struggle. However, on Tu Bishvat we reconnect to trees and to the Tree of Life. We grasp the eternity symbolized by the long-living trees. We glimpse what the Garden was and how life could be again—no thorns or thistles, no returning unto dust.

Originally, in the Garden we were only young children, not ready for the responsibility of the knowledge of good and evil. Indeed, after eating of the Tree, we were incapable of handling the knowledge, and so we ran and hid. Now, having experienced the festival cycle in all its aspects, beginning with our birth at Pesah and growing through the subsequent holidays, we are mature enough to eat again of the Tree of Knowledge.

On Tu Bishvat we return to the Garden, beckoned by the trees all around us pointing the way to the Tree of Life. We are ready to handle the responsibility of bringing about *tikkun olam*—a spiritual repairing of the world, restoring it to its whole form found in an eternal garden planted in Eden.

Thus the rabbis said, "If a sapling were in your hand, and you were told that the Messiah had come, first plant the sapling, then go out to greet the Messiah." For Tu Bishvat holds out this vision instead of the thorns of our present world:

"Behold the days are coming," says the Lord, "when the plowman shall overtake the reaper and the treader of grapes him who sows the seed; the mountains shall drip sweet wine, and all the hills shall flow with it.

"I will restore the fortunes of my people Israel, and they shall rebuild the ruined cities and inhabit them; they shall plant vineyards and drink their wine, and they shall make gardens and eat their fruit. I will plant them upon their land and they shall never again be plucked up out of the land which I have given them," says the Lord your God. [Amos 9:13–15]

PURIM
SELF-MOCKERY AND MASQUERADE

 urim (Adar 14) celebrates—with a stress on every syllable of the word—the victory of Mordechai and Esther over wicked Haman. The story is related in the Book of Esther, which is read during the holiday. The name Purim means "lots," for Haman used a lot *(pur)* to decide when to kill the Jews. The lot fell on the month of Adar. Therefore the rabbis stated: *"Mi-shenikhnas adar marbim be-simhah*—With the start of the month of Adar we greatly increase joy." The rejoicing on Purim for this victory is not limited by any sense of sacredness: For example, there are none of the prohibitions associated with the pilgrimage festivals. Though the story of Esther is in the Bible, it is not part of the Five Books of Moses, and hence is only of rabbinic origin. Its observance centers around the reading of the *megillah*—scroll—of Esther. Every time the name of the villain, Haman, is read, we make noise to drown out the name. Other mitzvot/rituals include a festive meal on the afternoon of Purim, sending gifts of food to friends *(mishloah manot),* and giving money to the poor *(mattanot le-evyonim).* The day is also celebrated with costumes, masquerades, plays, parodies, and a heavy consumption of liquor. All of these activities are meant to make Purim a day when everything is topsy-turvy, and a Mardi Gras spirit runs wild even in the most straight-laced sectors of the Jewish community.

The story in the Book of Esther is a melodramatic tale of court intrigue.

In the first part of the book, the stage is set by the banishment of the proud Queen Vashti and the choice of Esther in a beauty contest to be the new queen. The courtier, Haman, becomes grand vizier, but Mordechai, Esther's protector, refuses to bow down to him. Haman decides to take out his fury on all the Jews and convinces the rather silly king, Ahasuerus, to consent to a decree calling for the massacre of the Jews throughout the kingdom. Mordechai and Esther go to work to counteract this scheme. Esther entrances the king, wines and dines him, and then reveals that she is Jewish and pleads for her people. Haman is hanged and the Jews are allowed to turn the tables on their enemies. Mordechai and Esther live happily ever after—after instituting Purim as an annual holiday.

This charming tale has led to much debate among scholars who question its historicity. Certain facts in the story are contradicted by other historical evidence: For instance, it is known that Persian kings of that period married women only from the seven leading families of Persia, therefore the king's marriage to Esther would have been impossible. Because of these questions, some scholars believe that Purim harks back to an ancient pagan festival that was transformed by the Jews. As evidence to support their views, they point out the striking correspondence between the names Mordechai and Esther and Marduk and Ishtar, two of the important pagan gods of the ancient Near East.

THE STORY AS FARCE

Even without these scholarly questions, an examination of the story provokes doubts about its literal truth. Perhaps the first hint of the story's farcical nature is in the first chapter when the king and his advisers decide they have to get rid of Queen Vashti in order to keep all the wives in Persia obedient to their husbands. What could be more farcical than a group of men issuing a decree that they must be obeyed by their wives!

The numerous plot devices also point to the whimsical nature of the story. Why does Vashti refuse to come before the king? Why is Esther told to keep her identity a secret? Why is Mordechai not immediately rewarded for saving the king from a plot against his life? Why does Mordechai refuse to bow down to Haman? The answer, of course, is that without these contrivances the plot could not have reached its grand conclusion.

The scholar H. L. Ginsberg surmises that the name of God nowhere appears in the Book of Esther because it would be irreverent to mention God in such a comic setting. The Book of Esther is, then, the first of a genre of Jewish literature, the Purim parody.

Whether the story really happened or is pure fantasy or an exaggerated version of a historical incident, the Book of Esther and Purim have become accepted by the Jewish people as part of the festive cycle. The levity of the book imbues the day with its basic character of joyousness; at no moment is the threat to the Jews in the story taken seriously. Yet the Book of Esther is

also seen in the light and shadow of the Jewish people's experience in exile. Haman's description of us as "a certain people scattered about and dispersed among the other peoples" has had a deep resonance for each generation of Jews. The tale of a group of Jews living in the Diaspora at the mercy of the whims of their rulers has been often repeated. All too frequently, we have faced Hamans and the conclusion of the story has not been happy. Purim affirms the bright moments of victory and denies the long, bleak centuries of persecution.

Purim, then, has remained a time to feel good and to let loose, a time to masquerade as someone other than yourself. The spirit of Purim is best captured in the Talmudic dictum "It is the obligation of each person to be so drunk [on Purim] as not to be able to tell the difference between 'Blessed be Mordechai' and 'Cursed be Haman.'" Although later scholars tried to explain away this obligation, the Talmud's statement is unequivocal. To drive home the point, the Talmud enters into the Purim spirit by following this dictum with this story:

> Rabbah and Rabbi Zera joined together in a Purim feast. They became drunk and Rabbah arose and killed Rabbi Zera. On the next day, he prayed on Rabbi Zera's behalf and brought him back to life. Next year, Rabbah said: "Will your honor come, and we will have the Purim feast together." Rabbi Zera replied: "A miracle does not take place on every occasion." [*Megillah* 7b]

Many rabbinic scholars had difficulty with the talmudic statement that it is an obligation to be drunk on Purim. Some thought it was not a commandment but only a suggestion. Others decided that it meant to drink a little more than usual. Some felt that you only had to drink enough to be unable to recite a very complicated piyyut. Still others thought it meant that you should drink only until you fell asleep. The rabbis explained the Talmud's preoccupation with drinking because so much of the plot revolves around drinking, from Vashti's disgrace to Haman's downfall. Despite all these attempts, no explanation could really detract from the statement's encouragement to fully celebrate the holiday.

TRADITIONS

Purim is preceded by Ta'anit Esther—the Fast of Esther—which was instituted in remembrance of the three-day fast by the Jews of Persia at Esther's request (see Esther 3:12; 4:16). Interestingly, the three-day fast in the *megillah* took place during the Passover of the year before rather than the day before the events of Purim occurred. The Jews were engaged in battle with their enemies on Adar 13 of that year. In an earlier time, the thirteenth of Adar was actually a minor festival called Yom Nikanor, which celebrated the victory of Judah the Maccabee over the Syrian army led by Nicanor. Since it was a minor fast not mentioned in the Bible (unlike the other minor fasts

It is not often noted that the precedent for masquerading on Purim is set by the Scroll of Esther itself. Esther the Jewess dresses up as queen, and Mordechai takes on regal garb. See the Jews dressing up like Persian royalty!

E.GR.

In order to understand the holiday's full significance in the eyes of the rabbis, we should note the special Torah and prophetic readings chanted on the Sabbath before Purim in the synagogue. We read, first, the paradoxical commandment to remember to blot out the memory of Amalek. The enemies who attacked our weak and our stragglers as we went forth from Egypt must be remembered—to be forgotten. In the haftarah we read about Saul, who forgot to remember. For reasons that are unclear but seem less than pious, Saul neglected to execute the Amalekite king Agag, and the job had to be done by the prophet Samuel. Mordechai, we are told, is a Benjaminite—like Saul. Haman is an Agagite—Amalek. On Purim we have the chance to do the job of remembering right.

How? The only way to blot out the memory of Amalek once and for all is so to perfect the world that the evil attributed to Amalek becomes inconceivable—as inconceivable as such a perfected world seems when we live under Amalek's sway. We are not yet able to fulfill the commandment in that way. We are rather, as the Book of Esther hammers home in 3:6, in exile. Chance rules here, not mitzvah; the fate of peoples is decided by one queen's failure to do a striptease, and another's success in a beauty contest; by a king's insomnia, and a bedside supplication mistaken for attempted rape. It would be funny if it were not so serious. It *is* funny, though it is serious.

How then can we remember properly to forget? Stay tuned.

A.E.

—see "The Three Weeks"), the rabbis were lenient about its observance. Today, outside traditional circles, the fast is not observed.

Purim begins at sundown of Adar 14. After ma'ariv, the *megillah* is read from a handwritten scroll (similar to a Torah scroll). Three blessings are recited before the reading and one after by the person reading the *megillah*. They are as follows:

> Praised are You, Lord our God, Ruler of the universe, who has sanctified our lives through His commandments, commanding us to read the scroll [of Esther].

> Praised are You, Lord our God, Ruler of the universe, who performed miracles for our ancestors, in those days, in this season.

> Praised are You, Lord our God, Ruler of the universe, for giving us life, for sustaining us, and for helping us to reach this moment.

After the *megillah:*

> Praised are You, Lord our God, Ruler of the universe, who has championed our cause and passed judgment on our behalf, taking vengeance for us, and punishing all our mortal enemies as they deserve. Praised are You, Lord our God, who saves His people Israel from all their enemies, for You are a redeeming God.

Whenever Haman's name is read, everyone breaks out in loud noise to literally fulfill the curse *Yimah shmo*—May his name be erased (or in this case drowned out). While any kind of noisemaking device is fine, a graf (rattle) is traditional. Since the Purim story revolves around proclamations and the holiday itself was promulgated through dispatches, it is customary to fold the scroll as it is read like a letter rather than rolling it up as is done with a Torah scroll. Certain verses are recited by the congregation and then repeated by the reader (Esther 2:5; 8:15, 16; 10:3). The *megillah* has its own special *trop* (cantillation). The verses listing the ten sons of Haman (Esther 9:7–10) are recited in one breath because they were hanged together.

All our other Purim rituals are based on Esther 9:22: "They were to observe them as days of feasting and gladness, and as a time for sending gifts to one another and presents to the poor." "Feasting and gladness" becomes the Purim seudah eaten late in the afternoon. This expression is also the basis for the encouragement of drinking on Purim. "Sending gifts" is *mishloah manot*, while "presents to the poor" is *mattanot le-evyonim.*

Mishloah manot involves sending gifts of food to friends. This usually means putting together some hamantaschen, cake, fruit, nuts, little bottles of wine, or whatever on plates, which are then delivered to various friends and acquaintances. The plates range from simple (two kinds of food is the mini-

And it was so, when the king saw Esther the queen . . . she obtained favor in his sight and the king held out to Esther the golden sceptre that was in his hand.

Esther 5:2

mum) to extensive. There is even a folk-art tradition of using specifically decorated plates for the *mishloah manot.* Today, most people use paper plates and confine themselves to what can fit on the plate.

Mattanot le-evyonim is a mitzvah to give to poor people. This practice is part of the theme of celebration that those less fortunate should be able to enjoy the festival and, more broadly, their lives. This gift on Purim (minimally to two poor people) is beyond the general mitzvah of tzedakah (charity). The giving is usually done through the various charities that assist indigent Jews.

Another custom related to giving to the poor is *mahatzit ha-shekel*—half of a shekel coin. In biblical times, each Israelite was supposed to donate a half-shekel toward the maintenance of the temple in Jerusalem. This practice was continued after the temple's destruction as a way to support the religious institutions of Palestine. Today, the giving of the half-shekel is usually done before the *megillah* reading at night. A silver dollar is used, and each person puts some money on a plate and then borrows the silver dollar, which is then donated back to the plate. Some people use three coins because the term *half-shekel* appears three times in Exodus 30:13, 15. The money collected in our day is given to the poor.

Purim comes to an end with the Purim seudah, which in the tradition ranks second only to the Passover seder in importance as a special meal. The seudah does not have any rituals similar to the seder's; it is simply a time for friends and family to gather. The seudah takes place late in the afternoon rather than at lunchtime. In some communities, Purim skits take place at this meal. While kiddush is not recited on Purim, some people recite a Purim kiddush consisting of a nonsensical stringing together of biblical verses linked by the use of the same word in two verses. The following is the beginning of one Purim kiddush. (It makes more nonsense in the Hebrew.)

> The sixth day [Gen. 1:31] were finished the heavens [Gen. 2:1] proclaiming [Ps. 14:1] the glory which fills the universe, His ministering angels ask one another [musaf amidah] is Sarah your wife? [Gen. 18:10] . . .

This kiddush is an example of "Purim torah." Purim torah consists of various forms of making fun of the tradition. There exist elaborate parodies of the Talmud as well as other standard traditional texts. A favorite theme of many of these parodies is why you are allowed to drink only wine and why water is bad for you and basically not kosher! In some yeshivot (rabbinic schools of higher learning) a Purim rabbi was elected who gave lectures parodying his teachers. On Purim, the traditional respect for rabbinic teachers is cast aside and they become the targets of biting satires. Perhaps this is all to say that it is important to be able to make fun of the Torah, which we hold so sacred during the rest of the year, lest we become sanctimonious about it.

Purim is also a time of Purim carnivals and masquerades. In Israel, a huge parade of costumed merrymakers takes place annually and is called *adloyada* from the dictum that you should be so drunk that you are not able to tell the difference between *(ad lo yada)* cursed Haman and blessed Mordechai. Those watching the parade are in constant danger of being bonked by the ubiquitous plastic hammers carried by troublemakers during Purim.

This is how we remember to forget Amalek's awful but all-too-normal behavior. We drown it out by screaming as loudly as we can. We celebrate the one time that we can remember when we, without God's direct aid, defeated Amalek at his own game. Then, exhausted by noisemaking, tired out by our merriment, we forget Amalek conclusively in the only way this imperfect world allows us. We get drunk. So drunk that we can't tell Mordechai from Haman, good from evil. For one day in 365 we forget the easy way—so that the other 364 we can work on the harder path to real forgetting: *tikkun olam.* It starts on the day of Purim itself, with the feeding of the poor. Amalek would simply let them starve.

A.E.

I would not be surprised if the custom of chanting the names of Haman's ten sons in one breath was invented by an expert *megillah* reader to enable him to show off his skills, much as many musical compositions for solo voice and instrument include sections that lack musical profundity but allow for the demonstration of technical virtuosity. A knowledgeable congregation will often ooh and ah following such a virtuoso achievement.

E.Gr.

A heightened sense of imagination and fantasy is what the Scroll of Esther and its festival of Purim are essentially about. The lighthearted tone of the story, which you do well to point out, bespeaks the carnival atmosphere in which the scroll emerged, as the first Purim Torah. Unlike some Christians and even some Jews who find the book offensive, most Jews have always heard the Scroll of Esther in a Mardi Gras context and have therefore taken it as fun and fantasy. The banishment of Vashti and the Jews' slaughter of 75,000 Persians, not to mention mass conversion to Judaism by the Persian populace, are cruel or absurd when taken at face value. But Jews, who have suffered the cruel caprice of and persecution by gentiles time after time, permit themselves the fantasy of imagining themselves in the gentile role and the gentiles in the Jewish role. As Mordechai replaces Haman in the Persian administration, we replace the gentiles in the scheme of the world. Fantasies don't hurt their victims; they mitigate the tensions of those having them.

The Scroll of Esther deals with an abiding serious issue for Jews in the Persian, or any, Diaspora. Jews are unlike anyone else. They are a nation living among all the nations, with ways of their own, loyalties to each other and to their traditions, and yet asserting their loyalty to the nations in which they reside. Gentiles, having no one to compare the Jews to, are understandably mystified. How can the Jews be loyal to their own nation and also loyal to ours? The Scroll of Esther "proves" that the Jews can. Mordechai remains a pious Jew and yet takes great pains to save the king from assassination. He demonstrates that he is a loyal steward of Persian interests and is rewarded with a high post in the government. Esther, or Hadassah, is the queen of Persia. She had been queen for years before letting on that she was Jewish. Of course a Jew can be loyal to the nation and loyal to her or his people—look at Esther! She is Hadassah with regard to her tradition and people, but she is Esther to us.

E.GR.

SHUSHAN PURIM

Because the Jews of Shushan fought against their enemies for an extra day and did not rest until the fifteenth of Adar, they observed Purim on the fifteenth of the month rather than on the fourteenth. The rabbis ruled that all cities walled at the time of Joshua would observe Purim as in Shushan. Either to honor the land of Israel or out of a belief that the only walled cities at the time were in the land of Israel, this is applied only to Jerusalem, where Purim is observed on Adar 15. Other cities in Israel, such as Acco, are in a doubtful category. Shushan Purim is observed in Jerusalem in the same way it is observed elsewhere on the fourteenth.

SPECIAL PURIMS

For Jews in many ages, it was easy to see the Purim story as a metaphor of Jewish history. The story takes place during the Exile, and the Jews are at the mercy of a whimsical local ruler. God's outstretched arm is nowhere apparent to save them from an anti-Semitic plot. It is the combination of their own efforts and chance—that is, God working behind the scenes—that brings about redemption. Not surprisingly, a custom arose that whenever a Jewish community was saved from its enemies, it would celebrate the event annually with a special local Purim. These days were known as Purim Katan—Little Purim. The celebration was modeled after that of Purim: (1) fasting the day before, (2) reading a *megillah* that recounted the story of the salvation, (3) reciting hallel and *al ha-nissim* prayers. In some communities a special feast was held and charity was given to the poor just as was done on Purim.

The *Encyclopaedia Judaica* lists over a hundred such special Purims. For example, until recent times the community of Frankfurt-am-Main celebrated a special Purim called Wintz Purim on the twentieth of Adar. In the year 1614, Jews were driven from the city by an anti-Semitic mob led by Wintz Fettmilch; but the emperor intervened on behalf of the Jews, Fettmilch was executed, and the Jews were allowed to return to their homes. There even are special Purims observed by a family because an ancestor was saved from death. One of the better-known is that of the Heller family of Prague who to this day still gather on the first of Adar to read a scroll describing how Yom Tov Lippman Heller, rabbi of Prague, was saved from a death sentence in 1629.

FROM PURIM TO PESAH

The last seven days of Adar (Adar 23 and on) are called "the days of dedication" because according to tradition the *mishkan*—sanctuary—was dedicated during this time, with its final dedication rite taking place on the first of Nisan.

Shabbat Parah and Shabbat ha-Hodesh occur during this period (see p. 183).

As mentioned, Nisan is the first of all months. Pesah's character infuses it, making it a time of rejoicing over the exodus from Egypt. It is also a joyous time because the tradition holds that just as we were redeemed from Egypt in the month of Nisan, so too will the final redemption take place during this month.

Nisan as a time for preparing for the holiday of Pesah is described in the Pesah chapter. There are also a number of customs unrelated to Pesah that occur in this month.

- The following blessing is recited when we see the first blossoming tree of the year:

    Praised are You, Lord our God, Ruler of the universe, who has withheld nothing from this world and has created beautiful creatures and beautiful trees in it, so that people may delight in them.

- According to tradition, the sanctuary was dedicated in the desert beginning with the first of Nisan. Each day the prince of one of the twelve tribes would bring offerings to the sanctuary (see Numbers, chapter 7). A few synagogues follow the custom of reading from the Torah each day the appropriate portion for each prince. Others read these sections without the blessing recited for aliyot. Still others read these sections from a Bible rather than from the Torah scroll. On the thirteenth of Nisan, we read the portion that begins "When You light the lamps . . ." (Num. 8:1, 2) in honor of the tribe of Levi who served in the sanctuary.
- Every twenty-eight years the Blessing of the Sun—*birkat ha-hamah*—occurs on the first Wednesday of *tekufat Nisan*. (The solar year is divided into four parts called *tekufot*, thus *tekufat Nisan* is not identical with the month of Nisan.) By traditional reckoning, on this day the sun returns to the same position it occupied in the sky on the fourth day of creation. The next blessing of the sun is in the year 2009.

Then took Haman the apparel and the horse, and arranged Mordechai, and caused him to ride through the streets of the city, and proclaimed before him:"Thus shall it be done unto the person whom the king delights to honor. "

Esther 6:11

And Haman's daughter looked out of the window and saw the procession below. Assuming the one leading the horse was Mordechai, she emptied the chamber pot on him, her father.

From the midrash

K A V V A N O T

Purim is a holiday that should not be relegated only to children. The joyous breaking of bounds is particularly important for adults, who usually feel constrained from acting out. The central event of Purim is the reading of the *megillah* on the evening of Purim. The evening begins with the ma'ariv service, which in some places is sung to High Holiday or other festival tunes, or even to the latest jingles from television. Next comes the reading of the *megillah,* accompanied by noisemaking every time Haman's name is read. To go beyond the traditional grager, you should let your imagination run wild, keeping in mind that the noisier the better. Some interesting noisemakers I have seen include trumpets, a shofar, drums, a piano or organ playing appropriate or inappropriate music, a cookie tin filled with nails, wooden blocks beaten against each other, and balloons with Haman's name on them to be popped. A traditional twist on the stamping of feet (resorted to by those without noisemakers) is to write Haman's name on the soles of your shoes and to stamp until the name is erased. Booing, hissing, and appropriate shouts are also good last-minute resorts for the unprepared. An old custom, no longer observed, was the burning of Haman in effigy. Many observances encourage the wearing of costumes during the reading and at some point in the evening holding a parade of costumes.

The tradition of Purim plays and skits dates back to the Middle Ages. Many synagogues and groups stage performances ranging from silly songs to plays, which are done before, during, or after the reading of the *megillah.* Most of the skits retell the Purim story or poke fun at the members of the synagogue or group. It is in the character of the day to satirize things and people usually held in respect—for example, the rabbi. Care should be taken not to draw out the reading too long, especially if young children are present. On the other hand, the *megillah* reading in and of itself is long and some may feel that songs or skits can serve as a useful change of pace. In some places the reading is followed by a party or even a concert of Jewish music, with dancing.

Let everyone make masks before the *megillah* reading, using strips of surgical plaster-cast material that comes in rolls. After soaking the strips, place them on your face in a thin layer and cut out eyeholes, etc. Half-masks can be made for those with beards, and the masks can be painted when dry.

It can be disconcerting to see yourself in a mask. The year we did this, we ended up discussing other people's masks and our own masks and masks and masks.

Z.S.

Turn the *megillah* reading into a play by assigning one person Haman's part, another Esther's, another the narrator's, etc.

Z.S.

Work is not prohibited on Purim, but, if possible, take the day off anyway and celebrate it as a festival without any restrictions. This will enable you to pay attention to the rituals of the day, which tend to receive short shrift. Traditionally, the *megillah* is read again during the morning services, though this always seemed to me a boring repetition rather than an enhancement of the Purim spirit. However, the rituals of *mishloah manot* and the Purim seudah, which take place during the day, are important enhancements of Purim. *Mishloah manot* is a nice way to exchange gifts with friends and provides a Purim activity for the day. In traditional circles, it is customary for children to deliver the plates and receive an edible "tip" from the recipient. This ritual is most evident in Hasidic neighborhoods where the streets are full of children traveling back and forth delivering *mishloah manot* (and, in general, fooling around). Even in other communities, *mishloah manot* can be a fun activity, especially for families or groups. Some people have taken it upon themselves to deliver these plates of food—and, more important, of good cheer—to those who need them most, such as people in nursing homes. A few have combined this with the notion of skits and have re-created the practice of traveling troubadours who sing Purim songs and deliver *mishloah manot.*

FOOD AND CRAFTS

The two craft items for Purim are gragers and, less prevalently, the *mishloah manot* plates. There is also a tradition of illuminating the *megillah.* The crafts involved are fairly technical, though simpler versions for children are possible, such as decorating the *mishloah manot* plate with crayons, "illuminating" their own *megillah* scroll, etc. Simpler gragers such as dried beans in a grager-shaped container made of cardboard or aluminum pans, or any kind of noise-maker, are good projects to do with children.

For the more ambitious, there are directions for grager-making in *The First Jewish Catalog,* p. 138. If you cannot find the wooden spool mentioned in those directions, you can make your own by drilling a hole through a small block of wood. You might also want to "double the recipe" by substituting a lath strip for the tongue depressor, using wood that is ¾" × 2½" × 17¾" for the top and bottom and making a larger center spool. This will give you a hefty two-handed grager.

Another area of craft activity involves the preparation of costumes. There is also an old folk custom of making posters to announce the month of Adar, which heralds the joy of Purim. A prominent motif is fish since Adar coincides with the zodiac sign of Pisces.

The Purim food is hamantaschen, triangular cookies (supposedly reminiscent of Haman's hat) filled with any number of things, though prune and poppy-seed fillings are the most popular. Other traditional foods are variations of a similar sweet, such as the orecchi di Haman (Haman's ear) cookies of Italian Jewry. (For a recipe, see *The Classic Cuisine of the Italian Jews* by Edda Servi Machlin [New York: Dodd, Mead, 1981]).

It is also traditional to eat kreplach on Purim, perhaps because it, too, is triangular—or because Jews seem to want to eat kreplach whenever they can. Traditionally, they are also eaten on Hoshana Rabbah and the day before Yom Kippur (and Shavuot).

According to one tradition, Esther, in order to keep kosher, ate only seeds and legumes, which has given rise to a custom of eating chick-peas and other such foods, or at least foods that contain seeds or nuts, such as baklava. Since the country of Hodu—India—is mentioned in the *megillah,* some Jews in Eastern Europe eat turkey, which is called the "Hodu bird" *(tarnegol hodu).*

DERASH

PURIM VISION I

As we saw in the chapter on Shavuot, there is a cycle of the law that runs throughout the festival cycle and at the same time resonates with the historical experience of the Jewish people. The cycle begins with the giving of the Torah on Shavuot. Sinai is a unique moment in the life of the Jewish people. But the heights of Sinai last only a brief forty days before the descent to the sin of the golden calf. In the calendar, forty days after Shavuot comes the seventeenth of Tammuz, which initiates the Three Weeks, a period marking the depths of the Jewish historical experience. The golden calf is the first of many betrayals of the Covenant leading ultimately to the destruction of the temple in Jerusalem and our exile from the promised land.

Having descended from Shavuot to the Three Weeks, we begin our ascent as we seek reconciliation with God during the month of Elul. As the prelude to the High Holidays, this is a period during which we strive for forgiveness for our sins. This movement in the festival cycle is reflected in the traditions surrounding the golden-calf incident. Moses spends forty days pleading with God not to destroy the Israelites because of their sin. Finally God relents and commands Moses to come up to the mountain for another forty days to receive the second set of tablets. Moses descends carrying the tablets, the sign of God's forgiveness, on the tenth day of Tishri, known to us as Yom Kippur.

Having been reconciled, we rejoice during the holiday of Sukkot, but this, too, fades as we descend into Heshvan, the month without holidays, which marks the approach of winter. Only at Hanukkah, with its ever-increasing light, do we begin to emerge from the wintry depths. Tu Bishvat, with its imagery of growth, then leads us to the end of the festival cycle, Purim. That Purim comes at the end of the festival cycle apparently makes it end with a bash rather than a confrontation with a crucial spiritual theme. Yet underneath the hilarity lies an important reason why Purim closes the festival cycle. The cycle began with Pesah, when God alone—not an angel, a seraph, nor any other agency—redeemed us from the depths of Egypt. The cycle ends with a salvation during which God has retreated behind the curtain and the human actors have come center stage. *We* have learned how to bring about

So they hanged Haman on the gallows that he had prepared for Mordechai.

Esther 7:10

This is redemption? Yes and no. It is like the exodus from Egypt: survival that makes more-than-mere-survival possible, the liberation from oppression that lets us choose our own way— God's. *This* kind of redemption we "have learned to bring about." But the other? It eludes us still. The lessons start almost at once—at Pesah.

A.E.

our own redemption. Even Hanukkah, with its military victory, still has its miracle of lights. Purim is the work of the Jewish people, and of Mordechai and Esther in particular. If Pesah is to show us by example that redemption is possible, then Purim demonstrates that we have learned the lesson.

Purim also brings to a culmination the cycle of the giving of the Torah begun on Shavuot. According to the midrash, at Sinai God suspended the mountain over the heads of the Israelites and ordered them to accept the Torah or else. The nature of the giving of the Torah at Sinai partakes of the nature of imparting rules and values to children—that is, there remains the essential aspect of a mountain hanging over their heads, no matter how willingly or cooperatively they acquiesce to those rules and values. Only when we have grown up through the festival cycle to Purim, when we can effect our own redemption without God's miracles, can we, as adults now, fully accept the Torah.

Concerning the midrash about the suspended mountain of Sinai, Rabbi Aha bar Jacob states: "The fact that the mountain hung over their heads would serve as a valid excuse for denying culpability for violating the Torah since the covenant was accepted under duress!" But Rava says: "Nevertheless the Jews accepted the Covenant willingly in the time of Ahasuerus, as it says: 'The Jews affirmed and accepted [see Esther 9:27]'—that is, they affirmed now what they had accepted earlier."

Finally, the Torah is accepted out of free will. As a sign of this, we humans make the Torah ours by adding to it the holiday of Purim. Purim is the fulfillment of the real message of Pesah and Shavuot for we take both redemption and the process of Torah and grasp them firmly in our hands.

And yet, by Purim, we are almost at the end of the festival cycle. In a month we begin again with Passover, a new birth, as the story of slavery and Sinai recommences. Symbolically, then, we fully accept the Torah for only a brief moment before we are again immersed in the new/old cycle of the giving, abandoning, and final receiving of the Torah.

PURIM VISION II

Why must we seriously fulfill the commandment to be crazy on Purim?

The Jewish festival cycle is full of different moods—the bittersweet joy of Pesah, the mourning of the Three Weeks, the awe of Yom Kippur, the rejoicing of Simhat Torah, among others. Each of us in his or her our own life experiences the same range of feelings, and part of the festival cycle's effort is to provide a context for those feelings. Each of us probably has difficulty expressing one or more of them—for example, grief or joy or guilt. Surprisingly, perhaps, many people find it less difficult to feel contrite on Yom Kippur than to act the joyous fool on Purim. Purim calls upon us to give free rein to that dimension of our personalities signified by the phrase *ad de-lo-yada*. *Ad de-lo-yada*—the state of not knowing the difference between Haman and Mordechai—is a time when all our rules and inhibitions are swept

Very sly, our author. Shall I confess? Until I realized that this put-on is an outstanding example of "Purim Torah" at its most improbable, I was almost taken in by it. Now, of course, I realize that our good author is here quite carried away by the spirited beverages recommended for Purim, and has imbibed to such an extent that not only can he no longer distinguish Haman from Mordechai; he can no longer distinguish the human from the Divine, the creature from the Creator, the redeemed from the Redeemer. *"We* have learned how to bring about our own redemption."

That, friends, is Purim Torah of a very high order! I wish I knew what brand the author swills to slake his thirst; its mental effects are as miraculous as the Purim melodrama itself.

Alas, not having this magical brew in my liquor cabinet, when I look at our vaunted twentieth-century efforts to "bring about our own redemption," I am anything but cheered.

E.GE.

And Parshandatha, and Dalphon, and Aspatha, and Poratha, and Adalia, and Aridatha, and Parmashta, and Arisai, and Aridai, and Vaizatha, the ten sons of Haman . . . slew they.

Esther 9:7–10

Ingenious: And so, by mocking law and authority this one day, we testify to our submission to them all the rest. The sacred order contains our inevitable drive to cast it off, by letting us do so for one day, and then calling us back to business. Even knowing how it works, we have a great time tearing down the barriers we will simply put back up—and reinforce—the very next day.

A.E.

I like the good/evil symbolism. But the idea is not that good and evil cannot be recognized in their pure states, in Mordechai and Haman, say. It is only in the grayer areas of life, most of them, that we must sort out the evil and the good.

E.Gr.

Or is it the flip side of Purim, the Day of Atonement, Yom Kip-purim—"like Purim"? On both days, Purim and Yom Kippur, we step outside ourselves completely, one to rise, one to fall. Then we step back in and get back to the business of life—living. With each other, before God, well.

A.E.

away, when the superego is pushed aside by an untrammeled id. We enter the world of the drunk, a world of blissful ignorance of reality.

The state of *ad de-lo-yada* also enables us to see how easy it is to change from Mordechai into Haman, from a crusader for justice into simply a crusader. That is why the Talmud says that we fully accept the Torah only on Purim, for only when we can mock the tradition can we fully accept it. Only then are we safe to do so; otherwise we make the tradition into an idolatry rather than a smasher of idols, into frozen-in-stone dogma of what once was rather than a living faith. The threat of the mountain of Sinai hanging over our heads evaporates as do all mirages at the laughter of the Jews on Purim. All the smoke and sound of Sinai vanishes and we see clearly the Torah, its great potentials and great dangers. We accept the Torah knowing that once a year on Purim there will be a time to laugh at our own self-righteousness. We can live by that Torah all the rest of the year because for one day we can let out our repressed feelings as we overturn all the rules, even turning the Torah itself upon its head. Both for the sake of Torah and ourselves, we need Purim to laugh at what we value and thus paradoxically gain a real sense of self-worth.

Ad de-lo-yada has another level of meaning as well. It is not an animalistic state of stupor, but rather a higher degree of consciousness. It is a messianic/-mystical moment when there is *no* difference between Haman and Mordechai, good and evil, for both are found in the Holy One "who created light and darkness, made peace and created evil" (Isa. 45:7).

Which is it then—Purim the nihilistic holiday of unbounded joy, or Purim the climax of the festival year by its fulfillment of the message of Pesah and Shavuot? Which is it, Haman or Mordechai? *Ad de-lo-yada*—I leave it to you to distinguish which is the real Purim.

When all the other festivals will be abolished [in messianic times], Purim will remain. [*Midrash Mishle 9:2*]

And the cycle begins again.

COMMENTATORS

Arnold Eisen received his Ph.D. in modern Jewish thought at Hebrew University. He is an associate professor of Jewish thought at Tel Aviv University and the author of *The Chosen People in America.*

Everett Gendler is the rabbi of Temple Emanuel in Lowell, Massachusetts, the Jewish chaplain and instructor in philosophy and religious studies at Phillips Academy, and does small-scale farming.

Arthur Green is the dean of the Reconstructionist Rabbinical College, a member of the faculty at the University of Pennsylvania, and the author of *Tormented Master: A Life of Rabbi Nahman of Bratslav* and other writings.

Edward L. Greenstein is associate professor in Bible at the Jewish Theological Seminary of America; author of monographs, articles, and reviews; and coeditor of the forthcoming volume *The Hebrew Bible in Literary Criticism.*

Zalman Schachter-Shalomi is professor of religion and Jewish mysticism at Temple University, founder and leader of the B'nai Or community, and the author of *The First Step: A Guide for the New Jewish Spirit.*

All are active in the *havurah* movement.

AUTHOR

Michael Strassfeld is a coeditor of the *First, Second,* and *Third Jewish Catalogs,* coeditor of the annual *Jewish Calendar,* and editor of *A Passover Haggadah.* He received a B.A. and an M.A. in Jewish studies from Brandeis University. He currently serves as Director of Programming and Development at Temple Ansche Chesed. He resides in Manhattan with his wife and two children.

ILLUSTRATOR

Betsy Platkin Teutsch is a leading Jewish artist working in gouache, ink, and serigraph. Born in Fargo, North Dakota, Ms. Teutsch has a B.A. in Jewish studies from Brandeis University and an M.A. from Hebrew Union College. She resides in Manhattan with her husband and son.

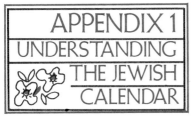

APPENDIX 1
UNDERSTANDING THE JEWISH CALENDAR

An understanding of the workings of the Jewish calendar will be helpful in reading this book. This calendar is fundamentally a lunar one—that is, based on the cycles of the moon. The moon completes its cycle of phases every twenty-nine and a half days (approximately), thereby creating months. Since this is an uneven number, some months have twenty-nine days and others have thirty.

Rosh Hodesh—the first day of the new moon/month—is a minor holiday marked by hallel, a special Torah reading, and by a musaf (additional) amidah. In biblical times, Rosh Hodesh was more of a festival than it is today, though recently some people, especially women, have celebrated it as a day marking the feminine aspect of Judaism. There is an old custom of women not working on Rosh Hodesh and some have seen that custom as reflecting the striking resonances of the phases of the moon with the menstrual cycle and the imagery of the swelling belly of pregnancy. (Since Rosh Hodesh and Shabbat occur frequently, I have decided not to include them in this book, because both intrinsically belong to the daily and weekly life cycles of the Jew and as such await treatment in a book devoted to them.)

A twenty-nine-day month is followed by one day of Rosh Hodesh. A thirty-day month creates two days of Rosh Hodesh—that is, both the thirtieth day of the month of Nisan, say, and the first day of Iyyar are Rosh Hodesh (since the month has twenty-nine and a half days, part of the thirtieth is Rosh Hodesh). Nisan, Sivan, Av, Tishri, Shevat, and in leap years Adar I are thirty-day months. Iyyar, Tammuz, Elul, Tevet, and Adar (Adar II in leap years) are twenty-nine-day months. Heshvan and Kislev vary year to year from twenty-nine- to thirty-day months.

There are twelve months, in general, in the Jewish calendar, which totals 354 days in a year. Being more than eleven days short of the solar year, the Jewish year creates a problem for the Jewish festivals. Left as is, the holidays would move back eleven days each year so that Passover, the festival of spring, would come to be celebrated in winter, autumn, and summer as well; hence, all the festivals would lose their connection to the natural/agricultural cycle. To keep the holidays in their appropriate seasons, a "leap month" is added to the calendar at regular intervals. This leap month (Adar II) is added seven times during a nineteen-year cycle, thus occurring every two or three years. The discrepancy between the number of days in the lunar and solar years also explains why all of the holidays shift from year to year: For example, Hanukkah can occur anytime between early and late December.

YOM TOV SHENI: THE SECOND FESTIVAL DAY

In the period of the second temple, the new moon and its month were proclaimed by the high court in Jerusalem when it appeared in the sky to eyewitnesses instead of by calculation. This created a problem for telling the Jews in the Diaspora when the holidays would fall, since the new moon (Rosh Hodesh) could fall on either one of two days. If one did not know exactly when the first day of Nisan was, for example, it would be unclear when Passover was to occur. To let the outlying Jewish communities know the times of the new moon, various systems were devised, such as a network of signal fires. However, there were problems with each of these systems, and some communities were too distant to be reached by any method.

The rabbis consequently devised Yom Tov Sheni Shel Galuyot—the second festival day of the Diaspora. This meant that for most full festival days, an additional day was observed to cover both of the days on which the festival could occur: For example, the seventh day of Sivan became the second day of Shavuot. Thus, a second festival day was added to the first and seventh day of Passover, Shavuot, the first day of Sukkot, and to Shemini Atzeret. These second days, with very minor exceptions, maintained all the restrictions and all the ritual obligations of the first days. Because fasting for forty-eight hours would be difficult, Yom Kippur remained only one day. The second day was also not applied to the rabbinic holidays of Purim and Hanukkah. Rosh ha-Shanah has a unique status that is discussed in the Rosh ha-Shanah chapter.

Even after the calendar was set by calculation rather than by eyewitness testimony, the rabbis decided to maintain the practice of second-day festivals. The reasons for doing so are not very clear, yet until modern times the second day was universally observed in the Diaspora—although, with the exception of Rosh ha-Shanah, Jews in the land of Israel during all this time observed only one-day festivals.

Recently, a number of authorities have come to question the two-day practice. The basic argument against the weight of tradition is that there is no longer any doubt about the holiday calendar. Also, it is detrimental to repeat the same rituals twice. (Why ask "Why is this night different?" if it is not any different from the previous night?) It is also argued that the observance of the first day will be strengthened by the abolition of the second. Whatever the merits of these arguments, Orthodox Jews still observe the second day, Reform Jews do not, and practice varies among Conservative Jews. A good source for this question is *Conservative Judaism* 24 (no. 2, Winter 1970).

APPENDIX 2
HALAKHAH OF THE HOLIDAYS

This section contains a detailed discussion of various laws and customs related to the festivals. I rely mainly on the classic code of Jewish law, the *Shulhan Arukh,* which dates from the sixteenth century and is the work of two scholars: Rabbi Joseph Karo, a Sephardic scholar, who composed it, and Rabbi Moses Isserles, the RaMA, who added Ashkenazic opinions to the text. Other traditional scholars whose authority I draw upon are identified by the century. For contemporary opinions, I often refer to the Rabbinical Assembly Law Committee (RALC), a body of Conservative rabbis. Other Conservative opinions come from the late Isaac Klein, author of *A Guide to Jewish Religious Practice,* and Seymour Siegel, author of *The Jewish Dietary Laws.* The Orthodox point of view is represented by J. David Bleich, who teaches at Yeshiva University, and Shimon Eider, who teaches at the Lakewood (New Jersey) Yeshiva.

This section begins with a description of the laws for festivals in general and then follows the order of the book in discussing each festival individually.

A WORD ABOUT HALAKHAH

It has often been said that Judaism is short on dogma and long on practice. While this is not entirely true, the practice of halakhah has been central to Judaism at least since rabbinic times. There has been and still is much debate about the nature of Jewish law and its development. In fact, attitudes toward halakhah are often used to differentiate among Orthodox, Conservative, Reconstructionist, and Reform Judaism. These range from the conviction that the law in its unchanging, binding totality was given at Sinai, to the conviction that halakhah is no longer binding and serves only as a resource from which to choose what we wish to observe today. There are countless gradations between these two extremes. Each of us has to decide his or her approach to halakhah. This book presents much of the traditional halakhah but at times suggests practices that are at variance with the tradition. It also suggests many contemporary customs that have not yet been either accepted or rejected by traditional halakhic authorities. All of this material is meant to serve as a source of knowledge rather than a prescriptive guide for the reader.

It may be useful to the reader to understand something about the broad categories of Jewish law. According to traditional view, there are three such categories: biblically ordained commandments *(de-oraita)*, rabbinically ordained commandments *(de-rabbanan)*, and customs (minhagim). Biblically ordained commandments are those dos and don'ts explicitly stated in the Five Books of Moses: for example, "Keep the Sabbath day." These are commanded by God and must be carefully observed. The second category includes all laws either deduced by the rabbis from the Torah—that is, those not explicitly stated—or promulgated by rabbinic decree. While not of divine origin, the traditional view obligates us to observe them. The third category, customs, includes practices that the people of Israel or its sages devised over time to enhance Judaism. These carry no obligation except for the weight of tradition.

Unfortunately, it is not so simple, for there are laws that, although not explicitly stated in the Bible, the rabbis believed were implicit in the biblical text and therefore biblically ordained. In fact, there is no single agreed-upon list of the 613 commandments that the tradition ascribes to the Torah. Similarly, there is no universal agreement about what is rabbinically ordained and what is biblically ordained, or what is rabbinically ordained and what is established by custom. Over time, many customs became law, while for some authorities customs began to have a binding force all their own. This book tries to make clear what practices belong to each of the three categories, to assist you in establishing your observance.

A final note: In our time there is a spectrum of observance across denominational lines. I use the term *traditional Jews* instead of *Orthodox Jews* since there are Jews of other denominations who also observe the practice being described.

HALAKHOT OF YOM TOV

Certain rules apply to all full festival days. For example, work is prohibited on the first and last day of Passover, Shavuot, Rosh ha-Shanah, Yom Kippur, the first day of Sukkot, and Shemini Atzeret. Where there is a second festival day (see above), this prohibition also applies to the second and eighth day of Passover, the second day of Shavuot, the second day of Sukkot, and Simhat Torah (which is the second day of Shemini Atzeret). The prohibition is basically similar to that of Shabbat, thus many kinds of activities related to work are restricted. However, there is one major difference: The kinds of work needed to prepare food are permitted on festivals—cooking, carrying, lighting fire from an existing source (and therefore, smoking cigarettes). The last example means that you cannot strike a match but you can light a match from a stove burner left on before the festival began. (Yom Kippur is an exception to this, and is treated like Shabbat.)

Two positive aspects that all these festivals share are *kavod* (honor) and *oneg* (pleasure). Traditionally, *kavod* involves honoring the festival day by making yourself clean and wearing your best clothes. *Oneg* involves pleasurable activities, especially eating good food and drinking wine, for festivals are meant to be times of rejoicing.

The festivals are also *mikra'ei kodesh*—days of holy assembly—and to mark this holiness, these days are introduced with candlelighting and the recital of kiddush (sanctification) over wine. They are also ended by havdalah marking the transition from the holy to the ordinary weekday.

These rules do not pertain to the rabbinic holidays of Purim and Hanukkah.

EIRUV TAVSHILIN

While cooking is permitted on a full festival day, it is forbidden to cook and prepare food during yom tov that will be eaten on Shabbat (or for that matter on a weekday). This causes a problem if the full festival days are Thursday and Friday, because food would have to be prepared on Wednesday for Shabbat! However, the rabbis decided that if the preparation of food is symbolically begun before the festival (on Wednesday), it can be continued during the festival. The ritual of *eiruv tavshilin* was created for this purpose. Some cooked food and a piece of bread (matzah on Pesah) are set aside for the purpose of being eaten on Shabbat, thereby permitting the preparation of additional food for Shabbat during the festival. The ritual involves setting aside the food and reciting:

> Praised are You, Lord our God, Ruler of the universe, who has sanctified our lives through His commandments, commanding us concerning the *eiruv*. By means of this *eiruv* we are permitted to bake, cook, warm, light candles, and make all the necessary preparations during the festival days for Shabbat—we and all who live in this place.

This ritual is observed in traditional circles.

HALAKHOT OF PESAH

BEFORE PESAH

If you are going on an extended trip during the thirty days before Passover, you should do bedikah before you leave. If you can't do it the night before Pesah, then perform it after Passover in order to find any *hametz she-avar alav ha-pesah* (since hametz owned by a Jew during Pesah becomes forever forbidden). The blessing *al bi-ur hametz* is recited only for bedikah done the day before or during Passover, not thirty days before or after Pesah. (Synagogues, schools, etc., require bedikah but not *bittul.*)

Because of the rabbinic interpretation of the word *akh* in Exodus 12:15 (also Deuteronomy 13:3), the day before Pesah was divided in half. During the first half of the day, we are allowed to eat hametz; during the second half, we are forbidden. The second half of the day in temple times was devoted to bringing the Pesah sacrifice to the temple, where it would be slaughtered. The rabbis, concerned lest someone make a mistake—particularly on a cloudy day when the sun couldn't be used to tell time—shifted the prohibition of hametz one hour earlier. (NOTE: Hours in this context refer to halakhic hours, which are calculated by adding together the minutes between sunrise and sunset and dividing that number by twelve. Thus, the length of an hour will be longer in the summer, since there is more daylight, and shorter in the winter.)

The *siyyum* custom for the Fast of the Firstborn is for someone to finish studying a text the morning before Pesah. Other firstborn (even those who have not studied the rest of the text) join in the study of the last lines. This is followed by a meal. While originally the *siyyum* was supposed to celebrate the end of a text that had been studied for much of a year, the study has become very pro forma. Often relatively brief texts (e.g., the mishnah of a tractate) are studied during the week before Pesah in order to arrange for a *siyyum.*

If Passover falls on Sunday, the fast is on Thursday. If Passover falls on Saturday, the fast is on Friday. A father is supposed to fast for a firstborn son who is not old enough to fast. (There is disagreement as to whether the prayer *aneinu* should be said in the Amidah for this day.)

THE LAWS CONCERNING HAMETZ

Besides Exodus 12:15 quoted earlier, the prohibition against hametz is found in the following verses:

No leaven shall be found in your houses for seven days.
For whoever eats what is leavened, that person shall be cut off from the assembly of Israel, whether he is a stranger or a citizen of the country.

You shall eat nothing leavened, in all your settlements you shall eat unleavened bread.

Remember this day, on which you went free from Egypt . . . no leavened bread shall be eaten.

Throughout the seven days unleavened bread shall be eaten; no leavened bread shall be seen with you, and no leaven shall be seen in all your territory.
[Exod. 12:19, 20; 13:3, 7. See also Deut. 16:3, 4.]

The hametz laws are derived from these verses, which the rabbis regarded as intentionally repetitive. There is a positive commandment to remove hametz (in Exod. 12:15) and there are negative prohibitions against eating it (for example, Exod. 13:3) —a double emphasis. Further, we note that the punishment for violation of the commandment is *karet*—the cutting off of the offender from the people of Israel—one of the only two times such a punishment occurs for violating a positive commandment in the Torah.

The rabbis interpreted these verses to mean that not only was eating hametz forbidden by the Torah but gaining benefit from hametz was forbidden as well. For instance, you can neither sell hametz nor use it to feed your pets during Pesah. This is more stringent than the laws concerning nonkosher foods—for example shrimp or nonkosher meat, which, while forbidden for a Jew to eat, can nonetheless be bought and sold.

Further, it is forbidden even to own hametz during Pesah. This is a unique law derived from two verses (Exod. 12:19 and 13:7) and is called *bal yera'eh bal yimatzeh*— "Hametz should not be seen nor found in your possession." (Actually, these are two prohibitions, but they are always referred to together.) Therefore, we must search for and remove all the hametz we own. Even if you own hametz that you have no access

to during Passover—for example, in a summer house or locked away in a friend's house—you are still violating the principle of *bal yera'eh bal yimatzeh,* for it is the fact of owning hametz, not the use of it, that is forbidden by this law.

Bal yera'eh bal yimatzeh applies only to *your* hametz; it does not forbid you to see bread on TV or in the supermarket—in fact, you could have a whole stack of bread in your house as long as it belonged to someone else and you bore no responsibility for it. On the other hand, the prohibition against eating or gaining benefit from hametz applies to *any* hametz, whether you own it or not.

Another way in which the laws of hametz are more stringent than other dietary laws is in regard to the amounts of hametz that are forbidden. Hametz is forbidden *be-mashehu*—even in the tiniest amounts. This is different from the injunction against pork or a mixture of milk and meat, which the Torah forbids in quantities of *ke-zayit* (larger than the size of an olive). The rabbis, however, extended the prohibition by outlawing the eating of any amount of pork or milk-and-meat mixtures. What then is the practical difference? The difference is related to the principle of *bateil* (nullification).

If *by accident* a forbidden food falls into a permitted food or creates a forbidden mixture (e.g., if milk is spilled into a pot of chicken soup), the rabbis have provided us with a series of rules to clearly indicate when the forbidden food becomes nullified by the larger quantity of kosher food. For instance, a little milk in chicken soup would be nullified if the soup had a 60:1 or greater ratio to the milk. While the rules change with different circumstances and substances, this principle of nullification is relied upon to make the kosher laws more flexible. It allows for the possibility of accidents and spares people the hardship of discarding a whole pot of soup because a little milk fell into it. *Bateil* also allows us to be less concerned with the possibility of small quantities of forbidden food being mixed into processed foods. Thus, even if a rabbinic supervisor at a factory turns his back for a moment, during which time a no-no falls on the conveyor belt, we can depend on the principle of *bateil,* in many circumstances, to nullify the problem.

Hametz, however, is forbidden *even in the smallest amounts* and the principle of *bateil* does not apply to it. Therefore, additional care and rabbinic supervision are required for anything we eat during Pesah, and many foods that do not require rabbinic supervision during the year require it for Pesah.

In buying certain foods before Passover, especially liquids, some people rely on the fact that *bateil* does apply before Passover. According to this view, while hametz in the tiniest amount is forbidden on Passover, before Passover it is nullified in mixtures of 60:1. Therefore milk or even cans of tuna fish packed only in water are bought by some people before Passover. If there is a bit of hametz in the milk, it becomes nullified before Passover begins, thus allowing its use during the holiday itself. Some authorities question whether something that is *not forbidden* (hametz before Passover begins) can be nullified. Others wonder whether once Passover begins and hametz becomes forbidden, it becomes "unnullified" *(hozeir ve-na'or);* and therefore if there is hametz in the milk, the milk is forbidden. The consensus of traditional opinion is that while the hametz remains nullified for liquid foodstuffs such as milk, it regains its hametzhood for solids.

There is one other unique aspect to the laws of hametz—the principle *hametz she-avar alav ha-pesah,* according to which any hametz owned by a Jew during Pesah becomes irrevocably forbidden to him or her forever afterward. This rule was instituted by the rabbis as a penalty for those who thought they could hold on to their hametz through Passover and then consume or sell it afterward. To prevent this the rabbis forbade such hametz to all Jews forever. (This principle, of course, does not apply to hametz owned by a non-Jew during Pesah. This may be used as soon as Passover is over.)

What Is Hametz? Leavened bread occurs when water is mixed with flour from any of the five grains—wheat, barley, spelt, rye, and oats. If left alone for eighteen minutes or more, enough rising will occur simply from molecules in the air for the mixture to become hametz.

There are three other categories of hametz:

1. *Se'or:* yeast, since it speeds up fermentation. In talmudic times, people would mix a warm, already fermented dough in with a new batch of dough to speed up the fermentation.
2. *Ta'arovet hametz:* a mixture of hametz with permitted food. As explained above, any amount of hametz is forbidden even if found in a large amount of permitted food.
3. *Hametz nuksheh:* hametz unfit for human consumption (or, alternatively, hametz fit to be eaten only by a dog). This category covers those things made with flour and water and yet not consumed as food.

The category of *hametz nuksheh* is very complicated and technical. In general, those substances that fall into it can be *owned* during Passover since they are not considered food for humans. One subcategory is substances unfit even for dogs to eat and therefore permitted *to be used* during Passover—for example, ink, paint, and certain cosmetics. Another subcategory is called *ahsheveih*—substances that are "eaten" (e.g., lipstick). Are these "foods" or not?

There is much debate about these questions. In general, the most problematic substances in the rubric of *hametz nuksheh* are those made from grain alcohol. Despite being consumed, most medicines are permitted even by strict authorities because they are not food fit for a dog and they are not eaten in the normal manner—that is, they are swallowed without being chewed. Any medicine needed because of a threat to life is, of course, permitted. (If in doubt about a medicine, consult your druggist and/or rabbinic authority.) There are some questions as to whether chewable tablets may be used during Passover. Liquid medicine can be even more problematic because of grain alcohol, used especially in cough medicine. Rabbi Klein states that saccharin, aspirin, and digitalis are permitted. He also says that the principle of *bateil be-shishim*—nullification if more than a 60:1 ratio—does apply to *hametz nuksheh.* It should be noted that isopropyl alcohol is not a grain alcohol and is permissible.

Many rabbinic authorities state that grain alcohol is a problem only in liquid form, such as perfumes and mouthwash, and is permitted as a solid—for example, in creams and ointments. Rabbi Eider lists both permitted and problematic substances. It is permitted to use nail polish, hand lotion, cold cream, baby lotion, shampoo, shoe polish, ink, paint, air fresheners, talcum and baby powder, powder or stick deodorants, eye shadow and liner, mascara, blush, rouge, lipstick, soap, and toothpaste. (Note: Some people use kosher soap for washing dishes, though there is no obligation to do so.) Substances that are problematic and need to be checked for their ingredients are perfume, cologne, toilet water, hair spray, shaving lotion, mouthwash, liquid and roll-on deodorants. Perfumes containing ethyl alcohol should be considered actual hametz and be sold or removed before Passover.

RELATED MATTERS

Kitniyot Ashkenazic Jews do not eat from another category of foods, called *kitniyot,* during Passover. *Kitniyot* consist of legumes—beans, peas, lentils, rice, etc. (see a complete list at the beginning of the Pesah chapter). Sephardic Jews, however, do eat *kitniyot* on Passover.

For those who do not eat *kitniyot,* it is forbidden only to eat them, not to own or benefit from them. The usual reasons given for avoiding *kitniyot* on Passover are as follows:

- The kernels of *kitniyot* and grain are easily confused.
- Cereal and other foods made from *kitniyot* look similar to the same foods made from grain.
- Bread can be made from some of these legumes, which could lead to possible confusion.

(Because of the last reason, at one time potatoes also were not eaten by some people during Passover, since potato flour can be used to make bread. This custom, however, is no longer observed.) There is disagreement as to whether the oils of *kitniyot* are permitted—for example, corn oil, peanut oil, etc. Many authorities permit the use of these oils, and some regular brands are available with rabbinic supervision for Passover.

While widely observed among traditional Jews today, the custom of *kitniyot* was a source of disagreement for many years (see "Legumes on Passover" by Marc Rosenstein, *Central Conference of American Rabbis* [Reform] *Journal,* Spring 1975, pp. 32–40). It is a particular problem for vegetarians, for whom beans are an important source of protein. The ban also makes many canned foods problematic since both fruits and tuna fish are sometimes canned in oil made from *kitniyot.*

The Question of Egg Matzah—or, Kosher in English, Restricted in Hebrew! There is a long-standing debate about matzah made from flour mixed with eggs or fruit juices. According to one body of opinion (including Joseph Karo and Maimonides), flour mixed with eggs or fruit juices (without any water) never becomes hametz. Many others argue that eggs or fruit juices with water (and flour) can become hametz. Some argue that in fact the eggs or fruit juice speed up the fermentation process. The RaMA states that only those too sick or old to digest matzah comfortably are allowed to eat egg matzah on Pesah. Following a general tendency of late to be more restrictive, most Orthodox authorities today follow the RaMA's opinion.

We may wonder, then, why all the matzah companies produce egg matzah and state in bold letters on every box, "Kosher for Passover." Since the status of the product is questionable—for there *are* some opinions that permit it—the rabbinic supervisors apparently are willing to acquiesce in its sale. Yet, clearly these rabbinic supervisors do not really feel that egg matzah is permissible, since if you look at the fine print (usually on the side of the box) you will find important qualifications written in Hebrew or cryptic references to the *Shulhan Arukh.* No brand clearly states in English that according to many rabbinic authorities egg matzah can be eaten only by the old and sick. It is hard not to see this practice by the matzah companies, and those prominent rabbis and kashrut organizations who supervise them, as unethical and deceptive. At least a clear explanation would leave it to the consumer to decide whether to eat egg matzah on Passover or not. (NOTE: Although most authorities today forbid egg matzah, there is strong precedent to permit it if made without any water. If made with water, some authorities still permit it if baked quickly, since eggs are supposed to speed up the leavening process. In any case, egg matzot, according to all opinions, should not be used at the seder unless one is too sick to eat regular matzot, for it is not considered *lehem oni*—the bread of affliction—as matzah is referred to in the Haggadah text.)

Humras Passover seems to bring out the compulsive side of Jewish behavior. There are many stringencies (*humras*) that people have adopted, some of which later authorities can find no justification for (such as not eating garlic, dried fruit, or unwashed eggs). One *humra* observed in very traditional circles is *gebrokhts*—refraining from eating broken matzah in liquids. The fear is that fermentation may take place if any liquid is added to matzah; therefore, people observing this stringency don't eat *k'neidlah*—dumplings—in soup or anything else made from matzah meal mixed with water (such as most brands of gefilte fish). Since the eighth day of Passover has only rabbinic status (see the second day of Yom Tov, p. 202), they do not observe this stringency on that day and will eat matzah in liquid. Other authorities believe that once flour and water are made into matzah, "it can soak in all the water in the world and can never become hametz."

This whole tendency toward restrictions has been taken so far that there are a few people who eat matzah only at the seder to fulfill the commandment, but do not eat matzah the rest of the week out of fear that the matzah may not have been baked properly. We come then to the ultimate Jewish absurdity—refraining from eating matzah on Passover lest you be eating hametz by mistake!

MORE ON PASSOVER KASHERING

If you do not have all the utensils you need for Passover, you may want to kasher some of your year-round (hametz) utensils for Passover use. This can be done by using the basic principles outlined on p. 11, but you must also take into account the kind of material the utensil is made from:

- Metal, stone, wood, and natural rubber can be kashered.
- China, earthenware, porcelain, and synthetic rubber *cannot* be kashered.
- Corningware, Pyrex, plastic, nylon, and Teflon give rise to different opinions.
- Glass is in a category of its own, for it is the easiest to make kosher.

Why the difference in acceptability of these materials? It has to do with the principle of absorption. Materials such as metal, which absorb food particles under heat but also exude them, can be kashered. Materials that absorb food particles but do not exude them again even under heat cannot be kashered—for example, earthenware. Then there are those materials, such as glass, that do not absorb food and therefore do not require heat to be kashered. There is also another principle that affects kashering: If a material might be damaged by the kashering process—for example, thin plastic, which would melt under heat—then we are not allowed to try to kasher it.

The status of the materials in the third category is debated by scholars. Some strict authorities do not allow the materials in the third category to be kashered for Passover even though they might allow a *nonkosher* utensil of that material to be made kosher during the rest of the year. Rabbi Eider states that everything in category three, plus Correlle, Duralex, and Melmac, *cannot* be kashered. However, according to Rabbi Klein, Pyrex, Teflon, and agate can be kashered. According to Rabbi Siegel, Pyrex and Corningware should be treated as glass.

How to Kasher If a pot is used to cook water or liquids, then scrub it clean and wait twenty-four hours. After filling the pot with water and bringing the water to a boil, some people then drop a heated stone or piece of metal into the water to

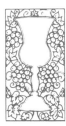

retain heat and to cause the water to overflow. In this way the outside of the pot is kashered in the manner that it was used—that is, by an occasional spilling over of the contents of the pot. A widespread custom is to rinse the pot with cold water after it is kashered.

When kashering many pots, first kasher a big pot, as above, then simply place smaller pots inside the larger pot, which is filled with boiling water. Make sure the whole surface of the smaller pot is covered with the water. The pot used to kasher others should be kashered again before using it on Pesah.

Similarly, to kasher silverware, drop the pieces *one at a time* into a pot of boiling water. Silverware with wooden handles or not made of one piece of metal is problematic since food gets into the joints and is impossible to clean out completely.

If a utensil is not used with liquids—for example, spits or baking pans—then a different procedure, called *libun,* is required. Following the principle that a utensil is kashered in the same manner as it is used, a blowtorch or charcoal is used to make the utensil as red-hot as it could become in normal use. In certain cases *libun kal* is sufficient—i.e., making the utensil only hot enough to make paper burn (rather than red-hot). *Libun kal* can be achieved by putting the utensil in an oven. In the case of *libun,* you do not have to wait twenty-four hours after using the utensil to kasher it, nor is it necessary (though it is still preferable) to clean the utensil. This is because *libun* destroys the hametz particles in the utensil; it does not draw them out. (The custom is not to rinse in cold water afterward.)

Glass, being nonporous, is in a special category. Heat is not required to kasher it, but there are two opinions on what is required. Both opinions say that first the glass must be thoroughly cleaned. Rabbis Eider and Klein state that it should be soaked in water (e.g., in a bathtub) for seventy-two hours with the water changed every twenty-four hours. The second opinion (RALC, Sephardic) states that since glass is nonporous, it need only be thoroughly scoured and rinsed to be made kosher.

A few authorities believe that fine translucent china *can* be used for Passover if it has not been used for food for over a year. It should be thoroughly scoured and rinsed with hot water (RALC).

Mention should also be made of those people who do not believe that the method outlined in the Pesah chapter for kashering the oven is adequate. They use a blowtorch to heat the walls of the oven. (Care should be taken when using this method, especially with a gas stove.) Some even go one step further and, after performing one of the methods of kashering, install a liner that completely covers the inside of the oven.

In all of the above, we are discussing utensils that were used with hot food. Utensils used *only* for cold foods or liquids, such as soda glasses or salad bowls (even if made of china), require only a thorough cleaning to be kashered. The two major exceptions are liquor glasses and utensils used in baking bread (rolling pins, etc.). In both cases the utensil has come into frequent contact with pure hametz even if it was cold. Also, there is a belief that the strong flavor of alcohol is absorbed in some measure even by glass and even if cold.

Dishwasher While the stringent authorities state that plastic-sided dishwashers cannot be kashered and that metal-sided ones require new dish racks, others (RALC) state that a dishwasher can be kashered by not using it for twenty-four hours and then running it through a full cycle. (NOTE: All the notions of absorption, etc., are laid down by the rabbis and, while bearing some resemblance to scientific principles, are really religious ones that need not and frequently do not coincide with scientific findings.)

SHABBAT EREV PESAH

When the day before Passover falls on Shabbat, a number of problems arise. We cannot burn hametz or kasher the stove utensils since lighting a fire on Shabbat is prohibited. While the simplest thing would be to convert our households to Pesah beginning Friday night, it is customary to eat two hallot—loaves of bread—with the first two Shabbat meals (Friday-night dinner, Shabbat-afternoon lunch). We cannot use matzah for the *lehem mishneh* (the name given to the double portion of hallot needed for these meals) since, as mentioned earlier, we do not eat matzah during the day before Passover. Therefore, the following procedure is followed during those years when Erev Pesah falls on Shabbat:

- The search for unleavened bread takes place Thursday evening. In general, we treat the thirteenth of Nisan (Thursday night to Friday) as if it were Erev Pesah. Some people say the formula of nullification after the search; others do not.
- The burning of hametz takes place Friday morning during the fifth "hour" after sunrise. We follow the practice of burning during the fifth hour so as not to cause even more confusion about what we do in regular years and Erev Pesah/-Shabbat years. The selling of hametz should be completed by then as well. (In actuality, hametz is not forbidden on Friday and either the burning or the selling could take place until Shabbat begins.) The kitchen is made ready for Passover. The food for Shabbat should be prepared in Pesah dishes. The only non-Pesah-dik thing in our homes should be the hallot for the two meals.
- The Fast of the Firstborn takes place on Thursday (beginning Thursday morning) since fasting on Shabbat is prohibited.
- On Shabbat, the hallot should be kept on a separate dish and care should be taken not to mix the bread with the rest of the food. Some advise using disposable plates and utensils, though decorative ones in honor of Shabbat.
- On Shabbat morning, hametz can be eaten until the end of four "hours" after sunrise. Since the second meal is eaten after morning services, some people hold services earlier than usual in order to have enough time to eat the second meal before hametz is prohibited. After the second Shabbat meal, all hametz should be disposed of (for example, flushed down the toilet) and any non-Pesah utensils put or thrown away. The formula for *bittul* should be recited during the fifth "hour" even if no second meal has been eaten. (Interestingly, Maimonides maintains a minority opinion and states that the hallot should be covered over and burned during the intermediate days of Passover.)
- The third Shabbat meal, eaten in the afternoon, should not include hametz or matzah but should consist of fruit, vegetables, or dairy foods.
- Since we are not allowed to prepare things on Shabbat to be used when it is not Shabbat, any preparations for the seder (e.g., salt water, haroset, shank bone, egg, ground horseradish) should be done before Shabbat or after yom tov candles are lighted when Shabbat is over.
- If you are afraid to or cannot use hallot, it is permissible to use egg matzot. Rabbi Bleich suggests that since there are halakhic doubts about whether egg matzah is a cake or bread, a large quantity, seven ounces, of egg matzah should be consumed. (Halakhah considers eating a large quantity of cake the same as eating bread.) This is about four or five matzot a meal, and can be regarded as training for the seder.

    On the other hand, eating egg matzah beforehand weakens the significance of eating matzah at the seder. It makes sense to me to forgo *lehem mishneh* altogether at the second Shabbat meal as a sign of the imminent arrival of Passover.

HALAKHOT OF THE OMER

The blessing is recited every night, not just the first night. If you forget to count at night, you may count the next day without the blessing, and the next night you may resume counting with a blessing. If, however, you forget to count either at night or during the day for a whole day, then you must continue to count but can no longer recite the blessing. This is because the counting is seen as one whole unit and to miss a whole day raises doubts as to whether the blessing should be recited. (In cases of doubt, blessings generally are not said.) If you are unsure whether you counted yesterday, then you are allowed to continue with a *berakhah.*

Because of the word *temimot*—meaning full or complete—in Leviticus 23:15, the counting is done when it is actually nighttime rather than at twilight, so that each day counted will be a full one. If your synagogue prays ma'ariv early (i.e., right after minhah), then the omer should be recited later at night. In the synagogue, the omer is recited after the kiddush Friday night, but before havdalah on Saturday nights.

Since the ritual consists of counting, we are warned to be careful not to recite the number for that day before saying the blessing. If someone asks you what day in the omer it is (before you have counted that night), you should respond by saying that last night was the fifteenth day in the omer, thus implying that tonight is the sixteenth. If you do recite the number, you have already fulfilled the mitzvah and cannot count again that night with a blessing.

The emphasis on counting puts a premium on being exact; therefore, no attention is paid to the doubt underlying the second festival day of the Diaspora—we count as though there is no doubt that the second night of Passover is just that. Because of this notion of exactitude, some authorities state that the counting should be done in a language you understand (i.e., English), even though in most liturgical commandments recitation in Hebrew is given precedence.

OTHER OMER PERIOD LAWS

If Lag B'Omer falls on Sunday, even if you are observing the mourning customs you are permitted to get a haircut on that Friday in honor of Shabbat.

If Yom ha-Atzma'ut falls on Friday or Shabbat, its celebration is moved up to the preceding Thursday to prevent any violation of Shabbat and to allow for a full day of festivities.

Some of those people who still observe the Monday-Thursday-Monday fast of Iyyar postpone it until after Yom ha-Atzma'ut occurs.

HALAKHOT OF SHAVUOT

Because it lacks a specific ritual, Shavuot does not have many distinctive practices. One group of its laws/customs concerns the changes in the liturgy if you have stayed up all night on Shavuot for the tikkun.

- The following morning prayers are omitted: *birkhot ha-torah* (the blessings over Torah study), *elohai neshamah* (a paragraph thanking God for our life "restored" to us after sleep), and the blessing over *arba kanfot* (the fringed garment worn under the shirt).

- The ritual washing of hands upon rising in the morning is performed, but without the customary blessing. The blessing should be recited after using the bathroom, along with the blessing of *asher yatzar* (the blessing traditionally recited after every use of the bathroom).
- Some authorities state that all of the *birkhot ha-shahar* (a series of blessings thanking God for giving us strength, making our feet walk, etc.) should not be said unless there is someone there who did sleep and can lead that part of the service.

One old custom was to read Ruth on the Shabbat before Shavuot. Another was to read one-half the first day, one-half the second. Some believe it should be read from a parchment scroll accompanied by the blessing *al mikra megillah.* The Gaon of Vilna adds that *she-he-heyanu* should be recited.

Those places observing two days of Shavuot divide the azharot—liturgical poem —into two halves—the positive commandments the first day and the negative the second day. On the second day, some Ashkenazic congregations recite the piyyut *yetziv pitgam.*

While many people begin Shabbat and festivals early—before sunset—particularly during late spring and summer, on Shavuot it is customary not to begin the holiday (lighting candles, davening ma'ariv) before sunset. As noted, the verse commanding the counting of the omer uses the word *temimot,* meaning complete, and to reach seven full weeks, we wait until the forty-ninth day of the omer is completely over before we begin Shavuot. At the beginning of the holiday, candles are lighted with the blessing. The *she-he-heyanu* blessing is recited at candlelighting and/or at kiddush.

The second day of Shavuot used to be known as yom tov of *matnat yad*—the festival day of giving—because of the Torah reading that includes the verse "but each with his own gift [*matnat yado*], according to the blessing that the Lord your God has bestowed upon you" (Deut. 16:17). A special *mi-she-berakh* (a prayer for good fortune recited for someone who receives an aliyah, is sick, etc.) was recited on behalf of those who contributed to tzedakah—charity. Some authorities state that this is why yizkor is said on the second day of Shavuot (and the last day of Pesah) since this portion reminds us to donate to tzedakah in honor of the deceased, an appropriate deed to accompany the recital of yizkor.

Halakhot of the Three Weeks

Seventeenth of Tammuz

There are few halakhot specific for this fast day. The Torah reading is Exodus 32:11–14 and 34:1–10. Exodus 32:12 and 34:6, 9 are first said aloud by the congregation and then repeated by the reader, because they ask for mercy. For a similar reason, they are chanted in the special High Holiday *trop.* The rest of chapters 32 and 33 are skipped because they relate the golden-calf incident, about which we do not want to remind God on a fast day.

If the Seventeenth of Tammuz (or any of the four fasts) falls on Shabbat, it is postponed until Sunday. Pregnant or nursing women as well as the sick are exempt from this fast day (and from any other of the *minor* fast days). Those not fasting should still eat simply. If you are not fasting, you do not recite *aneinu* in the amidah, nor should you take an aliyah at minhah.

The Three Weeks

Besides the mourning customs and the special haftarot, the following customs are practiced:

In some congregations, on Friday nights the hymn "Lekhah Dodi" (except for the last two verses) is sung to the melody of "Eli Tzion" (one of the kinot—penitential prayers—of Tisha be-Av). On Shabbat Hazon (the Shabbat before Tisha be-Av) the haftarah is often chanted almost in its entirety to the *trop* of Lamentations. Others chant only the verses of admonition to that *trop.* No *mevarkhim ha-hodesh*—announcing of the new month—takes place in shul on the Shabbat preceding the new month of Av.

The Nine Days As mentioned, there is a prohibition on swimming, washing, laundering clothes, or wearing fresh clothes. Sephardim observe these extra restrictions only during the week of Tisha be-Av itself, not for the whole nine days. You are permitted to wash yourself if you are dirty; you may even use hot water if necessary to remove the dirt. Most authorities permit wearing fresh clothes for Shabbat and washing your hands and face before Shabbat. Washing clothes for infants also is permitted during the Nine Days since they require many changes of clothes.

Although meat and wine are not consumed during the Nine Days, they are permitted on Shabbat even if Tisha be-Av falls on Shabbat (the fast is postponed until Sunday). Meat and wine are also permitted at a *seudat mitzvah*—a meal in honor of a religious event (e.g., a circumcision). Another kind of *seudat mitzvah* was held for a *siyyum*—the completion of the study of a tractate of Talmud or another body of work. Just as with the Fast of the Firstborn before Passover, some people arrange to finish studying a text during the Nine Days so as to have a meat meal. (For more details, see p. 207.)

Tisha be-Av Before Tisha be-Av begins, we eat a meal called *seudah ha-mafseket,* which marks the transition from a regular day to a fast day. A few people eat it while sitting on the ground. A few eat only bread, water, and lentils or hard-boiled eggs. Since a regular meal is permitted before minhah, this last meal may be mostly symbolic. While it is customary not to partake of wine or meat during the Nine Days, the halakhah forbids doing so during the *seudah ha-mafseket.* To emphasize the atmosphere of mourning, the *zimun* that is traditionally said as an introduction to Grace after Meals (if three or more people eat together) is not said after *seudah ha-mafseket.*

The common custom is to read the Book of Lamentations without any *berakhah,* though the Gaon of Vilna recited the blessing *al mikra megillah* as on Purim. There are those who chant the third chapter of Lamentations to a different melody from the preceding and following chapters. Another custom is for the reader to raise her or his voice at the beginning of each chapter.

Since it is customary to curtail comforts on Tisha be-Av, some people sleep on the floor. Every adult is required to fast unless too ill to do so. Women within thirty days of childbirth are exempt. Washing is forbidden even in cold water except if necessary to remove dirt from your hands, etc. Interestingly, a bride is allowed to wash her face for thirty days after her wedding, presumably to retain some of her "brideness."

Tisha be-Av ends with ma'ariv. There is a disagreement as to whether *kiddush levanah* (the sanctification of the new moon) should be recited at the end of Tisha be-Av. Most authorities say it should. If Tisha be-Av begins Saturday night, then *attah honantanu* is recited in the ma'ariv amidah, but no havdalah ritual is said. The blessing over fire *is* said alone upon seeing candlelight. At the end of a Tisha be-Av that falls on Sunday, havdalah is recited over wine, but neither the *berakhah* over fire or over spices is recited. Havdalah is postponed to the conclusion of Tisha be-Av because wine cannot be drunk on Tisha be-Av, nor is havdalah in keeping with its mood. (The blessing over spices is recited only on Saturday night.)

A mourner can leave the house of *shiv'ah* (seven days of ritual mourning) and go to the synagogue both in the evening and on the morning of Tisha be-Av.

There is some question raised about why we commemorate the destruction of the temple on the ninth of Av when it seems to have burned mostly on the tenth of Av. The usual rabbinic answer is that the catastrophe is marked at its beginning. Certain mourning customs are still observed on the morning of the tenth of Av. (Also, it should be noted that the rabbis decided to commemorate the breaching of the walls of Jerusalem by the Romans, which took place on Tammuz 17, rather than the breaching of the walls by the Babylonians, which took place on Tammuz 9).

Thus we are restricted from consuming wine or meat until noon on the tenth of Av. However, this is not the case if Tisha be-Av falls on Shabbat and therefore is postponed until Sunday. In that situation, you can bathe Sunday night and eat meat Monday morning.

HALAKHOT OF ELUL

Beginning with Elul 1, one set of shofar sounds *(tekiah, shevarim-teru'ah, tekiah)* is blown every day after shaharit services. The shofar is not blown on Shabbat, however, or on the day before Rosh ha-Shanah. The latter omission is to mark the distinction between the shofar blowing of Elul, which is only a custom, and that of Rosh ha-Shanah, which is biblically commanded.

Psalm 27 is recited at the very end of morning and evening services, beginning with the first day of Elul through Hoshana Rabbah. Ashkenazim recite it after shaharit and ma'ariv, Sephardim after shaharit and minhah. It is followed by mourner's kaddish.

Selihot—special penitential prayers—are recited every day during the week before Rosh ha-Shanah, beginning with Saturday night. If Rosh ha-Shanah falls on Tuesday or earlier in the week, the first selihot are moved up to the Saturday night of the preceding week in order to have at least four days of selihot. This minimum is related to the former practice, still maintained by a few people, of fasting throughout the ten days of repentance. Since there are four days during that period when one is not allowed to fast—the two days of Rosh ha-Shanah, Shabbat Shuvah, and the day before Yom Kippur—the four days before Rosh ha-Shanah are needed to make up the number ten. Hence the four days of selihot become the four extra fast days. Others interpret the four days of selihot as analogous to the practice of examining an animal for blemishes for four days before offering it as a sacrifice in the temple.

The first selihot service is said at midnight; subsequent selihot services occur early in the morning before sunrise. An Ashkenazic custom is for the service leader to wear a tallit even though it is not usually worn at night. Some service leaders use a borrowed tallit, which would not require a blessing in any case. It is customary for the same person to lead the services for selihot and shaharit. The thirteen attributes are said only in a minyan; therefore a person saying selihot alone would delete that part of the service.

A few people recite selihot either the whole month of Elul or from Elul 15 on. There is also a custom of checking your mezuzot and tefillin during this month to see that their parchment is still "kosher" (i.e., that the writing on the parchment has not faded).

For Tishri, there is no "blessing of the new month" on the Shabbat before the new moon. Two reasons are given for this. One is that everyone knows when Rosh Hodesh

Tishri falls because it is on Rosh ha-Shanah. The other is that the omission is to confuse Satan, who is eager to act as the accuser against the Jews during the ten days of repentance: If Satan does not realize it is Rosh ha-Shanah, then he cannot be the accuser. Beginning on Elul 25, some people read the account of creation in Genesis because according to one tradition God began to create the world on that day.

HALAKHOT OF ROSH HA-SHANAH

A number of additions to the regular liturgy are said on Rosh ha-Shanah and Yom Kippur. These include *zakhreinu le-hayyim* in the first *berakhah* of the Amidah, *mi kamokha* in the second, and a long insertion in the third *berakhah* of *u-vekhein tein pahdekha*. The third *berakhah* ends with *ha-melekh ha-kadosh*—the Holy King—instead of *ha-eil ha-kadosh*. In the next-to-last *berakhah* we add *u-khetov le-hayyim,* and in the last we add *be-sefer hayyim* and conclude with *oseh ha-shalom.* (Sephardim use the regular concluding formula.) These stress God's kingship and our desire to be inscribed for life. The word *le-eilah* is added to every kaddish to emphasize that God rules from high on his heavenly throne. Similarly the service leader begins the major part of the shaharit service at the end of *nishmat* with the word *ha-melekh*—the King—rather than with the opening words used for other festivals or Shabbat.

Avinu malkeinu is recited after the amidah, but not if Rosh ha-Shanah falls on Shabbat, since its petitionary nature is not appropriate to Shabbat. When the first day of Rosh ha-Shanah falls on Shabbat and the shofar is not blown, some piyyutim are shifted to the second day, while the words of others are changed from "a day of shofar blowing" to "a day of remembering the blowing of the shofar" *(yom zikhron teru'ah).*

THE SHOFAR

The shofar is made of a ram's horn, which is a reminder of the ram that Abraham substituted for Isaac. We use a ram's horn even though the horn of almost any kosher animal is permitted, except that of a cow or ox because it reminds God of the sin of the golden calf!

Usually the shofar is bent or curved to symbolize our humbleness on this Judgment Day. It should be free of holes or cracks. Since there are complicated rules about how much of a crack invalidates a shofar, an expert should be consulted.

Before the shofar is sounded, Psalm 47, which mentions *teru'ah,* is recited. The kabbalists of Safed instituted the practice of reciting the psalm seven times. God's name appears seven times in the psalm, and these sevens represent the seven *sefirot.* After the psalm, a number of verses are recited, six of which form an acrostic spelling *kra satan*—destroy Satan. Satan's role during the High Holidays is to defame the Jews in order to bring about God's condemnation. Therefore there are a variety of customs to confuse Satan and prayers like this one calling for his destruction.

The shofar is kept covered until it is used. Usually someone other than the service leader blows shofar. The shofar blower *(ba'al tekiah)* recites the blessing for shofar blowing and the *she-he-heyanu.* Someone calls out the order of shofar blasts to guide the shofar blower.

Some authorities have complicated rules for blowing the shofar, such as different lengths of the blasts. One opinion holds that the *tekiah, shevarim,* and *teru'ah* should all be the same length.

As mentioned earlier, there are a number of different customs for blowing the total of 100 blasts. The necessity for 100 blasts is itself unclear. The common traditional explanation is that the mother of Sisera, the enemy general killed in Deborah's time, used 100 letters in her lament for her son. To counterbalance her sorrow and "just complaint" against the Israelites (even though Sisera had come to attack Israel), we blow 100 blasts. Ashkenazim blow thirty after the torah reading, thirty during the repetition of musaf, thirty during *kaddish titkabeil* after musaf, and the final ten after mourner's kaddish. Sephardim blow thirty after the Torah reading, thirty during the silent musaf amidah, thirty during the repetition, and the final ten in *kaddish titkabeil*. The sequence of blasts to make thirty is *tekiah, shevarim, teru'ah, tekiah* (three times); *tekiah, shevarim, tekiah* (three times); *tekiah, teru'ah, tekiah* (three times). Each set of blasts ends with an extra-long *tekiah (tekiah gedolah)*. There is no difference between the blasts on the first and second days of Rosh ha-Shanah.

HALAKHOT OF THE TEN DAYS

The insertions into the amidah are recited during all of the services of the Ten Days with the exception of the long insertion of *u-vekhein tein pahdekha* in the third *berakhah*. This insertion is recited only on Rosh ha-Shanah and Yom Kippur. However, the conclusion of an additional *berakhah* in the amidah is changed. The conclusion of the eleventh *berakhah* (said only on weekdays) is changed to *ha-melekh ha-mishpat. Le-eilah u-le-eilah* is still recited in the kaddish. Some people change *oseh shalom* at the end of the kaddish to *oseh ha-shalom*. Some people say *mi-kol birkhata* instead of *min kol birkhata* in the kaddish to keep the number of words the same in the kaddish despite the adding of *le-eilah*. This is because medieval mystics gave significance to the number of words in each of the prayers.

Avinu malkeinu is said after the shaharit and minhah amidah except minhah Erev Shabbat, on Shabbat itself, and minhah Erev Yom Kippur. If Yom Kippur falls on Shabbat, then *avinu malkeinu* is said at shaharit on Erev Yom Kippur. Some people add Psalm 30 before the *barekhu*.

It is customary not to have weddings during the Ten Days.

If Tzom Gedaliah falls on Saturday, it is postponed until Sunday. Since it is a minor fast day, the fast always begins in the morning, not the evening before.

HALAKHOT OF YOM KIPPUR

The *seudah ha-mafseket* should be finished in time to begin Yom Kippur before sunset. It is customary to sing Psalm 126, *Shir ha-ma'alot,* before the recitation of Grace after Meals, to express our desire to see the return to Zion described in this psalm. Usually, this psalm is recited as an introduction to the Grace only on festivals and Shabbat.

Of the five prohibitions on Yom Kippur, the most strictly observed is the ban on eating and drinking. Unlike the minor fast days, everyone is encouraged to fast on Yom Kippur, except those excused for medical reasons. Children under nine are not allowed to fast; children over nine should begin to fast for a longer period each year. A woman who has given birth within three days is not allowed to fast; within four to seven days, she should follow her doctor's advice. A pregnant women who feels the need to eat despite understanding the importance of Yom Kippur should do so (Klein quoting Maimonides). Those not fasting should eat only enough to satisfy their needs. If Yom Kippur falls on Shabbat, we still fast.

The other prohibitions on Yom Kippur have less stringent sanctions than that of fasting. While washing is prohibited for pleasure, it is permitted for hygiene—for example, if your hands or feet became muddy. Similarly, you are allowed to wear leather shoes either for health reasons or because you have to walk through mud. An old rabbinic ruling permits a bride to wash if she has been married within the last thirty days.

As mentioned, the Kol Nidrei service should be begun while it is still daylight. Since a blessing over the tallit is not said at night, special care should be taken to don the tallit before sunset. If you put on the tallit after sunset, no *berakhah* is recited.

As mentioned, the phrase *Barukh shem kavod malkhuto le-olam va-ed*—"Praised be the name of his glorious majesty forever and ever"—which appears right after the Shema Yisrael prayer, is recited out loud. All during the year this phrase is recited silently, but on Yom Kippur it is said out loud in remembrance of the temple. As can be seen from the description in the *avodah* service of musaf, the people would respond with that phrase whenever God's ineffable name was pronounced. It also appears that this phrase was used instead of "amen" in the temple.

The viddui is recited during all the services of Yom Kippur. There is an old custom of beating your breast as you say each line of the confessional.

Another old custom, mostly fallen into disuse, was to remain in the synagogue after the Kol Nidrei service to recite psalms and other prayers. In fact, some stayed up all night in the synagogue.

Avinu malkeinu, a plea for God's compassion, is recited after each service except minhah. If Yom Kippur falls on Shabbat, then *avinu malkeinu* is not recited by Ashkenazim except in neilah. *Avinu malkeinu*'s petitionary nature was felt to be inappropriate to Shabbat, yet it was regarded as too important not to say it once at neilah. Some Sephardim say *avinu malkeinu* after each service even if Yom Kippur falls on Shabbat.

When prostrating during musaf, some people spread paper or some material on the floor, particularly if it is a stone floor, because of an ancient prohibition against bowing on a stone floor.

Havdalah is recited at the end of Yom Kippur. The blessing for spices and the introductory verses are omitted unless Yom Kippur falls on Shabbat. It is customary to light the havdalah candle from a flame that was burning during all of Yom Kippur. This is related to the complicated question of whether to say the blessing over lights in havdalah. This blessing is usually said only after Shabbat, for only on Shabbat is fire forbidden. As we have seen, Yom Kippur is in a category all its own and it was felt that lighting the havdalah candle from an already burning flame would solve a number of halakhic problems.

HALAKHOT OF A SUKKAH

BUILDING THE SUKKAH

The sukkah should have four walls, though theoretically you may have a sukkah made up of two walls and a part of a third. For some of the sukkah walls, you may use an already standing structure such as the side of your house.

The walls may be made of any material, but should be no higher than thirty feet, to reflect the temporary nature of the sukkah. On the other hand, the sukkah should be able to stand up to a strong wind. (It is a good idea to stake down the walls, especially if they are made of canvas or other such material. One of the memorable experiences of my life was being inside a sukkah as the wind began to fill the canvas, causing the sukkah to set sail for the distant horizon.) The rabbis set a minimum dimension for a sukkah of twenty-six square inches and more than three feet high.

The *skhakh* should be evenly spaced across the sukkah so that there is no large open space in the roof. While it should provide more shade than sun, you should be able to see the stars at night, and it is forbidden to have so much *skhakh* that rain will not enter the sukkah.

The *skhakh* should last for the duration of the holiday, not shrivel up and die. Therefore, many people use branches of evergreen. Canvas, metal, or even wood made into an object or utensil are not permitted as *skhakh.* This is derived from the verse "After the ingathering from your threshing floor and your vat, you shall hold the Feast of Booths for seven days" (Deut. 16:13).

According to the rabbis, anything that is made into a utensil is susceptible to ritual impurity. Anything which can be ritually impure cannot be used for *skhakh.* Only that which has been grown and harvested (i.e., that which could be found on the threshing floor) is suitable for use to celebrate the festival.

The *skhakh* also must be detached from the ground; therefore, a grape arbor or any growing vines cannot be used. For the same reason, it is better not to build a sukkah under a tree even if its branches are much higher than the sukkah's roof, unless the tree branches cover only a very small part of the sukkah. Some use the principle that if the shade of the *skhakh* is greater than the sun, even without the tree, it is permissible. Some will not sit in the section of the sukkah that is covered by the tree.

For all these reasons, as well as to have the sukkah open to the sky, it should not be built under an overhanging roof. *Skhakh* must be an organic unfinished material, which eliminates house roofs, gutters, etc. Therefore, just as with a tree, some people will not sit in the part of the sukkah that is under an overhanging roof.

Since the *skhakh* is the key to the sukkah, finish the walls before putting on the *skhakh.* If necessary, you can use a permanent structure for a sukkah as long as the roof is removable. During Sukkot, the roof can then be removed for the duration of the holiday. Some people have roofs that can be temporarily lifted by pulleys. Such a roof can be lowered when it rains and later raised again.

You are permitted to put some kind of covering (canvas, heavy plastic, or awnings) over the *skhakh* when the sukkah is not in use to keep the sukkah dry and the decorations intact in case of rain. These coverings should be removed, however, before you eat in the sukkah.

All of the construction and decoration of the sukkah should take place before the holiday begins. Once Sukkot begins, you may not remove any of the decorations. Rabbi Sheshet, a talmudic sage, interprets the verse "On the fifteenth day of this seventh month there shall be a Feast of Booths to the Lord for seven days" (Lev. 23:24) to mean that for all seven days the sukkah is consecrated to God. Therefore, it is forbidden to use the sukkah, its roof, and its ornaments for any other purpose. (In this sense the decorations, etc., are like objects labeled *muktzah* on Shabbat, such as money, which cannot be used nor even moved during Shabbat.)

USING THE SUKKAH

Certain categories of people are exempt from the mitzvah of sukkah:

- The sick and their attendants are exempt from eating in the sukkah, even someone who is only sick with a headache. Some authorities say that the sick person's attendants are exempt only if the patient needs them.

- Newlyweds and the wedding party are exempt. Some opinions hold that the newlyweds should go beyond the letter of the law and obligate themselves to eat in the sukkah (though since there is a doubt, no blessing is recited). The reason for this exemption appears to be the principle of not mixing two kinds of joy—that of the wedding and that of the sukkah. One could also speculate that the rabbis felt the sukkah was not the most comfortable environment for the couple's wedding night. The exemption continues for the traditional seven days of celebration after the wedding.
- Those involved in performing other mitzvot are exempt whether by day or night. Even if you are performing the mitzvah by day, you are exempt at night as well, since you are so involved in the mitzvah. This exemption is based on a more general principle that you are exempt from one mitzvah when preoccupied with doing another. The *Shulhan Arukh* gives the following mitzvot as examples of deeds that free you from the obligation to perform the mitzvah of sukkah: the study of Torah, redeeming captives, visiting your teacher. Perhaps, then, if we find ourselves in circumstances that make us unable to eat in a sukkah, we should engage in an important mitzvah—e.g. Torah study or charity. Transforming a meal by studying Torah at the table would at least acknowledge that it is Sukkot even if we are unable to eat in a sukkah.
- Daytime travelers are exempt both at night and during the day. The RaMA explains that they are exempt even at night because of the principle that the sukkah should be like your home. During the rest of the year, a traveler does not return home every night; so, too, during Sukkot, it is not necessary to change the pattern of the rest of the year and return home (i.e., go back to your sukkah). Perhaps this principle could be expanded to include those who work away from home during the day even though they return home every night (i.e., commuters). While they would still be obligated to eat in the sukkah at night (since they return home all year at night), during the day—that is, for lunch—they would be exempt from eating in a sukkah, just as all year long they do not eat lunch at home.
- A watchman of vineyards does not have to build a sukkah, because it would let robbers know where he is and they could then rob from other places in the fields!

(NOTE: Just because in certain cases you are exempt from eating in a sukkah does not mean that if you can eat in a sukkah you should forgo the opportunity. Thus if a traveler has the opportunity to eat in a sukkah, he or she should. Only when eating in a sukkah becomes an act of grim determination—such as eating in the rain—do the rabbis make the exemption almost a requirement that you *not* eat in the sukkah.)

You are permitted to eat a snack outside of the sukkah just as you eat snacks outside of your home during the year. In general, we are encouraged to do in the sukkah what we normally do at home (e.g., make havdalah on Saturday nights). To perform in the sukkah what we do not always perform at home is optional (e.g., prayer that takes place both at home and at the synagogue).

Some people follow the custom of the Ari (sixteenth century) and place Joseph after Moses and Aaron in the order of the *ushpizin*. Each of these figures is associated with one of the *sefirot*, which have their own order. Also in this arrangement, Moses is the *ushpizin* for the fourth day of Sukkot, which falls on the same day of the week as the seventh of Adar (the day when the tradition says that Moses died). The fifth day of Sukkot falls on the same day of the week as the first of Av (traditional day of death of Aaron). The seventh day of Sukkot falls on the same day of the week as the sixth of Sivan (traditional death date of David).

HALAKHOT OF THE FOUR SPECIES

The lulav is held in the right hand (symbolically the "better" hand, the stronger hand, etc.) because it has three species and so is more important than the etrog. For the same reason, only the lulav is mentioned in the blessing: Being more important, it includes all four species.

The *she-he-heyanu* blessing is recited on special occasions and when a mitzvah is performed the first time in a year. For instance, it is recited on the first night of Hanukkah or on Sukkot for the first time the lulav and etrog are taken. You might think it would be recited on the second day as well in the Diaspora because of doubt about which day is the festival. However, the rabbis stated that you are permitted to recite the *she-he-heyanu* even before the holiday, when you are putting your lulav and etrog together—for that, too, fulfills part of the mitzvah. Therefore, you fulfill part of the mitzvah and the saying of *she-he-heyanu* on the first day just by bringing the four species together, even if it should turn out that it was the day before Sukkot and not the first day of the festival.

Shaking the lulav is seen as an important part of the mitzvah. The lulav can just be shaken until its leaves rustle. Some shake it as it is done in hallel (in the four directions of the compass and up and down).

The rabbis decreed that the lulav and etrog are not used on Shabbat, out of fear that they might be carried in the public domain to the synagogue. If the first day of Sukkot falls on Shabbat, then *she-he-heyanu* is recited on the second day. The Talmud states that if Shabbat falls on the *first* day in which there is a special obligation to perform the mitzvah, you should bring the lulav and etrog to shul on Friday. But if you forget and carry the lulav by accident on the Sabbath, you are not culpable, because you are performing a religious act. Today we do not use the lulav on Shabbat even on the first day.

There is a dispute as to whether left-handed people should hold the lulav in the right hand or in the left (which for them is the "stronger" hand). The majority opinion is that they should hold it in the right.

The lulav should be bound with material of its own species; thus the ties are usually made from pieces of a palm branch. Besides the holder in which the myrtle and willows are placed, there are usually two or three rings placed around the lulav to help hold it together.

Because the verse states *Ve-lakahtem lakhem*—literally, "You shall take to yourselves" the four species—the halakhah stresses that the four species must be yours. This is especially required on the first day of the festival. Therefore, if you use someone else's lulav and etrog, it must be given to you as a present, not a loan, though with the condition that it be returned. The problem is with children, who as minors cannot really transfer ownership. Therefore, give it to a child last. After the first day when the obligation is only rabbinic, you can borrow and lend the lulav and etrog.

In hallel, the service leader shakes the lulav in each *hodu* a total of eight times. Sephardim shake the lulav only once in the first and last *hodu* and twice in *ana hoshi'ah*. If you are praying without a minyan you shake it only once in each *hodu* and at *ana hoshi'ah*.

BUYING THE FOUR SPECIES

As mentioned, some people go to great lengths to buy the perfect four species. We must each decide how much attention we will pay to the minutiae of the laws and customs that have grown up around the four species. There are many things that detract from an etrog's perfection, and yet some seem to have nothing to do with the concept of *hiddur mitzvah*—beautifying the commandment. For example, any little speck of brown or black on the etrog detracts from its perfection. I have seen people choose etrogim that are pale, lean, and scrawny over those that are round and bright yellow because of such a speck. After a number of years of minutely examining etrogim, I decided I preferred those that look good, even with a few tiny spots, to those that are spotless but look emaciated.

The basic rules to know are (1) that you need the authentic four species—that is, a citron, not a lemon; (2) the etrog should have its *pitom* (tip) still intact, because if that is broken off, the etrog is clearly *pasul* (invalid); and (3) all of the four species should look fresh, not dried out, and have the right color (e.g., green, not brown).

Lulav-and-etrog sets are available from synagogues and Jewish bookstores. In certain very Jewish neighborhoods, special stores open just to sell the four species. On the Lower East Side in New York City, there are street vendors selling the four species. When buying a set, you should know that the main item you are buying is the etrog. If a store has a large assortment and a range of prices, the prices are keyed to the quality (in halakhic terms) of the etrog. If the four species are being sold as a you-put-it-together package, it is like buying a stereo system with a number of components. In this case, you choose your etrog first, which sets the price, and then choose the rest of the four species. (There is usually no price difference for better-quality lulavim.) The price for the etrog includes the other three components of the four species, though in some places the *aravot* are sold separately for a small sum.

THE LAWS

Lulav Lulav should be at least fifteen or sixteen inches long—longer than the myrtles and the willows. It should be straight, not bent, and the top should not be broken off or split. The leaves should not be spread out, and should be green on the front side and flat and whitish yellow on the back. If there is some brown, dried-out material resembling dead leaves adhering to or simply stuck in between some of the branches, this is not a problem—it will come off when the lulav is shaken.

Hadasim (myrtles) and Aravot (willows) Each of these should be at least eleven to twelve inches long. The myrtles' leaves should be mostly *meshulash*—that is, occurring in groups of three rather than randomly placed; thus the leaves cover the twig. This is not always easy to find. Some say three clusters of three leaves near the top of the myrtle is the minimum amount.

The willows should have red twigs with long, smooth-edged leaves (though green twigs are permissible). Some prefer willows that have two leaves coming off the twig at the same level. Neither the willows nor the myrtle should be dried out—a particular problem with willows, which tend to dry out quickly, leaving you with brittle leaves. The willow is considered dried out in terms of halakhah when the green color is completely gone from the leaves.

Etrog As mentioned, the etrog must have its tip intact. However, there is a certain type of etrog that comes naturally without a tip and is permitted for Sukkot. These etrogim are from Corfu and are preferred by some, since they are known not to have been grafted (see below). The etrog should be wider at the bottom and taper upward like a pear, rather than being round like an orange. The surface should be rough and ridged, rather than smooth. It should not be green, unless it will turn yellow before the holiday, and there should be no spots or blemishes on the skin; if there are, the closer the spots are to the tip, the less perfect is the etrog. The shape should be basically symmetrical so that the tip *(pitom)* is directly above the stem at the bottom. A choice etrog has lengthwise ridges extending from the bottom toward the *pitom*.

Since there is a prohibition in the Bible against grafting plants, some people are concerned about unwittingly buying etrogim that grew on grafted trees. Grafted *(murkavim)* etrogim can be recognized because their skin is smooth like a lemon's and thin rather than thick as a "kosher" etrog's is.

HALAKHOT OF SHEMINI ATZERET/SIMHAT TORAH

There is much rabbinic discussion over determining whether Shemini Atzeret is independent of Sukkot or not. The Talmud refers to six signs that Shemini Atzeret is independent, and these have been interpreted in a number of ways. They are (1) the different rotation of the priests in the temple; (2) the recital of *she-he-heyanu;* (3) no mitzvah to dwell in the sukkah or use the four species; (4) calling the day Shemini Atzeret, not Sukkot; (5) a different order of sacrifices; and (6) a different psalm for the day recited by the Levites. Each of these marks a difference between Shemini Atzeret and Sukkot.

SIMHAT TORAH

Since traditional Jews go to synagogue first, daven ma'ariv, and then eat supper, on Simhat Torah there is no opportunity to eat until very late, after the hakkafot are over. Therefore, in traditional synagogues, people individually go to another room during the hakkafot, make kiddush and eat something (cake, perhaps) and then return once again to the fray. If kiddush is not made in the synagogue, then it is made at home (*not* in the Sukkah).

Because the morning service is so long, many people customarily make kiddush after they receive their aliyah. This creates a problem for *birkat kohanim*—the priestly blessing that takes place in traditional synagogues on festivals. This ritual consists of someone of priestly descent standing in front of the congregation and blessing the worshipers with the *yevarekhekha* blessing. It is forbidden for a priest to perform this ritual while intoxicated, and there is a fear that this might happen because of kiddush. Therefore, some synagogues have a priestly blessing at the end of the shaharit amidah rather than in its usual place at the end of the musaf amidah. Others continue to have it in musaf and simply require the priests to be careful. Still others do not allow the priests to make kiddush until after services are over.

A variation of the procedure for the special Torah readings comes between the end of the Deuteronomy reading and before the recital of the blessing when some congregations recite three times: "We have merited to complete it in peace, may we merit to begin it and complete it in peace." Then Genesis 1:1–5 is recited by heart, followed by the final blessing, which is recited by the *hatan torah.* The maftir (Num. 29:35–30:1) is then read from the third Torah scroll; the haftarah is the first chapter of Joshua, which begins appropriately "Now it came to pass after the death of Moses. . . ." Some authorities maintain that a different reader should chant the last eight verses of Deuteronomy to show the special character of these verses, which describe the death of Moses. If Moses, according to tradition, wrote the whole Torah, did he write these verses as well? There are two traditional answers: (1) Joshua wrote these verses, or (2) Moses wrote them before his death and wept as he did so. To mark this special character, a second reader should be used.

HALAKHOT OF HANUKKAH

The preferred time to light the menorah is during the half-hour after sundown, because in talmudic times not many people were still out in the streets after that hour, and since the purpose of the lighting is *pirsum*—to proclaim the miracle—it should be done when people will see it. Today's practice has changed for two reasons. First, some authorities argue that the *pirsum* is for the members of the household, not those outside on the street; therefore the menorah need not be lighted near a window, and is best lighted when all the members of the household are at home and awake. While it is considered preferable to light it right after sundown, it is perfectly correct to light it later as long as people have not gone to sleep.

Others argue that the *pirsum* is still for the people passing in the street, but that due to street lamps, etc., people are out on the streets much later than in talmudic times; indeed, depending on where you live, the time people are "on the streets" can continue for a number of hours.

Both sides agree therefore that while the menorah should be lighted early in the evening, it can be lighted anytime until midnight. According to most authorities the menorah can be lighted with the blessings even after midnight, until sunrise, but some say it should be done without blessings. The commandment cannot be fulfilled during the day since the light will not be visible and no *pirsum* will be possible.

Originally the menorah was placed outside the dwelling next to the doorposts. Since this became dangerous because of anti-Semitic neighbors, the law was changed. Nowadays the menorah is most frequently placed on a windowsill or on a table in the room. Another custom is to place the menorah near the doorpost on the inside. It is placed on the left so that on one side you have the mezuzah and on the other the menorah, thus symbolically surrounding you with mitzvot.

The general custom today is to begin with one candle and add one each night until you reach eight. The Talmud states that the mitzvah consists of lighting one candle each night per household. It then mentions a disagreement: The School of Hillel states that you should kindle one light the first night and add one each night; the School of Shammai believes that you should kindle eight lights the first night and decrease by one each night. The halakhah follows the School of Hillel on the grounds that you should increase rather than decrease that which is holy.

Unlike Shabbat, any candle or oil is "kosher" for the Hanukkah lights. The purpose of the lights is to proclaim the miracle. Since we do not read by them, the quality of their illumination is not important. (On the other hand, only certain waxes and oils can be used on Shabbat to prevent anyone from adjusting the light to improve its illumination, an act that would violate Shabbat laws.)

The correct number is important not only for proclaiming the miracle but also for designating which day of Hanukkah it is. If you do not have enough candles for, let us say, the fifth night, you are supposed to light one rather than three or four since one candle will not be as confusing to people (and one candle is the primary mitzvah).

It is important that we begin the lighting with the additional candle, which marks the new day and signifies that the miracle became greater day by day. In tractate *Yoma,* the method of sprinkling the blood on the altar is described as follows: "All your turnings should be to the right." Therefore, we light the newest candle and then turn right and light the next, proceeding from left to right until all of them are lighted.

She-he-heyanu is recited only on the first night. If you are prevented from lighting the menorah the first night, it is recited the first time you light the menorah. If on any night you are prevented from lighting the menorah (and know you will not get a chance later that night) but see another person's lighted menorah, you should recite the second blessing, " . . . who performed miracles. . . ."

Hasidic customs vary for prayers recited after candlelighting. The Munkacs recite Psalms 90:17 and 91 seven times, sing "Ma'oz Tzur," then recite Psalm 30; a piyyut called *or ha-ganuz; emet ve-yatziv* (the *berakhah* following Shema in the morning) through *ezrat avotainu,* ending with *mi kamokha* (an acrostic for Maccabee). The Belz recite *barukh adonai yom yom* (from Shabbat zemirot); the *Shir ha-ma'alot* psalms (Pss. 120–134), and Psalms 111 and 112. The Bratslav recite Psalms 90:17 and Psalms 91, 67, 30, 33, 111, 112, 100, and 150, then *yedid nefesh* and *el mistateir* (from Shabbat zemirot), ending with the piyyut *or ha-ganuz.*

The candles or oil should burn for half an hour or more. However, the consensus of halakhic opinion is that the commandment of the Hanukkah menorah is fulfilled by the lighting of the candles. Therefore, if the candles do not burn for a half-hour, or if they are accidentally extinguished, you have still fulfilled the mitzvah. Even those who say you should relight them agree that the blessing should not be recited again.

On Friday night, Hanukkah candles are lighted before Shabbat candles. Once Shabbat is ushered in with the kindling of Shabbat candles, it is forbidden to light Hanukkah candles. Since traditionally Shabbat candles are lighted eighteen or more minutes before sundown, it is customary to use bigger candles or more oil so that the Hanukkah lights will still burn for thirty minutes *after* sundown.

There are a number of customs about the order of havdalah and lighting of Hanukkah candles on Saturday night. The most commonly observed pattern is as follows: For the lighting in the synagogue, Hanukkah candles are lighted first and then havdalah is recited; at home, havdalah is made first and then Hanukkah candles are lighted. The arguments on this are complicated but rest on whether havdalah, which occurs every week, should take precedence over Hanukkah, which happens only once a year, or whether proclaiming the miracle is more important and therefore the menorah should be lighted first. The latter position also rests on the desire to postpone the departure of Shabbat as much as possible. It should be remembered that, according to all opinions, one form of havdalah is recited in the amidah of ma'ariv *(attah honantanu),* which should precede the lighting of the menorah. If it has not been said, the havdalah service should be recited before lighting the menorah.

THE MENORAH IN THE SYNAGOGUE

Most place the menorah itself on an east-west axis, but some place it on a north-south axis: The difference reflects a debate on how the menorah was placed in the temple. On Friday afternoons, some light the menorah before minhah; some after.

Rosh Hodesh Tevet occurs during Hanukkah. Kislev is one of the two months that can still vary in the calendar from twenty-nine to thirty days. Therefore, sometimes there are two days of Rosh Hodesh Tevet (Kislev 30, Tevet 1) and sometimes only one (Tevet 1 following Kislev 29). This means that the last day of Hanukkah can be on Tevet 2 (if there is an extra day of Kislev) or on Tevet 3.

HALAKHOT OF THE ARBA PARSHIYYOT

Each special portion is read after the regular Torah reading. There are special haftarot for each of these Shabbatot. If the new moon of Adar or of Nisan falls on Shabbat, three Torah scrolls are taken out of the ark and read in the following order: (1) the regular portion, (2) the Rosh Hodesh reading, (3) Parshat Shekalim or ha-Hodesh.

If Rosh Hodesh Adar falls on Friday, then Shekalim is read on the last Shabbat

of the month of Shevat. Zakhor is always read on the Shabbat preceding Purim. If Rosh Hodesh Nisan falls on a weekday, then Parah is read on the Shabbat following Purim. If Rosh Hodesh Nisan falls on Shabbat, then Parah is read on the last Shabbat of the month of Adar.

Some rabbinic authorities believe the reading of Parshat Zakhor is a biblical commandment, and a few believe that the reading of Parshat Parah is one as well.

HALAKHOT OF PURIM

If Purim falls on Sunday, the Fast of Esther is observed on the preceding Thursday. This fast is of less status than the four fasts concerning the destruction of the temples; therefore, pregnant or nursing women and people whose health would suffer are exempt from fasting.

If no *megillah* written on parchment is available, then the *megillah* can be read from a printed text without reciting the blessings. Similarly, since the reading of the *megillah* is important, it should be read even without the special cantillation if no one knows that *trop.* It can even be read in English, though this halakhah is not practiced today. It should be read in a minyan, but it can be read even for one person.

The reader stands while chanting the *megillah,* and it is customary for the reader to raise his or her voice for the following verses, which are turning points in the story: 1:22; 2:4, 17; 4:14; 5:4; and 6:1. The verse 2:6 is read to the cantillation of Lamentations since it describes the destruction of Jerusalem.

Because every word of the *megillah* should be heard, care should be taken to confine the noisemaking to mention of the name Haman.

Tradition views the daytime reading of the *megillah* as the more important of the two (contrary to current attitudes). There is a disagreement over whether *she-he-heyanu* is said before the reading in the morning. Some authorities state that you should say it, while keeping in mind the other mitzvot of the day, such as the Purim seudah and *mishloah manot.*

Liturgically, *al ha-nissim* is added to every Amidah and Grace after Meals. However, Hallel is not recited on Purim. A variety of explanations are given for this omission. One is that the *megillah* takes the place of Hallel. Another is that the Jews were still subjects of Ahasuerus and thus not fully free. A third reason is that Hallel is not said for events that take place outside the land of Israel.

There is a difference of opinion concerning the practice of mourners sitting *shiv'ah.* The most common practice is for the mourners to come to the synagogue and sit in their regular places. Mourners can also wear shoes to synagogue. However, Purim counts as one of the seven days and mourning in private is still observed.

Most authorities permit weddings on Purim, but some do not on the principle of not mixing one joy with another.

Some people light candles without reciting a blessing at the Purim seudah.

Shushan Purim is observed on the fifteenth of Adar in Jerusalem. There are doubts about whether Jaffa, Safed, Acco, Tiberias, and Lud were walled in ancient times, so the *megillah* is read on the fourteenth and the fifteenth. However, on the fifteenth it is read only at night and without the blessings.

When the fifteenth of Adar falls on Shabbat, *purim meshulash*—the "three-sided Purim"—is celebrated. Some Purim practices are moved up to Friday; others are postponed to Sunday; and some remain on Shabbat. Thus the *megillah* is read on the fourteenth (to prevent its being carried on Shabbat) and presents are given to the poor. The prayer *al ha-nissim* and the Purim Torah reading are still read on Shabbat. The seudah and the giving of *mishloah manot* are moved to Sunday.

APPENDIX 3
TORAH READING CHART

This chart sets out the Torah reading divided by aliyot for the festivals. It follows the Ashkenazic ritual; there are slight differences in Sephardic ritual and in the customs in Israel. (NOTE: The readings are divided by aliyot. It is useful to remember that there are seven aliyot on Shabbat, six on Yom Kippur, five on full festival days, four on *hol ha-moed* and Rosh Hodesh, three every other day—e.g., fast days. A single / signifies a reading from a second Torah scroll. A double // signifies the maftir reading. A double // following a single / signifies the use of three Torah scrolls. Alternate readings or special occasions are signified by the use of parentheses.)

Day	Torah Reading
Pesah (Day 1)	Exod. 12:21–4, 25–8, 29–36, 37–42, 43–51//Num. 28:16–25. Haftarah: Josh. 5:2–6:1
(If falls on Shabbat)	Exod. 12:21–4, 25–8, 29–32, 33–36, 37–42, 43–47, 48–51//Num. 28:16–25. Haftarah: the same.
Pesah (Day 2)	Lev. 22:26–23:3, 23:4–14, 15–22, 23–32, 33–44//Num. 28:16–25. Haftarah: 2 Kings 23:1–9, 21–25.
Hol ha-Moed (Day 1)	Exod. 13:1–4, 5–10, 11–16/ Num. 28:19–25.

Day	Torah Reading
Hol ha-Moed (Day 2)	Exod. 22:24–26, 22:27–23:5, 23:6–19/ Num. 28:19–25.
Hol ha-Moed (Day 3)	Exod. 34:1–10, 11–17, 18–26/ Num. 28:19–25.
Hol ha-Moed (Day 4)	Num. 9:1–5, 6–8, 9–14/ Num. 28:19–25.
Shabbat Hol ha-Moed	Exod. 33:12–16, 17–19, 20–23, 34:1–3, 4–10, 11–17, 18–26//Num. 28:19–25. Haftarah: Ezek. 37:1–14. (Note: If Shabbat falls on the third day of *hol ha-moed,* the readings for the third, fourth, and fifth days are moved ahead.)
Pesah (Day 7)	Exod. 13:17–22, 14:1–8, 9–14, 15–25, 14:26–15:26// Num. 28:19–25. Haftarah: 2 Sam. 22:1–51.
(If falls on Shabbat)	Exod. 13:17–19, 20–22, 14:1–4, 5–8, 9–14, 15–25, 14:26–15:26// Num. 28:19–25. Haftarah: the same.
Pesah (Day 8)	Deut. 15:19–23, 16:1–3, 4–8, 9–12, 13–17//Num. 28:19–25. Haftarah: Isa. 10:32–12:6.
(If falls on Shabbat)	Deut. 14:22–29, 15:1–18; the rest is the same.
Shavuot (Day 1)	Exod. 19:1–6, 7–13, 14–19, 19:20–20:13, 20:14–22// Num. 28:26–31. Haftarah: Ezek. 1:1–28, 3:12.
Shavuot (Day 2)	Deut. 15:19–23, 16:1–3, 4–8, 9–12, 13–17// Num. 28:26–31. Haftarah: Hab. 3:1–19 (or 2:20–3:19).
(If falls on Shabbat)	Deut. 14:22–29, 15:1–18; the rest is the same.
Fast Days	Exod. 32:11, 34:1–3, 4–10.
Fast Days—Minhah	Same Torah reading. Haftarah: Isa. 65:6–66:8.
Tisha be-Av (A.M.)	Deut. 4:25–29, 30–35, 36–40. Haftarah: Jer. 8:13–9:23.
Tisha be-Av—Minhah	Same as other fast days.
Rosh ha-Shanah (Day 1)	Gen. 21:1–4, 5–12, 13–21, 22–27, 28–34//Num. 29:1–6. Haftarah: 1 Samuel 1:1–2; 10.
(If falls on Shabbat)	Gen. 21:1–4, 5–8, 9–12, 13–17, 18–21, 22–27, 28–34// Num. 29:1–6. Haftarah: the same.
Rosh ha-Shanah (Day 2)	Gen. 22:1–3, 4–8, 9–14, 15–19, 20–24//Num. 29:1–6. Haftarah: Jer. 31:1–19.
Yom Kippur (A.M.)	Lev. 16:1–6, 7–11, 12–17, 18–24, 25–30, 31–34//Num. 29:7–11. Haftarah: Isa. 57:14–58:14.
(If falls on Shabbat)	Lev. 16:1–3, 4–6, 7–11, 12–17, 18–24, 25–30, 31–34//Num. 29:7–11. Haftarah: the same.
Yom Kippur—Minhah	Lev. 18:1–5, 6–21, 22–30 (alternate: Lev. 19:1–4, 5–10, 11–18). Haftarah: Jon., Mic. 7:18–20.
Sukkot (Day 1)	Lev. 22:26–23:3, 23:4–14, 15–22, 23–32, 33–44//Num. 29:12–16. Haftarah: Zech. 14:1–21.
(If falls on Shabbat):	Lev. 22:26–33, 23:1–3, 4–8, 9–14, 15–22, 23–32, 33–44//Num. 29:12–16. Haftarah: the same.
Sukkot (Day 2)	Same Torah reading as the first day (weekday). Haftarah: 1 Kings 8:2–21.

DAY	TORAH READING
Hol ha-Moed (Day 1)	Num. 29:17–19, 20–22, 23–25, repeat 17–22.
Hol ha-Moed (Day 2)	Num. 29:20–22, 23–25, 26–28, repeat 20–25.
Hol ha-Moed (Day 3)	Num. 29:23–25, 26–28, 29–31, repeat 23–28.
Hol ha-Moed (Day 4)	Num. 29:26–28, 29–31, 32–34, repeat 26–31.
Shabbat Hol ha-Moed	Exod. 33:12–16, 17–19, 20–23, 34:1–3, 4–10, 11–17, 18–26//The maftir changes depending on what day of *hol ha-moed* Shabbat falls: On the first, the maftir is Num. 29:17–22; the second, Num. 29:20–25; third, Num. 29:23–28; fourth, Num. 29:26–31. Haftarah: Ezek. 38:18–39:16.
Hoshana Rabbah (Day 5)	Num. 29:26–28, 29–31, 32–34, repeat 29–34.
Shemini Atzeret	Deut. 14:22–29, 15:1–18, 15:19–16:3, 4–8, 9–17//Num. 29:35–30:1. Haftarah: 1 Kings 8:54–66.
(If falls on Shabbat)	Deut. 14:22–29, 15:1–18, 15:19–22, 16:1–3, 4–8, 9–12, 13–17//Num. 29:35–30:1. Haftarah: the same.
Simhat Torah at Night	Deut. 33:1–7, 8–12, 13–17, 18–21, 22–26.
Simhat Torah (A.M.)	Deut. 33:1–7, 8–12, 13–17, 18–21, 22–26, 33:27–34:12, Gen. 1:1–2:3//Num. 29:35–30:1. Haftarah: Josh. 1:1–18. (NOTE: In Israel, the above readings for Simhat Torah are read on Shemini Atzeret instead of the listed readings for Shemini Atzeret.)
Hanukkah (Day 1)	Num. 7:1–11, 12–14, 15–17 (alternate: 7:1–4, 5–11, 12–17).
Hanukkah (Day 2)	Num. 7:18–20, 21–23, 24–29 (7:18–20, 21–23, repeat 18–23).
Hanukkah (Day 3)	Num. 7:24–26, 27–29, 30–35 (7:24–26, 27–29, repeat 24–29).
Hanukkah (Day 4)	Num. 7:30–32, 33–35, 36–41 (7:30–32, 33–35, repeat 30–35).
Hanukkah (Day 5)	Num. 7:36–38, 39–41, 42–47 (7:36–38, 39–41, repeat 36–41).
Hanukkah (Day 6, Rosh Hodesh)	Num. 28:1–5, 6–10, 11–15, 7:42–47 (the same).
Hanukkah (Day 7)	Num. 7:48–50, 51–53, 54–59 (7:48–50, 51–53, repeat 48–53).
(If Rosh Hodesh)	Num. 28:1–5, 6–10, 11–15, 7:48–53 (the same).
Hanukkah (Day 8)	Num. 7:54–56, 57–59, 7:60–8:4 (the same).
Shabbat Hanukkah	Regular portion of the week// Hanukkah reading of the day. Haftarah: Zech. 2:14–4:7.
(Shabbat Hanukkah II)	Same as the above for Torah and maftir reading. Haftarah: 1 Kings 7:40–50.
(Shabbat Rosh Hodesh) Hanukkah	Regular portion of the week (six aliyot)/ Num.

Day	Torah Reading
	28:9–15//Hanukkah reading for the day. Haftarah: Zech. 2:14–4:7.
Purim	Exod. 17:8–10, 11–13, 14–16.
Special Sabbaths	
Shabbat Shuvah	Regular portion. Haftarah: Hos. 14:2–10, Mic. 7:18–20, or Hos. 14:2–10, Joel 2:15–27.
Shabbat Shekalim	Regular portion//Exod. 30:11–16. Haftarah: 2 Kings 12:1–17.
(If it is also Rosh Hodesh)	Regular portion/ Num. 28:9–15//Exod. 30:11–16. Haftarah: the same.
Shabbat Zakhor	Regular portion//Deut. 25:17–19. Haftarah: 1 Sam. 15:2–34.
Shabbat Parah	Regular portion//Num. 19:1–22. Haftarah: Ezek. 36:16–38.
Shabbat ha-Hodesh	Regular portion//Exod. 12:1–20. Haftarah: Ezek. 45:16–46:18.
(If it is also Rosh Hodesh)	Regular portion/Num. 28:9–15//Exod. 12:1–20. Haftarah: the same.
Shabbat ha-Gadol	Regular portion. Haftarah: Mal. 3:4–24.

APPENDIX 4
THE COMMON
HEBREW
BLESSINGS

The blessing recited before bedikat hametz (the search for the hametz) begins:

בָּרוּךְ אַתָּה יְיָ אֱלֹהֵינוּ מֶלֶךְ הָעוֹלָם אֲשֶׁר קִדְּשָׁנוּ
בְּמִצְוֹתָיו וְצִוָּנוּ עַל בְּעוּר חָמֵץ.

The *bittul* (nullification) formula recited at night:

כָּל־חֲמִירָא וַחֲמִיעָא דְּאִכָּא בִרְשׁוּתִי, דְּלָא חֲמִיתֵּהּ
וּדְלָא בַעֲרִתֵּהּ, וּדְלָא יָדַעְנָא לֵהּ, לִבְטִיל וְלֶהֱוֵי
הֶפְקֵר כְּעַפְרָא דְאַרְעָא.

The *bittul* formula recited in the morning while the hametz is burned:

כָּל־חֲמִירָא וַחֲמִיעָא דְּאִכָּא בִרְשׁוּתִי, דַּחֲמִיתֵּהּ וּדְלָא
חֲמִיתֵּהּ, דְּבַעֲרִתֵּהּ וּדְלָא בַעֲרִתֵּהּ, לִבְטִיל וְלֶהֱוֵי
הֶפְקֵר כְּעַפְרָא דְאַרְעָא.

The blessing for *sefirat ha-omer* (the counting of the omer):

בָּרוּךְ אַתָּה יְיָ אֱלֹהֵינוּ מֶלֶךְ הָעוֹלָם אֲשֶׁר קִדְּשָׁנוּ
בְּמִצְוֹתָיו וְצִוָּנוּ עַל סְפִירַת הָעֹמֶר.

The greetings for the High Holiday period:

During Elud: לְשָׁנָה טוֹבָה תִּכָּתֵבוּ   or   שָׁנָה טוֹבָה

or   לְשָׁנָה טוֹבָה וּמְתוּקָה תִּכָּתֵבוּ   or   כְּתִיבָה טוֹבָה

The response: גַּם לְמַר   or   גַּם לְךָ (male)   or   גַּם לָךְ (female)

During the Ten Days of Repentance: לְשָׁנָה טוֹבָה תִּכָּתֵבוּ וְתֵחָתֵמוּ

On Yom Kippur: גְּמַר חֲתִימָה טוֹבָה   or   חֲתִימָה טוֹבָה

The prayer recited when dipping apples in honey on Rosh ha-Shanah:

יְהִי רָצוֹן מִלְּפָנֶיךָ יְיָ אֱלֹהֵינוּ וֵאלֹהֵי אֲבוֹתֵינוּ,
שֶׁתְּחַדֵּשׁ עָלֵינוּ שָׁנָה טוֹבָה וּמְתוּקָה.

The blessing for eating in the sukkah (if it is the first time this year, the *she-he-heyanu* is recited—see * at bottom of page 235):

בָּרוּךְ אַתָּה יְיָ אֱלֹהֵינוּ מֶלֶךְ הָעוֹלָם אֲשֶׁר קִדְּשָׁנוּ
בְּמִצְוֹתָיו וְצִוָּנוּ לֵישֵׁב בַּסֻּכָּה.

The blessing for the four species (if it is the first time this year, the *she-he-heyanu* is recited—see * at bottom of page 235):

בָּרוּךְ אַתָּה יְיָ אֱלֹהֵינוּ מֶלֶךְ הָעוֹלָם אֲשֶׁר קִדְּשָׁנוּ
בְּמִצְוֹתָיו וְצִוָּנוּ עַל נְטִילַת לוּלָב.

The blessings for lighting the Hanukkah candles (if it is the first time this year, the *she-he-heyanu* is recited—see * below):

בָּרוּךְ אַתָּה יְיָ אֱלֹהֵינוּ מֶלֶךְ הָעוֹלָם אֲשֶׁר קִדְּשָׁנוּ
בְּמִצְוֹתָיו וְצִוָּנוּ לְהַדְלִיק נֵר שֶׁל חֲנֻכָּה.

בָּרוּךְ אַתָּה יְיָ אֱלֹהֵינוּ מֶלֶךְ הָעוֹלָם שֶׁעָשָׂה נִסִּים
לַאֲבוֹתֵינוּ בַּיָּמִים הָהֵם בַּזְּמַן הַזֶּה.

The blessing recited upon seeing the first buds on the trees in Nisan:

בָּרוּךְ אַתָּה יְיָ אֱלֹהֵינוּ מֶלֶךְ הָעוֹלָם שֶׁלֹּא חִסַּר
בְּעוֹלָמוֹ דָּבָר וּבָרָא בוֹ בְּרִיּוֹת טוֹבוֹת וְאִילָנוֹת טוֹבִים
לְהָנוֹת בָּהֶם בְּנֵי אָדָם.

The blessing for candlelighting for festivals:

בָּרוּךְ אַתָּה יְיָ אֱלֹהֵינוּ מֶלֶךְ הָעוֹלָם אֲשֶׁר קִדְּשָׁנוּ
בְּמִצְוֹתָיו וְצִוָּנוּ לְהַדְלִיק נֵר שֶׁל
(On Friday night add שַׁבָּת וְשֶׁל) יוֹם טוֹב.

The blessing for candlelighting for Yom Kippur:

בָּרוּךְ אַתָּה יְיָ אֱלֹהֵינוּ מֶלֶךְ הָעוֹלָם אֲשֶׁר קִדְּשָׁנוּ
בְּמִצְוֹתָיו וְצִוָּנוּ לְהַדְלִיק נֵר שֶׁל
(On Friday night add שַׁבָּת וְשֶׁל) יוֹם הַכִּפּוּרִים.

(NOTE: The blessing for candlelighting is followed by the *she-he-heyanu*—see *
below.)

*The *she-he-heyanu* blessing recited the first night(s) of holidays and the first time
rituals are performed:

בָּרוּךְ אַתָּה יְיָ אֱלֹהֵינוּ מֶלֶךְ הָעוֹלָם שֶׁהֶחֱיָנוּ וְקִיְּמָנוּ
וְהִגִּיעָנוּ לַזְּמַן הַזֶּה.

Kiddush for festivals. The words in parentheses are said when the festival
coincides with Shabbat. Kiddush is followed by *she-he-heyanu* unless the person
reciting kiddush has already recited it at candlelighting.

(וַיְהִי עֶרֶב וַיְהִי־בֹקֶר

יוֹם הַשִּׁשִּׁי. וַיְכֻלּוּ הַשָּׁמַיִם וְהָאָרֶץ וְכָל צְבָאָם. וַיְכַל אֱלֹהִים
בַּיּוֹם הַשְּׁבִיעִי מְלַאכְתּוֹ אֲשֶׁר עָשָׂה, וַיִּשְׁבֹּת בַּיּוֹם הַשְּׁבִיעִי
מִכָּל מְלַאכְתּוֹ אֲשֶׁר עָשָׂה. וַיְבָרֶךְ אֱלֹהִים אֶת יוֹם הַשְּׁבִיעִי
וַיְקַדֵּשׁ אֹתוֹ, כִּי בוֹ שָׁבַת מִכָּל מְלַאכְתּוֹ אֲשֶׁר בָּרָא אֱלֹהִים
לַעֲשׂוֹת.)

סַבְרִי מָרָנָן וְרַבּוֹתַי.
בָּרוּךְ אַתָּה יְיָ אֱלֹהֵינוּ מֶלֶךְ הָעוֹלָם בּוֹרֵא פְּרִי הַגָּפֶן.
בָּרוּךְ אַתָּה יְיָ אֱלֹהֵינוּ מֶלֶךְ הָעוֹלָם אֲשֶׁר בָּחַר בָּנוּ מִכָּל עָם,
וְרוֹמְמָנוּ מִכָּל לָשׁוֹן, וְקִדְּשָׁנוּ בְּמִצְוֹתָיו. וַתִּתֶּן־לָנוּ, יְיָ
אֱלֹהֵינוּ, בְּאַהֲבָה (שַׁבָּתוֹת לִמְנוּחָה וּ)מוֹעֲדִים לְשִׂמְחָה,
חַגִּים וּזְמַנִּים לְשָׂשׂוֹן, אֶת יוֹם (הַשַּׁבָּת הַזֶּה וְאֶת יוֹם)

	Shemini Atzeret and Simhat Torah	Sukkot	Shavvot	Pesah

חַג הַמַּצּוֹת   חַג הַשָּׁבֻעוֹת   חַג הַסֻּכּוֹת   הַשְּׁמִינִי, חַג
הַזֶּה, זְמַן   הַזֶּה, זְמַן   הַזֶּה, זְמַן   הָעֲצֶרֶת הַזֶּה,
חֵרוּתֵנוּ,   מַתַּן תּוֹרָתֵנוּ   שִׂמְחָתֵנוּ   זְמַן שִׂמְחָתֵנוּ,

(בְּאַהֲבָה) מִקְרָא קֹדֶשׁ, זֵכֶר לִיצִיאַת מִצְרָיִם. כִּי בָנוּ בָחַרְתָּ,
וְאוֹתָנוּ קִדַּשְׁתָּ מִכָּל־הָעַמִּים, (וְשַׁבָּת) וּמוֹעֲדֵי קָדְשֶׁךָ
(בְּאַהֲבָה וּבְרָצוֹן) בְּשִׂמְחָה וּבְשָׂשׂוֹן הִנְחַלְתָּנוּ. בָּרוּךְ אַתָּה
יְיָ, מְקַדֵּשׁ (הַשַּׁבָּת וְ)יִשְׂרָאֵל וְהַזְּמַנִּים.

If a festival begins on Saturday night, a special havdalah is added to the kiddush.

בָּרוּךְ אַתָּה יְיָ אֱלֹהֵינוּ מֶלֶךְ הָעוֹלָם בּוֹרֵא מְאוֹרֵי הָאֵשׁ.
בָּרוּךְ אַתָּה יְיָ אֱלֹהֵינוּ מֶלֶךְ הָעוֹלָם הַמַּבְדִּיל בֵּין קֹדֶשׁ לְחֹל,
בֵּין אוֹר לְחֹשֶׁךְ, בֵּין יִשְׂרָאֵל לָעַמִּים, בֵּין יוֹם הַשְּׁבִיעִי
לְשֵׁשֶׁת יְמֵי הַמַּעֲשֶׂה. בֵּין קְדֻשַּׁת שַׁבָּת לִקְדֻשַּׁת יוֹם טוֹב
הִבְדַּלְתָּ, וְאֶת יוֹם הַשְּׁבִיעִי מִשֵּׁשֶׁת יְמֵי הַמַּעֲשֶׂה קִדַּשְׁתָּ;
הִבְדַּלְתָּ וְקִדַּשְׁתָּ אֶת עַמְּךָ יִשְׂרָאֵל בִּקְדֻשָּׁתֶךָ. בָּרוּךְ אַתָּה יְיָ,
הַמַּבְדִּיל בֵּין קֹדֶשׁ לְקֹדֶשׁ.

At the end of kiddush, as noted, *she-he-heyanu* is recited. It is not said following kiddush of the seventh and eighth day of Pesah.

בָּרוּךְ אַתָּה יְיָ אֱלֹהֵינוּ מֶלֶךְ הָעוֹלָם שֶׁהֶחֱיָנוּ וְקִיְּמָנוּ וְהִגִּיעָנוּ לַזְּמַן הַזֶּה.

At the end of kiddush on Sukkot, the blessing for the sukkah is recited.

בָּרוּךְ אַתָּה יְיָ אֱלֹהֵינוּ מֶלֶךְ הָעוֹלָם אֲשֶׁר קִדְּשָׁנוּ בְּמִצְוֹתָיו וְצִוָּנוּ לֵישֵׁב בַּסֻּכָּה.

Traditionally we wash our hands and recite this blessing before eating bread:

בָּרוּךְ אַתָּה יְיָ אֱלֹהֵינוּ מֶלֶךְ הָעוֹלָם אֲשֶׁר קִדְּשָׁנוּ בְּמִצְוֹתָיו וְצִוָּנוּ עַל נְטִילַת יָדָיִם.

Festival meals begin with the *motzi*—the blessing recited over hallot or matzah:

בָּרוּךְ אַתָּה יְיָ אֱלֹהֵינוּ מֶלֶךְ הָעוֹלָם הַמּוֹצִיא לֶחֶם מִן הָאָרֶץ.

Havdalah is recited at the conclusion of festival days. It is similar to the ritual that concludes Shabbat, but deletes the blessings over spices and fire. No havdalah is recited if a festival is followed by Shabbat (e.g., a festival that occurs on Friday). Havdalah is said at the conclusion of a festival day followed by an intermediate day of the holiday.

סַבְרִי מָרָנָן וְרַבּוֹתַי.
בָּרוּךְ אַתָּה יְיָ אֱלֹהֵינוּ מֶלֶךְ הָעוֹלָם בּוֹרֵא פְּרִי הַגָּפֶן.
בָּרוּךְ אַתָּה יְיָ אֱלֹהֵינוּ מֶלֶךְ הָעוֹלָם הַמַּבְדִּיל בֵּין קֹדֶשׁ לְחֹל,
בֵּין אוֹר לְחֹשֶׁךְ, בֵּין יִשְׂרָאֵל לָעַמִּים, בֵּין יוֹם הַשְּׁבִיעִי
לְשֵׁשֶׁת יְמֵי הַמַּעֲשֶׂה. בָּרוּךְ אַתָּה יְיָ, הַמַּבְדִּיל בֵּין קֹדֶשׁ
לְחֹל.

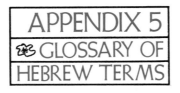

APPENDIX 5
GLOSSARY OF HEBREW TERMS

aleinu   the concluding prayer for all services

aliyah/aliyot   being called up for the Torah reading

amidah   the central portion of all services; also known as *shemoneh esrah*

amot   a Talmudic measurement

barekhu   the call to prayer that precedes the main part of the morning and evening services

berakhah   a blessing

bimah   the raised platform in the synagogue from which the Torah is read

davening   praying

devar torah   a speech/sermon about Torah

eil maleh rahamim   a prayer recited in memorial to the dead

erev 1.   the day before (e.g., Erev Shabbat is Friday); 2. the evening of (e.g., Friday night)

Gemara   the later rabbinic material that is part of the Talmud

gematria   a system that assigns a numerical value to each letter in the Hebrew alphabet

haftarah   the selection from the prophets that is read after the Torah on Shabbat and holidays

halakhah   Jewish law

hallah/hallot   the loaf/ loaves of bread customarily eaten at the beginning of meals on Shabbat and holidays

hallel   a collection of psalms recited on festivals

havdalah   the ritual marking the end of Shabbat and holidays

kabbalah   the mystical tradition in Judaism

kaddish   a prayer recited at various points in the liturgy; one version is recited by mourners.

ketubah   the Jewish marriage contract

kiddush   the sanctification of the day recited over wine at the beginning of festivals and Shabbat

kohanim   priests

levi'im   members of the tribe of Levi who were temple servitors

ma'ariv   the evening service

maftir   the concluding portion read from the Torah on Shabbat and festivals

megillah/megillot   scroll(s); refers to the Book of Esther as well as other books such as Song of Songs, Lamentations, etc.

midrash   interpretations of or homiletics on Jewish texts, particularly the Bible

mikveh   ritual bath

minhag   custom

minhah   the afternoon service

Mishnah   the early rabbinic material that is part of the Talmud

mitzvah/mitzvot   commandment(s)

musaf   the additional service recited on Shabbat and holidays

piyyut   a liturgical poem

sefirah/sefirot   the ten spheres that make up the world(s) in the kabbalistic view

shaharit   the morning service

she-he-heyanu   the blessing recited at special occasions

Shekhinah   the indwelling presence of God, sometimes the feminine aspect of God

shema   Hear, O Israel, the Lord your God, the Lord is one.

siddur   a prayer book

tahanun   a penitential prayer in the daily service deleted on joyous occasions

tallit   prayer shawl

tefillin   phylacteries

teshuvah   repentance

tzedakah   charity

yahrzeit   anniversary of the date of death

yizkor   memorial service for the dead

yom tov   a festival

APPENDIX 6
DATES OF THE HOLIDAYS: 5762–5776 (2001–2015)

The following chart gives the dates of the holidays and the day of the week the holidays fall on until the year 2015. Only the first day of each holiday is listed (e.g., Shemini Atzeret but not Simhat Torah). It should be noted that when Yom ha-Atzma'ut falls either on a Friday or Saturday, or if Yom ha-Shoah falls on a Friday, it is moved up to the preceding Thursday. Similarly, if the fast of Tisha be-Av falls on a Saturday, it is postponed to the following day, Sunday.

	5762–2001/2	5763–2002/3	5764–2003/4	5765–2004/5	5766–2005/6
Rosh ha-Shanah	T Sept. 18	S Sept. 7	S Sept. 27	Th Sept. 16	T Oct. 4
Yom Kippur	Th Sept. 27	M Sept. 16	M Oct. 6	S Sept. 25	Th Oct. 13
Sukkot	T Oct. 2	S Sept. 21	S Oct. 11	Th Sept. 30	T Oct. 18
Shemini Atzeret	T Oct. 9	S Sept. 28	S Oct. 18	Th Oct. 7	T Oct. 25
Hanukkah	M Dec. 10	S Nov. 30	S Dec. 20	W Dec. 8	M Dec. 26
Tu Bishvat	M Jan. 28	S Jan. 18	S Feb. 7	T Jan. 25	M Feb. 13
Purim	T Feb. 26	T Mar. 18	Su Mar. 7	F Mar. 25	T Mar. 14
Pesah	Th Mar. 28	Th. Apr. 17	T Apr. 6	Su Apr. 24	Th Apr. 13
7th Day of Pesah	W Apr. 3	W Apr. 23	M Apr. 12	S Apr. 30	W Apr. 19
Yom ha-Shoah	T Apr. 9	T Apr. 29	Su Apr. 18	Th. May 5	T Apr. 25
Yom ha-Atzma'ut	W Apr. 17	W May 7	M Apr. 26	Th May 12	W May 3
Shavuot	F May 17	F June 6	W May 26	M June 13	F June 2
Tisha be-Av	Th July 18	Th Aug. 7	T July 27	Su Aug. 14	Th Aug. 3

	5767–2006/7	5768–2007/8	5769–2008/9	5770–2009/0	5771–2010/1
Rosh ha-Shanah	S Sept. 23	Th Sept. 13	T Sept. 30	S Sept. 19	Th Sept. 9
Yom Kippur	M Oct. 2	S Sept. 22	Th Oct. 9	M Sept. 28	S Sept. 18
Sukkot	S Oct. 7	Th Sept. 27	T Oct. 14	S Oct. 3	Th Sept. 23
Shemini Atzeret	S Oct. 14	Th Oct. 4	T Oct. 21	S Oct. 10	Th Sept. 30
Hanukkah	S Dec. 16	W Dec. 5	M Dec. 22	S Dec. 12	Th Dec. 2
Tu Bishvat	S Feb. 3	T Jan. 22	M Feb. 9	S Jan. 30	Th Jan. 20
Purim	Su Mar. 4	F Mar. 21	T Mar. 10	Su Feb. 28	Su Mar. 20
Pesah	T Apr. 3	Su Apr. 30	Th Apr. 9	T Mar. 30	T Apr. 19
7th Day of Pesah	M Apr. 9	S Apr. 26	W Apr. 15	M Apr. 5	M Apr. 25
Yom ha-Shoah	Su Apr. 15	Th May 2	T Apr. 21	Su Apr. 11	Su May 1
Yom ha-Atzma'ut	M Apr. 23	Th May 8	W Apr. 29	M Apr. 19	M May 9
Shavuot	W May 23	M June 9	F May 29	W May 19	W June 8
Tisha be-Av	T July 24	Su Aug. 10	Th July 30	T July 20	T Aug. 9

	5772–2011/2	5773–2012/3	5774–2013/4	5775–2014/5	5776–2015/6
Rosh ha-Shanah	Th Sept. 29	M Sept. 17	T Sept. 5	Th Sept. 25	M Sept. 14
Yom Kippur	S Oct. 8	W Sept. 26	S Sept. 14	S Oct. 4	W Sept. 23
Sukkot	Th Oct. 13	M Oct. 1	Th Sept. 19	Th Oct. 9	M Sept. 28
Shemini Atzeret	Th Oct. 20	M Oct. 8	Th Sept. 26	Th Oct. 16	M Oct. 5
Hanukkah	W Dec. 21	Su Dec. 9	Th Nov. 28	W Dec. 17	M Dec. 7
Tu Bishvat	W Feb. 8	S Jan. 26	Th Jan. 16	W Feb. 4	M Jan. 25
Purim	Th Mar. 8	Su Feb. 24	Su Mar. 16	Th Mar. 5	Th Mar. 24
Pesah	S Apr. 7	T Mar. 26	T Apr. 15	S Apr. 4	S Apr. 23
7th Day of Pesah	F Apr. 13	M Apr. 1	M Apr. 21	F Apr. 10	F Apr. 29
Yom ha-Shoah	Th Apr. 19	Su Apr. 7	Su Apr. 27	Th Apr. 16	Th May 5
Yom ha-Atzma'ut	Th Apr. 26	M Apr. 15	M May 5	Th Apr. 23	Th May 12
Shavuot	Su May 17	W May 15	W June 4	Su May 24	Su June 12
Tisha be-Av	Su July 29	T July 16	T Aug. 5	Su July 26	Su Aug. 14

INDEX